D1525531

STAGESTRUCK

STAGESTRUCK

The Business of Theater in Eighteenth-Century France and Its Colonies

Lauren R. Clay

CORNELL UNIVERSITY PRESS
Ithaca and London

First published 2013 by Cornell University Press
Printed in the United States of America

Library of Congress Cataloging-in-Publication Data

Clay, Lauren R.
   Stagestruck : the business of theater in eighteenth-
century France and its colonies / Lauren R. Clay.
      p. cm.
   Includes bibliographical references and index.
   ISBN 978-0-8014-5038-9 (cloth : alk. paper)
   1. Theater and society—France—History—
18th century.   2. Theater and society—West Indies,
French—History—18th century.   3. Theater—Economic
aspects—France—History—18th century.   4. Theater—
Economic aspects—West Indies, French—History—18th
century.   5. Theater management—France—History—
18th century.   6. Theater management—West Indies,
French—History—18th century.   7. France—Social life
and customs—18th century.   8. West Indies, French—
Social life and customs—18th century.   I. Title.
   PN2633.C56 2013
   792.0944'09033—dc23   2012032827

Cloth printing   10 9 8 7 6 5 4 3 2 1

For my grandmothers

The first noticeable effect of this establishment [a public theater] will be . . . a revolution in our practices which will necessarily produce one in our mores.

Jean-Jacques Rousseau, *Letter to M. d'Alembert on the Theatre*, 1758

The Englishman shows himself in all his glory at Parliament and at the stock exchange, the German in his scholar's study, and the Frenchman at the theater.

Nicolaï Karamzine, *Lettres d'un voyageur russe*, 1792

CONTENTS

ILLUSTRATIONS

Acknowledgments

This book has been many years in the making. It is with great pleasure that I can now express my gratitude to those who have supported and encouraged me along the way. My initial research was funded by the Mellon Foundation, the Fulbright Program, and the University of Pennsylvania. At Texas A&M University, the Melbern G. Glasscock Center for Humanities Research, the College of Liberal Arts, and the History Department provided research funding and leave that enabled me to ask new questions and take the manuscript in new directions. With a summer stipend from the National Endowment for the Humanities, I was able to visit additional archives in France. The Center for Renaissance and Baroque Studies at the University of Maryland welcomed me as a visiting scholar. An NEH Fellowship and Vanderbilt University supported a crucial year of writing. Vanderbilt also provided a subvention to underwrite this book's publication. I thank all of these institutions for their generosity.

In France, knowledgeable and efficient archivists and librarians in Bordeaux, Châlons-en-Champagne, Le Mans, Lyon, Nantes, Paris, Reims, Rouen, Saumur, Strasbourg, Toulouse, Valenciennes, and Vincennes helped me to navigate their collections, responded to queries, and facilitated the reproduction of images. I am especially grateful to the Bibliothèque-Musée de la Comédie-Française for allowing me to use their collections and to Jacqueline Razgonnikoff, who during my very first weeks of research in France located invaluable sources and helped me to decode the handwritten letters of eighteenth-century actors, while sharing her enthusiasm for my project. In the United States, the librarians at the New York Public Library, the Newberry Library, and the libraries of Harvard University and the University of Pennsylvania proved to be tremendously helpful. I also thank the indefatigable interlibrary loan departments at both Texas A&M and Vanderbilt, who did a heroic job responding to my countless requests.

I had the great good fortune to begin studying the French theater industry at the University of Pennsylvania with Lynn Hunt as my adviser. As valuable to me as Lynn's critical insight and astute advice has been her constant faith that this project would, in fact, make a book. Over the years she has continued to give generously of her time, reading chapters of this manuscript with care, for which I offer my thanks. At Penn, Lynn Lees and Alan Kors challenged me to think about culture, commerce, empire, and urban life during the age of Enlightenment in new ways. Joan DeJean and the French Cultural Studies seminar provided inspiration for interdisciplinary inquiry, and allowed me to present my early findings on the eighteenth-century stage. Friends and colleagues including Ellen Amster and Catherine Bogosian Ash helped to make my Philadelphia years intellectually exciting as well as fun. I am also grateful to professors Suzanne Marchand and Theodore Rabb, who first opened the doors of the Bibliothèque nationale for me.

In France, colleagues including J. P. Daughton, Richard Keller, Katherine Kuenzli, and Lara Moore helped me to get this book off the ground in conversations that were most often conducted over good wine and delicious meals. Roger Chartier graciously allowed me to attend his seminar, and Martine de Rougemont offered her expert advice. Luc Poirier extended his friendship and hospitality. In Cambridge, Massachusetts, Alexis Albion and Brian DeLay reached across disciplinary boundaries to read my work, as did Laurel Thatcher Ulrich.

At Texas A&M University, my colleagues in the History Department made College Station a warm and intellectually engaging environment in which to begin writing this book. Walter Buenger was supportive and accommodating. My appreciation goes to Cyndy Bouton, Chester Dunning, Rebecca Hartkopf Schloss, Troy Bickham, Jim Rosenheim, Lora Wildenthal, Daniel Bornstein, and the members of the Junior Faculty Reading Group for reading my work and offering valuable suggestions. Christian Brannstrom helped me to create preliminary maps.

In Nashville, I was welcomed into another collegial and intellectually vibrant academic community. At Vanderbilt University, my department chairs, Liz Lunbeck and Jim Epstein, and Dean Carolyn Dever have supported my research with enthusiasm. I offer my thanks to Catherine Molineux, Eddie Wright-Rios, Holly Tucker, Jane Landers, Gary Gerstle, Joel Harrington, Celso Castilho, Marshall Eakin, Ole Molvig, Colin Dayan, and Jérôme Brillaud for their advice and recommendations, as well as for their encouragement and camaraderie. Sarah Igo has been a scholarly inspiration as well as a supportive friend. Bill Caferro not only read parts of the manuscript, he also provided countless morale boosts. At a crucial moment, Katie Crawford helped me to remap the book's organization. Matt Ramsey read the entire manuscript. Rachel Early, Thomas Liwinski, Beatrix Brockman, and Cecilia Bilyk assisted me with research.

Over the years, I presented aspects of this research at meetings of the Society for French Historical Studies, the Western Society for French History, the American Society for Eighteenth-Century Studies, the Social Science History Association, and the French Colonial Historical Society, as well as at the conference "Diversité et modernité du théâtre du XVIIIe siècle." I also presented chapter drafts to the Baltimore-Washington Old Regime Group and to the works-in-progress seminar organized by the Center for Renaissance and Baroque Studies. The participants in these forums, as well as those in colloquia and working groups at Penn, Harvard, Texas A&M, and Vanderbilt, provided me with valuable feedback that has helped me to refine my arguments. I especially thank John Shovlin, David Bell, Greg Brown, Bill Weber, Jeremy Popkin, Sue Peabody, Paul Cohen, Clare Crowston, Sharon Kettering, Gay Gullickson, Cyril Triolaire, Philippe Bourdin, Denise Davidson, Gene Ogle, and Nina Kushner for their suggestions, insights, and encouragement. A special thanks goes to Bernard Camier, who shared results from his own research and even mailed me copies of archival documents that he thought might be valuable for my research. (They were.) When called upon, Jen Popiel and Jen Sessions applied their critical abilities to improving chapters, lent a sympathetic ear, and rallied my spirits. I am especially grateful to Jeff Ravel, who read the manuscript twice, offering expert advice and helping me to sharpen its arguments. He is a valued mentor. The anonymous readers for Cornell University Press also deserve recognition. Their detailed reports challenged me to undertake important changes that, I believe, have made this a better book.

At Cornell, John Ackerman's early enthusiasm for the project helped to carry me through the lengthy revision process. Going above and beyond the call of duty, John even applied his extraordinary talents as an editor to the book's introduction. I thank my manuscript editor, Susan Specter, for skillfully guiding my manuscript through to publication. My copyeditor, John Raymond, did terrific work on the manuscript. Dave Prout compiled the index.

Portions of this book have previously appeared in published form. Chapter 1 draws on my article "Patronage, Profits, and Public Theaters: Rethinking Cultural Unification in Ancien Régime France," *Journal of Modern History* 79 (December 2007): 729–71. © 2007 The University of Chicago. All rights reserved. An earlier version of chapter 5 was published as "Provincial Actors, the Comédie-Française, and the Business of Performing in Eighteenth-Century France," *Eighteenth-Century Studies* 38, no. 4 (2005): 651–79. I thank the editors of these journals as well as the American Society for Eighteenth-Century Studies, Johns Hopkins University Press, and the

University of Chicago Press for granting me permission to reprint, with changes, this material.

On a personal note, this book would never have been written without the extraordinary support that I received from friends and family. Carmen Scheffler, Shannon "Nano" Albrecht, and Denae Gaunce cared for and loved my children during the many hours that I was at my computer. Korin Brody, Mary Young, and Ingrid Burkett have stepped in to save and brighten the day. In Chicago, John Chambers, Sara Rosheger, and Susan Noble encouraged my passion for the stage. Meredith Barber not only taught me a thing or two about the everyday realities of a modern-day career in the theater, she has also been the truest friend, a source of encouragement, laughter, and resolve. The Vandy moms have been there to commiserate and celebrate.

The most important part of my production team, though, has been my immediate family. My parents, Hollie and George Clay, my sisters, Karen and Sarah, and my brother Tom have offered unflagging moral support. My sons, Joshua and Nathaniel, and my daughter Naomi have been a source of joy for me throughout. I thank them for their understanding and for their cheerleading. I am thrilled to announce that mom's book is finally done! My husband and colleague, Leor Halevi, understands the labor involved in writing this book all too well. As my live-in editor, he carefully read the manuscript many times. As my co-parent, he kept the show going. As my companion, he kept me sane. Some debts can never be repaid, but I offer him my thanks and appreciation.

I dedicate this book to my grandmothers, Mary Reynolds Clay (1911–2011) and Edith Foster Hicks, who inspired me from a young age with a passion for the French language and culture, and who invested materially and emotionally in making it possible for this book to reach a public.

STAGESTRUCK

Introduction

The Making of a French Theater Industry

"Never has talent been so rare among us," complained theater director, dramatist, and talent scout Charles-Simon Favart. Writing from Paris in the early 1760s, Favart maintained that all of France was facing an acute shortage of able and experienced actors, actresses, and singers for hire. "We are beating the drum to find them," he observed, "and if our capital, which is their usual rendezvous, lacks them today, one cannot hope to find them elsewhere."[1] Favart, who corresponded widely with performers and auditioned talent in provincial cities as well as in Paris, understood France's changing talent market well. In recent years, the salaries demanded even by performers he considered mediocre had escalated rapidly, rising "in proportion to need and rarity." Demand for qualified personnel exceeded supply and the reason was clear. "Each provincial city wants to have a troupe," he explained, "and they recruit all the way to our [Paris] boulevards." Moreover, France's expanding theater industry, Favart felt certain, was only gathering momentum. With the Seven Years' War finally coming to an end and peace almost sure to stimulate economic growth, he predicted that the number of French theater troupes "is going to multiply . . . to infinity."[2]

Favart's lifetime spanned from the reign of Louis XIV to the French Revolution, most of it working in the theater business, so he occupied a particularly good vantage point from which to witness the profound transformations sweeping the performance industry in France. Yet his contemporaries also noticed the enthusiasm for theater that was taking hold in provincial cities and its consequences for everyday life. The French, it seemed clear, were stagestruck. "The public theaters, although innumerable, do not suffice, we construct them in villages, in the armies, . . . in private homes," complained a Catholic moralist living in Montauban, a city that had acquired its first dedicated playhouse only in 1760: "We run to them, we go in, we perform there, we spend our lives there."[3] Moreover, as this author and others noted, this growing passion for theater was not restricted to the metropole. Plays, published accounts of the latest theatrical happenings, and even actors crossed the Atlantic and Indian oceans to reach cities throughout the empire.[4]

This book is a history of the making of a French theater industry in the late Old Regime. I use the term "French" because this study examines why and how professional public theater became a regular aspect of cultural and social life for city dwellers throughout France and its colonies, a phenomenon that was rooted in the eighteenth century. In comparison with Spain, Italy, and England, professional theater came late to France. The first troupes of Italian actors began to stage commedia dell'arte in French cities during the 1570s. French actors soon followed their lead, and by the 1630s Parisians had begun to enjoy regular public theater. Outside of the capital, however, professional performance long remained on the margins of urban public life.[5] When King Louis XIV founded the Comédie-Française, France's royal dramatic theater company, in 1680, only a single provincial city enjoyed a dedicated playhouse, Toulouse. Yet between the 1680s and 1789, at least seventy metropolitan cities and eleven cities in France's colonies celebrated the inauguration of their first public *salle de spectacle* (theater).[6] (See appendix.) On the eve of the Revolution, more French cities boasted theaters than universities, chambers of commerce, royal academies, or local newspapers.[7] Together, these provincial and colonial playhouses could accommodate as many as fifty-seven thousand customers on any given evening, an estimate that swells to seventy thousand when Parisian theaters are included.[8] In these auditoriums, spectators who had long made do with sporadic and often brief visits by traveling acting troupes began to enjoy regular seasons of theater and opera. By the late 1780s, large resident performing arts companies entertained audiences with comedy and tragedy, musical theater and opera year-round in over a dozen French cities that stretched from Lyon to Rouen to Cap Français, in the Caribbean colony of Saint-Domingue (modern-day Haiti). During the final decades of the Old Regime, France's theater industry came to surpass even that of highly commercialized and theater-loving England, where all troupes outside of London toured for much of the year.[9]

The consequences of this expansion were striking. Theaters emerged as the most prominent and prestigious new cultural institutions of the century. France's leading architects reimagined the public playhouse as a monument to the performing arts. The theater companies that took to these stages entertained hundreds of thousands of men and women living in cities throughout France and its empire. To sustain operations on this scale, theatrical production became big business.[10] In the seventeenth and early eighteenth centuries, professional theater in most of France was performed by small acting troupes of twelve to fifteen members who traveled from city to city. By the 1780s, in contrast, the cast and crew for the theater company in Lyon numbered more than 150. Their customers purchased a few hours of entertainment, but also much more. With their tickets, spectators bought the opportunity to approve or disapprove of the performance, opinions that were expressed loudly through applause or whistles and catcalls. They also gained the opportunity to participate directly in literary and cultural networks that fostered a shared cultural heritage, one that was self-consciously located in the domain of "elite" culture. What is more, as diverse audiences numbering in the hundreds and even thousands gathered regularly under the watchful gaze of local and royal authorities, theaters became key urban sites in which social, political, and, in the colonies, racial relationships were articulated, contested, and redefined.

The creation of this theater industry has important implications for our understanding of Enlightenment society, the consumer revolution in France, and the absolutist state. The French state has historically played a particularly prominent role in cultural production. Indeed, historians often privilege the state as the primary cultural actor in France, a model that has been applied widely—from the age of absolutism to the modernizing Third Republic to the "Cultural State" (*État culturel*) of the late twentieth century.[11] The historian Pierre Nora has argued strongly for the cultural agency exercised by the government: "French culture," he has written, "flowed into the social fabric of France only through the channels the state had carved for it."[12] The roots of this French cultural exceptionalism are traced, as often as not, back to the distinctive relationship between cultural patronage and political authority so successfully cultivated by Louis XIV. With his minister Jean-Baptiste Colbert, the absolute monarch implemented an array of ambitious and carefully coordinated cultural policies that would establish him as the most important patron of the performing arts in Europe. The "cultural system of the Old Regime," scholars have argued, was marked by "the progressive capture by the State of the disciplines and the institutions that govern cultural production."[13]

Given Louis XIV's skillful use of performance and spectacle at Versailles and in Paris to enhance his prestige and authority, one might well expect the Sun King and his successors to have been committed to patronizing the performing arts elsewhere in the kingdom. Theater, after all, featured centrally in the political agenda of absolutism. "Sovereigns," the abbé d'Aubignac counseled in *La Pratique du théâtre*, first published in 1657, "can do nothing more advantageous for their glory and for the good of their subjects than to establish and to support theater . . . in an orderly manner and with munificence worthy of their crown."[14] The young Louis XIV apparently took such sentiments to heart, staging elaborate court festivities including theater and dance performances in which he took on starring roles. He patronized Pierre Corneille, Jean Racine, and Jean-Baptiste Poquelin, better known as Molière, now recognized as France's greatest playwrights, as well as Jean-Baptiste Lully, the composer who founded the French operatic tradition. Later in life, he established three royal theater companies in Paris: the Paris Opera, the Comédie-Française, and the Comédie-Italienne. Just as the palace at Versailles was designed to proclaim the king's grandeur and manifest his authority, the king's engagement with theater, music, and spectacle constituted a means to stage royal power.[15]

Working within this state-centered framework, scholars have traditionally embraced a top-down vision of cultural change, proposing that royal authorities essentially imposed theaters on France's cities, even at times against the will of their residents.[16] In this book, in contrast, I will argue that the unparalleled expansion of French theater in the eighteenth century was not founded on a court-based culture of patronage and political coercion. In Paris, it is true, Louis XIV and his successors used royal patronage and authority to put their privileged theater companies to work "in the service of the king."[17] Outside of the capital, however, a markedly different picture emerges, one in which the king appears relatively disinterested in the new theaters that received his stamp of approval, provided they did not tax the royal treasury. Although royal governors, intendants, and military commanders proved eager to encourage theater in cities under their authority, most notably in France's garrison and port cities, these representatives of the crown confronted financial limitations that significantly restricted their ability to patronize local stages. The prestigious royal theater companies, for their part, provided inspiration for provincial and colonial actors and audiences. As we will see, they supplied nearly all of the theatrical and operatic repertory performed on French and French colonial stages, and they defined professional standards for actors and directors working throughout French domains. The King's Players (*comédiens du roi*) even toured the new theaters, making themselves into national stars. Nonetheless, the three royal stages, which were administered as part of the King's Household (*Maison du roi*) and benefited from royal patronage and privilege, hardly offered viable models for directors struggling to generate a sufficient audience even in France's second-largest city, Lyon, an important center for banking and silk manufacturing with a population that swelled by the late eighteenth century to over 150,000, let alone in a city such as Lorient, a commercial port on the Atlantic coast with fewer than eighteen thousand residents.[18]

If state policies and political pressure contributed to the widespread estab-lishment of public theater in eighteenth-century France, they were not the primary force behind theater's success. In most French cities, professional public theaters resulted from local initiative and were paid for with private funds. Moreover, in all but a few cases the entrepreneurs and investors who built these playhouses—as well as the directors with whom they contracted to perform in them—operated theaters as businesses that they expected to earn a profit. France's new stages owed more to the market than to the court. If in theory the state wielded tremendous authority over the new playhouses and theater companies springing up across France, in practice the individu-als who created, managed, and oversaw them enjoyed a significant measure of autonomy—and were often left to their own devices. It is telling that the theatrical profession was never granted the corporate status enjoyed by almost all other urban trades and professions in France. This suggests the extent to which theaters in their everyday practices operated in tension with the corporatist and hierarchical order that constituted the very foundation for politics and society during the Old Regime.

The notable successes of eighteenth-century French theater were founded, above all, on a literal buying in to the pleasures of the stage. This book, there-fore, presents a study in the commercialization of culture. The professional stage represents just one of many arenas in which cultural production was commercialized in seventeenth- and eighteenth-century Europe. Theater's rise to widespread popularity took place in the context of an ongoing con-sumer revolution, in which demand for nonessential commodities such as colorful clothing, cosmetics, wigs, furniture, books, and an array of luxury goods and "populuxe" products—cheap knockoff versions of elite com-modities—expanded significantly, including among people of the middling and popular classes. Important studies by Daniel Roche and many others have brought to light the changing ownership patterns and new relation-ships to consumer goods that together signaled the "birth of consumption" in France. Between the reign of Louis XIV and the Revolution, individuals ranging from the wealthiest aristocrats to artisans and day laborers began to purchase more consumer goods of greater value, especially clothing.[19] This increased spending, together with developments in style and production, disrupted the traditional hierarchy of appearances founded on the belief that one was what one wore and owned. From Paris to small villages, contemporaries noted uneasily that nobles and their servants were nearly indistinguishable when wearing their Sunday best.[20] Critics lamented this increase in luxury consumption among those outside of the traditional elite, which they claimed created a confusion of ranks that threatened the stability of the social hierarchy. Scholarship in this area has focused primarily on material culture. Yet paid entertainment can—and I suggest must—be evaluated within this same context. I approach an evening at the theater as a cultural commodity that came to be produced, distributed, and consumed in new ways in the eighteenth century.

Public theater constitutes a particularly valuable case through which to explore commercialization, a process that remains relatively understudied for France. Unlike most newly available goods, professional theatrical performances were produced as well as consumed in a public, social setting, under the keen eyes of urban audiences, public authorities, and cultural critics. As a result, sources ranging from city regulations to travel diaries to labor complaints filed by actors cast light on the varied experiences of commercialization and the meanings that process held for those creating and participating in the business of theater. Furthermore, because theater troupes operated within professional, cultural, and commercial networks that extended throughout France and its colonies, theater provides a framework for analyzing trends in commercialization as a broad urban phenomenon.[21]

At the same time, the development of a French theater industry stands to inform our understanding of the "bourgeois public sphere." Jürgen Habermas's concept of a sphere in which private individuals exchanged opinions and engaged in open debate—a space that opened up within the very confines of the absolutist state—has provided scholars with an appealing model for conceptualizing the emergence of public opinion as a political force during the late Old Regime and Revolution.[22] Theaters proved particularly important in constituting the public sphere because, as Jeffrey Ravel has explained, this "was the only public space in Old Regime France where a socially heterogeneous selection of the King's subjects regularly gathered to pass judgment on matters of theatrical—and increasingly political—importance."[23] Ravel has emphasized the need to look beyond the realm of discourse and the medium of print to evaluate lived behaviors in the physical spaces where members of "the public" gathered.[24] I build on this foundation by evaluating newly inaugurated playhouses, struggling theater companies, and outspoken spectators in the context of the emergent public sphere. At the same time, I hope to offer a corrective to scholarship on the public sphere that typically slights the influence of changing consumer behaviors and commercial practices on the public and the opinions it expressed. Colin Jones has rightly criticized the "de-economized" interpretation of Habermas that has dominated scholarship on the French Old Regime, one that obscures the intimate connections between the "commercialization of cultural production" and the emergence of a confident and demanding public.[25]

In this book I turn to the stage to describe and analyze the development of a commercial public sphere, one that engaged a remarkably diverse array of individuals from the urban community. French theaters drew in servants and nobles, women and men, and, in the colonies, blacks and whites. As theatrical production was commercialized, theater professionals and their customers in cities across France and the empire began to perform new economic, social, and cultural roles. Aware of the possibilities but also the very real pressures of the market, they made choices and defended them, asserted their rights, and even at times explicitly contested the symbolic authority of the royal government.

The rise of a national theater industry transformed cultural relations in France in significant ways. As entrepreneurs, investors, and civic leaders defined these new institutions, they found themselves engaging not only with the royal theaters of Paris but also with theaters and theater professionals in other cities in France. Each new playhouse and theater troupe became a node within this rapidly evolving and increasingly dense cultural communication network, one that came to resemble a spider web more than spokes of a wheel with Paris at its hub. For this reason, I seek to locate cultural developments in provincial cities, in France's colonial cities, and in Paris within the same analytic framework. Embracing a broader geographic perspective on this cultural phenomenon, one that deliberately eschews a Paris-*province* or metropole-colony divide, I argue, sheds light on the processes by which city dwellers came to participate in a common cultural marketplace and to share common sets of social and cultural practices.[26] To put it another way, the making of a theater industry has quite a lot to tell us about how members of the bourgeoisie—in the traditional sense of urban citizens—became French.

If, as Benedict Anderson has argued, nations are constructed as "imagined communities," playhouses and theater companies powerfully staged for audiences their membership in a larger French national community.[27] France's proud heritage of dramatic literature, opera, and dance, as well as the experience of going to the theater, became important elements in eighteenth-century conceptions of Frenchness, a fact acknowledged by residents and foreigners alike.[28] Far-flung audiences clamored to enjoy the same hit plays and opéras-comiques, and even to cheer the same stars. As royal actors, drawn by the lucrative possibilities of this expanding theater market, began appearing on stages throughout France, they achieved a celebrity that would have been impossible a half century earlier. Directors expressly marketed the experience of cultural simultaneity to boost revenues.[29] Commercialization, in this way, can be seen as promoting a "nationalization" of the French theater industry.[30]

At the same time, approaching theater on a national and imperial scale forces us to reconsider the role of the capital in defining commercial culture. French culture was not simply produced in Paris and then acquired or imitated (poorly, in the opinion of many contemporary Parisians) elsewhere.[31] Plays, librettos, and scores could be imported from the capital, and they were, by the hundreds. When it came to their performance, however, cultural production was required to take place locally. As directors, entrepreneurs, and civic leaders quickly discovered, the capacity to adapt and invent was often necessary to establish and sustain an active local theater. Circumstances in the varied provincial and colonial cities that were home to more than 90 percent of France's urban population differed in important ways from those of the capital.[32] As a result, these locales became important sites of innovation in areas ranging from financing to theater architecture to business practices. Although Paris was undoubtedly the most influential city producing and mediating performing arts culture in eighteenth-century France, it was not the only player. In fact, the theater arts constituted one arena in which Parisian cultural hegemony could be disrupted and even, on occasion, openly contested.

Provincial and colonial theaters stood alongside academies and Masonic lodges as key institutions of Enlightenment culture and sociability. Indeed, because theaters did not require literacy, social status, or substantial wealth as criteria for participation, they engaged larger publics and a broader cross-section of the population than perhaps any other institution of the public sphere.[33] For these reasons, among others, the theater of the Old Regime and the Revolution has captured the attention of historians, literary scholars, sociologists, and musicologists. Their rich and varied scholarship has established the significance of the professional stage for French politics, culture, and society.[34] Yet since Max Fuchs's groundbreaking study first drew attention to the vitality of provincial theater nearly eighty years ago, there has been no serious scholarship evaluating professional theater on a national scale.[35] Drawing on these new historical and theoretical perspectives, and armed with new evidence, we can reconsider the causes and especially the consequences of theater's success.

To discover why and how this unparalleled investment in theater took place, as well as what consequences it had for audiences, performers, and governing elites, I traveled to municipal and departmental archives in cities from Lyon to Le Mans. In Paris, the archives of the Comédie-Française offered up invaluable evidence on these questions; so too did the archives of the French army at Vincennes and the colonial collections at the Archives nationales. I considered a wide array of sources, ranging from architectural plans to the bylaws of joint-stock societies to police reports concerning audience misbehaviors. Rather than approaching the history of French theater through a small number of case studies, I set out to compare the evolution of theatrical practices in many different cities. This approach, I found, revealed patterns and trends within the developing industry as a whole that would not otherwise have come to light. It also suggested the profound influence that developments in various locales such as Bordeaux and Lyon had on other cities—including Paris—and on practices in France more broadly. This type of analysis was possible only because in addition to my own archival research I was able to draw upon a host of local studies in which nineteenth- and twentieth-century scholars painstakingly reconstructed the history of a single public theater.[36] These works constitute an invaluable source of information on playhouses, troupes, theater regulations, and audience practices in individual cities throughout France, to which this book, as the endnotes will attest, is deeply indebted.

Early on in my research, I confronted the fact that eighteenth-century theaters were complex and multifaceted institutions. To contemporaries, *le théâtre* might signify a building, an esteemed cultural institution, a career path, an investment opportunity, a social meeting place, an evening of dramatic entertainment, and more. To accommodate this complexity, I chose to evaluate the establishment of a French theater industry from multiple perspectives, with each chapter investigating the role played by a different set of participants in this process.

Focusing primarily on the decades of theater's greatest expansion, from the 1750s to the 1780s, this book consists of seven chapters. The inauguration of buildings dedicated for performance purposes constituted the first step in the institutionalization of theater in urban life. For this reason, I begin with playhouses. The first three chapters evaluate the roles played by key groups—entrepreneurs and investors, municipal governments, and the state—in funding, designing, and operating new public theaters in provincial France. Chapter 1 investigates those who paid for playhouses, focusing especially on the local entrepreneurs and investors in joint-stock companies who provided the capital and the drive to construct a substantial majority of France's new public theaters. Chapter 2 examines the architectural evolution of the French playhouse as it rose from humble origins in the late seventeenth century as a simple and inexpensive wooden structure, often a converted *jeu de paume*—an indoor tennis court—to achieve monumental status in the mid-eighteenth century in the large and elegant theaters erected in cities such as Lyon, Bordeaux, and Nantes. Taking the perspective of urban authorities, who paid for several of the largest and most architecturally striking playhouses of the era, this chapter casts new light on a more familiar narrative by exploring the civic aspirations and intercity competition that often motivated local municipal governments to fund public theaters. Chapter 3 asks what role the French state—here defined as the royal government and representatives of the crown, including military commanders—*did* play with regards to these new stages. Royal agents promoted provincial theater in a variety of ways, for personal reasons as well as for reasons of state. To the extent that the French state was complicit in the creation of a theater industry, however, this was primarily because royal officials encouraged, protected, and at times even collaborated on theater projects that had important roots in the private domain.

Next, I turn to the business of performing on these new provincial stages, particularly during the later decades of the Old Regime when resident theater companies became increasingly widespread. Chapter 4 focuses on the theater directors who drove the establishment of resident acting and opera troupes. These businessmen and women developed a new organizational model for theatrical production, and in the process they filled France's new public playhouses with growing numbers of patrons. Chapter 5 highlights the actors who did the work of entertaining these burgeoning provincial audiences. As they took to the stage, actors found themselves responsible for mediating between the entrepreneurial aims of their directors and the desires of the public. Here, labor history, viewed through negotiations between actors and directors over contracts, wages, and working conditions, reveals the profound impact that commercialization had on the acting profession throughout France, including in Paris. Chapter 6 turns to audiences and their theater practices. Spectators in cities across France became savvy cultural consumers, confidently asserting their "right" to comment on performances and demanding an ever greater say in casting and repertory decisions. Authorities' persistent attempts to order and discipline theater audiences often failed, most spectacularly when spectators embraced commercial tactics such as consumer pressure—including full-fledged theater boycotts—to make their voices heard.

The final chapter examines the establishment of public playhouses and professional acting troupes beyond the Hexagon, in the colonies of the French Caribbean. Directors, patrons, and colonial administrators self-consciously portrayed the public theaters established in cities in Saint-Domingue beginning in the 1760s as direct participants in the theater culture and practices of metropolitan France. I chose to consider colonial playhouses, performers, and audiences separately from those of the provinces for two reasons. First, colonial theater constitutes a comparative case with which to evaluate the arguments presented here. Considered separately, provincial and colonial stages throw into relief commonalities and differences marking the institution of theater in these two "peripheries." Second, staging performances in the tropical slave plantation societies of the French Caribbean involved political, economic, and social considerations quite different from those of provincial cities. The operations of these theaters therefore must be located within the specificities of the colonial situation. As spaces that gathered white planters, traders, artisans, and soldiers, as well as free people of color, the playhouses of Saint-Domingue played a prominent role in negotiating colonial identities and racial boundaries. Approaching theaters as cultural businesses subject to the commercial pressures of the market, this chapter devotes particular attention to the unmatched opportunities that the stage afforded free people of color, who participated not only as spectators but also as directors, patrons, and actors in colonial theaters.

For much of the last century, cultural discourse has cast the commercialization of culture—and the widespread consumption that accompanied it—in a negative light. The French have been particularly vociferous critics of what is often depicted as a dehumanizing process that undermines creativity, discourages agency, and leads to cultural decline and alienation.[37] Yet, in the cities of eighteenth-century France and its colonies, the commercialization of theatrical production offered new opportunities for entrepreneurial, civic, and professional engagement to women as well as men from a variety of backgrounds. Spectators, for their part, drew on their authority as consumers to shape theater offerings and the theatrical experience in unprecedented ways. From the standpoint of the director struggling to keep out of bankruptcy, the actress negotiating for a higher salary, or the shareholder putting his or her money into a joint-stock theater company, commercialization did not unfold in an impersonal and structurally determined process. Even during its heyday theater proved a risky business. Bankruptcy was common. A theater's success, when it happened, was the result of personal ambitions and community initiatives by individuals who, despite the economic perils of the enterprise, succeeded in balancing the books. This study brings to light the experiences of the often-anonymous cultural intermediaries whose efforts made France into Europe's leading arena for the performing arts. Eighteenth-century theater entrepreneurs and their customers emerge here not as passive recipients of cultural practices imposed on them from the capital or as victims of a process of cultural centralization directed by the state, but as active participants in commercial cultural networks that they helped to create and to define.

In writing this book my goal has been not simply to suggest that a different framework is necessary for understanding cultural production in the cities of France's "peripheries," or to argue that innovations rooted in these "peripheries" in turn influenced theatrical life in the capital (although I do hope to do both). Rather, I propose that what took place both behind the scenes and in the auditoriums of new provincial and colonial playhouses merits our attention because during the decades preceding the Revolution these theaters introduced new cultural and commercial practices into urban public life that reshaped contemporary values and social norms.

Jean-Jacques Rousseau recognized the potential for theater to do just this in his *Letter to M. d'Alembert on the Theatre*, in which he famously opposed the introduction of professional public theater into his native city, Geneva. Writing in 1758, in the midst of the rapid expansion of France's theater industry, Rousseau warned that "the theatre has rules, principles, and a morality apart" that would nonetheless serve as a powerful model for local society.[38] Rousseau was hardly the first to condemn the stage. Antitheatricality had deep roots in France, where the Catholic Church officially placed actors under a ban, denying them burial in sacred ground.[39] Rather than reiterating the threats that actors and their profession posed to religion, however, the author of the *Letter to M. d'Alembert* emphasized the moral and social influence that theater would have on the urban population. He presciently anticipated that spectatorship would foster luxury consumption and the desire for emulation; that theater would offer women a more prominent role in society and in public life; and that customers, even those with bad taste, would demand to "play the connoisseurs and arbiters" of the theater and "to decide for [their] money."[40] Establishing public theater as a regular part of urban life, Rousseau believed, would bring about a "revolution" in contemporary mores.[41]

In recent decades, scholarship on the French Revolution has largely abandoned the search for a unified causal framework of this signal event, embracing instead the exploration of the Revolution's "cultural origins," defined by

Roger Chartier as those "changes in belief and sensibility that would render such a rapid and profound destruction of the old political and social order decipherable and acceptable."[42] There is no doubt that philosophical essays, political libels, legal briefs, newspapers, advertisements, and even plays and librettos all had a role in bringing about significant changes in the ways that contemporaries conceived of the traditional social and political order and their place within it.[43] Nevertheless, this book adopts the perspective—one that is shared by many in the theater business—that actions speak even louder than words. Theater investors, directors, actors, and spectators, as we will see, claimed the relative liberty, authority, and equality that could be exercised in this emerging cultural marketplace years before they would claim these rights in the political sphere as revolutionary citizens.

CHAPTER 1

Investing in the Arts

In late 1774, residents of Le Mans, a city of about fourteen thousand located to the southwest of Paris, complained in the local newspaper, the *Affiches du Mans,* that their city was now "the only one in the whole [region] deprived of the pleasure of a theater."[1] Many other French cities had recently dedicated public playhouses, but those acting companies willing to travel to Le Mans rented space in a private house to stage their performances. Although a group of citizens had petitioned the city government in 1768 to build a municipal theater, their request had been refused. Le Mans, officials explained, simply did not have the funds, "the meagerness of patrimonial revenues having always prevented the municipality from being able to provide this amenity to the citizens."[2]

In the absence of financial support from the municipality or the state, a local judge named Mathieu Chesneau-Desportes joined with several other prominent residents to pursue a new plan: they would construct the theater through private investment. They organized a Society of Shareholders for the Construction of a Playhouse in the City of Le Mans, a joint-stock company that proposed to sell shares of 150 livres each in order to raise the eighteen thousand livres needed to build a public theater. In December 1774, the *Affiches du Mans* first advertised the project to provide the city with a theater described as "nicely decorated without luxury."[3] The society would operate the theater, with members receiving a share of the proceeds made from renting the stage to traveling acting and opera troupes as well as to popular performers such as tightrope dancers and musicians who played the glass harmonica. The city agreed to donate use of land for the theater and the theater-building society began recruiting investors. More than a hundred individuals came forward to purchase a share in the enterprise.[4] Their efforts proved a success. The city celebrated the theater's inauguration in 1776. Local residents began enjoying theatrical entertainment on a regular basis, and the society-operated theater remained the city's primary performance venue, to the profit of its investors, well into the nineteenth century.[5]

For eighteenth-century cities like Le Mans theater in and of itself was hardly novel. Public performance had long enlivened urban life in France.[6] From the Middle Ages into the middle of the sixteenth century, the Catholic Church, together with religious confraternities and trade guilds, had patronized the performance of religious works that included passion plays and mystery plays. Secular drama had made its debut in France in the thirteenth century. During the Renaissance, societies of amateur actors had performed bawdy, satiric farces that proved popular among urban crowds. In the seventeenth century, Jesuit colleges had begun to stage annual student productions of classically inspired works. Even professional theater already had a rich history, for traveling acting companies had begun entertaining urban audiences by the late sixteenth century. In fact, in Paul Scarron's bestselling seventeenth-century novel *Le Roman comique*, the author recounted the adventures of a troupe of strolling players beginning with their arrival in the city of Le Mans, where Scarron had resided in the 1630s.[7]

What was new in the eighteenth century was the public playhouse. For decades, itinerant acting companies performed wherever they could find space. Most often, this was on a temporary stage erected in a jeu de paume, a building that housed a playing court for an early form of tennis. Actors also performed in private residences, in city halls, and even outdoors in courtyards or on plazas. The introduction of buildings dedicated expressly and permanently for the purposes of performance and entertainment provides an important indication of the changing status of theater in urban life. In 1671, an inn in Toulouse known as the Logis de l'Écu established what scholars consider to be the first dedicated public theater building outside of Paris.[8] Although the inn had already hosted performances of farces and comedies by traveling troupes in one of its outbuildings for perhaps half a century, the hall had served as little more than a space in which actors put up their own stages for the duration of their stay. At this point, however, the "Salle du Logis de l'Écu" was endowed with a permanent stage as well as box seats from which the Capitovls, or city magistrates, could enjoy performances with

In metropolitan France, by 1789 spectators attended theatrical performances in dedicated public playhouses in at least seventy-two cities.

greater comfort and distinction. Cities such as Lyon, Marseille, Montpellier, and Lille—among France's wealthiest and most populous in the late seventeenth century—inaugurated their first permanent public playhouses and opera houses in the 1680s and 1690s.[9] In the early decades of the eighteenth century they were joined by a handful of key administrative and garrison cities such as Strasbourg, Metz, and Dijon. Yet as late as 1730, only ten cities in all of France enjoyed a dedicated performance space that was open to the public. This number would reach just twenty by midcentury.

Beginning in the 1750s the number of new playhouses in France began to accelerate rapidly. By 1789 spectators in no fewer than seventy-two metropolitan cities could spend an evening at their local public playhouse. When taking into account those theaters built to replace stages that were antiquated or that had been destroyed in fires, new playhouses opened in at least sixty-six of these cities during the final four decades of the Old Regime alone.[10] By the 1770s and 1780s, a significant number of these new stages were to be found in middling and smaller cities. Even in municipalities with populations of fewer than ten thousand, such as Quimper, Saint-Quentin, and Mâcon, audiences were able to attend performances in a dedicated salle de spectacle.

The establishment of dozens of new playhouses in eighteenth-century France raises questions concerning who established them, how, and why. To account for the dramatic growth of French theater during this era, most scholars have endorsed a vision of provincial assimilation by an expanding state in which representatives of royal power have played the defining role.[11] The initiative demonstrated by the civic leaders and investors of Le Mans, however, calls into question this interpretation. To what extent should the establishment of public theaters in France be seen through the lens of patronage and pressure from the royal government, with change stemming from "above"? Or, to what extent should these new cultural institutions be seen as commercial operations that sold access to a cultural commodity in new and growing markets? To find answers to these questions, we need to begin by considering who built, paid for, and operated France's new public playhouses. In most cases, the crown, agents of the royal government, and even municipal officers did not initiate and realize theater-building projects. Rather than resulting from a directed and centralized process of expansion, most provincial playhouses, like that of Le Mans, were locally motivated and privately funded.

Arts Funding and the State during the Old Regime

A systematic examination of who paid to construct France's theaters helps to illuminate the impetus behind the widespread adoption of this institution.

Contemporary sources identify the individuals or groups that paid to build eighty-three playhouses constructed in sixty-three provincial cities between 1671 and 1789.[12] Only two of these theaters, the Théâtre de la Marine in Brest and the theater in Besançon, another midsized city with a sizeable garrison, received significant direct financial assistance from the crown. In three cities noble-sponsored theaters were opened to the public: Nancy, Lunéville, and Mâcon. Municipal backing proved more common, with city governments paying for the construction of twenty-three of these new theaters. Municipally owned theaters were among the most impressive theaters in eighteenth-century France and by the late eighteenth century a significant number of these enjoyed a resident theater and opera company. Perhaps for these reasons, many contemporaries shared the belief that "in effect the playhouses in France are furnished either by His Majesty or built on the municipality's dime."[13] Yet this was not, in fact, the case. Of these eighty-three theaters, fifty-six—or more than two-thirds—were constructed using private funds.[14] To understand why, we first turn our attention to royal and municipal involvement in provincial theater-building.

The challenge facing all those who wanted to erect a new public theater in their city, from France's provincial governors and royal intendants to military commanders to municipal officers, was money. Building a public theater, especially one that might bring honor to a city, was expensive. Although aristocratic patronage had provided a vital support to the traveling acting troupes of the mid-seventeenth century, this traditional patronage was not in most cases a viable means to supply a city with a public theater. The settling of the court at the palace of Versailles, along with hundreds of France's most powerful and wealthiest aristocrats, and the establishment of royal theater companies in Paris seem to have discouraged nobles from supporting their own theater troupes. The number of companies bearing the names of royal family members and other high-ranking nobles had declined precipitously by the early eighteenth century. For those acting and opera troupes that continued to bear the name of a governor or another powerful patron throughout the eighteenth century, as in Marseille and Lyon, this distinction did not necessarily imply any financial support.[15] In fact, theater companies became so independent from this traditional source of patronage that by the middle of the eighteenth century, when provincial governors began to assert their authority to select the acting company or companies that were permitted to perform in their province, the troupe's director was often required to pay the governor for this privilege. In 1777, for example, a group of actors paid four thousand livres to the governor of Brittany, the duc de Penthièvre, for the rights to the exclusive theatrical privilege for Nantes for a year.[16]

The few prominent nobles who had the means and desire to build a stage usually intended them for private, rather than public, use. For example, in Nancy, Léopold, the duc de Lorraine, erected an opera house in the gardens behind the ducal palace in 1708–09 for the use of his court. Only decades later, after the court and its theater had been removed to Lunéville, was this theater opened to the public. His successor, Stanislas, then supported the construction of a new public theater in Nancy in 1755.[17]

For most royal representatives, their relationship with Versailles did not provide a direct solution to the money problem. Louis XIV and his successors focused their attention on the Paris stages, taking surprisingly little initiative regarding theatrical life in provincial cities. Unlike the British state, which established Theatres Royal not only in London but also in Bath, Norwich, Bristol, and several other important provincial cities, the French monarchy authorized no royal dramatic theaters beyond the capital.[18] Although in France the approval of the King's Council was necessary for the construction of new provincial theaters, the monarchy provided significant funds for such projects only in the rare instances mentioned above, cities that were important military garrisons lacking playhouses. (In fact, the state even made it a general rule to deny tax relief to cities building or rebuilding a theater.[19]) Only in Brest, a case that will be discussed in chapter 3, did the royal government go so far as to claim ownership of a provincial public theater.

It is true, however, that royal agents such as provincial governors and especially intendants, administrators who reported directly to the crown, wielded influence in their relations with municipal governments that proved instrumental in resolving the financial challenges of theater- building. During the reign of Louis XIV, the king granted intendants substantial authority over the finances of most municipalities, making these administrators responsible for overseeing all major capital projects.[20] It to be expected, therefore, to find intendants and other royal agents closely involved in promoting theaters in cities such as Montpellier, Clermont-Ferrand, and Bayonne, all cases in which the municipality paid for the building.[21] If an intendant could win the approval of the King's Council, these individuals could use their authority to demand, more or less, that city governments pay for projects ranging from a *place royale* to a new official residence for the intendant to a new theater.[22] Provincial governors, too, might exert a great deal of influence. In Metz, the maréchal de Belle-Isle was closely involved in the building of the municipal public theater. In Bordeaux, scholars argue, the governor of Guyenne, the duc de Richelieu, willed the city's construction of the lavish Grand Théâtre.[23] Still, the fact that representatives of the crown could resort to coercive techniques does not mean that most did so. Recent scholarship on seventeenth- and eighteenth-century urban building emphasizes the extent to which royal representatives worked with municipal governments or private individuals to realize projects that can be seen as mutually beneficial.[24]

For agents of royal authority such as intendants, building a new theater certainly offered political advantages. Like their king, intendants sought to benefit from the display of status and authority that was staged during a performance. They maneuvered, along with military commanders, judges of provincial parlements, and other political notables, to claim one of the most prominent boxes from which to enjoy performances, those located adjacent to the stage. These seats often gave a poor view of the performance, since the sightlines were awkward and the stage lamps could be blinding. The spectators seated there had the advantage, however, that they were the most visible to the audience. From this prestigious position, an intendant could demonstrate his authority as the king's representative.[25] Some, as we will see, even explicitly used theater seating to assert their rank over political rivals. Beyond such aims, however, intendants often seem to have seen in a public theater the opportunity to provide a new center for elite sociability, to promote urban renewal and civic pride, and to integrate the city into developing cultural networks, attitudes they shared with municipal authorities, private patrons and investors, and other urban leaders. It seems hardly coincidental that by 1789 the seats of thirty of France's thirty-four intendancies enjoyed a public theater.[26]

Municipally owned playhouses caught on slowly in France, picking up momentum only after the first waves of entrepreneurial public theaters. The municipal playhouses that were built in provincial France during this era expressed an intensification of the city government's traditional oversight of local public entertainment. In the seventeenth and early eighteenth centuries, the municipality exercised the right to approve or deny performances by traveling troupes, and they also took responsibility for maintaining public order at performances.[27] Over time, and as theater companies began to spend longer seasons in residence, a number of municipalities began providing and maintaining a performance space. In many cases, these were second-generation public theaters, replacements for run-down or defunct privately operated stages.

Although cities had often allowed traveling actors to set up a temporary stage in the city hall or another municipal building, based on this evidence only six city governments—those of Lyon, Bordeaux, Toulouse, Dijon, Nancy, and Strasbourg—acquired or converted a dedicated public theater during the first half of the eighteenth century. During the final four decades of the Old Regime, as theater gained popularity and prestige, these municipalities were joined by some fourteen others representing a broad spectrum of urban communities, including not only growing commercial centers such as Nantes and garrisons such as Metz and Besançon but also small cities such as Agen and Saint-Quentin that were establishing their first dedicated playhouse.[28]

Initially, these municipal playhouses might be located inside the city hall, as in Toulouse, or converted from a warehouse or jeu de paume, as in Strasbourg and Lyon.[29] Beginning in the mid-eighteenth century, however, municipalities such as Metz, Montpellier, and Lyon, and later Bordeaux and Nantes began forming more ambitious plans for playhouses, signaling the advent of a new era in theater architecture that will be the subject of chapter 2 of this book. As municipal governments in these cities and others began to invest in purpose-built theaters, building costs escalated exponentially. Whereas early in the century theaters even in large cities were usually built for just a few thousand livres, around midcentury city authorities began to replace these simple structures with new playhouses costing tens and even hundreds of thousands of livres. By the 1770s, construction costs escalated even higher.[30]

Proposals for theater-building projects reveal a variety of motivations that inspired municipalities to invest in new theaters, from beautifying the city and providing citizens with a much-desired cultural amenity to helping the city manage gambling and other social ills. Contemporaries, citing the dilapidated conditions under which performances were taking place, frequently argued that an existing structure posed a public health risk. To promote attendance, a proper playhouse was needed that would provide for the safety as well as the comfort of the audience.[31] Size was another concern. A small theater accommodating only a few hundred spectators would hardly generate enough revenue to cover the operating expenses of most acting troupes, let alone provide enough profit to draw them to town and keep them there for an extended period. Especially in middling and smaller cities, a safe, sizeable, and welcoming public playhouse was often presented as a necessary step to cultivate a thriving theater scene locally. According to this logic, if the city would build a theater, both actors and audiences would come. Local demand may also have influenced the decisions of city governments to invest in theaters. By the 1760s and 1770s, a public theater was no longer considered a luxury: it was increasingly presented as a social and cultural necessity. As was the case in Le Mans, in cities where there was no public theater, citizens often turned first to the municipal government to provide one. Finally, with more cities enjoying new playhouses, civic pride and a sense of intercity competition became increasingly important factors driving both the construction and, as we will see, the design of new playhouses. To make sense of such seemingly all-inclusive agendas, we need to read petitions promoting theaters as part of the eighteenth-century discourse of *embellissement*. To contemporaries, *embellissement* encompassed not only beautification but also improvements to urban infrastructure and concerns for promoting public health, maintaining order, and encouraging commerce.[32]

Nonetheless, not all municipalities were able or willing to take financial responsibility for local entertainment. Some saw paying for a public theater as a poor investment, while others, such as Le Mans, just could not afford to do so. Despite the influence exerted by governors, intendants, and even their own populations, municipal governments could and did find ways to resist the pressure to take the theater in hand. In La Rochelle, for example, the city refused to purchase and renovate the city's theater as the intendant had hoped. The municipal government, likely worried about expense, justified its refusal by focusing on the administrative responsibilities this would have created: "These officers, occupied with serious affairs in the interests of the king's service and the good of their city, are they obliged . . . to interrupt their deliberations to descend into the base and minute details of the theater?"[33] Theaters, they implied, should be left in the hands of professional managers more familiar with these responsibilities and of a more appropriate social station to undertake them. The La Rochelle playhouse remained in private hands.

Nor should royal support for such municipal theater-building projects be taken for granted. In fact, as the growing expense and potential risks involved in theater-building became clear, the royal government actively discouraged the plans of certain cities to build a theater with municipal funds. When the mayor of Lorient solicited royal approval in 1774 to take municipal loans necessary to build a new theater in this Breton port, the King's Council responded that Lorient was neither "significant enough nor peopled enough to possess an institution of this nature." Versailles denied Lorient's request.[34]

Entrepreneurs and Playhouses

To understand the proliferation of French theaters during the late Old Regime, therefore, it becomes necessary to look beyond the state to consider private initiatives. Beginning in the late seventeenth century, new modes of private entrepreneurship emerged to exploit the potential for profit in professional entertainment. Local businessmen and women, alone or in groups, were typically among those establishing France's earliest public theaters. This was the case in France's largest cities, such as Lyon, Lille, Marseille, and Nantes, as well as in many smaller provincial municipalities.

The earliest playhouses were often converted from contemporary indoor tennis courts. The frontispiece of *Le Jeu royal de la paulme* by Charles Hulpeau (1632) shows the interior of a seventeenth-century jeu de paume. Courtesy of the Bibliothèque nationale de France.

In the seventeenth century, when traveling acting companies rented indoor space to perform, the owners of a jeu de paume did not always allow the actors to have use of their courts during the daylight hours, when they might be filled with tennis players. In such cases, actors were required to set up anew every evening, severely limiting their options for establishing a stage, seating, and sets. By the later seventeenth century, as the popularity of theater rose and the sport declined, acting and opera companies increasingly arranged to rent these buildings for weeks at a time. They then paid to build a stage on which they would perform. For example, in Auxerre in the summer of 1671, a group of actors paid a carpenter "to make them a stage in the city's jeu de paume . . . with a trap door in the middle and a place for the actors to dress—this within three days, for the sum of sixty-six livres."[35] An acting troupe contracting for a temporary stage in La Rochelle in 1689 agreed to pay one hundred and eleven livres for a more elaborate stage equipped with cables and pulleys, presumably for a stage curtain and possibly scenery, as well as a loge (or box) next to the stage for the violins. They planned to use the theater for a month and a half. At this point, the agreement specified, the stage would be demolished and the wood returned to the builders.[36] In Metz, too, in the 1680s, it was common practice for a visiting acting troupe "to have a theater put up" in a local jeu de paume for the duration of its stay.[37] Sources concerning these early temporary stages make little mention of seating for audiences. A painting from the 1710s by Jean-Baptiste Coulom depicts a scene from Scarron's *Le Roman comique* in which an actor performs on a hastily constructed wooden platform for spectators who are sitting on chairs or stools or standing around, an informal setting that may well have greeted some provincial spectators into the early eighteenth century.[38]

Around the 1680s, some entrepreneurs began gambling that permanently converting a jeu de paume or another large building into a theater could be lucrative. When France's first dedicated provincial theaters opened in cities such as Toulouse in 1671, Marseille in 1685, Lyon in 1688, Montpellier in 1692, and Lille in 1699, they were established by private entrepreneurs.[39] These early playhouses were hardly designed with luxury in mind. Through the first decades of the eighteenth century, frugality and practicality seem to have been the primary concerns for those establishing a public theater. In Montpellier, for example, when the director of a traveling opera company made arrangements in the 1690s to permanently convert one of the city's jeux de paume into a playhouse, the building's owner agreed to build only a simple stage, not one equipped with machines that moved sets and produced special effects. He consented to construct an *amphithéâtre*, or an area with bench seating located behind the parterre, and two rows of boxes along each side of the structure, all out of pine and all for "the most meager expense possible."[40] In 1712 one of the Metz jeux de paume was finally given a permanent stage as well as boxes and an amphitheater, the physical infrastructure that contemporaries deemed "necessary for the performance of comedies." All this was built for a cost of just thirty-five hundred livres.[41]

Given these modest beginnings, it may come as little surprise that among early theater entrepreneurs we find a number of jeu de paume operators, as well as those in the building trades. Jeu de paume owners were involved in theaters in Metz, Rennes, Douai, and Tours. In Quimper the theater was built by a wood merchant (*marchand de bois*), in Alençon by a building contractor (*entrepreneur de maçonnerie*), and in Soissons by a master roofer (*maître couvreur*).[42] A second group included those who might be placed in the service sector. For instance, in the 1740s a Nantes innkeeper (*aubergiste*) named Tarvouliet turned a concert space that he had initially constructed to host guests into a theater. In Abbeville a café owner and his wife bought an adjacent lot in order to establish a theater that also featured a café along the street front. A tiny 150-seat theater was set up by a hairdresser in Saint-Étienne.[43] Finally, some theater entrepreneurs were professional performers themselves. A musician named Gautier opened Marseille's first public theater to provide a space in which his opera company could perform. Women directors also established playhouses. In the early 1730s, Mademoiselle Dujardin hired three entrepreneurs, including an architect, a master carpenter, and a master joiner (*maître menuisier*), to build and operate a provisional playhouse in Bordeaux. In the 1770s and 1780s, Mademoiselle Montansier built new public theaters in the cities of Versailles and Le Havre.[44]

To understand how these individuals might benefit from building a theater, it is helpful to compare the operations of theatrical entertainment in provincial cities with those in Paris. Unlike in Paris, where the system of royal monopolies guaranteed that each theater or opera house became home to a single company that featured only a specific genre of entertainment, provincial playhouses typically hosted an array of genres.[45] Entrepreneurs negotiated monopolistic privileges with the city, the provincial governor, or sometimes the royal government, and these privileges typically assured that their theater would be the city's only venue for paid entertainment.[46] Sometimes this included all performances of theater, opera, and ballet; other times it was extended to popular performances by marionettists, acrobats, and the like. Many theaters hosted balls and dances, as well, especially during the Carnival season. This was the case in Abbeville, where the entrepreneurs proposed that their playhouse to be used "to perform comedies, to hold public balls, to play goblets, to rope dance, and [to] give all other entertainments."[47]

In a small city such as this one, owners might charge for the use of the building by the performance, whereas in larger municipalities contracts were often negotiated for longer periods.

Although this privilege offered some degree of protection, builders had no guarantees that acting companies would in fact come to the city and rent the theater. As late as 1786, the owner of the relatively new theater in Laval complained that "for three years he was able to have on his stage only two troupes who moreover gave very few performances, which reduced the profit of the theater to very little."[48] Theater entrepreneurs who proved successful at filling their theater with acting troupes and other performers, however, stood to make a relatively comfortable living off of their investment.

This was the case because once the theater was built the owners operated more like landlords, with the troupes that rented from them taking on most, although not all, of the risk. Rental contracts between the Nantes theater owner Tarvouliet and various directors demonstrate that, from the late 1740s through the 1770s, he charged directors three thousand livres a year to rent his theater and its furnishings. These contracts were made on a yearly basis, even though the actors did not at that point perform in Nantes year-round. As additional perks, he and his wife and children were granted free entry to all performances, and he was given three additional free tickets for each performance and ball.[49] In Marseille, in the late 1730s the Gay family earned about five thousand livres a year from the use of the theater they had built in 1733 as well as from the rental of an apartment and café located within the building. Although the theater itself rented for seven hundred livres a month, their income seems to have fluctuated depending on how much of the year the theater actually hosted acting and opera companies, and whether these troupes in fact paid their rent.[50] In the 1770s, this same theater, now owned by a lawyer named Chomel, rented for a steady seventy-two hundred livres a year. In the early 1780s, when concerns arose about the potential public safety in the now-outdated structure and plans began taking shape to build a new theater, Chomel sought in vain to defend his privilege. This theater, he wrote, constituted "the main object of [my] fortune," and the means by which he supported his family. Could the city "refuse to an honest citizen, a father of a family, the upkeep from his profession?"[51] Theaters like that of Marseille, these cases suggest, provided substantial income for entrepreneurs, enough so that the Marseille city government investigated purchasing the playhouse to operate it, although it ultimately decided not to do so.[52]

Most of the buildings erected or converted by these provincial entrepreneurs ranged from minimally utilitarian to modestly distinguished. Mademoiselle Montansier's theater in the city of Versailles, rather exceptionally, was truly fit for a king: Louis XVI and Marie Antoinette attended opening night in 1777.[53] All, however, operated as commercial enterprises. Their owners, like the professional acting companies that they solicited to rent them, were committed to selling a cultural commodity—an evening of entertainment—in these emerging markets. In his landmark scholarship on consumption in France, the historian Daniel Roche has highlighted the role that local merchants played in transforming early modern buying practices.[54] In similar fashion, these theater entrepreneurs provided an important impetus for the adoption of new leisure practices in urban France.

Joint-Stock Companies

Beginning in the 1760s, private engagement in public entertainment took on a second—and substantially different—form. Between 1760 and 1789, groups of private investors came forward to finance public playhouses or resident acting companies in at least twenty provincial cities.[55] The theater societies they created were typically *sociétés par actions*, joint-stock companies similar to those created to generate capital for many different kinds of businesses during the Old Regime.[56] In the seventeenth century, most joint-stock companies had been created by the royal government to finance overseas trade and colonization, as in the case of the French East India Company. Beginning in the eighteenth century, however, a significant number of private companies were formed on a similar basis. Theater societies, like other joint-stock companies involved in trading, mining, or manufacturing, required royal approval for their creation, usually granted by the King's Council. The first of these theater societies was created in 1760 by the duc de Richelieu to finance an acting and opera company that would provide year-round entertainment in Bordeaux. This approach was later emulated in cities ranging from Toulouse and Marseille to Le Havre and Perpignan. The influence of private arts investment on performance companies, and the successes and challenges these investors encountered, will be considered in a later chapter. What matters here is that the joint-stock model was quickly applied to the building of playhouses, and with remarkable success. Between 1766 and 1789, private individuals founded joint-stock companies to finance the building of new public playhouses that opened in Toulon (1767), Grenoble (1768), Rochefort (1769), Le Mans (1776), Rouen (1776), Reims (1777), Lorient (1779), Lille (1787), Marseille (1787), and Saumur (1788).[57] In several other cities, including Cambrai, Pau, Nantes, and Angers, local residents also expressed interest in building a theater through subscriptions or shares, although these projects were not realized.[58]

The organization and aims of these theater societies differed according to local needs and abilities.[59] Some joint-stock societies involved small numbers of very wealthy investors, each contributing several thousand livres to the project. Others included more than a hundred investors whose participation required a much smaller contribution. In some cities, such as Le Mans, a theater society raised funds to build a city's first playhouse. Elsewhere, such as in Lille, local elites used the joint-stock organization to generate enough capital to replace an old and decrepit playhouse with a stately and modern theater. In still other cases, such as in Marseille, a privately funded new theater served as the centerpiece of an extensive project in speculative land development. The crown embraced such initiatives. In Lorient, not long after the royal government rejected the city's proposal to build a municipal public playhouse, the mayor and fifteen others established a joint-stock company to raise the capital to

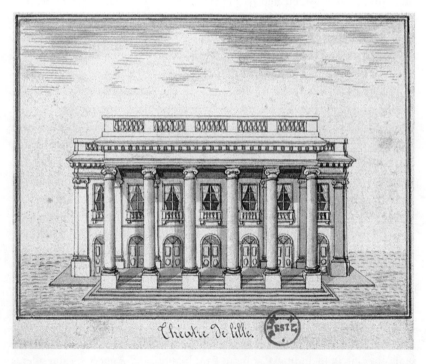

With its columns and classical styling, the Lille playhouse (inaugurated in 1787) demonstrates that joint-stock theater societies, influenced by contemporary architectural trends, also built monumental theaters. Théatre de Lille, courtesy of the Bibliothèque nationale de France.

pay for the construction costs themselves. This time the King's Council approved the project, and Lorient received a theater.[60]

Most theater-building societies adapted the investment formula known as a tontine, a variation on an annuity that offered lifetime revenue in exchange for an investment of principal.[61] Royal tontines had begun as strictly financial ventures concerned with raising revenue for the crown, but the tontine concept was here adapted to new purposes. Shareholders paid to construct, furnish, and maintain the building. The city government usually provided the land for the theater at no charge, with the agreement that at the death of the last designated heir the building would become the property of the city. According to some contracts, the liability of shareholders was limited expressly to the initial amount invested, protecting the investors from poor project management.[62] Each investor and, after his or her death, a designated heir received a share of the revenue generated from renting the theater, whether to a local acting and opera company or to traveling troupes and entertainers. The share could be passed down a single time only. As a result, as the number of living shareholders diminished over time, rental revenue was shared by fewer survivors, benefiting disproportionately those who were long-lived. Given the popularity of gambling in eighteenth-century France, such a proposition may well have appealed to the gambler's willingness to take a risk with the possibility of a significant payoff.[63] For those lucky heirs, their stake in a theater might prove lucrative indeed. When the last shareholder in the theater-building tontine in Lille died in 1864, this individual was the sole recipient of all rental income from the Lille theater.[64]

Members of theater societies did more than simply pay to erect public theaters. They also played an important role in managing the operations of these cultural institutions. The recruitment processes, social makeup, and business tactics of these little-known arts organizations, therefore, provide insight into the processes of cultural change in the cities of eighteenth-century France.

Membership and Recruitment

Who invested money in public theaters? The theater societies of Le Mans, Lille, and Saumur maintained detailed records regarding their membership and operations, enabling the reconstruction of the social background of more than 85 percent of investors in each project.[65] Of ninety-nine identifiable investors in Le Mans (out of a total of 108), the nobility came out most strongly in support of the project, with thirty-six nobles purchasing shares. They were joined by thirty-one lawyers and royal or local officeholders.[66]

Affiche listing the members of the Society of Shareholders for the Construction of a Playhouse in the City of Le Mans in 1777, with handwritten additions. With permission, Archives départementales de la Sarthe 111 AC 611, "Tableau de la société d'actionnaires."

Yet the relatively modest cost of a share, just 150 livres, also placed this opportunity within reach of thirty-two others, including not only *négociants* (elite wholesale traders) and merchants, but also an apothecary, an architect, three ironmasters, two grocers, a watchmaker, a surgeon, and a printer.[67]

Such social diversity also characterized the joint-stock theater society in Lille, as well as that of Saumur, which combined a theater with a new covered market. In Lille, a much larger city with a population of nearly seventy thousand, shares cost the substantially larger sum of fifteen hundred livres. Consequently, wealthier investors tended to be more strongly represented. Of the seventy-two identifiable investors there (out of seventy-six who bought shares), twenty-four were nobles, yet only seven lawyers or officeholders participated. In this important center for textile manufacturing and trade, the commercial bourgeoisie was particularly prominent. The twenty-four négo-ciants who bought shares constituted nearly one-third of all participants. Yet in Lille, too, another seventeen came from more modest backgrounds, includ-ing a master locksmith, a printer, an apothecary, and a brewer.[68] In Saumur, cavalry officers took the initiative in forming the theater society. Among the hundred investors whose social or occupational status is known (of a total of 116), these *carabiniers* were strongly represented.[69] In all, twenty-five military officers purchased one of the three-hundred-livre shares. They were joined by only one additional member of the nobility. Thirty-one investors held offices or practiced law. The remaining forty-one investors came from other professions and from the commercial and artisanal classes, including négo-ciants, entrepreneurs, and merchants, but also a surgeon, a café owner, a jew-eler, a candy maker, two engineers, a baker, and a domestic servant. Perhaps most surprising is the involvement of two priests who, despite the Gallican church's hostility toward the stage, supported the enterprise.[70]

In order to draw in such large numbers of investors, these societies recruited through personal networks as well as through more public means. In Le Mans, the theater project was advertised repeatedly in the local news-paper, and public meetings were held to promote interest.[71] In Saumur, a city without a local newspaper, recruitment began by mobilizing support within existing social networks. A form letter circulated in 1783 read as follows:

Monsieur,

The repeated cries of the public and the vows that you have cer-tainly made to have in Saumur a more proper theater than the current one, where one runs great risks to life, make me believe that you will not hesitate to sign the enclosed form, which is a promise to buy one or several shares of three hundred livres each for the construction of a new theater.[72]

If social connections served as a primary means of locating investors, the Sau-mur organizers nonetheless went out of their way to clarify that all investors would be welcome: "Persons who desire to buy shares, and who will not have received a copy of this letter are asked to believe that this is an omis-sion."[73]

The success of each of these three projects, it is evident, hinged on the creation of a heterogeneous coalition including the provincial nobil-ity, administrative and professional elites, prominent business leaders, and a healthy range of investors of the "middling sort." These projects were truly collective in nature: only rarely did individuals purchase more than four shares in the enterprise, and the vast majority of investors purchased just a single share.[74] Contemporaries publicly acknowledged the broad-ranging social support these theater societies garnered. The police ordinance for the new Saumur theater was prefaced with the announcement that "this edifice [is] uniquely destined for the public, of which the different classes contributed to its construction."[75] Because anyone with the funds was encouraged to purchase a share, membership in theater societies proved significantly more socially inclusive than membership in provincial academies, in which potential academicians needed to be elected by a membership drawn predominantly from notables: the nobility, the clergy, and the professions. Furthermore, despite the fact that Masonic lodges, often held to be the most egalitarian of provincial institutions, typically excluded women from membership, women constituted a small but significant number of shareholders—approximately ten percent—in each of these theater societies.[76]

Patronage, Profits, and Civic Leadership

By enabling a group of civic-minded individuals to pool their money in order to build a theater deemed "necessary to the status of this city," theater societies helped to give rise to a new form of local arts patronage.[77] In at least one case—Reims—shareholders made a no-interest loan toward the building of the theater. Shareholders there agreed to provide "funds in renouncing all interest on their advances and in submitting that they would only withdraw them little by little after the complete payment of the construction and of all the furnishing that followed."[78] The theater was a gift to the community. After the initial investments had been repaid, whatever monies came from renting the building would go to charity.[79] Even in the majority of cases for which profit was not renounced, these institutions frequently presented their mission in terms of the public good, reflecting the value placed on civic duty and "public utility" during the age of Enlightenment.[80] As private organizations established to contribute to the improvement of local urban life, theater societies have certain parallels to the *musées*, emulation societies, and secular philanthropic organizations also created in the last decades of the Old Regime.[81]

Why did individual shareholders or contributors choose to put their money into theaters? Beyond the desire—civic-minded or more perhaps more selfish—for a nicer venue in which to enjoy performances and to socialize, the primary motivation for most of these investors can likely be found in the cultural capital that could be gained from joining in such an effort.[82] Theater patrons can be seen as emulating the actions of the seventeenth-century high aristocracy, perhaps in hopes of receiving some of the same admiration and legitimation. In fact, these very traditional aristocrats sometimes played a leading role in these eighteenth-century projects. The first of the joint-stock theater-building companies, in Rochefort, was supported financially as well as politically by the provincial governor, the maréchal de Senecterre, who "placed himself at the head of this establishment" by purchasing the first share.[83] Participation in such a venture was a natural extension of traditional noble leadership in urban affairs as well as in the new civic institutions such as academies. It also reinforced the status of nobles who, especially during and after the Seven Years' War, became increasingly concerned with demonstrating their merit through acts of utility and benevolence.[84]

For those from professional and commercial backgrounds, the desire for entrée into the world of arts patronage seems to have been especially strong. Scholars have argued that for provincial professionals, membership in local cultural institutions, along with other cultural activities, "played an important role in the construction of . . . masculine social identities and in representing their status and rank."[85] For doctors and lawyers, then, but perhaps especially for wealthy négociants, whose membership in provincial academies remained restricted, theater societies presented a novel terrain in which to demonstrate cultural accomplishment and to exert civic leadership.[86] Purchasing a share in one of these organizations may have served as a means to buy recognition and membership in the cultural elite to which many of these individuals sought to belong.

Yet, for a significant number of those involved in such projects financial opportunity was also likely an important motivation. According to Colin Jones, growing civic-mindedness posed little conflict with "a developing 'market consciousness.'"[87] The elite investors in Lorient, for example, embraced both in tandem. In making the case for their endeavor, they noted the importance of providing safe and regular entertainment for the growing city, as well as their desire to endow Lorient with something "useful" and "pleasant."[88] At the same time, these shareholders approached their theater as a commercial enterprise. According to the contract of the Lorient joint-stock society, the theater and its café were to be rented at rates that would, ideally, assure each investor an annual 5 percent return on his investment.[89]

Recent scholarship on eighteenth-century credit markets demonstrates that wealthy nobles and well-off artisans alike kept their eyes open for potentially profitable places to invest their money.[90] France's nobility as well as the commercial elite invested heavily in joint-stock companies for industrial and manufacturing ventures, and were comfortable with this framework.[91] Moreover, financial investments were shaped not only by their earning potential but also by their social implications. It is well documented that many French elites took their money out of more lucrative but riskier investments to invest in the more prestigious and more stable areas of land and *rentes*, which typically yielded a 5–6 percent annual return.[92] (As we shall see, on average those of the theater society in Le Mans actually exceeded this amount.) Among investors in the Saumur theater society, it is telling that, military officers aside, nearly one-fifth listed their residency not in the local area, but in cities as far away as Rouen, Lyon, and Bayonne. For these shareholders, who were unlikely to attend the new theater and had less obvious social motivations, their investment decision may well have involved economic considerations. Finally, the social diversity characterizing membership in these organizations suggests a diversity of motivations on the part of shareholders. Despite the fact that an investment in a theater held none of the guarantees of a *rente* or a state-run tontine, the widow, apothecary, baker, and servant who bought shares in these operations may well have approached this as an investment in their future—and perhaps especially that of their children.[93]

Ultimately, in order to succeed as patrons of the arts, those organizing and leading these societies had little choice but to learn to run these theaters as businesses. Constructing a theater held no guarantees that troupes would rent it or that the enterprise would operate in the black. Because their operations depended on renting the theater at favorable rates, theater societies had good reason to be invested in seeking out directors and troupes and establishing a viable public. In Le Mans, Mathieu Chesneau-Desportes began to seek out directors in the months before the theater was completed to encourage them to perform in the city. He also undertook research on other regional theaters. In February 1776 he sent Pierre Pinchinat, the painter commissioned to decorate the interior of the playhouse, to visit the theater of Rouen, still under construction, as well as the theater in Caen, about a decade old, to gather ideas about interior design. Pinchinat also investigated their business practices. He wrote back with advice about how to rent the theater:

> I do not doubt that you, as well as your other commissioners, are thinking hard so as not to make a bad plan for renting the theater; don't speak of twelve livres per performance, nor of twenty, because they will take it for a *gargote* [a cheap and vulgar eating establishment]. [The theater] of Le Havre, where there aren't half the resources of Le Mans, is rented for fifteen hundred livres for just six months. These entrepreneurs have more resources than you think.[94]

Pinchinat's letter illuminates ways in which information ranging from theater designs to business strategies was shared laterally through France's urban
network. In the end, the society ignored Pinchinat's advice. They rented the
theater to performers on a sliding scale: acting and opera companies paid fifteen livres per performance, while popular performers paid between six and
nine livres. The concessioner also paid one livre for each evening of performance for the opportunity to sell refreshments. During the decade after the
theater's inauguration, the theater regularly hosted performances seventy-five
to eighty-five days a year. When the society had earned its first profits, the Le
Mans shareholders decided that the first dividend would be spent decorating
the theater. Beginning in 1778, shareholders began to receive a regular return,
on average about 6-7 percent of their investment.[95]

Not all theater-building ventures operated quite so smoothly as those in Le
Mans, Lille, and Saumur. In Marseille, the investors involved in constructing
a new public playhouse in the 1780s faced significant financial challenges.[96]
In a deal brokered by the governor and the monarchy together with the city,
an investment company had agreed to spend six hundred thousand livres to
construct the theater, a sum already considerably larger than those spent by
theater-building societies in other provincial cities. In this case, the deal was
founded on land speculation. To attract investors, the authorities offered
to grant them a larger amount of land than was necessary for a playhouse.
The shareholders intended to develop and sell this additional property in the
neighborhood immediately surrounding the theater, which they anticipated
would appreciate significantly in value once this important structure was
completed. The catch was that the shareholders did not enjoy the freedom
to select the architect and develop a plan to meet their needs as well as those
of the city. Instead, according to the terms of the land concession, a contest
was held in which the Royal Academy of Architecture in Paris selected the
winning design, which was then approved by the royal governor. When the
plan that the investors themselves commissioned from the architect Claude-
Nicolas Ledoux was passed over for a more traditional—and expensive—
design by Charles Joachim Bénard, these initial investors grew skeptical that
such a theater could be built for the agreed-upon amount. They withdrew
from the project. At this point a second group of investors came forward
to construct the theater. They incurred cost overruns that nearly doubled
their expenditures. Despairing, the members of this investment society found
themselves saddled, collectively, with a 1,100,000 livre bill.[97]

The Marseille investors shared with those in cities such as Lorient a desire
to do well by doing good—or, at the very least, to do well enough. If money
was not, as they claimed, their primary motivation, it did figure into their

calculations. In 1785, the group explained optimistically that the desire of a great number of citizens for a new theater persuaded them to take on this project despite the fact that "it is as good as demonstrated that we will only make an ordinary profit."[98] Three years later they were chastened. They had not anticipated, they wrote, that the privilege to build and run this theater would be purchased "at the expense of our peace of mind and of our fortune."[99] In crisis, the shareholders who owned the playhouse attempted to pass along their financial burden to the shareholders of the city's resident theater and opera company by raising the rent to eighty-two thousand livres a year—well over ten times the amount the troupe paid to rent the previous playhouse. In response to this outrageous demand, the theater troupe called for mediation by the police. Through negotiations, the rental price was lowered to thirty thousand livres a year, still among the highest in all of France.[100] Investing in theater, they learned the hard way, carried risks.

In the long run, at least in the cases for which financial sources are available, the investment of theater-building societies in the local community seems to have paid off. This was certainly the case in Le Mans, where the investment society's playhouse remained the city's principal performance space, to the continued benefit of investors, until 1842, when a new and larger municipal theater was inaugurated.[101] In Lille, those investors or heirs who were still alive in the 1840s and early 1850s earned dividends that steadily increased from two hundred to almost five hundred francs a year.[102] In Saumur, surviving heirs continued to share the revenue from the theater through 1861.[103] Even in the case of Marseille, the theater, which later served as the city's opera house, remained in private hands until 1882, when it was purchased by the city for more than a million francs.[104]

Those participating in such ventures had the opportunity to take pride in their contribution to urban life and to enjoy attending the new theater they helped to build. But theater societies also enabled members to participate in managing the enterprise and in the process to take part in a new institution of "civic sociability."[105] The society of Le Mans provides one example of how this could work. In contrast with theater-building projects directed by municipal governments, governors, and intendants, the Le Mans theater society invited participation from the beginning. When organizers first introduced the project, they immediately solicited comments concerning possible designs. They promised that "they will be collected with care; & we will only begin the project model after having examined them, & having given them all the attention that without doubt they will merit."[106] In late January of 1775, a scale model (*plan en relief*) of the theater was then placed on display for the public, along with a preliminary estimate of the costs, at the home of the treasurer, M. Rey.[107] Those who purchased shares had the opportunity to become quite involved in the project. Nearly sixty shareholders attended a meeting in February to approve the bylaws for the society and elect four representatives.[108] During the period of organization and construction, the shareholders gathered regularly in assembly to discuss membership, finances, and the progress of the construction. After the theater was completed, shareholders continued to meet "to deliberate on various affairs of interest to the society," including rental arrangements, the acquisition of sets and props, and upkeep of the building.[109] The *Affiches du Mans* advertised these shareholder meetings, summarized the proceedings, and even, by the 1780s, printed reminders to shareholders to stop at the house of M. Rey to receive their share of the profits.[110]

At these meetings, each shareholder was given a vote on society affairs. The Le Mans theater society was not alone in this democratic organization, which was shared by those in Reims, Saumur, and other cities.[111] In voting rights, theater societies were more inclusive than many other joint-stock companies, in which shareholders often needed to hold a significant financial stake in order to receive a vote, and where many important decisions were made by the professional staff and merely endorsed by the shareholders.[112] In the societies of Le Mans and Lille, elected leadership positions, it seems, were often filled by nobles, tax farmers, and other notables.[113] Still, the social implications of such an organizational framework are noteworthy. Shareholders in the Saumur theater such as Anne Poperin, a domestic servant, and Jacques Ainard de Moreton, the comte de Chabrillan, could both, at least in theory, attend meetings and cast their vote on theater policy.

In sum, joint-stock theater societies helped to bring together a remarkably heterogeneous group of private investors to collaborate on an enterprise that embraced civic, cultural, and financial goals. In doing so, they created new opportunities for civic leadership and for the status acquisition with which arts patronage was traditionally associated—opportunities that are more often associated with the "bourgeois leisure" of the nineteenth century.[114]

The commercial orientation characterizing France's privately run provincial theaters may seem surprising to those more familiar with the cultural landscape of Paris, where royal patronage continued as a defining force throughout the Old Regime. There, we have seen, the royal theater companies actually constituted part of the King's Household.[115] The king provided each of the three royal troupes with a Parisian monopoly over drama, opera, or commedia dell'arte and opéra-comique, as well as with the tremendous prestige that came with the designation as a royal company. This royal protection enabled these troupes to recruit the best talent from all over France, to serve as the principal venue for the debut of new stage works, and to suppress and exploit competition from theaters in the fairgrounds and on the Boulevard du Temple. Even with such support, the Paris Opera remained chronically insolvent.[116]

Yet, these privately financed provincial playhouses were perhaps not so very different from the royal theaters of Paris as one might think. The monarchy, too, faced financial constraints in its cultural patronage, and direct financial support from the crown had its limits. In fact, in 1687, when Louis XIV forced the Comédie-Française to vacate its theater on the rue Guénégaud, the players found themselves collectively responsible for building their own new playhouse, which they constructed on the rue des Fossés-Saint-Germain-des-Près at a cost of nearly two hundred thousand livres.[117] Nearly a century later, when the Comédie-Française finally moved to an elegant new theater, the troupe's new home—the present-day Odéon theater—had been constructed neither by the king directly nor by the royal theater company. This time the new Paris theater, the centerpiece of a speculative land-development project, was financed by private investors.[118]

Culture Brokers in the Late Old Regime

Studying theatrical production in eighteenth-century France from the local perspective brings to light an unexpected—and unexpectedly diverse—array of culture brokers. Of the theaters constructed in provincial France from the 1680s through the 1780s, approximately two-thirds were established by private individuals or groups. The cohort of theater owners included significant numbers of entrepreneurs such as carpenters, café owners, and professional directors, as well as the hundreds of members of the new joint-stock theater societies established in the later decades of the Old Regime. Although traditional elites played a prominent role in endowing cities with theaters, so too did professionals and middling men (and women) whose entrepreneurial drive and civic values motivated them to invest in projects that allowed them to become patrons of the arts. The establishment of public playhouses in provincial France was not the realization of the ambitions of a centralizing absolutist state. Instead, the decision to erect a permanent stage—whether a simple converted jeu de paume playhouse or, as in Lille, an elaborate "theater-temple"—most often came from local initiative.

The individuals who built these stages, as we have seen, did so for varied reasons. Collectively, however, their efforts brought results, helping to launch institutions that significantly shaped everyday urban sociability during the late Old Regime. By the 1770s, dedicated public theaters had become so common in France that actors in traveling troupes griped when they were asked to perform in cities that lacked a proper dedicated playhouse. One actress considered it entirely unjust for her director to bring her to a city such as Niort, where the troupe was expected to perform in a space that she derided as a "stable."[119]

Prior to the opening of the new public theater in Le Mans, local audience support for the performing arts, by all accounts, was lacking. In the early 1770s, one theater director discouraged a colleague from taking his troupe to perform in the city, warning him that there were at most forty to fifty enthusiasts who followed the theater.[120] The determined founder of the Society of Shareholders for the Construction of a Playhouse in the City of Le Mans, and others like him, believed that a dedicated public theater could change this. As work got under way, the theater did in fact capture the attention of curious local residents. They began to crowd the construction site to watch the building go up, getting in the way of the workers and at times posing a hazard to themselves and others. In the *Affiches du Mans*, the builder announced that he would begin giving public tours of the building site on Sundays and holidays, but he asked in return that locals keep out of the way during the week.[121] As the inauguration of the playhouse, scheduled for late May of 1776, drew near, the builder declared that he and his crew were forced to close the doors to the public entirely during the final two weeks because "the crowds hinder them considerably, & distract them from their work."[122]

The playhouse that enthralled passersby in Le Mans was modest compared to many others of the era. Only forty feet by eighty feet, it accommodated no more than six hundred spectators and cost less than twenty thousand livres, a fraction of the cost of the signal theaters of the era.[123] Yet the building's façade was ornamented with a balcony, columns, and representations of the muses of comedy and tragedy. The appointments of the new theater were described enthusiastically in the local newspaper, which celebrated the luxury customers would find within. The investors even went so far as to bring a painter from Paris to decorate the auditorium and to paint the stage curtain featuring Voltaire, the most celebrated living playwright.[124] As clearly as the spectacular playhouses constructed in cities such as Lyon, Bordeaux, and Nantes, the society's playhouse in Le Mans proclaimed to residents the new importance accorded to theater in urban public life. Although built by private investors, this theater, too, served as an emblem of civic pride.

Chapter 2

Designing the Civic Playhouse

For the mayor and city councilors of Nantes, the inauguration of an impressive new municipal playhouse shortly after Easter in 1788 was an event long in the making. For several decades these magistrates had wanted to give the city a new theater to replace the dilapidated privately operated playhouse that had hosted performances in the city since the 1740s. As early as 1766, a master plan for urban renewal commissioned by the city featured a new public theater. Several parties came forward in the 1770s and early 1780s to point out the many deficiencies of the existing playhouse and to propose the construction of a new stage.[1] According to one pamphlet, "Everyone agrees that the theater is too small and poorly situated. The stage is almost always crowded [with spectators], even during regular performances, in such a way that it is impossible ever to have a good sense of theatrical illusion." The playhouse, which was constructed of wood and had inadequate exits, was a veritable firetrap, threatening spectators as well as the surrounding neighborhood. Yet what made a new playhouse in a better location an "indispensible necessity," the pamphlet argued, was the impressive growth in recent years in Nantes's population, its wealth, and in particular the large numbers of visitors drawn to the city to conduct business.[2] The existing theater—a far cry from the new ideal for a public theater that had been realized in cities such as Metz, Montpellier, and especially Lyon in recent decades—had become an embarrassment.

40

Then, in 1779, a wealthy tax farmer and businessman named Jean-Joseph-Louis Graslin had approached the municipal government with an offer it could hardly refuse. Graslin offered to donate to the city a sizeable plot of land in a desirable location, a gift whose value was estimated as high as two

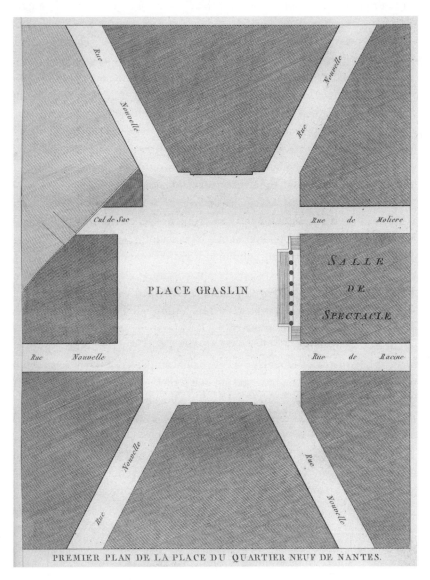

PREMIER PLAN DE LA PLACE DU QUARTIER NEUF DE NANTES.

This early proposal by Graslin offers an initial plan for the placement of the new Nantes theater within a new neighborhood (today's *quartier* Graslin). Aside from the salle de spectacle and plaza, almost the entire map represents proposed roads (listed as *Rues Nouvelles*) and buildings to be developed, demonstrating the extent to which the new theater defined the neighborhood that was built around it. "First map of the plaza of the new quarter of Nantes," published with permission from the Archives municipales de Nantes DD 231 n. 3.

hundred thousand livres. He agreed to build a public plaza onto which the theater would face, and even to construct the adjacent roads and necessary sewers. In exchange, he asked the city to pay to build a new public theater on this land. Graslin, anticipating that property values in the vicinity would rise through proximity to an elegant new playhouse, planned to develop a new upscale neighborhood anchored by the theater (today's quartier Graslin).[3]

Yet Nantes's new theater was not to be just any theater. The playhouse, designed by the municipal architect Mathurin Crucy, was intended as a monument celebrating all that Nantes had achieved in recent decades—and perhaps even more so what the city hoped to become in the future. Graslin aggressively promoted his plan. In numerous pamphlets, he appealed to the civic pride of the city magistrates as well as his fellow citizens: "The taste for embellishments has won over all the big cities; ours already emulates them with its commerce and its population, would you want for it always to remain so far behind them in matters of taste and pleasure, and only ever to contest them the advantage of wealth?"[4] Embracing Graslin's plan as well as his vision, the municipal government spent an estimated 265,000 livres constructing the building alone. The sculptures, painting, and other interior decorations cost an additional 185,000 livres.[5] When completed, the new Nantes theater boasted elegant columns, a white stone exterior, and elaborate gilding that emphatically proclaimed the city's commercial successes and its rising fortunes. Arthur Young, an English traveler who chronicled French life on the eve of the Revolution, recorded his impressions of the newly inaugurated Nantes playhouse, while conveying his astonishment at how luxurious French theaters had become: "Within all is gold and painting, and a coup d'oeil at entering that struck me forcibly. It is, I believe, twice as large as Drury Lane [London's leading theater], and five times as magnificent."[6]

When travelers like Young visited France's new playhouses during the 1780s, they had reason to be impressed by the new directions taken in French theater design. For decades the French had relied almost exclusively on theaters converted from jeux de paume and other buildings, constructed in most cases with minimal imagination and expense. Beginning in the mid-eighteenth century, however, the French playhouse was transformed into one of the most significant buildings in the urban landscape.[7] In the 1750s, the royal architect Jacques-François Blondel announced this new era for the institution when he declared that "nothing so contributes to the magnificence of cities as public theaters; these edifices must by their grandeur and their exterior disposition announce the importance of the cities where they find themselves erected."[8] Between the 1750s and the 1780s cities such as

Metz, Montpellier, Lyon, Bordeaux, and Nantes erected elegant monuments to the performing arts, with construction costs rising into the hundreds of thousands of livres and even, in the case of Bordeaux, into the millions.[9] Over the course of the eighteenth century, municipalities engaged in a large number of ambitious urbanization projects, busily constructing roads, public gardens, stock exchanges, covered markets, *places royales*, and more. Among these projects, however, the public theater emerged as the "worthy monument" of the late Old Regime.[10]

The rise of the theater to monumental status, although familiar to architectural historians, merits closer attention when viewed from the perspective of the making of a French theater industry. As contemporaries recognized, the physical structure of the playhouse greatly influenced the operations of theaters as cultural institutions and as businesses. For directors and actors, the building provided the stage on which they rehearsed and performed before a paying audience. The size, location, and amenities of the building all played a significant role in determining how much a theater company, as well as the owners of the theater, might earn from performances. For spectators, this was the site where they purchased their ticket and took their seat in a loge or balcony or jostled for a spot in the parterre, a standing-room-only pit located on the main floor. It was there that they cheered or jeered at the actors. This building, in other words, served as the site where theatrical production and cultural consumption took place. A theater's façade and decor, its interior spaces for gathering such as salons and cafés (or lack thereof), and the arrangement of seating within the auditorium all informed the experience of theatergoing and its meanings. With this new generation of buildings, urban leaders and municipal governments self-consciously set out to redefine the experience of dramatic and lyric entertainment, while celebrating civic pride and commercial success.

The evolution of the playhouse is illuminating for a second reason. It provides a means to study more closely the involvement of local city governments in promoting the expansion of professional theater during this era. Over the course of the eighteenth century, as we have seen, the magistrates of at least twenty cities approved, supervised, and paid for the building of new public playhouses. Although this constituted a minority of the new public theaters inaugurated in Old Regime France, these did include several of the most expensive, ambitious, and influential playhouses in France, most notably the theaters of Lyon, inaugurated in 1756, and of Bordeaux, inaugurated in 1780. Although scholars have traditionally emphasized the "fundamental role" of representatives of royal authority in eighteenth-century urban building projects such as theaters, this chapter argues that municipal authorities also need to be seen as central, if underappreciated, participants in establishing new standards for the design, elegance, and utility of the French playhouse.[11] Their actions supported an escalation in expectations in cities large and small that influenced all theater-building projects, public as well as private. This is all the more significant because in the domain of theater architecture the royal government was not the primary trendsetter. As the playhouse was reinvented in the second half of the eighteenth century, the most spectacular innovations took place outside of Paris.

From Jeu de Paume to Monumental Theater

"I cannot . . . complain enough of the little care that they have in France of making theaters worthy of the excellent works that they perform there, and of the nation that delights in them," Voltaire remarked in 1748 in his *Essay on the Tragedy of the Ancients and the Moderns*. Plays such as "*Cinna*, [and] *Athalie*," he continued, "deserve to be performed somewhere other than in a tennis court, at the end of which some decorations of the worst possible taste have been put up, and in which the spectators are placed, against all order and against all reason, some even standing on the stage, others standing in what we call a parterre, where they are uncomfortable and indecently crushed up against one another, and where they sometimes throw themselves in tumult one against the other, as in a public riot."[12] Voltaire was hardly exaggerating the conditions under which French audiences experienced dramatic entertainment. In the late 1740s, in the vast majority of those cities that boasted a dedicated playhouse, spectators attended performances in a converted building that had formerly served as a jeu de paume, warehouse, or other structure. Even those salles de spectacle that had been substantially renovated retained the shape of their earlier functions. These rectangular structures usually stood adjacent to other buildings, and featured simple exteriors. The results were long, narrow halls with a stage at one end. Box seats or galleries stacked in tiers, one above another, lined the walls of the auditorium. Hundreds of spectators typically stood in front of the stage in the parterre, while particularly distinguished spectators often watched the performance from the stage itself. At the same time, as we have seen, audiences in smaller cities and towns still frequently made do with temporary or makeshift accommodations.

Voltaire's frustration about the poor quality of France's theaters was directed at the theaters of Paris no less than at those in provincial cities. Even in Paris, home to France's first dedicated public theaters, existing structures had been renovated and permanently converted to the purposes of performance. At the time of his writing, the Paris Opera and the Comédie-Italienne

still performed in buildings that had not been originally constructed as theaters. When a new Paris Opera house finally opened in the Palais-Royal in
1770, it became the first new royal theater constructed in the capital in over
eighty years.[13]

The Comédie-Française was the exception. When the King's Players,
having been evicted from their previous home, hurriedly built themselves a
new playhouse in 1688-89, it became the first permanent public theater in
France constructed specifically for the purposes of performance.[14] Yet the
Comédie-Française theater did not significantly improve on existing jeu de
paume designs. It was located in the middle of a block of buildings. The
exterior, distinguished by little more than a few modest decorations, hardly
announced the prestigious players within. Foreign travelers expressed little
enthusiasm for the home of the leading dramatic theater company in Europe.
On his first visit to France in 1751, the renowned Shakespearean actor and
director David Garrick, no doubt comparing the theater with his own Drury
Lane theater in London, noted simply that "the Appearance of the house was
not so bad as I expected from the report of others."[15] His assessment twelve
years later, following a substantial renovation of the theater, was little better:
"The alteration of the Play house since I was there before, is much for the
better, but it look'd so dark & dirty that I was hurt at my first Entrance."[16]
The Comédie-Française finally abandoned this stage in 1770, and moved
into the theater in the Tuileries Palace while its members continued their
decadelong lobbying effort for a more distinguished home.[17] When Mrs.
Thrale, a British author and patron of the arts, attended a performance in
this temporary residence in 1775, she readily acknowledged that "the Actors
are really excellent; *better than our own*," but she found their playhouse a
"Wretched one, Foote's little Theatre [in London] is a Palace to it, for size,
magnificence and Elegance of Decoration." When the queen appeared at
the theater one evening, Thrale "wished her a better Theatre & handsomer
box to sit in."[18]

Given the esteemed reputation of French playwrights and actors throughout Europe, the relatively poor physical state of France's theaters for much of
the eighteenth century was unexpected for many visitors. Yet France lagged
behind England and especially the Italian cities in theater design. When
Blondel wrote his survey of French architecture in 1752, he considered elim-
inating playhouses entirely, believing that the theaters of ancient Greece and
Rome and those in contemporary Italian cities so clearly surpassed those of
France.[19] The architect and machinist André-Jacob Roubo acknowledged
that "for a long time, we complained in France of our theaters' poor design
and the lack of comfort, & quite justifiably so."[20] "We were in a way used to

it," the architect Pierre Patte explained concerning the poor state of French theaters, "and more than a century passed before we dreamed of remedying it."[21]

Within a few decades of Voltaire's critique, however, public theaters would come to occupy a place of honor within the French urban landscape, although not at first in Paris. Beginning with the inauguration of new theaters in Metz, Montpellier, and Lyon in the 1750s—all projects at least nominally undertaken by municipal governments—French theater design entered an era of rapid development.[22] Whether municipal authorities set out to endow their city with its first theater or to replace a decaying jeu de paume playhouse, growing numbers did so with a new ambition to distinguish their city. As Daniel Rabreau has shown, new theaters came to feature prominently in the urban planning projects that marked the era. Frequently used to anchor broader development projects, playhouses were often situated on esplanades and plazas or near bourses and public gardens.[23] The most influential theaters of this era, the Lyon theater designed by Jacques-Germaine Soufflot and the Bordeaux theater designed by Victor Louis, illuminate these new departures in theater design, as well as urban authorities' role in the invention of the modern French playhouse.

As in most other cities in France, Lyon's actors and singers performed until midcentury in a jeu de paume theater. In 1728, the city had acquired the *jeu de paume de la Raquette royale*, which it used to host the opera company that entertained Lyonnais for at least several months of every year.[24] Twenty-five years later this simple wooden playhouse was badly decayed. The city found itself "forced to build a new playhouse because of the total degradation of the building that currently serves this purpose."[25] Yet if necessity largely drove the construction of the new Lyon theater, civic pride determined what kind of new theater this would be. Criticizing the existing jeu de paume playhouse as "poorly proportioned to the grandeur of the city and to the number of its citizens," the city government decided to endow Lyon with a large and impressive new theater to be located on a plaza adjacent to the city hall, on land that was formerly a garden.[26] The municipality committed over six hundred thousand livres for a public building dedicated to arts and leisure, at the time an unprecedented investment in urban cultural life.[27]

The theater's architect Jacques-Germaine Soufflot would later achieve renown for his work as a royal architect, most notably as the architect of the Church of Sainte-Geneviève (now the Panthéon) in Paris. In the early 1750s, however, he was the official architect of the city of Lyon, having held the position of controller general of buildings and public embellishments for nearly a decade. Soufflot's vision for this theater was primarily influenced by

the theaters of Italy, where he had studied during formative years of his training. He studied contemporary opera houses in cities such as Parma, Rome,
and Venice, but also took a special interest in the theaters and amphitheaters
of the Roman Empire. Soufflot presented his plans for the new theater to
the Lyon Academy together with an essay explaining and justifying a project
that was ambitious for its day. In it, he explicitly rejected the French tradition,
in which even purpose-built theaters resembled converted jeux de paume.
Instead of following that path, he wrote, he aimed to benefit from the advantages of antique and Italian theaters, while improving on them.[28]

The resulting theater defined new standards for design and functional-
ity while raising the status of the French playhouse as an edifice. Several of
aspects of Soufflot's design proved especially influential. To begin with, the
Lyon theater was among the very first French playhouses designed to be an
independent, freestanding structure.[29] This served several practical purposes.
Theaters were notorious fire hazards because of the countless candles and oil
lamps required to light the stage as well as the house. The isolation of the
Lyon theater improved the security of the entire neighborhood by containing the risk that might be posed to adjacent buildings, while also providing
for more exits for its customers.[30] A freestanding theater also catered to the
comfort of wealthy patrons by offering more extensive street access for those
arriving and leaving by carriage. From an aesthetic standpoint, moreover, a
theater set apart from other buildings and situated on a plaza was more visually imposing.

Soufflot brought neoclassicism, influential in the design of other important public buildings of the era, to bear on the theater.[31] His playhouse was
proportional and symmetrical: a simple yet stately façade featured a long
decorative balcony framing the main entrances. Above, along the roofline,
the theater featured seven statues depicting Apollo, the god of music and
poetry, and numerous winged putti representing the arts. Inside, Soufflot's
elliptical auditorium brought the audience closer to the stage, in contrast to
the deep U-shaped auditoriums characteristic of jeu de paume theaters that
marked the recent playhouses of Metz and Montpellier.[32] Finally, he matched
the interior design of the playhouse, including its entrance hall, staircases,
salons, and even the auditorium, with the "restrained elegance" of the theater's exterior.[33]

Soufflot's efforts, more than those of any other contemporary architect,
established a model for the theater as an impressive public monument.[34] The
theater did more than receive widespread acclaim.[35] It marked a watershed
in French theater design. For the next three decades, when provincial cities
decided to build a theater, most looked to Lyon for inspiration. Even before

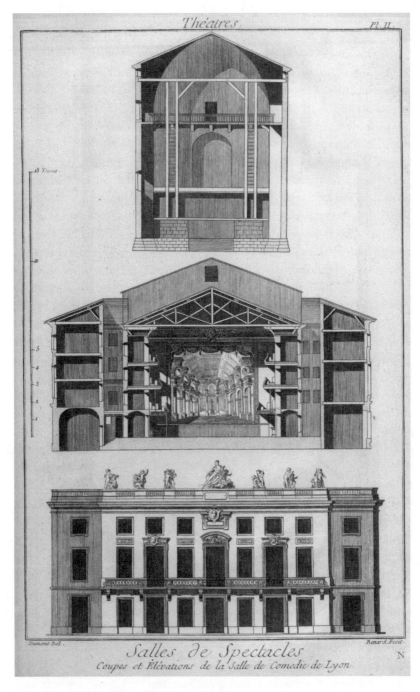

Views of the Lyon theater, designed by Jacques-Germain Soufflot and inaugurated in 1756, from *Recueil de planches, sur les sciences, les arts libéraux, et les arts méchaniques, avec leur explication*, volume 10. Courtesy of the Rare Book and Manuscript Library, University of Pennsylvania.

the inauguration of the Lyon theater, the architect Antoine Le Carpen-
tier advised the intendant in Clermont-Ferrand to consult Soufflot's theater
rather than that of the Opéra-Comique in Paris as a model for his city's new
playhouse. By the 1770s, exterior and interior views of the theater had been
reproduced widely in the *Encyclopédie* as well as in treatises on theater design.
When the city of Bordeaux began planning for a new theater in the 1770s,
the local architect who was initially favored for the project wrote to Soufflot
to ask for his advice on what style they should adopt. In 1781, the architect
for the Valenciennes theater sent an agent to Lyon to copy the architectural
plans for the theater. A hand copy of Soufflot's plan for the Lyon theater can
even be found among the plans for the new Nantes theater, inaugurated in
1788.[36]

During the decades following the inauguration of the Lyon theater, the
definition of a public theater changed in the minds of contemporaries. Pub-
lications about theater architecture proliferated in the last twenty-five years
of the Old Regime, constituting a new genre within architectural writings.
Collectively, these treatises clearly express this rapid reorientation in attitudes
toward the stage. Architects including Gabriel Dumont, Charles-Nicolas
Cochin, Pierre Patte, André Jacob Roubo, and Victor Louis published illustrated works on theater design, while also discussing their approaches in pub-
lications such as the *Journal de Paris*.[37] Confirming the theater's rising status
in the field, the Royal Academy of Architecture held its first ever grand-prize
competition for a dramatic theater in 1768. The requirements the academy
established for this project are revealing, for they suggest the extent to which
pragmatic matters of theatrical production were also shaping theater design.
All plans entered into the competition were required to feature "a theater for
a large city isolated between two plazas and two streets . . . in this space [the
contestant] will make rooms for meetings and for rehearsals, rooms where
actors and actresses can dress, warehouses for storing [and] for painting the
decorations, and for locking the costumes, a foyer, a café, housing for the
concierge and a few small accommodations for the Swiss guards, the porters,
and the stagehands."[38] With regard to the exteriors of public theaters, architectural consensus aimed for the monumental. Theaters, now conceived of as
centerpieces of the city, were often situated on plazas with calculated views.
As the number of design opportunities rose, many leading architects fixed
their attention on the provinces. Already in 1765, when Cochin published
architectural plans for a salle de spectacle, he explained that his proposed
design was not principally created with Paris in mind. "If some provincial
cities would want to construct theaters," he wrote, because their playhouses
would be "smaller than those of the capital, they would be even more likely
to benefit from this new plan."[39] Whereas Old Regime playwrights looked

toward the royal stages of the capital for the opportunities that might establish them as successful writers, architects regularly looked to France's provincial cities.[40]

The trends marking theater design reached their fullest expression a quarter century later in the Grand Théâtre of Bordeaux. A site of extensive urbanization, Bordeaux by the 1770s boasted a new *place royale*, stock exchange, and customs house as well as new quays and a new public garden. It was the new theater, however, that would prove the most prominent feature of the cityscape. Designed by the architect Victor Louis and built between 1773 and 1780, it featured a more elaborate exterior than earlier French theaters, one ornamented by a columned façade and by decorative arcades and galleries along the sides. Louis also lavished attention on the theater's interior. The auditorium was nearly circular, bringing the entire audience, but especially the boxes, closer to the stage. Notably, he dramatically increased the size and elegance of the spaces devoted to social interaction. The opulent entry hall and staircase that spectators ascended to enter the auditorium were strikingly original.[41] The Grand Théâtre became the new home for the city's successful theater, opera, and ballet company. According to the shareholders of the theater troupe, the opening of the theater attracted such a "prodigious crowd"

VUE PERSPECTIVE DE L'ENTRÉE PRINCIPALE

"Perspective view of the main entrance" of the Grand Théâtre of Bordeaux, from Victor Louis, *Salle de spectacle de Bordeaux* (Paris, 1782). Courtesy of the Billy Rose Theatre Division, The New York Public Library for the Performing Arts, Astor, Lenox, and Tilden Foundations.

that the seventeen hundred tickets were quickly distributed. Many had to be turned away that first evening.[42]

The city's role in the construction of this new theater is a complex one. By the early 1770s, it is true, a new municipal theater had long been on the agenda in Bordeaux. The city had owned a series of stages, beginning in the 1730s with an inexpensive wooden structure that was soon replaced by a stone theater built in the garden of the city hall.[43] In 1755, when this theater burned, the city hastily commissioned a temporary theater. This playhouse, located near the Porte Dauphine just outside of the old city walls, cost about one hundred thousand livres.[44] Located in a former rope factory, it was designed to meet immediate needs. The city magistrates continued to consider building a more elaborate salle de spectacle, but they took no action. Only after a powerful group of private investors, including the governor Richelieu, obtained royal permission in 1772 to use land from an old royal fortress to construct a new playhouse on the city's behalf did the municipal officers finally resolve to undertake such a project directly.

Unlike the cases of Lyon and Nantes, however, in which the municipalities and their architects determined the plans and directed the building of the playhouses, in Bordeaux the city would find itself accepting a project that was defined by Richelieu and one for which it had insufficient resources. In fact, of all the theaters built by municipal governments, the Grand Théâtre of Bordeaux would be the one that most clearly reveals the politics of privilege at work in the Old Regime.[45] The history of this "theater-temple" has filled volumes; here, it will only be sketched briefly. Richelieu, determined to leave behind a monument for posterity, promoted his protégé, Victor Louis, over the local architects that the city put forward. The governor then instructed Louis to make his already elaborate plans even more grandiose. When building finally began, construction problems and cost overruns plagued the project. In a city that was transformed over the course of the eighteenth century with many impressive building projects, none would match the extravagance of the resulting theater, which would cost the city over 2,400,000 livres. The mounting costs for a theater that even Bordelais criticized as a "scandalous luxury" made Louis no small number of enemies in the city, including the city officers themselves.[46]

Yet, even in this case the mayor and city council fought determinedly to retain responsibility over the construction of the playhouse and to take credit for the result. They repeatedly refused offers by private investors to take over responsibility for the project, arguing that "it is more advantageous to the city to undertake the construction itself." They postponed plans to build a new city hall that had already received royal approval and for which the money had already been borrowed. Instead, they diverted these funds to the theater, putting other major construction projects on hold, and they raised taxes to pay for this project, the most ambitious in the city's history to that point.[47] Even as the city's management of the project drew harsh criticism, the mayor and aldermen resisted surrendering to closer royal oversight. Bitter battles over the pace of construction and its difficult financing reached a head in 1774, when the crown effectively stripped the city of authority over the building project, which was to be closely managed by two intendants, Charles-François Esmangart and Nicolas Dupré de Saint-Maur.[48] Slowly and painfully, the theater reached completion. Only in 1779 did the king finally restore the authority of the city over the Grand Théâtre and grant it complete ownership of the nearly completed structure. Do these complex power contests serve to confirm the city's almost complete lack of authority over this grandiose project? Should the construction of the Grand Théâtre, as some have argued, be seen as an act of "blind despotism" on the part of this powerful governor?[49] Or can it be that the city officers, jealous to hold on to their traditional authority over the performing arts and eager to endow the city with an impressive theater, agreed to realize an ambitious monument for which they grossly underestimated the complexity and the expense?

In the end, Bordeaux's municipal authorities—and the people of Bordeaux—took responsibility for the burdensome and unpopular construction costs. The mayor and councilmen continued to clash bitterly with Richelieu in the 1780s concerning jurisdiction over the theater and their rights within the playhouse.[50] At the same time the playhouse immediately drew national and even international admiration as the largest and most elaborate theater in France, a fact that the mayor and city officers celebrated from seats of honor in a prominent box reserved for their private use. Even the intendant Dupré de Saint-Maur, who had the unhappy responsibilities of acting as intermediary between the architect Louis and the Bordeaux city council and of locating the funds to keep construction going, was confident that the theater would be "one of the most beautiful of Europe" and that this was "an edifice that would give honor to the Nation."[51] When Arthur Young arrived in Bordeaux, he concurred, describing the Bordeaux theater as "by far the most magnificent in France," adding, "I have seen nothing that approached it."[52]

With their impressive theaters, Lyon and Bordeaux played an especially critical role in establishing the playhouse as a symbol of distinction for cities throughout France. In cities making do with older, smaller stages, authorities and private citizens alike felt inspired—even compelled—to emulate the new standards that had come to define the public theater. In a memoir promoting a new theater for Marseille in the early 1780s, a private investor justified the need for an ambitious structure by referring not to the capital, but to these two rivals: "The city of Marseille, more populous than Bordeaux, more commercial than Lyon, is one of the most flourishing in the kingdom, and yet one finds there neither the amenities nor the decorations that ornament these two cities." In place of the existing Marseille playhouse, which dated from the 1730s and was "very far from what one expects to see in a city of this importance," this would-be builder proposed "to procure for his *patrie* a monument worthy of it."[53] In response to such urban developments elsewhere in provincial France, the intendant residing in Lille lamented in the early 1780s that a city of Lille's importance boasted no monuments "that could fix the gaze of foreigners," and "no *public edifice that announces or inspires artistic taste.*"[54] In his plan to restore Lille to a position of prestige, a new public theater featured centrally. By the end of the decade, stately neoclassical theater-temples graced both of these cities, built in each case by joint-stock companies. (See image of the Lille playhouse on page 28.)

Such intercity competition contributed to an escalation of expectations that reached even middling and small cities.[55] Take, for example, Saint-Quentin, a city with a population of less than ten thousand in the province of

Suggesting the influence of the Lyon theater in its façade, this small but tasteful playhouse was intended to embellish the city of Châlons-sur-Marne, where it was inaugurated in 1771. It was built by a group of private investors. "Façade de la salle de spectacle de Chaalons," engraving by Varin. Bibliothèque municipale Georges Pompidou de Châlons-en-Champagne, n. 1238.

Picardy in northern France. The municipal government was spurred to build the city's first playhouse in 1773 when it learned that Saint-Quentin would host a festival and competition that would draw delegates from all fifty companies of French arquebusiers, historic military companies organized on the municipal level. With individuals arriving from cities throughout the kingdom, this opportunity to establish a positive impression of their municipality could not be missed. In preparation for the festivities, the city initially planned to build a simple theater comparable to one that had recently been inaugurated in its slightly larger neighbor, Cambrai. The plan soon escalated, as did the cost, which rose to over ninety thousand livres. In the advertisements for the event, distributed widely throughout France, the magistrates proclaimed grandly that "the municipal officers just constructed a theater that equals the most beautiful of the kingdom, and in which a select troupe of excellent actors will give the most amusing plays."[56] Although small cities such as Saint-Quentin could not realistically hope to match the majestic theaters of wealthy provincial capitals, many such communities took pride in a modestly elegant playhouse whose columns or decorative balconies both beautified their city and raised its cultural status.

Commercialism, Urban Growth, and Civic Identity

When the architect Roubo set out to explain why theaters were rapidly transformed from buildings "of a design and even a decoration below mediocrity" into the stately edifices of the late eighteenth century, he pointed to the changing socioeconomic conditions in France. Previously, he explained, "the big cities were neither so populous nor so opulent as they are now, and they were only lived in by people whose condition and occupations hardly ever brought them to these sorts of amusements."[57] The decisions of municipal governments to stake their city's reputation—and its funds—on a public theater must therefore be located in the context of the population growth and rising commercial wealth that marked eighteenth-century urban life.

Even as population growth slowed in Paris in the eighteenth century, it accelerated in many provincial cities, with the effects concentrated in major commercial centers. Between 1700 and 1780, the populations of Lyon and Bordeaux grew by more than 50 percent, to an estimated 152,000 and 83,000, respectively. This pace of growth was matched by cities such as Versailles, Brest, and Troyes. Nantes, Rouen, Toulouse, Amiens, and Reims, among others, grew by as much as a third. In some cases, the growth was even more remarkable: Metz, Nancy, Dunkerque, and Nîmes doubled in size.[58] The significance of this urban growth is brought into relief when

France's cities are compared with those of Europe as a whole. During this era, of the forty-eight European and British cities with populations larger than forty thousand, nine were French. Only the Italian states featured more early modern metropolises than France. Already by the mid-eighteenth century, nearly two million French men and women lived in cities with a population of ten thousand or more, well over twice as many as any other continental European state.[59]

During this same era, France's economy entered a period of rapid growth, boosted by a dramatic expansion of Atlantic trade focused on the Caribbean colonies. Supported by a trade monopoly binding France's colonies with the metropole, French merchants made fortunes selling to plantation owners in Saint-Domingue, Martinique, and Guadeloupe the slaves, foodstuffs, and manufactured goods they needed, and in reselling the sugar, tobacco, indigo, and other commodities they purchased in the colonies.[60] Profits from this international trade generated extensive new wealth that was particularly concentrated in commercial port cities. Yet, economic growth was not limited to these locales. Throughout France, as we have seen, urban populations from aristocratic elites to their servants consumed more goods and enjoyed a higher standard of living in the eighteenth century.

From these developments two consequences stand out. First, although economic and demographic growth was widespread, its uneven distribution enabled fast-growing trading centers to disrupt France's urban hierarchy. Bordeaux quickly graduated from the nation's sixth largest city to its fourth. International trade out of Bordeaux expanded twenty times over during the course of the century.[61] Cities that experienced only modest growth, such as Rouen, or whose population stagnated, as in Aix, often came to feel that they were being surpassed.[62] As rising cities sought recognition and respect for their new status, their counterparts struggled to maintain a fading prestige.

Second, this eighteenth-century prosperity helped to drive new ways of "imagining the town," resulting in a new urban model that highlighted cultural amenities.[63] As a French guidebook published in 1760 explained, theater, concerts, art galleries, public gardens, and the like had recently become "the hallmark of a thriving city."[64] When magistrates in various cities extended their support for the theater arts, they followed influential philosophes such as Voltaire, Jean Le Rond d'Alembert, and Denis Diderot, who argued strongly in favor of theater's positive influence on society. D'Alembert's arguments in the *Encyclopédie* regarding the benefits of professional theater for the city of Geneva could easily be applied to striving provincial cities as well. Professional theater, he suggested, "would form the taste of the citizens and would give them a fineness of tact, a delicacy of sentiment, which is very difficult to acquire without the help of theatrical performances." With a theater, he continued, the city of Geneva would soon achieve the "urbanity of Athens."[65] In the eighteenth century, the arts and letters in general—and theater in particular—constituted a terrain in which cities and urban elites staked claims to prestige.

For municipalities invested in fashioning a new public image, a playhouse provided a prominent canvas with which to represent a city's history, wealth, and honor. This act of patronage also provided a means to transform newly acquired wealth into distinction. This sentiment was especially pronounced in the cities of Nantes and Bordeaux, where theater decorations became a medium through which these communities delivered a rehabilitative message about commerce and commercial wealth, which they celebrated as the foundation for their rising cultural status.[66] In Nantes, the theater's architect Mathurin Crucy designed an elaborate allegory for the stage curtain that represented Nantes as a city made prosperous from trade that now devoted its attention to the arts. Spirits presented medals honoring famous men in Breton history, calling special attention to the heroes of naval victories. A nymph of the Loire River represented one source of the city's wealth and geographic identity. The muse of astronomy represented the navigational sciences so essential to the overseas trading at the heart of the local economy. The city itself was personified together with Mercury, the god of commerce, and with the muses of comedy, tragedy, and their sisters. Allegories of architecture and painting presented the city with the plans for the theater, which Crucy described as an "eternal monument of its munificence." The artist acknowledged the deliberate association of commerce and cultural distinction in his description of the curtain: "To put the surplus of riches to noble use, the city of Nantes calls arts and letters to its bosom."[67]

In the auditorium of Bordeaux's new theater, an elaborate ceiling painting by Jean-Baptiste Robin paid an even more direct tribute to the commercial foundations of that city's prosperity.[68] Here, too, the artist brought together imagery celebrating the city, its success in commerce, and the flourishing of the arts. The painting featured allegorical representations of Bordeaux, the Garonne River, and the Atlantic Ocean. The new theater was depicted as a temple to the arts watched over by Apollo and welcomed by the nine muses, who bestow laurels on favorite local actors and actresses. Yet, in a departure from this predominantly allegorical approach, the city's commerce was represented mimetically. Ships crowd Bordeaux's harbor, and dockworkers load and unload goods. Most strikingly, a central grouping in this montage featured a ship captain holding a flag and pointing to three African slaves, presumably en route to the Americas. Two dark-skinned men and a woman were depicted bowing in submission, bare-breasted and with their hands tied. Featuring such an explicit tableau within this prominent public building should be seen as a deliberate effort to legitimize trade—including the slave trade—as the primary source of the wealth that paid for the theater and thus made Bordeaux even more culturally prominent. Bordeaux's commerce was here represented as honorable and a central aspect of civic identity.

In theaters such as these the "union of commerce and the arts" was celebrated not only visually through interior decorations, but also with inaugural performances featuring specially commissioned plays that took up these same themes.[69] In this way playhouses explicitly welcomed commercial elites—who frequently encountered resistance to their participation in other cultural institutions such as academies—to claim these spaces as their own.[70] Moreover, in commercial cities invested in burnishing their public image, lavish temples to the arts seemed to hold out the promise of refocusing cultural values and practices. As one Bordelais explained upon the inauguration of the Grand Théâtre:

> Foreigners reproach us that in our city commerce seems to absorb all; but alas! The mediocrity of our enjoyments in the Beaux-Arts, doesn't it excuse a bit our indifference? I dare to hope, Monsieur, from the superb monument that I just described for you a happy revolution in our tastes: sculpture, dance, music, painting and other pleasant talents seem to express a new desire to shine in the superb frame that is destined for them; appearing henceforth in all their glory, without doubt they will have to pique our attention, excite our enthusiasm, and wrest our praise.[71]

Urban Sociability in the New Public Playhouse

This new generation of public playhouses quickly came to function as multifaceted cultural, social, and even commercial centers, accommodating a wide variety of uses by the urban community. Developments in interior design made this possible. The earliest provincial playhouses offered few opportunities for social distinction, as we have seen, with some featuring just a few boxes for the use of distinguished spectators such as the city magistrates. The opportunities for honorific seating, however, grew quickly as playhouses emerged as civic monuments. Already by the mid-eighteenth century most new theaters featured an array of half a dozen or more discrete seating categories. As in Paris, seating was organized hierarchically within the playhouse, ranked according to prestige as well as price.[72] The most prestigious and expensive seats in the house were those on the stage itself and in the first boxes, the lowest tier of loges ringing the auditorium. In the new dedicated theaters the most prominent first boxes, those located immediately to the right and left of the stage from the perspective of the audience, were typically reserved for political authorities. Known colloquially as the "king's box" (*la loge du roi*) and the "queen's box" (*la loge de la reine*), following their designations in the Paris theaters, these were larger and more sumptuously decorated than the rest. In larger theaters these boxes often included an adjacent private lounge. In addition to the stage and first boxes, nobles and other urban notables and their wives also sat on benches directly in front of the stage and in the amphitheater, a raised area of the main floor located behind the parterre. The second and third boxes traditionally accommodated bourgeois and middling spectators. Less expensive tickets provided standing room in the parterre, which despite its discomforts provided some of the best views in the house. Customers choosing the cheapest seats usually mounted the stairs to the highest balcony known as *le paradis* (literally "heaven"), the nosebleed seats of the era. Details differed from city to city, depending on the size and complexity of the playhouse, but almost everywhere in France theaters ordered the urban public according to a common set of organizational principles.[73]

Early jeu de paume and converted theaters had offered spectators little more than a space in which to enjoy a performance and an area for refreshments. For example, the Strasbourg theater inaugurated in 1701 featured a small entry vestibule and a café. Other than the auditorium, however, it offered no other formal public spaces where people could gather inside the building.[74] In contrast, the new Montpellier playhouse inaugurated in the 1750s housed both a theater auditorium and a separate concert hall. The theaters in Metz and Lyon included extensive foyers and several private salons for use by authorities and other notables. In Lyon, the theater also included a sizeable café and private apartments for the director and others.[75] Such innovation was encouraged by the advent of theaters that were built from the ground up, which freed architects from the constraints of designing a functional playhouse within a preexisting structure.

Victor Louis took these developments considerably further in the Grand Théâtre of Bordeaux, which featured an imposing stone staircase that audience members ascended to enter the theater, decorative foyers and lounges where spectators could enjoy refreshments and warm themselves in winter, and galleries and terraces where they could stroll in summer.[76] The distribution of space demonstrates an evolution in social functions accorded to the

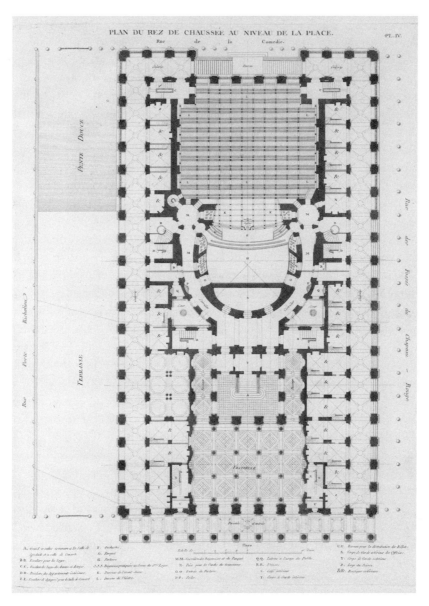

Overhead view of the ground floor of the Bordeaux theater at the level of the plaza, from Victor Louis, *Salle de spectacle de Bordeaux* (Paris, 1782). This plan suggests the evolution of the playhouse into a more complex social and cultural space, serving purposes beyond spectatorship. The theater's large entry hall *(vestibule)* opens onto its signature grand staircase, a sizeable café, and numerous boutiques opening onto the galleries that run along the sides of the exterior. With permission of the Billy Rose Theatre Division, The New York Public Library for the Performing Arts, Astor, Lenox and Tilden Foundations.

public theater. On the first few floors, nearly one-third of the interior was devoted to the entrance hall, various lobbies, salons, meeting rooms, cafés, a concert hall, and other areas not directly associated with the performance. To visitors, these amenities contributed to the grandeur of the theater.[77] At the same time, the building catered to the social and leisure needs of the Bordeaux elite. In fact, just months after its inauguration, the city learned that "a society of a hundred women from the commercial elite, and almost as many men" wanted to rent space in the playhouse to "hold their assemblies there."[78] Members of this circle valued the convenience of meeting in the theater, which enabled them to move freely between their private social gatherings and the public theatrical performances, without "displacing themselves."[79]

Commercial uses also came to be integrated into the design of theater buildings. Such a trend is already evident in Lyon's playhouse, in which Soufflot made use of the street frontage on the north side of the building to house a number of boutiques. The rent from theater dependencies, including these shops as well as storage areas, cellars, and several apartments, provided a substantial source of revenue over the next few decades.[80] Moreover, Soufflot's efforts seem to have encouraged the development of the immediate area as a commercial district that would be busy during the day as well as in the evening, when the theater would open its doors. In the 1760s, a decade after its inauguration, the municipality approved the construction of a row of boutiques along the rear of the city hall, facing onto the plaza directly in front of the theater. The city specified that these were to be rented to fashion retailers (*marchandes de modes*), print sellers, jewelers, and book sellers—those selling just the luxury and consumer goods that might appeal to wealthy and middling theater spectators.[81] Later architects emulated and even expanded on Soufflot's concept. The Lille theater included twenty-three boutiques.[82] Victor Louis integrated numerous private apartments, storage areas, cellars, and shops into the Bordeaux theater design, purportedly no fewer than 144 spaces that were rented out by the city until the middle of the nineteenth century.[83] One visitor to Bordeaux was delighted with the results: "All around reigns a gallery formed by arcades. One can walk there in all weather: it serves as an extension [*dégagement*] of the theater by many small doors that open onto it; there it is also a great pleasure to see merchants of all kinds."[84] In this case, the theater was transformed into a veritable shopping center, enlivening the neighborhood and catering to consumers while generating income for the city.

In addition, architects did not neglect audiences' aesthetic experience of the performance. New stages brought spectators closer to the actors and singers and generally improved sight lines and acoustics.[85] Larger and deeper stages—often as deep as the auditorium itself—were framed by proscenium arches to promote the "sense of theatrical illusion" that theater enthusiasts in Nantes and elsewhere demanded.[86] New theaters were also commonly built with complex stage machinery to move scenery and set pieces and to create special effects, bringing production capabilities in the provinces closer to those of Paris. In fact, to equip the Nantes theater with the most modern stage machinery the architect Crucy hired the machinist of the Comédie-Française in Paris.[87] Rather than continuing to rely on directors and actors to provide their own sets, as was long the practice with traveling theater companies, municipalities (and private owners) increasingly provided sets designed to fit the exact specifications for their new theaters. In Saint-Quentin, for example, the city rented the new theater to traveling acting and opera companies equipped with an impressive array of stage scenery including a house, a woods, a garden, a cave, a rustic cottage, and a public plaza, as well as set pieces and props for popular contemporary productions including André Grétry's comic opera *Les Deux Avares* and Pierre-Augustin Caron de Beaumarchais's *Le Barbier de Séville*.[88]

Perhaps the most significant effect of this new generation of playhouses for spectators was that they self-consciously located professional entertainment and the theatrical experience in the domain of high culture. A letter published in the *Mercure de France* observed, albeit rather optimistically, that the majesty of Bordeaux's Grand Théâtre had changed the behavior of the spectators who crowded into the new auditorium in the late spring of 1780:

> You know, Monsieur, how much external sensations influence our mores. The part of the building that I will call the theater proper offers us a striking example. During your visit to Bordeaux, you often complained that, despite the fairly numerous guards, our theater was one of the most boisterous of *province*. Without doubt the majesty of the space made more of an impression than the orders of the police. Today there reigns during the performance and even during the entr'actes, a calm and an air of well-being that, until now, were unknown to us. This sudden impression of respect and reserve is, in the eyes of the philosophe, the most beautiful homage that a nation can give to works of genius.[89]

The impact of this heightened elegance reached beyond the subjective outlook of the spectators by contributing to the formalization of distinctions between high and low culture in the performing arts, even as these playhouses invited much larger crowds become participants in the former. This is illustrated particularly clearly in Besançon, where the inauguration of an imposing new theater designed by Claude-Nicolas Ledoux spurred the city government to define just what kinds of performance would be permitted to take place there. Before 1784, acting and opera companies had shared the same venue with popular entertainments. When the magistrates established regulations for the new public theater, however, they relegated these "*petits spectacles*," such as acrobats, marionettists, and the like, to the old stage. Such popular entertainments could hardly appear in the new playhouse, they explained, "without offending the beautiful details and the effect of the decorations."[90] They reserved their new municipal theater for the more prestigious genres of drama, ballet, and opera. The Besançon theater, like many others, was consecrated as a domain of elite theater culture.

Funding Controversies

Given the unprecedented sums that urban authorities poured into building public theaters, it should come as little surprise that such use of municipal funds and land sparked criticism and protest. Controversy surrounding theater-building was inflamed by France's longstanding religious and moral concerns about the theater itself. France, to a greater degree than its European neighbors, nurtured a deeply contradictory relationship with its theater tradition, which was simultaneously celebrated as a cornerstone of French literary and cultural greatness and attacked as religiously suspect and morally degenerate.[91] In the seventeenth century, outspoken clergy began to attack professional theater as "the privileged domain of Satan," where spectators were tempted, distracted from their Christian duties, and robbed of innocence and virtue.[92] The Gallican Church went so far as to formally excommunicate professional actors and actresses, denying them access to the sacraments, although this was selectively enforced. Throughout the eighteenth century some clergy continued to oppose the construction of public theaters near convents and churches, although with diminishing success as theater became widely accepted.[93] Writing in his parish register in the 1780s, Père Le Feuvre, the rector at Saint Nicholas Church in Nantes, took note of progress on the new municipal theater that was transforming the urban landscape: "They admire the columns . . . and they announce superb decorations. This edifice passes for one of the most magnificent in the kingdom." The priest lamented the 450,000 livres in municipal funds spent for this project: "Is it possible that we pay so much for such establishments, and that we cannot find any money when it comes to repairing the temples of our Lord, which are all in such a pitiable state in Nantes! Gambling, luxury, theater, [and] pleasures of all types here absorb all the money."[94]

As traditional Catholic attacks on the stage waned during the eighteenth century, critics placed greater emphasis on the costs—social and moral, but also financial—associated with building a theater. The publication of Jean-Jacques Rousseau's influential antitheater polemic the *Letter to M. d'Alembert on the Theatre* in 1758 established new terms for the debates on the construction of municipal playhouses. A decade and a half later, when Saint-Quentin proposed to build its theater, an anonymous critic reiterated many of Rousseau's objections to introducing regular professional theater into urban life. "Yes, just two years of regular theater in our city and all is lost," the author predicted; "our society will be broken."[95] The pamphlet decried the changes in traditional city life and gender relations that the theater would certainly introduce, the debts actors and actresses would accrue and leave unpaid, and the jealousy that would be aroused among the poorer citizens who could not afford to attend. Would theater in this small city, as the author feared, become a "source of inequality"? Would it "weaken the citizen who is not rich" by tempting him with a seductive pastime that constitutes "a real increase of expenditure and a real reduction of work"?[96] Hardly less important for this author was the financial burden generated by a theater that he claimed the city could ill afford. His letter pointed out that the city hall received eighteen thousand livres in income and paid out an equal sum in expenses. In addition, Saint-Quentin already carried 100,000 livres in debt. A playhouse would mean thousands of livres a year in additional expenditures for the city for years to come.[97] Where would this money come from? Skeptical that the theater could become a profit-making venture, this author predicted that directly or indirectly local citizens would be forced to pay the price of this dangerous extravagance.

Moral arguments evidently did little to dissuade urban authorities (or others) from building theaters, yet municipal officers were not immune to financial concerns. Over time, various cities came to expect that these expensive structures should generate income to help pay for their cost and upkeep. In the 1770s, the municipal government of Lyon ended their policy of letting the resident theater company use the building for free and began demanding a hefty twenty thousand livres a year in rent. Following the inauguration of the Grand Théâtre, the city of Bordeaux established the rent for the theater at an exorbitant fifty-six thousand livres annually. The municipality drew an additional twenty-four thousand livres a year in revenue from the rental of the boutiques, cellars, and apartments located within the theater. When the new Théâtre Graslin opened in Nantes, the city charged the director fifteen thousand livres a year for its use, five times the amount charged for the previous privately owned stage.[98]

The decisions of French municipalities to begin paying to build public playhouses shed light on eighteenth-century urban priorities, because this constituted the primary means by which these cities supported the performing arts. Municipal governments during this era, evidence suggests, were not particularly keen on using their revenues to fund the performances taking place within these grand new playhouses. Although municipal subsidies for performances of theater and opera were not unknown during the eighteenth century, as we will see in chapter 4, the practice remained the exception rather than the rule. Only in the early nineteenth century did large numbers of French cities begin to provide substantial subsidies to a municipal opera or theater company. During the Old Regime, most urban authorities saw theatrical production as a business best left in the hands of professional directors.

Paris, *Province,* and the Modern French Playhouse

By the 1780s, when the city of Nantes collaborated with Graslin to build an impressive municipal playhouse, the royal architect Blondel's assertion that a public theater should be the standard by which a city is measured had become a reality. Memoirs written by French, German, Swiss, and British travelers demonstrate the extent to which this new civic monument came to serve as a basis for comparison between cities. When Madame de Gauthier traveled in France in the early 1780s, she attended the theater in a large number of provincial cities, recording her evaluations of each, from the impressive theaters of Lyon and Bordeaux—the latter described as too beautiful—to the pretty theater of Troyes to the large theaters of Tours and Auch. She deemed what passed for a theater in Orléans, one of the only sizeable cities without a proper playhouse, "very simply horrible."[99] Foreign visitors to France in the last decades of the Old Regime echoed many of Madame de Gauthier's opinions.[100] They, too, were often impressed with the theaters of provincial cities, as evidenced in Arthur Young's high praise for the theaters in Nantes and Bordeaux. Yet, they could also be unsparing in their criticism of those that fell short of the mark. Rouen, before the inauguration of its new theater, was stigmatized for its "wretched" playhouse. During her travels Mrs. Thrale remarked favorably on the theaters of Aix, Montpellier, and Rochefort, but described the 1730s-era playhouse still in use in Marseille as "old, large, and dirty" and the original Nantes playhouse, dating from the 1740s, as "small, decorated without taste, badly maintained."[101] When she passed by the construction site for the new Théâtre Graslin, however, she took notice: "Once finished, this will be an important construction."[102]

In studies describing the remarkable coming of age of theater architecture in eighteenth-century France, little notice has been paid to the fact that Paris did not serve as the principal inspiration and point of reference. Yet, according to most contemporaries, the modern French playhouse was invented and perfected elsewhere. In the second half of the eighteenth century, the wealth of a city such as Lyon and the ambitions of its magistrates created the preconditions for an unusual set of cultural circumstances in France. With the playhouse these municipal authorities discovered one domain in which they could successfully contest the cultural primacy of Paris.

As soon as Lyon's theater was inaugurated, comparisons between Soufflot's masterpiece and the aged theaters where the royal troupes performed in Paris became almost inevitable. "Have you seen the theater of Lyon?" inquired a character in Diderot's *Entretiens sur le Fils naturel*, published just a year after it opened. "I would only ask for a similar monument in the capital."[103] On a visit to Lyon, the abbé Coyer found the new playhouse "much preferable to the three jeux de paume where Paris watches its performances."[104] The author of a letter published in the *Mercure de France* delighted in reminding readers that the muses of comedy and tragedy "have a temple in Lyon that, despite its flaws, is preferable in all regards to those that have been erected to them in Paris."[105] A Parisian commentator, forced to agree, lamented "by what fatality, are [the theaters] of our capital so inferior" to those of "Italy, of Germany, and even of our provinces"?[106] More than twenty years after its inauguration, the widely traveled royal actor Henri Lekain still recognized Lyon's stage as "undoubtedly the most beautiful that there is in France."[107]

Even the inauguration of several new Parisian theaters in the 1770s and 1780s, including Marie-Joseph Peyre and Charles de Wailly's impressive new playhouse for the Comédie-Française, did not fully rehabilitate the capital.[108] The theater's distinctive design would certainly prove influential, and it was echoed as far away as Martinique.[109] Nonetheless, despite the fact that this long-awaited structure cost some two million livres, it opened to decidedly mixed reviews. The *Correspondance littéraire, philosophique, et critique* summarized public opinion about the new playhouse for readers: "The exterior façade of the building was generally found much too massive: nothing is more opposed to the elegant character that suits so well an edifice of this genre." Although the interior was impressive at first glance, spectators were met with many inconveniences in a theater in which more attention was paid to "luxury than to utility." The boxes were poorly distributed within the theater, and acoustics were problematic. Furthermore, on closer inspection the decorations, spectators found, were poorly executed.[110] Others corroborated the public's disappointment with the building on a number of counts, from the heaviness of the exterior to the small size of the boxes to the poor sightlines.[111]

In this context, Bordeaux's Grand Théâtre posed a provocative challenge to the capital. As fate would have it, in the early 1770s Victor Louis had submitted this design in the competition for the future home of the Comédie-Française, only to have it rejected.[112] During the construction period, the architect faced heated criticism from those who felt that his design was "above the magnificence appropriate for a provincial city."[113] In response to his critics, Victor Louis published a spirited defense of his controversial theater, which he celebrated as a theater for the nation.[114] "For the small-minded . . . who only allow anything great in Paris," Louis countered, "the monument that I proposed to raise in Bordeaux would have seemed a crazy idea." He justified his project by making an analogy between his theater and the monuments of the Roman Empire. In Rome's glory days, he argued, important aqueducts, bridges, and temples had been raised throughout the empire, and not in the capital alone.[115] Louis's beautiful book, which included a large number of full folio engraved prints of the playhouse, appeared with booksellers the very same year that the new Comédie-Française was inaugurated.

Ultimately, even Parisians reserved the highest laurels for the Bordeaux theater. Upon his arrival in Bordeaux in 1783, François de La Rochefoucauld noted with surprise that "overall, the luxury of the buildings is as great in Bordeaux as in Paris." Having visited dozens of French cities during the previous few years, he concluded that in Bordeaux "the theater is without peer, of all that I've seen."[116] According to the architect Pierre Patte, "the most magnificent of all modern theaters is unquestionably that which the capital of Guyenne [Bordeaux] just erected . . . the architect had complete liberty to give flight to his genius."[117]

The theaters of Lyon and Bordeaux are just the most prominent of the dozen or so monumental playhouses constructed in provincial cities and in the capital in late eighteenth-century France. Yet, by breaking new ground, these ambitious civic projects led the way in redefining what a public theater could be in the eyes of critics, travelers, and status-conscious urban notables. In a spirit of pride and competition, city governments and private theater societies from Saint-Quentin to Marseille to Nantes felt compelled to invest in a distinguished playhouse in an effort to achieve cultural distinction and honor for their city. The history of these playhouses and their reception points to the inadequacies inherent in the Paris-*province* relationship as it has been traditionally conceived: a reductive duality imbued with assumptions of Parisian cultural superiority and provincial immobility and backwardness.[118]

Cultural development in France need not be approached as a zero sum game in which the admittedly spectacular rise of Paris as the cultural capital of seventeenth- and eighteenth-century Europe is represented as having taken place at the expense of the provinces. On the contrary, an architectural gem such as the Grand Théâtre of Bordeaux, which to this day hosts operas and ballets, provides evidence that provincial cities, too, successfully asserted themselves as rising European cultural centers, influencing their neighbors and on occasion even outshining Paris.

The reinvention of the public playhouse during the eighteenth century—from humble, utilitarian structures to large, socially complex, and symbolically meaningful edifices—proved vitally important for France's emerging theater industry. This new generation of theaters literally set the stage for the new practices in theatrical production and consumption that we will turn to later in this book. Given the rising prominence of theaters in urban life, it is only to be expected that representatives of royal authority would seek to harness these institutions for their own political advantage.

CHAPTER 3

The Extent and Limits of State Intervention

In the summer of 1764, the naval commander in the port of Brest, the comte de Roquefeuil, wrote to Versailles with an unusual proposition. The wooden warehouse where acting companies performed in the city was badly decayed, and Roquefeuil proposed that the navy itself should construct a new playhouse to replace it.[1] When this ramshackle building burned down just a few months later, the commander pressed hard for the opportunity to enhance cultural and social life in the city, particularly for the noble-dominated officer corps. No garrison, he argued, should be without a theater. Roquefeuil, who had several thousand sailors and naval officers under his command, maintained that theatrical entertainment was critical for maintaining discipline and morale among these men while in port. "In a city of such importance, where so many different groups find themselves gathered together, a theater is of no small use in steering clear of gambling and quarrels," he argued, adding that "besides furnishing some education to young provincials who enter the navy, it also inspires less distaste among the officers to reside in the region."[2] Elsewhere, soldiers might enjoy performances in playhouses provided by entrepreneurs, joint-stock companies, or by the municipal government. In this remote city of about twenty-five thousand on the Breton coast, however, no other parties had come forward to make such an investment.[3] Roquefeuil sought permission from the secretary of state for the navy for the military itself to endow

France's most significant naval port with a public theater that could serve its needs.[4]

Roquefeuil's arguments must have resonated within a French military command struggling with declining prestige following the disastrous Seven Years' War in addition to growing discipline problems now that tens of thousands of men had returned to domestic garrisons. Faced with these postwar challenges, the state consented to experiment with a new level of engagement in provincial cultural affairs. The king approved Roquefeuil's request for a new theater in Brest, and agreed to provide both the land—a portion of the arsenal facing onto the parade grounds—and royal financing to construct the Théâtre de la Marine.[5] The new theater, however, was not a gift from the crown. The loan was to be repaid over several years through subscriptions by hundreds of naval officers.[6] When the new theater opened in late 1766, it was owned by the navy and operated under the personal authority and supervision of the naval commander.

If the navy might at first appear an unlikely patron for the performing arts, the Théâtre de la Marine can in fact be seen as the culmination of the close relationship between France's military and professional theater that dated back to the late seventeenth century. For decades, army commanders anxious to occupy, entertain, and even instruct their men took steps to promote theater in their vicinity. Already by the 1750s, officers as well as common soldiers constituted an important audience base and a key source of revenue for acting troupes in garrison cities. At the same time, military leaders and other royal agents in these cities pressed for greater prominence within new provincial playhouses and greater influence over what took place within them, to the displeasure of local ruling elites.[7] Scholarship on eighteenth-century urban history has traditionally emphasized the authority of the royal intendant in provincial city affairs, devoting relatively little attention to the influence weilded by France's army and navy. Yet studies of Europe's early modern "military revolution" have demonstrated the central role played by the rise of large-scale standing armies in the development and structure of the modern state and the relationship between the state and the people.[8] In France, military historians note, the army constituted the single largest branch of the royal government, as well as the largest employer in the kingdom.[9] For contemporaries living in cities where troops were garrisoned, the military was an imposing presence in public life. At the same time, the military vocation represented "the aristocratic preserve *par excellence*—a symbol of noble identity," with nobles making up an estimated 95 percent of the officers' corps.[10] Commanders such as Roquefeuil used their prestige, as well as their ability to marshal financial resources and political support, to catalyze cultural change in garrisons and ports throughout France. Perhaps nowhere was this influence more strongly felt than in the theater arts.

This chapter examines the involvement of representatives of royal authority in France's rapidly developing theater industry as a means to assess the extent as well as the nature of state engagement in professional entertainment. Even as the foundations were laid for France's new public playhouses, royal agents came to appreciate the opportunities that these theaters represented. Although officers of the crown did not typically build, own, or operate salles de spectacles, many did come to expect that they should demonstrate their authority within these newly prominent cultural venues and over the performances staged there. This chapter focuses on three areas of intervention that were particularly widespread. First, it examines the relationship of patronage that the French army and navy cultivated with acting troupes charged with entertaining their men during war as well as peace. Second, it examines the symbolic displays of political authority that took place within these playhouses, and the conflicts these sparked. Finally, it turns to the exercise of privilege in the domain of theatrical production, as royal governors used their authority to protect entrepreneurial directors and encourage them to expand their operations.[11]

When royal authorities began intervening in these domains, they trespassed on responsibilities and privileges that had historically fallen under the jurisdiction of the municipality. Theater therefore emerges as a lens through which to evaluate the long-term process of state centralization. Both the timing of this assertion of cultural authority and its provenance are significant. Frustrated municipal leaders loudly protested these incursions into the domains of urban culture and public life as late as the 1770s and 1780s, long after the absolutist state is often assumed to have asserted its dominion over provincial cities. Just as revealing, we find that this expansion of state involvement in the domain of the performing arts was rarely driven by the central administration. Rather, in case after case, military and political agents of the monarchy acted on their own initiative to institute changes that the crown later approved and endorsed.

Brest's Théâtre de la Marine provides a necessary starting point for this investigation. This theater, the only provincial playhouse built and directly administered by a branch of the royal government, embodied the fullest extent of royal authority over cultural production and consumption outside of Paris.[12] Roquefeuil not only arranged the financing and construction of the city's new playhouse, he took a personal hand in administering the year-round theater company that he assembled to entertain the officers, sailors, and soldiers in Brest. Then, as this overly ambitious theatrical enterprise lost money, he secretly appropriated tens of thousands of livres from the royal treasury to cover its shortfalls.

Ironically, the Brest case not only demonstrates the magnitude of royal intervention in provincial cultural life, it also serves to define its limits. Elsewhere, royal officers proved far more restrained in their involvement in local theater. Rather than attempting to emulate the king's patronage and direct administration of the royal theaters in Paris, most recognized certain boundaries in their relationships with the theater companies under their authority. Even as military commanders, intendants, and governors endorsed, protected, and rewarded directors and their performers by providing them with steady audiences, they also expected them to operate commercially, without relying on ongoing financial support from the royal government.[13] In time, the limits of state authority over the production of provincial theater became evident even to Roquefeuil. When details of his disastrous administration of the theater came to light in the early 1770s, Versailles finally cut off funding for the Brest theater company. Unable to make his bloated troupe commercially viable, the commander would watch in helpless distress as the bankrupted theater company dissolved and the Théâtre de la Marine went dark.

Theater and the Culture of Absolutism

Provincial public theaters were political spaces that intentionally highlighted the display of hierarchy and status that defined Old Regime politics and society. Given the importance of theater and theatrical self-presentation within the political culture of absolutism, it was only natural for representatives of the crown to look for ways to assert their authority within France's new provincial playhouses and over the expanding industry more generally.[14] As intendants, governors, and military elites took steps to fashion a closer relationship with the stage, they were influenced by the cultural practices of the court. To understand the motives of royal agents with regard to public theater, therefore, it is necessary to consider briefly the relationship between political authority and theater as defined by the king in Paris.

During the early decades of Louis XIV's personal rule, as we have seen, the Sun King and Colbert strategically sponsored and cultivated the arts as part of a cultural policy that was more than a display of largesse or an expression of the king's enthusiasm for literature, music, and the fine arts.[15] With the establishment of royal academies devoted to literature, dance, painting, sculpture, architecture, and music, France's most talented artists were enlisted to glorify the king.[16] Theater, too, featured prominently in this agenda. Although his father and grandfather had patronized acting troupes, even granting them the title "King's Players," Louis XIV associated himself with theater in a more spectacular way.[17] Consolidating the performing arts into three royal theaters, he granted each a privilege endowing it with a Parisian monopoly over its genre. Within the capital, the king accorded sole rights to perform opera and any vocal music to the Royal Academy of Music, spoken comedy and tragedy to the Comédie-Française, and commedia dell'arte to the Comédie-Italienne. He worked to centralize the creation of new dramatic works in the capital, encouraging and even demanding that France's greatest talents work for these stages.[18] By effectively controlling access to the Parisian public, as well as the wealth, prestige, and renown that success in Paris could bring, the king sought to establish himself as the primary arbiter of performing arts culture in France, if not in all of Europe.

At the same time, spectacle itself became a central aspect of the culture of absolutism, in the words of Jean-Marie Apostolidès "a necessity intrinsically linked to the exercise of power."[19] One of the hallmarks of the reign of Louis XIV was its theatricality. The king carefully staged his own self-representation for the nobles gathered at Versailles.[20] This was accomplished metaphorically, through the elaborate ritual that defined each of the king's days, beginning with the *lever*, his ceremonial morning rising before an audience of courtiers and attendants. But there was also a literal dimension, as the king personally starred in a number of theatricals staged at Versailles and enlisted courtly nobles to fill other roles.[21] Performances such as these glorified the monarchy while entertaining restless courtiers. Yet they also fostered a cultured sociability among aristocratic elites, while providing unique opportunities for the display of status. In a court society in which, according to Norbert Elias, "the compulsion to display one's rank is unremitting," maintaining status required constant effort to publicly assert one's place in the political and social hierarchy.[22] The personal display of rank not only at Versailles but also in Paris proved necessary for the effective exercise of political authority. Paris's public theaters, especially the prestigious Paris Opera, long provided some of the capital's most important sites for aristocratic sociability and the display of status. For those aristocrats who rented first boxes, theater-seating hierarchies held the potential to affirm their rank by reinforcing the social distance between themselves and those who, less privileged or wealthy, might be considered their inferiors.[23]

Traditionally, the king did not formally regulate theatrical performance outside of Paris. When Jean-Baptiste Lully took charge of the Royal Academy of Music in 1672, opera, which was considered to be the most prestigious of the dramatic genres, became the only type of provincial entertainment subject to indirect royal oversight. Louis XIV granted Lully sole rights to produce and perform French opera not only in Paris—as was the case with the other two royal theaters—but throughout France.[24] Lully, a savvy entrepreneur, used this kingdomwide monopoly to demand that provincial opera directors pay the Paris Opera for performance rights. This system was at least partially enforced until the mid-eighteenth century.[25] In contrast, dramatic theater companies—those performing comedy and tragedy—were not subject to such centralizing policies. Throughout the seventeenth and early eighteenth centuries, actors' and actresses' itineraries and performances were coordinated by the *chefs de troupe* and later by the directors who led their companies. Municipal authorities typically permitted or denied performances by itinerant troupes, approved repertories, and maintained order during the performance. Oversight of provincial theater long remained the responsibility of these urban oligarchs, who had exercised authority over public performance since the Renaissance.[26]

In recent decades, historians have thoroughly reassessed the politics of absolutism, reconsidering, among other things, the extent to which Louis XIV placed France's cities under the control of the state.[27] William Beik has described politics for provincial cities under absolutism in these terms: "Whereas power emanated theoretically from the crown, it was exercised through regional centers where concentrations of powerful subjects competed for shares of authority."[28] Eighteenth-century public playhouses, as we will see, offered a prime terrain upon which this competition for authority—symbolic as well as real—played out.

Cultural Patronage by the Military

Because the royal government did not as a rule directly initiate provincial playhouses or acting troupes, the most notable exceptions to this rule—the actions of the military—demand close attention. Over the course of the eighteenth century, theaters were constructed or converted in a sizeable number of cities that were home to army garrisons and naval ports. This included not only large, strategically located cities, such as Lille, Strasbourg, and Metz, but also those that were smaller and more remote, such as Perpignan, Rochefort, and Brest. In fact, by 1789 officers and common soldiers posted in at least eighteen of France's most important garrisons could attend performances in a dedicated playhouse.[29] Moreover, a significant number of these cities came to enjoy regular, year-round theater companies.

This correlation was no accident. The military played a decisive role both in institutionalizing public theater during the late Old Regime and in spreading enthusiasm for performances as it dispersed officers to training camps and garrisons across France and the French empire. As noble officers moved to new postings, many brought with them a set of expectations regarding elite sociability that made them important supporters of professional theater. When Lorient was established as a naval port in 1770, a group of navy officers paid to bring in an acting troupe, which performed in a warehouse.[30] In Saumur, as discussed in chapter 1, the officers in the *carabiniers* provided inspiration and funds to build the new public playhouse.[31]

As these cases suggest, the military's informal ties to the professional stage involved much more than spectatorship. (Army officers were even known to perform roles onstage alongside professional actors until 1772, when the king finally ordered this practice to stop, at least while these men were in service. Common soldiers, however, continued to perform on professional stages. They frequently worked as extras for large-scale theatrical productions in cities such as Metz, Lille, and Bordeaux, where they earned five sous per rehearsal and ten sous per performance well into the 1780s.[32]) It was the military's formal commitment to professional theater in the form of group subscriptions purchased on behalf of the officers and troops, however, that would most decisively influence the development of France's nascent theater industry.

The army's formal embrace of theater dates to the late seventeenth century, when opera and theater performances were encouraged by governors and then endorsed by King Louis XIV as a means to maintain order while the men were on campaign. In 1697, the final year of the War of the League of Augsburg, several French armies introduced a new policy of subscribing all officers and regiments for regular tickets for performances by the theater companies that accompanied the armies. This was specifically intended to keep the men occupied during the slow winter months.[33] As a kind of entertainment tax, deducted from the officers' wages, these subscriptions encountered some resistance from those who felt such contributions should be voluntary. Prior to this point, a governor might offer a gift to attract an acting company to a city or military camp, but those who wished to attend paid individually at the door.[34] The king upheld the practice that had been introduced by his commanders. He argued that withholding payment for subscriptions needed to be regulated, but that "it must be allowed to continue to amuse the officer, and to keep him from falling into the greatest dissolution."[35]

The use of performers to occupy soldiers and to raise their morale during wartime was more actively employed in the late 1740s during the War of the Austrian Succession. Several military commanders invited acting troupes to accompany their men. An officer from the northern campaign described roads to Antwerp that were filled with posters advertising three different theater companies. The soldiers even constructed a portable stage, which was carried with the army on twenty-five wagons when they decamped.[36] When the city of Namur was taken by the French in 1747, the comte de Lowendahl immediately undertook the construction of a playhouse there to house an acting company during his army's temporary residence.[37] Letters between the French commanders in Namur, Louvain, and Brussels exchanged information about singers, dancers, and popular performers whom they found especially entertaining.[38] During this campaign, the maréchal de Saxe hired Charles-Simon Favart to organize a musical theater company to accompany his men. The theater, Favart later recalled, "became a meeting place for all the officers. The taste that they took for the theater prevented them from succumbing to the passion for gambling, and maybe to other equally dangerous excesses."[39] If this was one of the maréchal's goals, there were others. Saxe explained his intentions for theater more expansively in a letter to Favart: "Do not believe that I regard it as a simple object of amusement: it enters into my political views and in the plan for my military operations."[40] At Saxe's request, Favart composed special impromptus to build confidence among the men, and on one occasion he even used the stage to announce an imminent battle.[41]

Many of the same concerns that prompted wartime associations with acting companies inspired the army and navy to support theatrical entertainments during peacetime as well. Commanders and city officials alike worried about the conduct of soldiers and perhaps even more so about that of officers, and for good reason. The maréchal de Saxe himself complained about the behavior of young noblemen from prestigious families who, despite a lack of training, felt entitled to command an infantry unit, only to find that "no sooner is the ceremony completed than they begin to get bored in the garrison and proclaim their boredom in all the neighboring towns."[42] Military authorities embraced theater as a way to occupy these young officers and to keep them from stirring up trouble. As early as 1750, the royal government authorized commanders of garrisons, should they wish to do so, to buy subscriptions to the local theater on behalf of their officers and soldiers.[43]

These peacetime subscriptions gave the military new means to promote theater locally. In Metz, for example, the effort to establish a year-round resident acting company to perform in the city's new public theater owed a great deal to the city's sizable garrison. When the theater troupe struggled, losing money, the governor wrote that the residents of Metz needed to be urged to do their share: "The troops that I established in the province and in the city, contributing as they do the principal part of the payment for this spectacle, should have engaged the citizens to follow their example, because it is this quantity of troops that procures the growth of commerce . . . and the wealth of the inhabitants of the region."[44] In 1753 and again in 1755, actors from the Metz theater company even traveled to military camps in the region to perform for the officers. Because of this dependence on military money, theater companies performing in garrisons were particularly vulnerable when the army mobilized for war. In 1756, when a group of actors negotiated to become the resident theater company in Metz, war was on the horizon. Their contract took this into account. They agreed that in times of peace they would perform in the Metz theater four days a week throughout the year, with the exception of the traditional two-week Easter holiday. In times of war, however, when the garrison was absent, they were permitted to close the theater for several months of the year. This allowed them to compensate for diminished revenue by traveling to perform in other cities for fresh new audiences.[45]

After France's defeat in the Seven Years' War, commanders confronted low morale among troops, public disdain, and a pressing need for reform. The army and navy both undertook sustained efforts to improve their effectiveness and professionalism, and to rehabilitate public opinion regarding military conduct, which reached its nadir around 1765.[46] As part of a broad program of military reform overseen in the mid-1760s by the secretary of state for the navy, the duc de Choiseul, officials in military posts such as Brest looked beyond instituting more rigorous training and greater discipline for officers in their official duties.[47] They looked to their private lives as well.

Concerns about officers' personal lives were twofold. First, commanders worried about the cohesiveness of the officer corps. Central to the military reforms of the 1760s was a deliberate reinforcement of the nobility's status in military leadership. New recruitment policies restricted entry into the officer corps to those with at least four generations of noble lineage. One unexpected result was greater tension between young courtier officers, favored by wealth, status, and connections, and the less affluent provincial nobility.[48] Faced with what scholars have described as "divisive social distinctions" among noble officers, commanders sought to lessen the role of money and other markers of social and cultural difference in the service. They also took steps to foster in the corps an environment in which merit—rather than status—would be rewarded.[49] By purchasing discounted theater subscriptions on behalf of all officers, who sat together according to military rank, the commanders of the French army and navy embraced theater as a common ground for socializing and relaxing. Meanwhile, in keeping with widely held Enlightenment sentiments, they endorsed the didactic potential of the stage. Many, like Roquefeuil, saw the theater as a means to educate young officers while providing them with a common frame of culture and civility.

The second concern facing military commanders in the 1760s was more pragmatic and yet no less pressing. During times of peace, when officers were not on campaign or out at sea, their exercises and studies occupied little enough of their time that they were left free nearly every evening to seek their pleasure.[50] Indeed, with hundreds of young men and adolescent boys gathered independently of their families and with some money to spend, the temptations of the city were only too well known.[51] Young officers earned a reputation for debauchery and womanizing. During the eighteenth century, prostitution, venereal disease, and illegal gambling became central concerns for the police of many of the larger provincial cities, but perhaps especially those with garrisons.[52] Because disciplinary actions achieved only limited success, military leaders also attempted to reform their men's behavior by providing alternatives to vice. When the naval commander at Toulon sought authorization from Versailles in 1767 to purchase subscriptions for the local theater, he emphasized "the large number of young officers of the navy and army who by their estate are required to reside here and who are usually very free [desoeuvrés] in the evening." Theater, he argued, was needed to "occupy them enough for them to avoid the bad company of the evenings that they spend in gambling dens or with the girls."[53] Whereas the theater appealed to many soldiers and officers as an enjoyable pastime and a social gathering place, to their superiors it was also a licit form of entertainment that might substitute for the illicit pleasures that created so many difficulties in policing the city and the arsenal.[54] At the theater, leisure was enjoyed in public, rather than in potentially compromising private settings that were nearly impossible to monitor. When attending theatrical performances, soldiers and sailors spent evenings under the watchful eyes of their commanding officers, frequently under armed guard.

It was in this context that the comte de Roquefeuil approached the secretary of state for the navy about strengthening the relationship between the navy and the stage. As the site for France's first (and only) military playhouse, Brest had a certain logic. Since its designation as a naval installation in the seventeenth century, the fortunes of this relatively isolated port city had been closely tied to the military's growing presence. Over the course of the eighteenth century Brest had become the most important of France's naval ports, with large numbers of army troops also passing through during times of war, as they embarked on transatlantic journeys to North America and the Caribbean. It was the site of a naval academy over which Choiseul took particular interest as he instituted the reforms that were intended to provide more rigorous education for future naval leaders. Meanwhile, the navy had already demonstrated cultural leadership in the city. Officers had established the Académie Royale de Marine in 1752. The navy had even provided the city with a theater of sorts, for it owned the warehouse in the arsenal in which theatrical performances took place during the early 1760s.[55] When Roquefeuil set out in 1762 to create a stronger theater presence in the city, he began by proposing that the officers stationed in Brest purchase group subscriptions. Although this practice had become quite common for army officers in garrison, it was novel for the navy.[56] Just two years later he began to advocate for a permanent new playhouse.[57] In Roquefeuil's vision, the theater, to be located in the arsenal on the parade grounds, would primarily serve the interests of the navy. Still self-conscious about its relatively recent origins under Colbert and resentful of the greater prestige accorded to the army, the navy would achieve a distinction that the army never had: a playhouse and theater company of its own.

Roquefeuil's close engagement with Brest's theater company and his letters about the project reveal his personal passion for theater. In addition, he must have anticipated the prestige he would garner from having endowed Brest with a distinguished playhouse. Nonetheless, when he presented his case for theater, he did so by stressing its necessity for his officers and soldiers. He argued that the subscription for the young guards was less than "the cost of an instructor of dance or of music, and would be for them a better education."[58] Language skills were another area of particular concern for Roquefeuil given that his officers, especially those from the poorer ranks of the nobility, may not have received extensive formal educations and may even have been raised speaking other languages and dialects. "The forty-eight livres that a family will pay . . . for a year of theater for a child in the naval guard," he wrote, "are not what they would pay a teacher of the French language, which this child often needs when sent to port."[59] Roquefeuil repeatedly described the theater as an educational supplement crucial for the formation of a military elite. Moreover, he suggested that for both senior officers and for those young recruits who had rarely left their province before joining the navy, theater would help promote a shared cultural identification that could encourage camaraderie.[60]

As was the case in garrisons elsewhere in France, the theater in Brest was not simply offered to the officers and sailors as one possible leisure activity that they could choose if so inclined. With the approval of the secretary of state for the navy, the administration purchased subscriptions that provided entry to all regular season performances for an entire year for the entire officers' corps, from senior captains to newly recruited guards. Beginning in

1765, the cost was automatically deducted from their monthly pay, regardless of whether they intended to enjoy the performances or even were in port.[61] The cost was graduated according to rank. Initially, captains paid seven livres a month, while the young guards paid four livres.[62] These amounts, Roquefeuil noted, were less than what officers in the army usually paid for their entrance to the theater. They were also significantly less than the cost of these same seats for other Brest residents, who paid almost two and a half livres per ticket for a single evening's entertainment in the first boxes and the amphitheater, and fifteen sous for the parterre.[63] When the resident theater company found itself struggling financially, however, subscription prices were raised for the more senior officers. Within two years ship captains paid ten livres a month, although guards still paid four.[64] Roquefeuil defended this increase, noting that even at these higher rates his officers still paid less than those of corresponding rank in most army garrisons.[65]

From its inception in the 1690s, the military's practice of subscribing men to the theater without their explicit approval had drawn criticism. In the 1760s, however, resistance to this increasingly common policy reached a new level, even sparking violence that stressed the already tense relationships between local citizens and royal soldiers. In Lille, when the colonels of the army garrison authorized that theater subscriptions be bought for their subordinate officers without their consent, a riot broke out.[66] On 17 May 1767, more than two hundred angry officers stormed into the theater at 4 p.m., about an hour before the show was to begin, and occupied the parterre. Once inside, they blocked entry to local townspeople and brutally ejected those who had found a way inside the playhouse. When the local residents protested, the officers responded by asking, "*Who requires you to come to the theater? As for us, they force us to, because they make us pay.*"[67] Dozens were injured in the melee. According to the police report, an important civilian patron of the theater was beaten viciously, and men were thrown against pillars. In the final count, thirteen townsmen of Lille filed official complaints against the officers. The city, scandalized, threatened to involve the minister of war. The army scrambled to reinstate order in its ranks, to repair this blow to public relations between the garrison and the city, and to respond to their junior officers' angry challenge to this policy. A British army officer traveling in France at the time was shocked to learn of the situation: "The officers are ordered to attend [the theater] merely (like children) to keep them out of mischief."[68]

As the violence in Lille suggests, the success of theater as a disciplinary force was hardly unqualified. Soldiers and officers proved unruly and strong-willed, ready to provoke conflict with the local citizenry, rival military

corps, and even at times their commanding officers. If commanders over-
estimated the power of professional theater to pacify their men and reinforce
order and hierarchy, altercations and even violent riots involving royal
soldiers in the theaters elsewhere, including Toulon and Calais, might well
have disabused them of that belief.[69] Even in the navy's own theater in
Brest, audiences could prove difficult to control. One evening a group of
high-spirited (and likely inebriated) young officers demanded that a benefit performance be given on behalf of their favorite actress. When their
request was ignored by the troupe's director, they responded by staging loud
and disruptive demonstrations on her behalf both inside and outside of the
playhouse. In doing so, they engaged in a battle of wills with the military
administrators of the theater that demonstrated a breakdown of hierarchy
and discipline, creating a very embarrassing situation for Roquefeuil.[70] In
spite of such events, however, theater was widely embraced as the lesser of
the potential evils. In fact, commanding officers in Brest and elsewhere
seem to have become increasingly convinced that an active theater was a
necessary and effective element in maintaining order in a city.[71] In 1768,
the crown issued an ordinance that standardized the practice of purchasing
army subscriptions. Under the subheading "On the Discipline and Police
of Troops in Garrisons," commanders were instructed to subscribe all regiments to the theater, provided one existed.[72]

With this action, the royal government, through France's military, offered
an important financial incentive to those who might build a playhouse in
smaller garrison cities, while also helping to recruit directors to perform in
these locales.[73] Subscriptions, after all, provided guaranteed income. Both
commanders and directors, however, understood the limits of this particular
financial commitment, which the king specified should be negotiated "at the
lowest possible price."[74] Roquefeuil alone among commanders took direct
financial responsibility for his garrison's playhouse and theater company.
Seemingly deliberately, he refused to take the necessary steps to cultivate a
diverse audience that would include significant numbers of civilian customers. He rebuffed the city's magistrates, for example, when they sought to
share authority over the institution. In his proposals, he suggested that the
subscriptions from military sources alone could fully support the year-round
troupe.[75] By operating the Théâtre de la Marine as an institution of patronage, he sought to insulate it from market forces, giving himself and the navy
the prestige and authority that a benefactor could claim. As he explained to
his officers, the navy could legitimately appear on advertising posters, enjoy
the best of honorific seating, police the hall, and oversee the acting company
and its repertory—rights that in other cities were typically reserved for or

shared with municipal officers—*only* because it owned the building and provided so much income to the troupe.[76]

In 1771, the deteriorating finances of the Brest theater company prompted an investigation by the crown, placing the special relationship between the navy and its stage in jeopardy. The secretary of state for the navy commanded Roquefeuil to poll his officers "to know if the support of the theater here by a corps subscription was really of the taste and the opinion of the greatest number in the department."[77] Roquefeuil complied. When gathering the opinions of his officers, he reminded them that maintaining an active theater was in keeping with the designs of the military "to make officers reside in the department as much as possible," and that it provided "a pretty pleasant means to dispel the ennui that this residence usually entails."[78] Roquefeuil sent the list of signatures to his superiors so that they might know the sentiments of the men themselves. Two hundred and twenty-nine of his officers signed the poll: one hundred and eighty-seven signed in favor of continuing the subscription to the theater, while forty-two voted against it. Those officers supporting theater constituted a majority of nearly five to one. Still, nearly 20 percent felt strongly enough to speak out against their commander's pet project. The fact that this petition was not confidential almost certainly shaped the results: with only a single exception, all those of the lower ranks of guard and ensign were in favor of the theater, while those who opposed the subscription were higher-ranking officers.[79] Perhaps these differences in opinion can be attributed to taste, to the higher cost of subscriptions for senior officers, or to the amount of time these men spent in port. Older and more senior officers were evidently willing to express dissent, while junior officers would have been more vulnerable to retaliation. Still, this poll seems to suggest that the younger generation of noble officers had been quite successfully converted to the stage. Roquefeuil for his part appeared very pleased that a strong majority favored "the support of the spectacle in the military."[80]

For Roquefeuil, the vote by the Brest officers to continue their subscription to the theater, even at the higher rates, served as a referendum on the importance of theater to the military more broadly. Did these men want to maintain theatrical entertainment in "the largest garrison of officers in the kingdom," Roquefeuil had asked, or did they want to be responsible for letting it fail?[81] Roquefeuil's appeal to the officer corps to dig more deeply into their pockets to pay the escalating expenses of the theater, however, can also be seen as an attempt to divert attention from problems of his own making. When the extravagant theater company that he created failed to support itself and successive directors went bankrupt, Roquefeuil refused to scale down his dream of year-round entertainment in Brest. Instead, he clandestinely diverted large sums from the navy's budget to cover the troupe's cost over-runs in order to continue operations. Roquefeuil may well have told himself that these transfers were a temporary measure, and that the theater's financial situation would soon improve. As we will see, the flow of state money to the Théâtre de la Marine, buried within the navy's budget, continued for several years before this unauthorized patronage was finally cut off.

The Politics of Display

In Brest, as in the dozens of other cities that inaugurated new playhouses during the late Old Regime, the distribution of honorific seating was no small matter. In fact, in the very letter authorizing funding for the construction of the Théâtre de la Marine, the secretary of state for the navy moved directly to address this issue: "The matters thus arranged, there is nothing more to decide than the establishment of the honorific boxes."[82] Such concerns were hardly new. Municipal officers, as we have seen, long embraced theater as an opportunity to display their status and authority within the urban community by watching performances from special boxes or prominent benches or seats specifically dedicated for their use.[83] Around midcentury, however, theater seating took on heightened significance as powerful political elites aggressively maneuvered to claim the most prominent seats for personal display. Conflicts over precedence pitted royal authorities against municipal officers and parlementary elites and even against one another. During the late Old Regime, such disputes became matters of state.

Seating conflicts proved especially common around the inauguration of a playhouse, when the transition to a new (and, increasingly, more prominent) building provided an excuse to challenge long-held traditions and to test the authority of rival powers. A lengthy and bitter conflict that erupted in Metz in 1752 when the nearly completed municipal theater was inaugurated illustrates the high political stakes of these contests over the use of boxes within a playhouse. In this case, the royal intendant and the first president of the Parlement of Metz, one of France's powerful regional high courts of law, entered into a dispute over which of them should rightfully occupy the queen's box, the second most prestigious in the house after the king's box, which the governor claimed. The theatergoers of Metz became the audience for a very public conflict between provincial judicial authority and royal administrative authority, one that played out over several years in the new municipal playhouse.[84]

Even before construction of the Metz theater had been completed, the intendant, Jean-François de Creil, seized the opportunity to claim the queen's box for himself. He obtained a personal key for the loge, and allegedly made it his habit "to occupy this box at all the theatrical performances from the moment that [the comedy] was established" and even during balls.[85] Mathieu de Montholon, who as the first president of the parlement had occupied the queen's box in the previous playhouse, wrote to the governor, the maréchal de Belle-Isle, to express his frustration at what he saw as a usurpation: "It is a matter of public notoriety that, as much for me as for my predecessors and for Madame de Montholon, this box has always been destined for the first president."[86] To substantiate that his claim should trump that of the intendant, Montholon went so far as to write to the other provincial parlements located in cities that enjoyed a public playhouse. In both Rouen and Nancy, he had been assured, his peers had use of the queen's box, and he was awaiting word from other parlements.[87] Meanwhile, Montholon warned Belle-Isle that "the public was aware of the affectation of M. de Creil."[88]

Under pressure from the governor to resolve the issue, the intendant visited his rival. Ultimately, the two agreed that neither would enjoy exclusive use of the queen's box, and that Montholon and his wife would reserve its use whenever they wished.[89] Still, the contest over precedence was not resolved. When a new intendant was assigned to Metz in 1754, without a box of his own, this successor chose to take a seat in the governor's box. This only exacerbated tensions, because it was regarded as added proof of the intendant's presumption. The new intendant, Antoine-Louis-François Lefebvre de Caumartin, wrote to Belle-Isle that the city's new playhouse was a success, but that "the two first boxes [are] causing offense to one another."[90] The special honors that the intendant received in the king's box only inflamed the rivalry. The first president's wife, Madame de Montholon, was angered that the intendant's box was illuminated during the performance, but not her own box, and that the theater company delayed the performance until the arrival of the intendant's wife, but not for her. The situation worsened when Montholon commanded the theater's director to give these honors to his wife, but *not* to Madame de Caumartin. Caumartin was keenly aware of the political fallout that resulted from this conflict, including "a lot of bad faith from the part of all the parlement, which kindles the fire. They say that the intendant is not made to be in the king's box, that he has no rank in a province, that there is a place for him in the amphitheater when the boxes are full, and steps on the staircases for him as for the others."[91]

When Caumartin, a theater enthusiast, began to take great interest in the day-to-day affairs of the theater company, rumors soon circulated that he enjoyed the favors of the actresses, that he spent evenings with them, and even that he took a lover into the notorious grilled box that was shielded from public view. These stories, he wrote in frustration, "spread to good society, and make me the butt of nasty jokes, from people from whom I believe to have the right to expect [high] regard either because of my name or because of my position. But I begin to understand that they are not accustomed in this city to respect either the position that I occupy, or those that fulfill it."[92] Rumors even reached the ears of his wife, straining his marriage. The only solution, he pleaded with the governor, would be to award him the queen's box. If not, to avoid becoming the object of the "mocking laughter of a parterre," he explained, he and his wife would have to bow to the pressure of a hostile public and stop attending the theater entirely.[93] "When certain societies have thoroughly humiliated me," he warned in one desperate letter, "I hope that the court will at least be happy with my administration."[94]

The resolution of this conflict, unfortunately, is not known. The struggle by these intendants in Metz to demonstrate their political power by attempting to claim theater boxes previously held by others, however, suggests the extent to which the assertion of royal authority over provincial cultural affairs was ongoing and contested as late as the 1750s. Disputes over seating honors between royal and local authorities continued, moreover, through the 1780s. In Nantes, for example, the municipal officers enjoyed use of the queen's box in the local public theater for more than four decades, having arranged in the early 1740s to have the city's coat of arms painted on the box. Yet just as the city prepared to inaugurate its impressive new public playhouse in 1788—paid for with municipal funds—the magistrates lost this prerogative. The city officers had made plans once again to adopt the second most prestigious box for their own use. When the provincial intendant, residing in Rennes, asserted his own claim to the box, the city protested and the dispute was ultimately taken to Versailles. The minister for the King's Household, the baron de Breteuil, determined that "in accordance with the order observed in all the theaters of the kingdom" the queen's box did in fact rightfully belong to the intendant. "If the arms of the city were painted on the queen's box," he instructed, "it will be easy to cover them and paint them on one of the other boxes of the municipal officers' choice."[95]

Not only *parlementaires* and municipal officers felt the pressure of the new symbolic claims put forth by royal authorities. In garrison cities, in particular, local residents shared similar concerns. This was the case because the claims of military officers regularly extended beyond the most prestigious boxes and well into the playhouse itself. Already by midcentury Versailles had agreed that military commanders should at minimum be granted prominent first boxes so as to receive recognition and "not to be confused [*confondu*] with the public."[96] By the 1770s, however, some commanders began to press that *all* officers be assured seats befitting their estate. This was achieved by setting aside whole sections of the auditorium for the exclusive use of the military. In these cases, contemporary conceptions of aristocratic honor served to reinforce France's hierarchical political culture with its emphasis on display. Rivalry between military branches, too, could play a role in extending this policy. This competition becomes clear in the dilemma confronted by the naval commander in Toulon. Although at first he had enthusiastically given his support for the construction of a local playhouse, he soon began to worry about where his men would sit. Given that army officers were stationed in Toulon in even greater numbers, the commander grew concerned that they would claim all the best spots in the theater, while his naval officers "would not know where to find decent and respectable seats." He informed the theater entrepreneurs that he would not authorize subscriptions for the navy unless they resolved this problem by reserving naval officers their own separate section of the theater.[97]

Because theater seating was used to reinforce rank within the military, superior officers claimed exclusive rights to especially prominent seats, often a bench located on the main floor directly in front of the stage, a section of the theater known as the parquet or the orchestra.[98] In some cases, first and second boxes were reserved for junior officers such as lieutenants, who might also appear in the parterre. Common soldiers were often seated in the fourth boxes (where they existed) or in the paradis. The army explicitly addressed the importance of such distinctions. The secretary of state for war, the comte de Saint-Germain, acknowledged that no ordinance or letter from his ministry mandated that a particular bench in theaters be designated for superior officers, and that "practices to this effect in almost all the garrison cities have to this point only been ordered by the commanders of the provinces."[99] Yet he defended the practice. "The form is necessary for subordination," he explained in a memorandum on the policing of theaters written in late 1776. "In the French armies where certain officers have taken to treating their leaders with equality and to forgetting all that they owe them, one cannot mark too much the differences that must exist between them, nor honor rank too much with public prerogatives."[100] The prince de Robecq justified reserving such prominent seats for those of higher military rank because "decency and the policing of the corps require that their superior officers not be confused with spectators so that one can have recourse to them at the moment where it is a question of interposing their authority to make the officers they command keep order."[101]

Even within the military, commanders encountered a certain amount of resistance in enforcing hierarchical theater seating, particularly among young and privileged junior officers.[102] In one such case, in the early 1760s an officer in Calais was asked to cede his seat on an honorific bench to a superior during a performance. He refused, responding "that they were all equal." This junior officer later apologized. The following day, however, the bench in question went missing. When the commander interpreted this as an assault on his authority, this apparent prank protesting hierarchical seating practices escalated into a significant disciplinary crisis.[103] Tensions over seating practices were exacerbated by the fact that in some garrisons strict seating hierarchies applied to military personnel only during regular season performances. For special performances, such as when royal actors visited from Paris, all subscriptions—including military subscriptions—were cancelled. During these shows, officers and even common soldiers who wished to attend purchased their own tickets and sat in whichever section they chose.[104]

Military claims to exclusive use of specific boxes, benches, and stage seating directly impinged on local citizens' own enjoyment of performances, not to mention their personal aspirations for seats of distinction. The expansion of military presence in the theater and especially the seating practices imposed by local commanders provoked protest in the 1770s and 1780s. In Valenciennes, for example, a bench theoretically reserved for the commanders of the military corps had become communal property as a number of nonmilitary notables had taken to sitting in this prime location. When the army began once again to restrict access to the bench, refusing seats even to city officers and their wives, a number of these urban elites felt humiliated and complained. In 1776, the city council protested that the city owned the theater, and that they, as the chiefs of civil authority, should have primary authority over seating within the playhouse, but to no avail.[105] The bench continued to prove a thorn in the side of the city. The magistrates protected their honor by publicly stating that they allowed the bench to be used by military leaders as a courtesy, even as the army provided a guard responsible for ensuring, albeit politely, that only the proper military elites sat there.[106] Only a move to a larger new playhouse in 1781 seems to have finally defused the tension surrounding the issue.

The complaints voiced in Valenciennes raised fundamental questions about public theater, questions that were posed even more directly in other French garrison cities during the final years of the Old Regime.[107] How far did military authority extend over spaces traditionally overseen by the municipality? Did not the citizen—the spectator—have certain rights as a consumer? This problem was confronted in Arras, where the city government spoke out in the 1780s against the practice of reserving the entire parquet of the theater solely for the use of the senior military officers stationed in the city. The magistrates argued that they were "persuaded that any person who goes to the theater, depending on the money that he pays to enter, has the right to put himself where he judges apropos."[108] City officials approached the commander with their complaint, arguing that theater should operate according to rules of the market, not according to the rules of the state. Their argument in fact won the day: "M. the Commander . . . lifted the ban and since then, each individual places himself indiscriminately in the parquet."[109] Just a few years later, when a new playhouse opened, the commander changed his decision and reinstated military honors and separate seating in the playhouse. This time, however, the community's conviction that the playhouse was a commercial space in which customers enjoyed certain rights was also taken into account. In a compromise, much of the interior of the playhouse—from the prestigious parquet to the modest paradis—was divided. Local citizens attended the theater on the left side, sitting according to the varying prices of the tickets they had purchased; the garrison occupied the right side, sitting hierarchically according to rank.[110] Thus, in the twilight years of the Old Regime, these two conflicting approaches to society and culture played out uneasily side by side in the public playhouse.

Royal Governors and the Theater Privilege

In addition to honorific seating, the right to authorize theatrical performances constituted a second area in which municipalities witnessed an assertion of royal authority in the mid-eighteenth century. Traditionally actors and other entertainers applied to each municipality to obtain permission to perform. When opera companies first began to perform in provincial cities in the late seventeenth century, the exclusive privilege that their directors paid to obtain from Lully and later directors of the Royal Academy of Music applied to opera alone, not comedy or tragedy. This permission from Paris to perform lyrical works, moreover, did not absolve these opera companies from obtaining local authorization. This began to change in the 1730s and 1740s when a handful of provincial governors started to issue their own theater privileges that granted specific directors exclusive rights for operatic or dramatic performances in cities such as Bordeaux and Montpellier for a specified length of time. By granting select troupes monopolistic privileges similar to those that the king granted to the royal stages in Paris, governors such as the duc de Duras used their authority to guard these concessioners from competition from other traveling troupes that might turn up, and to effectively guarantee them sole use of the city's public playhouse. In return for these guarantees, the directors agreed to various conditions, such as requirements that they perform for minimum periods of time.[111] In this way, governors used their clout to promote as well as control local theatrical life. By midcentury, a growing number of city governments—those whose governors had not asserted their authority to select theater troupes—had also begun to issue privileges authorizing theatrical performances by a single troupe or director for a portion of the year. As a result, in the late 1750s directors of traveling companies might need to obtain privileges in advance for a number of cities on their itinerary. In some cases, this required paying various municipalities thousands of livres to secure these exclusive rights.[112]

During the next few decades, as the use of theater privileges became more widespread, a few governors extended the geographic extent of the theater privileges they granted to encompass an entire province. This practice likely originated with the duc de Richelieu who, while serving as the governor of Languedoc and later Guyenne in the 1750s, expanded his theater privileges to cover the full domain of each of these provinces. At this time, the opera privilege granted by the Royal Academy of Music in both of these provinces already operated as regional concessions. Richelieu extended similar rights and protections on a provincial level to dramatic theater companies. This made it easier for theater companies to travel freely within these domains, because the governor's privilege guaranteed that local authorities must allow them to perform. In subsequent decades, this practice spread slowly as a number of governors and military commanders, likely emulating Richelieu, began to grant provincewide privileges in Picardy in the 1750s, Anjou, Brittany, and Lorraine by the 1760s, in Normandy around the 1770s, and in Bourgogne, Flanders, Hainaut, and Cambrésis by the early 1780s.[113]

When various royal governors assumed control of privileges, they denied municipal authorities their traditional right to select among the various directors and performers who proposed to entertain local residents, including the right to prohibit directors that they found objectionable.[114] A letter from the lieutenant general of police in Angers to the police of Bordeaux, written in the spring of 1766, conveys the response of one representative of local authority to this new prerogative claimed by the provincial governor and the impact it was having on theatrical production in the region. The right to authorize theatrical performances in Angers, the author complained, had always been the responsibility of the city's police lieutenant. In recent years, though, the governor had claimed the right to issue permissions to an acting troupe of his choice. This new privilege allegedly gave the troupe exclusive performance rights not only in Angers but throughout the entire province of Anjou. Such a system, the police lieutenant protested, entitled the privileged troupe "to do away with competitors." It performed freely in any city it wished "without any other troupe daring to present itself." He viewed this provincial privilege as an "attack" on the authority of the police and also on freedom of choice for the city and its residents. "It is certain that in the past," he maintained, "neither [the governor nor] the commanders of the provinces, resident or not," ever granted these sorts of privileges.[115]

Despite some local resistance, the establishment of theater privileges had a transformative effect on the French theater industry. By introducing, albeit incompletely and unevenly, a new level of regulation into France's cultural economy, the advent of the theater privilege brought the performing arts into line with most other forms of cultural production in contemporary France. According to the historian John Shovlin, the French economy in the late eighteenth century was "structured, through and through, by the exercise of political authority."[116] In this mercantilist era regulation was the norm. At the urging of the monarchy, most trades in French cities were organized into guilds that held exclusive rights to manufacture or sell specific goods or to provide specific services. "The essence of the guild system," one scholar notes, "was restriction of production."[117] Politically sensitive forms of cultural production such as printing and bookselling were already regulated by the royal government, and those seeking to establish a journal or newspaper needed to obtain a royal privilege.[118] Moreover, as we have seen, theatrical production in Paris already took place under an extensive system of restrictive monopolies. Outside of the capital, governors' introduction of the privilege promoted the expansion of the theater industry, encouraging the establishment of resident theater troupes by making such an enterprise somewhat less risky for directors, actors, and possible investors.

The privilege appealed to theater directors because it usually provided certain guarantees, such as access to local audiences, the availability of the local playhouse, and the certainty that no rival troupes would be cutting into their profits. Privileges often lasted for the fifty weeks of the traditional provincial theater season, which began shortly after Easter. The theater troupe, especially prior to the 1770s, was not always expected to perform in any one city for that whole period. For troupes that traveled, these yearlong contracts ensured that they could move into the public theater whenever they arrived in a new city and stay for as long as they found it profitable. They also made it more likely that local audiences, deprived of other theatrical entertainments, would be fresh and eager to attend. When it came to large cities such as Lyon, Marseille, Metz, and Lille, the privilege could extend for as long as a decade. When granting such a long-term contract for the theater in Lille, the governor explained that this extended length of time provided the director with greater security as he embarked on the risky and expensive undertaking of assembling a large troupe of performers, obtaining the sets, props, costumes, and other materials needed to perform.[119]

As theater troupes established themselves in cities on a longer-term basis, the scope of theater privileges expanded. Not infrequently, the privilege came to encompass not just opera or comedy and tragedy but all forms of performance and spectacle, including even dances and other entertainments for which audiences paid entry. This more expansively defined monopoly enabled privileged directors to reap an additional benefit, known to contemporaries as *"le quart des spectacles."* Directors whose privileges included this provision could require all others seeking to entertain in a city—and even, more controversially, throughout an entire province—to obtain their consent and to pay them one-fourth of their gross box office revenues.[120] The privilege for the Marseille theater company for the period beginning at Easter 1789 provides a clear example of this provision. It conveyed to the troupe the right to stage "exclusively of all others tragedies, operas, French and Italian comedies, comic operas and *opéra bouffon*, ballets, and all other spectacles of any type that there is, to give public balls in the accustomed places and circumstances and to be paid in keeping with custom one-fourth of the proceeds of the receipts of games or popular troupes, fireworks, and generally all spectacle for which the performance and the execution will take place in an enclosed space and for money in the city of Marseille and the suburbs."[121] In a city such as Lyon, directors applied this quart des spectacles no less liberally. In the 1780s, among the popular performers who paid the theater director a share of their proceeds we find marionettists, acrobats, and rope dancers, but also such sideshow spectacles as a little girl with no arms, a midget named Marie, a French giantess, and a man who broke stones with his teeth.[122] The payments from such entertainments constituted a significant boon to theater directors.[123]

By curtailing competition and setting up a system of subsidies in which a select theater company was funded in part by competitors and popular entertainers, the privilege encouraged directors to commit to longer performance runs and even, in some cases, to establish their troupes permanently in a city. In this way, the privilege proved critical for the development of the theater industry. In Nantes, the directors of the theater company explained the importance of the privilege for its operations in the late 1770s. They demanded that the municipality respect the provisions of the privilege "such as it is the practice in Bordeaux, Lyon, Marseille, Rouen, Toulouse, and in all the large cities where there is theater year-round, not to accord permission to any spectacle of any genre" unless this competitor had first come to terms with them and received their approval. Given the Nantes troupe's precarious financial situation, unauthorized competitors caused "immense harm."[124] The directors claimed that the exclusive right to performance, for which they had paid several thousand livres, was necessary for the very survival of their troupe, which was attempting to pioneer year-round performance in Nantes.

With the introduction of provincewide privileges, some directors began to assess the quart des spectacles on rival performers even in cities where their own troupes never performed. Confronting such tactics, smaller cities and those in more remote areas had particular cause to complain. The magistrates of Agen, one of five cities in the province of Guyenne with a public play-house, lamented that the privileged troupe found that it was not particularly profitable to perform there. At the same time, unprivileged troupes and entertainers were put off by the fact that they were taxed so heavily. The result for their community was little entertainment at all.[125] The practice of assessing the quart des spectacles in this way proved sufficiently controversial that the Comédie-Française was repeatedly asked to assess its validity. In their 1788 response, the King's Players looked unfavorably on what they viewed as aggressive profiteering. They concluded that directors could legitimately collect such a payment only in cities where they performed and only while they were in residence, unless their privilege very expressly stated otherwise. If a director managed to obtain this more expansive privilege, he or she would need to contact the police in every city and town large enough to attract performers to register their privilege in advance and to make their claims known before they could legitimately collect.[126]

As theater privileges became widespread, they helped to consolidate a more formal hierarchy of performance. Provincial theater was increasingly relegated into one of two broad categories. Opera, comedy and tragedy, comic opera, and ballet, on the one hand, were officially recognized and protected. These elite forms of theatrical performance, as we have seen, were appropriate to be performed in elegant new civic playhouses. On the other hand, alternate forms of entertainment or spectacle, ineligible for the privi-lege, were relegated to the category of popular culture. Yet, despite its provi-sions and costs, the privilege does not seem to have suppressed these more modest entertainments. Many flourished during this era. In fact, secondary popular theater companies even attempted to establish themselves on a more permanent basis in several of France's largest cities during the 1780s.[127]

The Cultural Politics of Assimilation

Nowhere was the influence of the privilege on the development of theatri-cal production more evident than in Strasbourg. Located close to the border with Germany, Strasbourg at the beginning of the eighteenth century was home to about thirty thousand residents most of whom commonly spoke Alsatian, a Germanic dialect. Troupes of German-speaking actors and Italian singers had long entertained the urban community. French theater companies first began to visit Strasbourg shortly after Louis XIV annexed the city to France in 1681.[128] The terms of the annexation addressed the cultural divide between Strasbourg's native population and the French administrative authorities and military forces that quickly converged there. Although in principle the city remained responsible for overseeing all theatrical entertainment, in practice the newly arrived representatives of royal sovereignty soon asserted their authority over French-language theater, while the city maintained authority over performances of greatest interest to locals, namely those in German and Italian.[129] To provide a home for French theater and opera, the city converted a warehouse into a municipal playhouse in 1701. When German actors and others came to Strasbourg, they performed on a second stage that was leased and managed by the city magistrates. The problem lay in the fact that both the military and the city recognized early on that Strasbourg was unable to support both kinds of troupes at the same time.[130] The military's determination to promote the French theater at the expense of local preferences, using the privilege to do so, would strain this cultural balancing act.

From its inception, the French theater in Strasbourg was intended above all to serve the interests and needs of the garrison. By the 1750s, commanders such as the marquis de Paulmy had come to consider theater in the city as "absolutely necessary," adding that the authorities should "neglect nothing that could contribute to supporting it and to making it suitable to satisfy those who go there."[131] The army extended the advantages it could offer, for example by purchasing subscriptions on behalf of the soldiers and officers of the garrison. The intendant de Lucé described the situation in a letter: "You know, dear friend, how necessary it is to have a theater in a garrison city as large as this one here. We have taken every measure to keep one here that was passable. We achieved this through the force of money and through the cares of a director that M. the marquis de Vibraye [lieutenant-general of the king's army], who involves himself in this detail here, had chosen and who had taken over the enterprise. We all pay him very high subscriptions."[132] Even so, the theater company struggled. When the garrison partly emptied in 1756 as soldiers mobilized for war, the director lost thousands of livres. Mired in debt, he fled the city, taking with him the box-office receipts, and was arrested.[133] Recognizing the challenging circumstances the director faced, the intendant hesitated to apportion blame for the theater's precarious situation: "Be it bad conduct on his part, be it a lack of resources in the colony of inhabitants, this entrepreneur was not able to finish the year."[134]

The military governors of Alsace further supported the French acting troupe in Strasbourg by extending to them the advantages of the privilege. As early as the 1740s, the maréchal de Coigny began requiring German and Italian troupes to pay the quart des spectacles for the right to perform in Strasbourg. These funds effectively subsidized the French-language troupe that he was hoping to establish more permanently in the city. Then, in response to pleas from the French players who felt threatened by the tremendous success of an Italian opera company, he curtailed performances by foreign actors and singers that might challenge the interests of the French theater. He forbade them, for example, from performing on Sundays, the most profitable day of the week.[135] These strategies proved particularly controversial, given that they violated the original terms that governed the division of authority over the city's cultural life. The city officers protested, arguing that Strasbourg needed "a spectacle that satisfies the inhabitants of this city," most of whom, after all, were not fluent in French. Whereas many Strasbourgeois could not understand performances of French comedies and tragedies, they did enjoy opera even when sung in Italian.[136] The municipal authorities expressed their concern that the financial burdens and restrictions placed on this opera and others seemed likely to drive away the unprivileged performers. The military paid the magistrates little heed, responding that the new policy "comes down to wanting to conserve a French troupe in preference to all others, tolerating and desiring however all other troupes that would not be prejudicial to it."[137] The city lost this political battle, and several others that followed. For more than thirty years, German and Italian theater companies were permitted to perform only during defined periods of the year, on days and at times when the French troupe was not performing. All the while they paid the privileged French players for the opportunity to do so.[138]

In the 1780s, when the French theater director began using the privilege to demand even greater authority over urban entertainments, the city magistrates once again felt compelled to protest. They complained that the director had "exceeded the limits and forced unheard of pretentions." Not only did the French troupe in Strasbourg seek to profit from visiting German and Italian troupes, it had begun to tax all spectacles and entertainments, and even attempted to prohibit concerts, parties during Carnival, dances in private homes, and the like. The magistrates demanded that these liberties be restored to the population. They asked that the quart des spectacles be lifted during the fairs that Strasbourg's residents enjoyed twice a year, and that exhibitions having to do with the arts, sciences, and natural history be exempted from this form of taxation because of their educational intent. While conceding that the German comedy troupe should not establish itself in the city year-round, the city officers proposed that the restrictions under which it operated be eased. They explained that "today, the large number of foreigners and the progress if not of wealth at least of luxury can support the two theaters together for a good part of the year."[139] Given strong public support for performances in German among city residents as well as by German visitors to the city, "the municipal government cannot resolve itself to participate in the destruction of an establishment to which the public attaches such interest and pleasure."[140] The magistrates even threatened to approach the king "to arrange this matter in a solid manner and to establish principles such that neither will your authority be compromised nor will the constitution of our city, which His Majesty confirmed and conserves until this day, suffer."[141]

This time the city fathers won some ground. The quart des spectacles was lifted during the fairs. Scientific and artistic exhibits could take place freely, as could events such as amateur concerts and dances. Yet, to their disappointment, restrictions on German theater companies remained, including a prohibition against their use of any song translated into German from French. The commander-in-chief of Alsace, the maréchal de Contades, explained that because "music is of all languages, that is what attracts those bourgeois who do not speak French" to the French playhouse.[142] Meanwhile, the restrictions in place ensured "that the preferential taste of the bourgeoisie of Strasbourg for these German amusements is not perpetuated by overly frequent occasions." In Strasbourg, the royal military commander explicitly viewed the French theater as a vehicle for assimilation of a population that even a century after annexation to France remained religiously, socially, and culturally distinct. Restricting and taxing German actors in the city was critical for ensuring the financial stability of what he described as the "national theater."[143]

The Limits of Royal Patronage and Authority

Given the importance that the monarchy accorded to theater and music, the fact of increasing state engagement in public theater outside of Paris during the eighteenth century is less surprising than its origins and its limitations. When governors, intendants, and military commanders asserted new claims over local theater, as this chapter has shown, they were not enacting policies originating with a king eager to consolidate his cultural control over French cities. Instead, representatives of royal authority such as the ambitious naval commander in Brest and the status-conscious intendants in Metz and Rennes frequently acted on their own initiative, leveraging their relationship with the crown when necessary to obtain support and approval for their plans. As a result, the lines of authority over the stage, the uses of privileges, and honorific practices within France's new public playhouses varied from province to province and from city to city. These differences inflamed the sense of injustice expressed by municipal authorities from Nantes to Valenciennes to Strasbourg as they confronted the erosion of their authority over public and cultural life.[144]

Even as royal authorities displayed themselves prominently in France's new public playhouses and governors claimed the rights to issue privileges to directors of their choice, they, like most agents of the crown, usually limited their engagement with theater to responsibilities that were largely regulatory and honorific. (Less frequently, these also extended into the domain of policing and public safety, which will be discussed further in chapter 5.) Unlike in Paris, where the monarchy directly administered the royal theaters as part of the King's Household, elsewhere in France political authorities almost always left matters of theatrical production to the professionals. Royal governors and military commanders took steps to ensure that provincial theater and opera companies might take root in a protected environment, subsidized by potential rivals and shored up by military subscriptions. Even with these protections, however, they could not ensure a theater company's success. Representatives of royal authority, to be sure, played an important supporting role in the making of France's theater industry. Yet it was directors who produced theatrical performances during the late Old Regime, developing the strategies that enabled theater companies to expand and to move into new markets. It was directors who took financial responsibility for the enterprise, whether in failure or in success.

Ultimately, the limitations of state engagement with provincial stages became clear even in Brest, where Roquefeuil's Théâtre de la Marine foundered in the early 1770s. Without the support of the local urban elite and a substantial civilian paying public, a year-round theater company with a sizable cast was simply too expensive to maintain. During Roquefeuil's tenure the new naval theater not only alienated city residents and sparked discipline problems, it also cost the royal treasury nearly eighty thousand livres in unauthorized debts that only grew over time.[145] The naval intendant instructed to investigate this financial catastrophe blamed unrealistic expectations and a misplaced desire for luxury for these escalating expenses. Once the stately new playhouse opened, he explained, it had seemed to call for "a spectacle that corresponded to the beauty of the playhouse and the decorations." Instead of making do with a modest troupe performing just comedy or opéra-comique, which was more fitting to the size and affluence of Brest, Roquefeuil and a coterie of supporters demanded a full and varied repertory, including even expensive genres such as ballet. From the intendant's perspective, this was what led to the theater's ruin.[146] When the crown discovered the full extent of these debts in the fall of 1771, royal funding was cut off. Versailles ordered Roquefeuil to repay to the royal treasury the sums that had been "indecently drawn from it." This would be done by continuing the naval officers' subscription payments, but diverting these funds to pay down the debts owed to the state. These officers were forced to pay the cost of Roquefeuil's grandiose dreams and managerial incompetence, a policy that met with outrage. Without the financial guarantees provided by military subscriptions, no director could be found who would risk taking on the privilege for Brest. In 1772, six years after it opened, the Théâtre de la Marine closed its doors. For several years the navy struggled to reopen it on a permanent basis.[147]

The spectacular failure of Roquefeuil's attempts to free the Brest theater from the constraints of the market and to operate it as an institution of naval patronage only reinforced the prevailing attitude at Versailles that provincial theater and opera troupes must operate commercially, under private management. The secretary of state for the navy defined the boundaries of the royal government's cultural policy with great clarity when he wrote to the new naval commander in Brest in 1776 that "the navy cannot take responsibility, as in the past, for the operations and the cost of this theater, and it must give these over to an entrepreneur." The commander, in response, reassured Versailles that in his dealings with directors he would abide by these limits and place theater operations in private hands: "The *Comédie* will be free: the director will be responsible for everything, will run all the risks, and will have nothing to demand of the navy."[148]

CHAPTER 4

Directors and the Business of Performing

In 1745, Jean Monnet, having abruptly lost his privilege to direct the successful Opéra-Comique theater at the Paris fairgrounds, left the capital to take up a new position as director of the Lyon stage. In order to secure the privilege for the theater of France's second-largest city from the duc de Villeroy, Monnet agreed to purchase the previous director's *magasin*—the sets, props, music, costumes, and other materials necessary to run such an enterprise—for twenty-five thousand livres. He also agreed to perform opera. Lyon enjoyed an operatic tradition dating back to the 1680s that had garnered political support from the city's ruling elite. As a business venture, however, the city's opera company had long struggled to sustain an annual season and performances, it seems, were intermittent. Opera was the most prestigious of eighteenth-century theater genres. It was also the most expensive to produce, requiring trained singers, a sizeable orchestra, and the lavish costumes, sets, and special effects that defined the French *tragédie en musique*. As Monnet acknowledged, several of his predecessors in this position had been ruined.[1]

To turn the Lyon theater into a financial and popular success Monnet recognized that he would need a new business plan. Unburdened by the genre restrictions that defined the Paris stages, he set out to expand the Lyon theater company's offerings to include not only opera but also comedy, tragedy, and the immensely popular new lyric genre known as opéra-comique. Whereas provincial opera companies at the time typically competed with traveling

97

dramatic theater troupes for customers and their money, he would attempt to profit by folding both into the same enterprise. To perform this expanded repertory, he hired opera singers as well as a parallel cast of dramatic actors and actresses who could also perform musical theater. Finally, with this larger and more versatile cast, he extended the troupe's performance schedule to entertain the city year-round. His goal was simple: use variety to draw in the largest possible paying public. "It is only a question of finding the means to satisfy the general taste of the Lyonnais," Monnet explained in his memoirs. "I succeeded by bringing opera together with comedy and opéra-comique."[2]

During the 1740s, however, even in a city as large and wealthy as Lyon, such an ambitious plan proved challenging to implement. Under Monnet's direction a talented and diverse company staged new works regularly in a variety of genres, to the delight of local audiences. Box office receipts rose sharply—yet so did expenses. To increase his revenue, Monnet took half of the company to perform in Dijon for a lucrative summer season. After his return, however, he still found himself struggling to pay the salaries of his cast. Within less than a year, Monnet became convinced "that it was impossible for an opera to sustain itself in the provinces." He convinced the city to drop opera from the repertory entirely, allowing him to slim his cast and focus on the more profitable comedy and opéra-comique. Monnet directed the Lyon theater for just few years before leaving for London and ultimately returning to Paris to reassume the helm of the Opéra-Comique when it was reinstated in 1752.[3] His polyvalent approach to theatrical production lived on, however, as later directors in Lyon and other provincial cities embraced similar strategies to transform theatrical production in France.

When Monnet undertook this bold experiment in the late 1740s, nearly every provincial city, including even large and wealthy cities such as Bordeaux, Marseille, Toulouse, and Nantes, continued to host traveling theater companies that specialized in either dramatic *or* lyric repertories.[4] Around midcentury, however, as provincial cities grew in size and wealth and as new consumer practices took hold, this traditional approach to theater production began to change. The inauguration of dedicated playhouses designed to accommodate substantially larger numbers of paying customers provided one incentive for directors to perform in cities for longer periods. The protections offered by theater privileges provided a second by encouraging directors to assemble larger, hybrid troupes capable of performing comedy as well as musical theater. Directors such as Monnet developed a new organizational model for commercial public theater that by the 1770s came to predominate in larger provincial cities. In the process they marketed and sold theatrical performances to unprecedented numbers of provincial consumers. Despite receiving only modest subsidies from municipal governments (when they received any at all), theater entrepreneurs succeeded by 1789 in establishing year-round theatrical entertainment in numerous cities throughout metropolitan France.

To this point, the business operations of France's theaters have received little attention from historians. Going behind the scenes to examine the organizational changes that made possible the expansion and institutionalization of professional public theater in urban France during this era enriches our understanding of performing arts culture, but it also does more. Because women featured prominently among provincial directors, the experiences of these directrices also contribute to our knowledge of women's workplace opportunities. Moreover, by examining the day-to-day business operations of professional directors and their troupes we can begin to appreciate the ways in which the creative and yet risky commercial expansion they launched in this era would redefine their relationship with the theater public. Before we turn to directors' new approaches to the business of theater, however, it is necessary to introduce these *entrepreneurs de spectacles*. This career, taken up by men and women of ambition, determination, and often considerable talent, was itself an eighteenth-century innovation.

From *Chef de Troupe* to *Entrepreneur de Spectacles*

It is difficult to pinpoint the moment when directors first took charge of theatrical production in France. What we do know is that from the origins of professional acting in France around the 1580s until the late seventeenth century, dramatic theater troupes were almost all small, often family-based ensembles. Although organized by a *chef de troupe*, these companies operated cooperatively on a profit-sharing basis. These itinerant troupes usually included about ten actors and actresses as members or *sociétaires*, while a few additional wage workers might help with sets and lighting, collecting entrance money, and performing small roles. Each member received a share in the company according to his or her status in the troupe, typically a half share or a full share. The *chef de troupe*, an experienced actor who usually owned the necessary sets and props, might receive as many as two shares in the enterprise. When joining a troupe, actors signed contracts that specified a fine for those who abandoned their fellow members, in some cases as high as a thousand livres or more. This fine, rarely enforced, was a symbolic gesture, reflecting actors' need to compensate for the instability of their lives through mutual reliance.[5] Seventeenth-century *chefs de troupe* were traditionally men. Actresses who were members of a company, however, enjoyed rights similar

In Paul Scarron's *Le Roman comique*, a fictional account of the adventures of a troupe of traveling players published in the 1650s, the actors transported themselves from city to city in an oxcart piled high with costumes, props, and set pieces, with the men walking on foot. This eighteenth-century engraving depicts an early scene in the novel when the troupe enters Le Mans, stopping near a jeu de paume where they would soon put on a show. "L'Arrivée des comédiens au Mans," Courtesy of the Bibliothèque nationale de France.

to those of the male members. All *sociétaires* participated in important troupe decisions. They typically discussed and voted on issues such as the choice of repertory and the recruitment of new members, settling matters by majority rule. This distinctive organization led Samuel Chappuzeau, a lawyer for the Parlement of Paris and a theater aficionado, to describe acting companies as "a manner of republic," in which members "all want to be equal."[6]

During the seventeenth century, this type of association served as the organizational framework for almost all French theater troupes, including those performing in Paris. In the 1680s, contemporaries estimated that there were twelve to fifteen such companies performing in the provinces in any given year, remaining in a city for anywhere from a few days to a few months.[7] With the exception of the more stable Parisian troupes and those patronized by members of the aristocracy, theater companies rarely maintained long-term cohesion, and many seem to have existed for only a year or two before dissolving and perhaps reestablishing with a different set of members.

Despite the fact that the Comédie-Française was integrated into the royal household when it was founded in 1680 and lost some of its autonomy to royal supervisors during the eighteenth century, the royal troupe maintained this cooperative organizational framework—directing itself, voting on issues, and sharing profits—throughout the Old Regime.[8]

The business of theater changed significantly with the emergence of the *entrepreneur de spectacles.* Directors first appeared at the helm of opera troupes. In contrast to dramatic theater, opera was centralized and hierarchically administered from the very creation of the Paris Opera in 1669.[9] To establish the first provincial opera company, founded in Marseille in 1684, the musician Pierre Gautier contracted with the director of the Paris Opera, Lully, to pay two thousand livres during the first year, and three thousand livres a year thereafter for this right. In the late 1680s and 1690s, the Royal Academy of Music granted directors privileges to perform opera in cities including Lyon, Dijon, Grenoble, Rouen, Bordeaux, Toulouse, Lille, Aix-en-Provence, Montpellier, Toulon, Arles, Nîmes, Nantes, and Strasbourg, as well as throughout the provinces of Brittany, Flanders, and Lorraine. Still, only a relatively small number of opera troupes performed at any one time, usually on circuits that included three or more cities.[10] Although provincial opera fell under the authority of a royal academy, these new opera directors cast themselves as businessmen and businesswomen who were concessioners of the Paris Opera. Indeed, in 1718, the city magistrates of Lille identified the city's first opera director, Claude Denis, as the "entrepreneur of the Royal Academy of Music."[11] In the 1740s and 1750s, in correspondence between provincial opera directors and the Paris Opera, these groups employed the terms *entrepreneur de spectacle* or *entrepreneur d'opéra* and director interchangeably.[12]

The *entrepreneur de comédie,* or director of a troupe performing dramatic repertory, debuted several decades later than his operatic counterpart, in the early eighteenth century.[13] Unlike the *chef de troupe*, the director assumed financial responsibility for the troupe as well as a much greater degree of authority over the cast and crew. Much more than a mere change in title, the advent of the theater director represents a critical turning point in the organization of theatrical production. Although directors assumed various artistic responsibilities, the position was largely entrepreneurial and managerial. Working alone or in partnerships, directors personally recruited and hired their actors and other personnel, set the troupe's itinerary, obtained the necessary privileges and permissions, rented the playhouse, determined the repertory, rehearsed the troupe, and marketed performances. As compensation for his or her efforts, the director might collect a salary and might also receive free housing inside the playhouse. Most significantly, the director claimed the profits the troupe might earn. At the same time, he or she also accepted responsibility for potential losses.[14] A director's wealth was often invested heavily in his or her magasin, built up over the course of a career. Appraising in the tens and even hundreds of thousands of livres, a theater magasin could be sold upon retirement or earlier if needed.[15]

With the advent of the professional director, actors began working for a fixed salary rather than a share of the profits. They typically signed contracts agreeing to work for the full theater year that began shortly after Easter and ended when theaters closed for the traditional two-week holiday break.[16] As a result, actors became *pensionnaires,* employees rather than voting members of a company, trading their authority within the troupe for greater stability and for higher pay. Such a profound restructuring of the theater industry did not take place overnight. *Chefs de troupe* appear in municipal registers throughout the first half of the eighteenth century, and some actors worked collectively *en société* into the Revolutionary era.[17] Nonetheless, letters to the Comédie-Française demonstrate that by the 1770s growing numbers of actors and singers worked as *pensionnaires* of a director who held the privilege for a city or province.[18] During the early Revolution, contemporaries observed that "the actors in the departments are almost all under a director; they are in the pay of entrepreneurs."[19]

This transition from collective, profit-sharing troupes to director-led dramatic theater companies was hastened indirectly by two midcentury developments. The first was the ongoing financial crisis confronting French opera. In the 1740s provincial opera directors regularly neglected to pay the Paris Opera for their privileges, citing financial difficulties. In 1750, the city of Paris, which had recently taken over administrative responsibility for the Opera from the monarchy, acknowledged that many provincial opera companies had proven unable to support themselves. The members of the city council apportioned some of the blame for this chronic indebtedness to the directors of the Royal Academy of Music, for "not having devoted all the attention to this matter that it merits."[20] The city's response to this crisis, however, was to intensify the Opera's policy of bureaucratic centralization out of Paris. It imposed a long list of conditions on local opera entrepreneurs intended to bind their troupes more closely to the Paris Opera and its operational model, ironically one that was founded upon "unparalleled visual and musical luxury."[21] Among other conditions, a director performing opera in Bordeaux, Bayonne, Toulouse, and Montpellier was required to hire a music master and a ballet master appointed by the Royal Academy of Music at predetermined salaries, to submit a cast list every three months, and to travel to Paris during each Easter holiday to account for the progress of his or her singers. Furthermore, the Paris Opera required the director to perform each opera as many times as possible, but at a minimum *fifteen* stagings in succession—at the time an extraordinarily long run for any work on a provincial stage.[22] Needless to say, such measures, which were expensive to implement and demonstrated little understanding of the circumstances these directors faced, did little to improve the economic situation for already struggling entrepreneurs.

Contemporaries began to argue that the problems confronting provincial opera troupes were rooted in the genre itself. After all, the economic troubles facing the opera companies in cities such as Lyon, Bordeaux, and Marseille were shared even in the capital. As one proposal for theater reform pointed out around 1750, Paris "is without a doubt the city of Europe the most capable of sustaining such an establishment, and yet the Paris Opera currently owes close to a million [livres]."[23] The anonymous authors of this plan praised Jean Monnet's decision to feature multiple genres in Lyon as "without doubt the most suitable" for a provincial stage. They also concurred that "the expense of the opera was . . . too heavy," and that these high production costs dragged the enterprise down.[24] Even in a city with the population and resources of Lyon, these authors concluded, for a theater company to sustain itself opera must be relegated to a very minor role: "We believe that one must establish a troupe . . . that will be capable of performing comedies, all the good opéras-comiques, [and] interludes of the old and new fairground theater and of the Comédie-Italienne. With the same performers we would be able to stage excerpts and acts of operas."[25]

As this proposal suggests, the crisis of opera coincided with a second development in the field of theater: the emergence of the wildly popular new genre, the opéra-comique.[26] Born in the Paris fairgrounds, opéra-comique merged song and comedy to entertain and amuse audiences from all backgrounds. In these works, a familiar cast of characters including sympathetic young maidens, eager suitors, simpletons, and villains sang bawdy or satiric vaudevilles, engaged in physical and bodily humor, and celebrated fantasy and marvel. Opéra-comique was far less technically demanding to perform than opera and even untrained singers could shine in character roles. In addition to being quicker, easier, and less expensive to produce, opéra-comique's catchy tunes and irreverent tone reached out to the artisans and aristocrats alike. During the 1750s and early 1760s talented librettists such as Charles-Simon Favart and Jean-Michel Sedaine raised the genre to even greater prominence. In fact, under the direction of Monnet and later Favart, the popularity of the Opéra-Comique theater in Paris became so great that in 1762 the king raised this upstart fairground troupe to the status of a royal theater by merging it with the Comédie-Italienne.[27]

During these decades, provincial directors quickly came to appreciate the benefits of combining popular musical theater with comedy in the repertory of a single troupe. The new hybrid troupes assembled by directors such as Monnet provided the flexibility, variety, and appeal necessary to entertain urban audiences for longer periods. Yet they also required a larger cast and additional musicians to accompany them. Already by the late 1760s and early 1770s provincial theater troupes had grown significantly in size, to include from about twenty-five *pensionnaires* for a company traveling between smaller cities to around ninety performers and musicians, as well as almost fifty additional crewmembers and staff, for the Bordeaux company. A decade later, even a traveling troupe could employ close to forty individuals. In 1787, the theater company of Lyon, when taking into account everyone from the cast members to hairdressers, stagehands, and ushers, employed one hundred and seventy-seven people.[28]

As the size of these new theatrical enterprises grew, so too did operating budgets. During the 1760s and 1770s, the costs of staging this expanded repertory could total over one hundred thousand livres a year, even for travel-ing troupes.[29] During the 1780s, the annual operating budget of the theater companies in Marseille and Lyon climbed above three hundred thousand and four hundred thousand livres, respectively. In Bordeaux it rose above six hun-dred thousand livres, an extraordinary sum at a time when the most expensive theater in Europe, the Paris Opera, spent just upward of a million livres a year.[30] The intimate, cooperative theater troupes of the seventeenth century blossomed in the eighteenth century into large and complex businesses that required not only expertise to run but also large amounts of capital. Inde-pendent directors predominated during the second half of the century. The resources of a single individual, however, were not always enough to finance operations on such a scale. This fact spurred investors to step into the field of theatrical production, usually with the goal of establishing a year-round resident theater company.

Private Investment Societies

During the 1740s and 1750s, the municipal playhouse in Bordeaux was a vibrant place, hosting in alternation an acting troupe and an opera company that the city shared with Toulouse. The quality of the entertainment was apparently uneven, however, and from time to time bankruptcies and con-flicts arose that left the Bordeaux playhouse unexpectedly dark. The duc de

Richelieu, who served both as the governor of the province and, in his capacity as First Gentleman of the King's Bedchamber, as an overseer of the royal theaters in Paris, determined that his capital city deserved better. In 1760, he organized a group of shareholders to finance a Bordeaux performance company that would combine dramatic and lyric genres and remain in residence throughout the year, to start after Easter in 1761. (Richelieu, whose experiences made him quite well informed about the commercial side of theater, listed comedy, opéra-comique, and concerts—but not opera—on the original contract.) Richelieu and eight others invested a total of sixty thousand livres in a joint-stock company that would make the performing arts a more prominent and integral part of public life in Bordeaux.[31] These shareholders represented different sectors of the Bordeaux elite, including, in the words of one contemporary, "the sword, the robe, and négociants."[32] In addition to Richelieu, the members featured one of the province's most distinguished aristocrats, the grand sénéchal de Guyenne; the city's vice-mayor and an ennobled member of the city council; two foreign consuls; the president of the parlement and another prominent *parlementaire*; and a high-ranking naval administrator. Richelieu correctly estimated that such an investment in local cultural and social life, the first of its kind, would be a sound one. As the site of a provincial parlement as well as a primary French port in the Atlantic trade, eighteenth-century Bordeaux sustained an increasingly wealthy population and attracted a growing number of visitors.[33] Indeed, the shareholders' success, both financial and artistic, was notable. For two decades, their joint-stock company proved to be a sustainable venture, with profitable years outnumbering those of deficit.[34] Under their management, the Bordeaux theater gained renown for its outstanding artists and high-quality productions. One of the very best stages in France, the Bordeaux theater emerged as a serious rival to Lyon and Marseille for the designation of France's second stage.[35]

The Bordeaux theater society, as noted in chapter 1, provided an influential example to those seeking to establish theater companies or improve entertainment elsewhere in France. Its success would be matched by that of a group of Marseille traders that managed the theater and opera troupe in the thriving Mediterranean port between at least the late 1760s and 1789. Little is known about this group and its operations. In 1770, however, when a Society for the Establishment of a Sedentary Theater set out to establish a resident theater company in Nantes, its members cited the success of similar efforts in Bordeaux and Marseille.[36] In the late 1780s this Marseille theater company held no outstanding debts and was turning a profit. Perhaps the strongest indication of the success of the Marseille venture was that the shareholders' ten-year theater privilege was set to expire in 1789 and they intended to renew it at the cost of ninety thousand livres.[37]

Private investment in provincial theater companies grew during the last three decades of the Old Regime. In Toulouse, the ballet master proposed establishing a joint-stock company to help him to finance a permanent troupe in the city as early as 1765.[38] During the late 1760s, local elites in Lille, Nancy, and Nantes took it upon themselves to attempt to establish regular entertainment locally.[39] In 1773, the Valenciennes theater privilege was taken over by shareholders. Around that time individuals in Le Havre did the same: a director explained that he sought the privilege for the city at the request of "a few négociants . . . who want to amuse themselves by running the risk of losing their money.[40] In Limoges, a group of ten leading citizens put together a company for opéra-comique, a strategy of direct action also taken up by local investors in Perpignan and Montpellier.[41] This model was even taken up in the colonies.

Yet, in contrast to the successful joint-stock tontines that built playhouses in cities from Le Mans to Lille, many of those financing theater troupes went bankrupt and closed down within a few years—and even, at times, within a few months. The theater society organized in Lille, for example, raised funds in 1767 to set the struggling local theater troupe on steadier footing.[42] It hired a company to perform a large repertory of theater and opera four evenings a week throughout the year, and it managed this troupe directly. Within months, however, the society was ruined. Its members requested the intervention of the governor, the prince de Soubise, to release them from their contractual obligations, although they continued to hold the theater privilege, which they subcontracted to others, for a number of years.[43] Similarly, when a group tried to bring year-round theater to Nancy in the late 1760s, it was quickly bankrupted.[44] In Nantes, the Society for the Establishment of a Sedentary Theater lost the staggering amount of 150,000 livres during the first three years of operations. The closure of France's theaters for several weeks in 1774 because of the king's illness and death seems to have finally done the organization in.[45] Ultimately, it seems, the only investment companies devoted to theatrical performance in the metropole to achieve long-term success were those in Marseille and Bordeaux.

As the many failures demonstrate, managing provincial theater troupes proved exceptionally challenging, especially in those cases where a theater society set out to pioneer regular entertainment in their city. In attempting to realize this desire, local notables often sought to accomplish what professional directors had not been willing to risk—or had already attempted and failed.

Not only did the local market for theater need to be sufficiently large and affluent, the company needed to be administered with great skill to provide quality dramatic entertainment of sufficient variety and appeal while also keeping costs as low as possible. Typically, those leading such initiatives, even if they were experienced businessmen, lacked expertise and knowledge in the field of theater management, which could generate tension with the actors, actresses, and others in their employ. Moreover, in many cases, investors' outsized ambitions for local entertainment seem to have interfered with their ability to focus on the bottom line. In Nantes, for example, where shareholders added a ballet corps to their theater company, this added expense put them on the road to bankruptcy.[46] When joint-stock theater societies closed down operations, however, professional directors almost always proved more than eager to step right in.

Directors and *Directrices*

Despite the fact that France's eighteenth-century theater directors held prominent positions in urban cultural life and managed sizable business enterprises, most have been all but lost from history. Jean Monnet was the only contemporary French theater director to publish his memoirs, and even his account reveals little about why and how he came to this profession.[47] Most directors left behind only traces in the source records, often little more than brief letters asking for permission to perform or references in municipal registers or police records. Gathering such traces nonetheless provides a starting point for evaluating the development of the profession. For eleven of France's largest cities between the 1680s and 1789, 182 different opera and theater directors can be identified by name.[48] Among those individuals whose previous employment can be determined, many came to directing with ample experience as actors, music masters, or troupe managers (*régisseurs*), and a substantial number continued to perform as actors or singers in their own troupes.[49] For most, their tenure as director of a city's theater company lasted between two and five years, although for some it was as short as a few weeks or as long as a quarter century.[50] A change of direction was frequently precipitated by financial difficulties, and bankruptcy was a common occurrence.[51] Yet directors also left this position to take charge of stages elsewhere in France, to return to performing, or even, when successful, to retire from the business altogether. By the 1760s, this evidence reveals, France's principal stages only rarely went dark for extended periods, and city residents almost never missed an entire theater season.[52] Even when directors were forced to hastily abandon an enterprise, running away in the night and leaving their debts unpaid, new entrepreneurs almost invariably came forward, in relatively short order, to try their hand.

Few individuals possessed the right mix of artistic vision, political acumen, managerial skills, and business sense required to excel at the helm of these complex cultural enterprises. Urban authorities often singled out such directors for praise, making special note of their commercial abilities. The magistrates of Amiens described M. Valville, whose troupe had performed in the city for three successive seasons, as "one of the most intelligent entrepreneurs that one could find: to a well-defined sense of business and vigilant efforts as a director, he unites the most distinguished talent in [performing] his own role."[53] Sieur Fages, who directed the Lille stage for five years in the 1780s, received recognition from the city for "his capability in such an enterprise," which was supported by "his talent and his good conduct." The local newspaper likewise applauded Fages, who "through hard work opened a path that his successors have only to follow, because he can take pride in having quite possibly created in Lille the taste for theater."[54]

Any list of the most successful provincial directors would almost certainly include Jean-Etienne Denesle, who directed the Nancy stage for six years and then codirected the Metz theater for eighteen more, and Joseph-François Gallier de Saint-Gérand, who as privilege-holder for theater throughout the province of Burgundy produced the winter season in Dijon for twenty years running.[55] The directors of greatest renown and influence, however, were both women. Marguerite Brunet, known as La Montansier, managed a theater empire stretching from the city of Versailles, where she directed the public theater troupe for twenty-one years, to numerous cities throughout northern and western France. She devoted the last decades of her career to theater in Paris. Madame Destouches-Lobreau (also known as Madame Lobreau) reigned over the Lyon theater for nearly twenty-five years.[56]

Their particularly well-documented careers shed light on the development of the profession, as well as on women's role in French society during the Old Regime.[57] Scholars such as Natalie Zemon Davis, Merry Wiesner-Hanks and others have argued that beginning in the sixteenth century, women's opportunities in the workplace declined as their legal and economic status eroded.[58] Yet theater at this time presented a new field of opportunity for enterprising women. Women assumed the role of director as early as 1699, when Jacqueline Philbert negotiated a ten-year privilege with the Royal Academy of Music to direct opera in Dijon, Lyon, and Grenoble. Over the course of the eighteenth century, French directrices worked widely, presiding over theater and opera companies in small cities and provincial capitals, as well as in the colonies. In the eleven cities noted above, the sixteen women who directed these stages constituted a minority, but a solid one: nearly 10 percent.[59] Moreover, as the experiences of Destouches-Lobreau and La Montansier demonstrate, over the course of the eighteenth century the visibility and influence of women directors increased substantially.

Madame Destouches-Lobreau was born Michelle Poncet-Destouches, one of three daughters of a Paris retail merchant, around 1720. She was not the only member of her family to go into theater: both of her sisters also directed provincial troupes. Paving the way was the eldest, Marie-Angélique Poncet, known as Destouches. This sister debuted at the Saint-Laurent fairgrounds in 1731 at about the age of sixteen and then performed in a traveling company in the provinces before returning to Paris for a position with the Opéra-Comique. At around age thirty she established her own troupe, which performed comedy and tragedy in Bordeaux and other cities in the late 1740s and 1750s. (Her younger half sister, known as Mlle Destouches cadette, would later succeed Destouches-Lobreau as one of the directors of the Lyon theater from 1782 to 1785.) Following in her older sister's footsteps, Destouches-Lobreau began her career first as a singer and then as an actress in Lyon in the later 1740s. After living briefly in Toulouse, she returned to Lyon where she began directing in the spring of 1752. She obtained the privilege for the Lyon direction in 1754, which she ran almost continuously until her retirement in 1780. In 1759, Destouches-Lobreau married a singer in her company named Jean Lobreau who was some ten years her junior.[60] During most of their twenty-seven year marriage, her husband continued to work as an actor under her direction.

Destouches-Lobreau managed an enterprise that grew to include six other tragic actresses (a role that she also performed), fifteen tragic actors, six female and eight male cast members for the opéra-bouffon, twenty-eight dancers, twenty-eight musicians, one machinist, fourteen set-builders and costumers, one wig maker, five rehearsal assistants and stagehands, five porters, five ticket-takers and ushers, a total of 124 employees in all.[61] Under her direction, the Lyon theater became one of the primary training grounds for actors and actresses for the Comédie-Française. Drawing on these connections with her former employees, Destouches-Lobreau invited royal actors and singers to Lyon for special guest performances and shrewdly marketed their celebrity to mutual advantage. In a memoir published in 1779, her lawyer recounted the story of her success: "By the felicitous choice of her actors, her assiduousness in training them, the pomp that always accompanied her spectacle, the taste & intelligence that reigned over it, the magnificence of her decorations & her costumes, she made her theater the rival of that of the Capital."[62]

Even for Destouches-Lobreau, however, the going was not always easy. In 1760, rumored to have fallen nearly one hundred thousand livres in debt, she leased out her privilege and returned to acting for several years. When she took up the direction again in 1764, her timing could not have been better, for the conclusion of the Seven Years' War ushered in a period of prosperity that drove theatrical consumption. By the mid-1770s, her theater company was making good money and the directrice was recognized as an affluent woman.[63] When Destouches-Lobreau retired from directing in 1780 at the age of sixty, she sold the privilege together with her magasin for 180,000 livres. After paying her debts, she came away with approximately one hundred thousand livres. She also received honor and recognition from the city, which bestowed upon her a gift of 120 gold medallions (*jetons*) marked with the arms of Lyon. Upon her death in 1786, the theater in Lyon went dark for an evening to mourn her passing, a mark of respect by her former actors.[64]

Marguerite Brunet, known as La Montansier, took a less direct path to the stage. Born in Bayonne in 1730 to a pinmaker who died when she was just five, Brunet came to Paris around the age of sixteen. There, she was introduced by her aunt into the demimonde of the capital and became a successful courtesan catering to the highest ranks. When one of her lovers received an appointment as a colonial intendant, Brunet accompanied him in 1750 to Martinique. After their ardor cooled, Brunet moved to Saint-Domingue, establishing herself as a *marchande de modes*. Upon her return to France in 1753, she presented herself as Mlle Montansier, and set about winning the affections of the courtly aristocrats who would later facilitate her success as a director. La Montansier turned to the theater only in her thirties, with the financial support and connections of her wealthy young lover, the marquis de Saint-Contest.[65] The evenings that the couple spent at the Comédie-Française and Comédie-Italienne likely planted the seeds for a new career for the aging courtesan. She debuted as an actress in Dunkerque and Nantes, performing the roles of queens and mothers. When audiences sent the message that her strong regional accent, among other things, would prevent her from achieving great success as an actress, she turned her efforts to directing. She put together a troupe and in 1766 set out to perform in Amiens, Caen, and Nantes. In 1768, La Montansier accomplished a coup when she acquired the privilege for theater in the city of Versailles as well as for entertainments for the court itself when it was in royal residences other than Paris or Versailles.[66] In the late 1760s and 1770s, La Montansier shrewdly snapped up privileges for stages throughout Brittany, Normandy, Picardy, and Anjou.[67] Meanwhile, she did not neglect her connections at court. In fact, unlike other provincial directors La Montansier managed her growing theater enterprise primarily from Versailles and Paris, with the help of another lover, an actor who became her lifelong business partner, Honoré Bourdon, known as Neuville.[68] La Montansier won over the affections of Louis XV's mistress Madame du Barry and, later, the young queen Marie-Antoinette. With the support of these powerful patrons, she obtained permission and land to construct a new public playhouse in the city of Versailles, in which her troupe performed.[69]

To serve such a large number of cities, La Montansier and Neuville took the unusual step of creating many troupes. As early as 1766 she employed troupe managers, beginning with the young Gallier de Saint-Gérand, to take over the many day-to-day responsibilities of theatrical production. Her theater companies in Versailles and, later, Rouen began to perform year-round, using the increasingly common mixed repertory of comedy, tragedy, and lyric genres. Most of her troupes traveled among the numerous cities under her authority, however, and specialized in either opera, opéra-comique, or dramatic repertory. She alternated these troupes in a circuit, giving audiences the opportunity to appreciate different performers and a change in repertory. This approach also gave her the flexibility to shift singers and actors in her employ from one troupe to another when necessary, and to adjust the amount of time troupes would perform in a particular city.[70]

In the late 1780s, La Montansier began shifting her attention to the capital. She began to build the Théâtre de la Montansier in the Palais-Royal, which she inaugurated in 1790, establishing a troupe there. Mlle Montansier survived the Revolution to entertain Napoleon as emperor. In 1800, at age seventy, she married Neuville, who died shortly thereafter. Near the end of her life, in a letter to King Louis XVIII, she called attention to her nearly fifty-year contribution to French theater. "I am the doyenne of the theater directors of all France," she proclaimed, before asking for a yearly performance in her benefit to support her in her old age.[71]

Within the theater business, female directors such as these two women do not seem to have met with opposition on the basis of their sex.[72] Abraham-Joseph Bénard, a comic actor at the Comédie-Française who went by the stage name Fleury, worked under both of these women early in his career. He remembered them both admiringly in his memoirs, describing La Montansier as "a charming woman . . . southern (*méridionale*) in all ways: southern in accent, in gestures, and in sentiments."[73] Her effusive personality, he suggested, contributed to her success: "This famous *directrice* was very good for her employees: fair, as much as her temper allowed her to be; but . . . not the least in the world a friend of order." Her direction of the Versailles stage occupied her days, but her passion for gambling consumed her nights.[74] In contrast, Fleury described Madame Destouches-Lobreau as "the perfect opposite of Mademoiselle Montansier." She was "just, clever, precise, a kind-hearted woman, a strict woman, a man in a petticoat concerning business management . . . a veritable monarch, but this was nothing to complain about, she held the scepter with a hand as steady as it was skillful: under her reign, the theater of Lyon could rival in magnificence and splendor the most brilliant of the capital."[75] This actor's choice of masculine descriptors for Destouches-Lobreau conveys his sense that she contravened traditional gender roles, yet without being viewed as transgressive.

Both of these directors displayed particular talent for navigating the patronage networks that exercised such influence in cultural politics during the Old Regime. If La Montansier, an intimate at Versailles, stands out in this domain, Destouches-Lobreau, too, proved adept in cultivating strategic relationships. She found enduring patrons in the ducs de Villeroy, particularly Gabriel-Louis-François de Neufville, who took great personal interest in a stage that he affectionately referred to as "my theater [*mon spectacle*]."[76] Particularly as governors began to claim the right to grant theater privileges, their patronage controlled access in many theater markets. When the municipal authorities in Lyon attempted to break her privilege in 1776 and give it instead to a group of entrepreneurs that offered to pay the city thirty thousand livres a year for rights to the stage, Madame Destouches-Lobreau called on her relationship with the governor—as well as her extensive knowledge of the theater business—as she fought to maintain her direction. During the legal standoff that ensued, she refused to grant the new directors use of her magasin, which was her personal property. Her performers, who were under contract to Destouches-Lobreau directly, refused to perform for the interlopers. Then, even though the king had already approved her competitors' new thirty-year privilege, she traveled to Versailles to present her case. At court, Villeroy interceded on her behalf and the king restored her privilege.[77] In what can be seen as a rebuke to the city, the governor later extended Destouches-Lobreau's privilege until 1793, in recognition "of the intelligence that she has continually shown in running the *comédie*, and of the satisfaction that said city has always had from this directrice as well as from her troupe."[78] As she approached her retirement, in 1779 she used her remaining influence to obtain an additional favor from the court. Destouches-Lobreau wrote to the duc de Richelieu to explain that her nephew was recently widowed and disconsolate, and that she wanted to bring him with her to live in Paris: "I would like to put him under your protection; it is, my adorable Maréchal, the reward that your protégé asks of you." She then invoked her long service to France's theaters: "I have given so many actors to the Comédie-Française that in gratitude you can well audition an actor who interests me."[79]

Richelieu instructed Denis-Pierre-Jean Papillon de la Ferté, the intendant of the Menus-Plaisirs (the division of the King's Household that administered the royal theaters), "to examine what we could do to oblige the poor Madame Lobreau, who merits our consideration." The matter was of such importance that Richelieu asked the intendant "not to forget to speak with him about it the first time that they see each other."[80] Her nephew François-Nicolas Dunant received a coveted *ordre de début*, a formal audition with the Comédie-Française.[81]

With their shrewd managerial abilities, these two women helped to define the position of director in France. They firmly asserted their authority over the actors they employed. When their *pensionnaires* violated their contracts, neither hesitated to hold actors and actresses accountable to the full extent of the law. Early in her career, in 1754, Destouches-Lobreau arranged for the arrest of Isabelle Jansolin, a dancer who had fled Lyon disguised as a man on her way to the London stage, six months before her contract was set to expire. "The directrice also pointed out to me," the royal commander of Lyon informed the lieutenant general of police in Paris, "that . . . it is only by examples that one can contain this type of people." After Jansolin's arrest, Destouches-Lobreau asked to have the actress transferred to a prison in Lyon in order to send a message to the other actors in her company.[82] La Montansier likewise confidently wielded authority over her actors. When Armand de Verteuil had skipped out on a three-year contract in one of her traveling companies for a more attractive appointment in Marseille without paying her the specified three thousand livre penalty, Montansier obtained a *lettre de cachet* to incarcerate him until his debts and obligations to her were paid. In the interim, the actor's wardrobe was confiscated. De Verteuil came to fully appreciate her resolve during "a month in captivity in the most dreadful prison . . . breathing the vapor of a pestilential air."[83] With her strong personality and unbending will, La Montansier was involved in numerous disputes with her actors and actresses. Yet, as with Destouches-Lobreau, her troupes were among the best, they usually made money, and her actors knew with certainty that they would be paid. These two directrices put their actors and singers through their paces as they set about enticing more customers to spend more of their money at the theater.

Variety, Novelty, and Theater Repertories

Eighteenth-century directors such as Destouches-Lobreau and La Montansier sold their customers an evening of theatrical entertainment, which almost invariably included a double feature of two different and complementary works. To entice as many individuals as possible to buy tickets, and, just as important, to return again and again, provincial directors offered audiences a broad array of choices. Indeed, for contemporary directors, variety and novelty provided two critical tools in achieving commercial success. Whereas the repertories of the Paris stages have drawn considerable attention from literary scholars, musicologists, and historians, our knowledge of provincial theater offerings during this era has long been hampered by source constraints.[84] Consistent repertory records for eighteenth-century troupes only rarely survived. Manuscript registers maintained by the theater companies of Lyon, Toulouse, and Bordeaux for periods during the 1780s therefore provide an extraordinary opportunity to compare and contrast a complete annual theater season for three different provincial stages.[85] In this way, it becomes possible to compose a sketch, albeit an incomplete one, of provincial directors' performance practices (and, accordingly, of their audiences' theatrical tastes) during the late Old Regime.

In all three cities, the directors followed remarkably similar strategies to sell this cultural commodity. To today's theater amateur, the pace of production as well as the sheer variety of the repertory presented by these companies is almost inconceivable. In the mid-1780s, during any given month the theaters of Lyon, Toulouse, and Bordeaux each staged upward of fifty *different* dramatic and lyric works. Over the course of the annual theater season that began and ended at Easter, each company offered more than 650 performances of two hundred or more different titles, not counting numerous ballets.[86] (In contrast, in 1787 the Comédie-Française, which also performed nightly double features, staged "only" 155 different works.[87]) This hectic pace of performance was driven by commercial interests. Traditionally, traveling theater companies presented much more limited repertories, performing a set of works to a series of new audiences in different cities on their route. As theater companies began to perform for longer seasons and eventually even year-round in a number of cities, the pressure for variety increased. Directors of these sedentary troupes faced the challenge of capturing the interest of a not unlimited audience pool—and keeping it indefinitely. Producing a diverse array of works in a variety of genres allowed theater companies to appeal to a wide spectrum of tastes among urban spectators. Essentially, directors wanted to offer something for everyone. At the same time, this diversity provided an incentive for regular customers to return frequently and perhaps even to purchase an *abonnement*, an unlimited subscription granting entry to all regular performances during a period of a month, six months, or the full annual season.

In addition to variety, novelty provided the second essential characteristic of theater repertories during this era. All three cities featured a steady
stream of new hits from the Paris stages, which served as the source for
the vast majority of the works in their repertories. The reason was simple.
Audiences flocked to the debuts of works that had never before been staged
locally. According to one authority in Lyon, "if the general repertory of the
year is well composed [and] if one adds to it at the right moment the novelties that are always desired by the public," the theater could always make
more money.[88] Box office receipts confirm the truth of this statement. In
Lyon, much anticipated debuts of new works from the Comédie-Italienne or
the Comédie-Française, particularly when performed on Sundays, regularly
brought in double or more the median daily box office receipts of about
426 livres.[89] In Bordeaux, 60 percent of these new productions were restaged
within less than a year of their Paris creation. Comedies and opéras-comique
could be picked up within a matter of months. Operas and tragedies typically took several years or longer.[90] According to the theater historian Henri
Lagrave, Bordeaux's repertory was "more recent than in Paris; they constantly
tried to rejuvenate it."[91]

Provincial directors holding the privilege, as we have seen, were free to
perform almost anything that might fill the house. Outside of the capital, genre hierarchies carried less weight: the practicality and profitability
of comedy, opéra-comique, and even popular works from the unprivileged
stages of the Paris fairgrounds and the Boulevard du Temple outweighed
the prestige value of opera and classical tragedy. The single most frequently
performed work of the 1786–87 season in both Toulouse and Bordeaux was
Richard Coeur-de-lion. This opéra-comique by André Grétry, now regarded as
a classic of the genre, had debuted to great acclaim at the Comédie-Italienne
in the fall of 1784.[92] Even this theatrical bestseller, however, was performed
only sixteen and seventeen times respectively during the entire annual season.
In Lyon, during the following season this popular work received fourteen
performances, putting it in second place. It was topped at fifteen by Louis-
Emanuel Jadin's *La Guerre ouverte, ou Ruse contre ruse*, which had opened just
six months earlier at the Variétés-Amusantes in Paris. In Toulouse and Lyon,
only ten works in all were performed ten or more times during this season.
In both cases, all but one of these was lyric, and eight of the ten had debuted
at the Comédie-Italienne. The only comedy to meet this threshold was a
recent provincial debut, *La Bonne Mère* by Jean-Pierre Claris de Florian,
which was picked up by the Comédie-Italienne in 1790. In Bordeaux, even
fewer works received a run of ten performances: just five during the 1786–87

season, and seven the following year. Tastes in that city were also, it seems, more varied. During those two years, alongside opéras-comiques such as Nicolas Dezède's *Blaise et Babet*, the Bordeaux directors offered longer runs of formal operas such as Étienne-Joseph Floquet's *Le Seigneur bienfaisant* and Grétry's opera-ballet *La Caravane du Caire*, as well as an original ballet choreographed by the dance celebrity Jean Dauberval.[93]

In these repertories, newly imported plays and operas stand out as box office winners that enjoyed particularly long runs. The majority of the two hundred or so different works that were performed each year on these stages, however, consisted of works that had emerged over time as classics, alongside crowd pleasers of more recent decades that aged well enough when kept alive in the era's equivalent of "reruns." During the seasons studied, Molière—France's most celebrated playwright and the father of Comédie-Française—was the third most frequently performed author in Toulouse, and the fourth most-performed in Lyon. In Bordeaux, according to Lagrave, during the 1770s and 1780s Molière's works were staged more often than those of any other playwright or composer.[94] This owed much, to be sure, to Molière's brilliance and the lasting appeal of his works. His esteemed reputation during this era, when he was celebrated as one of France's greatest cultural heroes, certainly added to the allure of his comedies and tragedies.[95] Yet there were other, more pragmatic reasons that also substantially shaped theater repertories. Actors could only be expected to learn so many new roles a year while they were also maintaining the extensive and varied repertories that were tied to commercial success. (The Comédie-Française also maintained a very extensive repertory of past successes that constituted more than 90 percent of the works staged in any given year.[96]) Provincial performers took their repertories with them when they changed troupes, which many did on a regular basis. A major challenge facing directors everywhere was to identify substantial numbers of works that their casts knew in common and could put up quickly, with minimal rehearsal time. Of the nearly six thousand plays and librettos published in the French language between 1610 and 1789, only a few hundred, it seems, made their way into this theatrical canon.[97] As this shared repertory base was identified by actors, singers, and directors, it was performed for theater publics in cities throughout the kingdom. In this way, French theater companies resembled contemporary English music societies, whose concert programs by the 1770s featured new works as well as a nascent canon of "ancient" music, by which they meant pieces that were more than two decades old.[98]

In all three cities, opéra-comique and comedy dominated the repertories. Together, they accounted for as much as two-thirds of all performances. In

Lyon and Bordeaux, comedy took top billing, whereas in Toulouse this honor went to opéra-comique. Ballet constituted the third most popular element of these repertories, with 162 dance performances that year in Toulouse and 131 in Bordeaux. Lyon's theater featured considerably fewer, with just thirty-seven stagings marked specifically as ballets, although other performances may also have featured dance. The *drame*, a new dramatic genre featuring emotional scenes depicting domestic dramas of the middling classes, played only a small role in these repertories, despite contemporaries' sense that it enjoyed a greater popularity in provincial cities than in the capital.[99] Nor did directors offer tragedies with great frequency. *Drames* and tragedies together accounted for about 10 percent of total performances in Toulouse, a number that was likely higher than usual due to a month of guest appearances by Mademoiselle Sainval aînée, one of the leading tragic actresses of the era and a former *sociétaire* of the Comédie-Française. In Bordeaux, these genres constituted slightly less than 10 percent of the repertory, and in Lyon just 5 percent. In spite of these variations, the commonalities in these directors' approaches to repertory—and in what seems to have appealed to these theater publics—remain striking.[100]

Although repertory records from Lyon and Toulouse provide just a one-year snapshot of stage offerings, Bordeaux's Lecouvreur manuscript records the company's repertory almost every year between 1772 and 1789. This provides an opportunity to examine performance trends over time. Several changes stand out. First, formal opera, at first deliberately excluded from the company's repertory, was reintroduced in the 1780s. The Bordeaux theater company did not perform any full-length *tragédies en musique* during the early 1770s. Following the move into the new Grand Théâtre in 1780, however, a new set of directors began to stage formal operas thirty or more times during the season. During the 1788–89 season the troupe offered sixty-five such performances. Second, the popularity of dance soared during this era. Dance comprised fifty to seventy performances a year in Bordeaux during the 1770s, but more than a hundred performances annually in the 1780s. Choreographed by Dauberval, a former first dancer with the Paris Opera, and with him and his wife performing the leading roles, dance became an ever more important component of the repertory. The number of ballets offered during the 1788–89 season rose to 178.[101]

Studying these repertories raises the issue of the relationship between theatrical production in the provinces and in Paris. Demonstrating continued royal commitment to securing Paris as the center of France's theater industry, the king declared in 1773 that it was unacceptable that plays destined for the capital be debuted elsewhere.[102] Beyond such political pressure, playwrights generally preferred the royal stages as the most professionally advantageous, as well as the most lucrative, places to debut. Writers, it is true, often grumbled about the rates of compensation that they received for works performed by the Comédie-Française, but outside of Paris playwrights and composers traditionally received no remuneration at all. Once a play or opera had been performed in Paris or was published, it was considered to be in the public domain.[103] For provincial directors, a further benefit of such works was that they had already passed the royal censor and thus did not require separate approval from municipal and military authorities. Finally, directors had the luxury of selecting only the best works from Paris—those that had proven to be hits and for which good reviews in the widely circulating *Mercure de France*, as well as in other newspapers and journals, would have already generated considerable publicity in their city.[104]

Despite efforts to fix dramatic innovation in Paris, provincial audiences did on occasion applaud works before they reached audiences in the capital.[105] Plays that were rejected by the royal theaters or that had a specific local interest might debut outside of the capital. In addition, some authors chose to introduce their works on other stages. Voltaire, for example, debuted *Le Fanatisme ou Mahomet le prophète* in Lille in 1741, and it appeared in Paris a year later. In the early 1760s Denis Diderot's *Le Père de famille* was performed in Marseille, Toulouse, Bordeaux, and Lyon before it was staged at the Comédie-Française.[106] Even after Charles Collé's *La Partie de chasse de Henri IV* was banned in Paris for what were seen as implicit unfavorable comparisons between the protagonist and King Louis XV, the work enjoyed success in cities from Bordeaux and Lyon to Abbeville and Amiens.[107] After heated public disputes with the Comédie-Française, the playwright Louis-Sébastien Mercier turned to Bordeaux, Dijon, Rouen, and even Saint-Quentin to perform his works. In cities such as these, *L'Indigent, Jenneval ou le Barnevelt français, La Brouette du vinaigrier*, and *Le Déserteur* debuted years before they were staged at the Comédie-Italienne.[108] "There is at least as much taste in the provinces as in Paris," Mercier argued, urging fellow playwrights to offer their works to audiences that were "more upright, less spoiled and more reasonable" than those in Paris.[109]

A final aspect of these theater repertories that merits consideration is the language in which these performances took place. On these privileged provincial stages, directors staged dramatic and lyric works in the French language, rather than in Italian, German, English, or, for that matter, the many other languages and dialects spoken widely throughout France at the time.[110] For this reason, the theater, René Merle has argued, operated as both "witness and agent of Frenchification (*francisation*)."[111] As seen in chapter 3, in a city such as Strasbourg where a thriving German theater tradition was deliberately marginalized, this was an explicit political and cultural objective. In most cases, however, directors' use of French-language repertory seems to have reflected longstanding theater traditions, audience preferences, and the realities of contemporary theater production. Given the celebrated and abundant supply of works in French, the fact that actors who were recruited from all across France were unlikely to be proficient in regional languages and patois, and these performers' lack of incentive to learn works that would have only limited geographic appeal, theater directors found little benefit in introducing other languages onto the eighteenth-century French stage. This was true even in a city such as Marseille, with its distinguished literary and even theatrical traditions in Provençal. On those infrequent occasions when the directors of the Marseille theater company did stage works using Provençal, typically short *divertissements* composed to celebrate a military victory or royal birth, such works only served to further normalize and distinguish the use of the French language. This was the case because by the late eighteenth century such pieces were almost universally bilingual: elite characters such as masters and négociants were scripted speaking in French, while peasants, sailors, and other lower class characters spoke in Provençal, often for comic effect.[112]

This comparison of theater repertories highlights the remarkable unity of the French theater industry in the late 1780s. Although it is based on an analysis of performance trends in three of France's largest cities, each home to a resident company, directors elsewhere, too, seem to have encountered similar preferences among the public. In Valenciennes, the *Journal du Hainaut* noted, "daily experience proves to us that the genre of performance that is generally preferred today is opéra-comique."[113] In Rouen, a letter to the editor of the local newspaper observed that, for local audiences, "rarity in all things interests, and choice captivates."[114] As theater companies set down roots in France's cities, directors embraced similar principles as they strove, like Monnet, "to satisfy the general taste" of the public—and, above all, to sell more tickets.[115]

Municipal Subsidies

Directors' ability to woo the theater public was critical because box office revenues and subscriptions were their primary—and in many cases their only—sources of income. Although municipal subsides for performances of theater and opera were not unknown during the Old Regime, the practice remained the exception rather than the rule. In fact, as we have seen, rather than supporting theater companies financially, some municipal authorities required directors to pay sizable amounts to obtain the local theater privilege or to rent the stage. Moreover, cities commonly required theater troupes to make significant contributions to support the urban poor.[116] This is not to say that cities did nothing to assist theater directors. In cases where the municipality owned the playhouse, some cities offered theater companies its use free of charge. In return, city councilors might demand free entry to performances for themselves as well as for other local dignitaries whom they wished to honor as well as their clients. A city might also offer a gift, a gratuity, or a pension to the director or to favored artists. In at least two cities, Metz and Strasbourg, urban authorities attempted to administer resident theater companies directly in experiments that proved costly and short-lived.[117] In those cities that did offer regular subsidies to theater troupes, the amounts—typically ranging from a few hundred to a few thousand livres—proved fairly modest in relation to these troupes' overall operating budgets.

The ambivalence that cities felt about using municipal funds to support theatrical production is illustrated in the case of Lyon, which was long among the most generous in supporting the performing arts. Until 1730 the city provided no regular subsidies for theater, with local authorities offering instead what they described as "passing help" to the local opera company.[118] After the city council took ownership of the jeu de paume playhouse in 1728, these unspecified gifts were supplemented by free use of the municipal theater. In 1730, however, the imminent bankruptcy of the opera company that had entertained local citizens for the past fourteen seasons, coupled with the announcement by several top singers that they were intending to leave Lyon, prompted the municipality to become more actively involved. Lyon "resolved and proclaimed to make an annual contribution in the sum of six thousand livres for the support of performance in this city," to begin in 1731. (This amount that was later reduced to five thousand livres a year.) In addition, they established pensions for the three most celebrated singers to entice them to stay.[119] After the inauguration of the city's large new playhouse in 1756, the officers of Lyon continued to allow the troupe to use the playhouse for free, while also granting the director additional income from the rental of the apartments, shops, and storage areas in the theater, which generated an estimated nine thousand additional livres yearly. In the 1760s, these two sources of financial support combined represented the equivalent of approximately 10 percent of the operating budget for the city's theater company.[120] This amount, though modest compared with the large subsidies offered by urban governments in the nineteenth century, provided a steady support that helped the Lyon theater company to flourish.[121]

Nevertheless, after more than forty years of steadily funding theatrical production the city of Lyon changed course in the 1770s. As we have seen, during an era when the city's budget was stretched thin, the municipal authorities began investigating whether the local theater company might in fact generate income for the city.[122] According to a report they submitted to the controller general of France, the playhouse had cost the city hundreds of thousands of livres to build, so "it was just that [Lyon] receive a revenue from this building."[123] The municipality determined that it might generate an additional twenty thousand livres a year in revenue by charging rent for the salle de spectacle. In 1777, when Destouches-Lobreau's privilege was reinstated, she and the city came to a new arrangement whereby she forfeited the subsidy that she had previously received, along with free use of the theater and its dependencies. Instead, she agreed to pay Lyon ten thousand livres a year for the use of the stage for the next two years, and twenty thousand a year thereafter.[124]

Financially speaking, the city came out ahead. Still, Lyon's new profit-seeking approach to the theater did not have quite the outcome that was hoped for. The new demands placed on the theater company, coinciding with the retirement of the talented Destouches-Lobreau, undermined the stability of the performing arts in the city. The 1780s witnessed a string of bankruptcies by Lyon directors. These financially strapped entrepreneurs lamented the imposition of what one described as "a crushing rent" that had led to "the decadence of the spectacle" and caused "enormous losses."[125] The author of this petition complained that the annual budget shortfall that he and previous directors had faced came to almost exactly the twenty thousand livres that directors were now required to pay the city, and he offered financial records to corroborate this claim.[126]

Based on surviving evidence, those cities that did offer various forms of support for the stage sought to delimit their commitment to public theater. In Strasbourg, the city's brief and financially disastrous attempt to directly administer the French theater company during the 1750s left the municipal authorities chastened. To extricate themselves from this unhappy situation, the city officers agreed not to charge rent for the French theater company's use of the municipal playhouse. The magistrates, under pressure from royal military authorities, also agreed to grant the director of the French company use of Strasbourg's secondary stage, which he rented out to German and Italian troupes as well as popular performers, keeping the proceeds. As part of this agreement, city officers received free tickets to performances in both venues. In this way, Strasbourg provided the city's privileged French troupe with an in-kind gift worth five hundred livres a year (the amount that the city paid to lease the secondary stage) for over three decades. In later decades, when the municipal officers encountered pressure to provide additional financial support to the city's French theater troupe, they balked. They argued that the city council had made such an arrangement precisely "to liberate itself from all contribution to [the troupe's] upkeep." In other words, the city opted for this fixed, in-kind donation to *avoid* committing to a regular—and likely escalating—cash subsidy.[127] Around midcentury, the city of Metz, also under political pressure, began to contribute the much larger sum of six thousand livres a year to support year-round theater, an amount later reduced to four thousand livres. Yet contemporaries suggested that the cities of Lille and Besançon, also home to large garrisons, offered their theater companies no support at this time. Several decades later, in the 1780s, the directors of the theater companies performing in Bordeaux, Marseille, and Lille attested that they, like the director in Lyon, received no municipal subsidies at all.[128]

Selling the Stage

To become a commercial success, a director needed customers—as many as he or she could entice into the playhouse. Theater companies brought in revenue in two ways. First, all directors sold individual tickets, good for a day's performances. These daily ticket sales, as we will see, provided the bulk of a theater's income. Second, as in Paris, provincial directors who were presenting a lengthy season usually offered subscriptions or *abonnements*. These tickets enabled subscribers to attend performances as often as they pleased for a discounted rate, typically for the full annual season. Advertising their productions as well as the advantages and appeal of theatergoing itself to the public, directors made use of posters, newspapers, handbills, and even appeals from the stage to encourage theatrical consumption.

Records for the Lyon theater provide the most detailed information concerning revenues. Only the wealthy could afford to pay the 120 livres for a subscription that entitled a male spectator unlimited entry to the playhouse, including the expensive first boxes, for a year in the 1760s and 1770s. (Women paid less.) At this rate, a subscription was financially advantageous to the purchaser only if he attended the theater in the first boxes at least forty times a year, or nearly once a week. Yet Madame Destouches-Lobreau and later directors signed on a growing number of annual subscribers, raising this customer base from 196 subscribers in 1761 to 788 in 1785. Without any increase in subscription prices, revenue from subscribers quadrupled to over one hundred thousand livres, contributing one-third of the total income for the theater company.[129] Lyon directors marketed subscriptions aggressively, even introducing a trial offer. At the start of the season a spectator could purchase a monthly subscription. Then, at the end of the month, this individual had the option to apply the cost of their monthly subscription to an annual subscription. They also introduced a discounted subscription for children.[130] Elsewhere, in cities with a smaller wealthy elite than Lyon or those that drew more travelers, subscribers constituted a smaller component of the audience—and a smaller share of the revenue. In Bordeaux, the income from *abonnements* amounted to about one-quarter of the total annual revenue. In Nantes, subscriptions made up less than one-tenth of the theater troupe's income.[131] In these cities and most others, daily ticket sales constituted the bread and butter of the industry.

To draw in the largest crowds, directors typically scheduled newer works with widespread appeal for Sunday evenings. On Sundays, merchants, shopkeepers, and artisans and their wives enjoyed greater free time to come to the theater. For this reason, Sunday tended to attract the highest turnout. In Lyon, Sunday daily ticket sales almost always brought in over one thousand livres. Occasionally, they reached as high as twenty-five hundred livres. In contrast, during a typical weeknight even the Lyon theater company often found itself performing to a small crowd that might bring in just two hundred to three hundred livres, and at times even less.[132] Financial records from the theater company in Nantes, which had less than half Lyon's population, demonstrate similar trends for this smaller-budget operation. In 1784, while still performing in the cramped 760-capacity playhouse on the rue Bignon-Lestard, the troupe brought in just over one thousand livres on its strongest Sundays, compared with less than one hundred livres on a slow weeknight.[133]

To advertise these shows, directors relied primarily on *affiches*, small posters listing the works that would be performed that day. Each morning, the troupe's *afficheur* posted these throughout the city at busy intersections, public plazas, government buildings, and private townhouses.[134] Directors might also print handbills that they could distribute to the homes of their subscribers and regular customers. The establishment of local and regional newspapers, particularly during the 1760s and 1770s, provided an additional means to draw attention to the local stage. Editors published theater reviews, poems, letters from spectators and directors, and occasional announcements about special performances. By the late 1780s, newspapers in cities such as Bordeaux, Marseille, and Lille also advertised performances in advance, although not regularly.[135] Finally, the stage itself served as a platform for advertising. In compliments delivered on the opening and closing nights of each season, the troupe sought to build loyalty among the spectators already present by

A rare surviving advertising poster, or *affiche,* for a 9 March 1775 performance in Valenciennes. Courtesy of the Bibliothèque municipale de Valenciennes.

urging them to make theatergoing a regular practice. In addition, at the end of each evening's performance actors announced from the stage which works they would perform the following evening, encouraging regular customers to return and generating interest through word of mouth.

Although most theater advertising reached out to an anonymous general public, directors specifically courted female spectators. In cities such as Lille, Valenciennes, and Angers, posters and printed invitations featured poems and addresses "to the ladies" that invited women to "come give their luster to an enchanted performance."[136] Inaugural performances for new playhouses entreated women that "your true temple is the theater / Come preside here often."[137] Most directors offered women monthly and yearly subscriptions that were significantly less expensive than those for men, often only about two-thirds the price.[138] Women took advantage of these offers, though even so they attended in smaller numbers than men.[139] Whether this discrepancy resulted from women's more limited access to the leisure time and spending money necessary for regular theater attendance, or from the perceived moral dangers stemming from theater's tarnished reputation, we may never know.[140] Directors were well aware that the libertine representations of actresses in contemporary culture—representations grounded to a certain extent in reality—shaped attitudes toward professional theater. Actresses, after all, figured among the most prominent kept women during this era.[141] Courtesans and prostitutes regularly flaunted their wares in eighteenth-century playhouses. Concerns that attending the theater might call into question the reputation of a "respectable" woman could drive away female clientele.

To combat such moral concerns, directors deliberately promoted the image of the theater as a virtuous pastime. In speeches, inaugural plays, and letters to the public, directors and their troupes drew on Enlightenment traditions that promoted theater as a didactic tool and a force for moral instruction, often paraphrasing the protheater sentiments of Denis Diderot and Jean Le Rond d'Alembert.[142] The theatrical performances they offered to the public, they assured audiences, were neither the coarse, licentious entertainment of the fairgrounds, nor a dangerously decadent luxury reserved for the aristocratic elites. Rather, directors positioned theater as a respectable leisure activity and even a means of self-improvement. Directors and their actors repeatedly praised the theater for its utility, namely its unique ability to combine "instruction" with "pleasure."[143] Audiences were told that "of all the arts that you encourage, the art of theater is, I dare to believe, Messieurs, that which best combines the pleasant and the useful. Acts of virtue which painting can only show from one point of view appear in full extension in the moving canvases of the great Corneille and his successors."[144] Attending the theater, spectators were told, could be beneficial to themselves as individuals and to urban society as a whole. As the directrice Mlle Destouches cadette declared in a letter to Lyon subscribers: "One no longer calls into question if theater is useful, and even necessary in a big city. The stage, in purifying itself, has become a school for taste, for the purity of language and of mores, and the theater is today the meeting place of good society."[145]

Finally, directors adopted one of the same strategies that urban magistrates used to promote the construction of new playhouses: they appealed to the civic pride of theater patrons. In a speech delivered from the stage in Rouen in 1786 and later published in the local newspaper, La Montansier's troupe praised the judgment of the local theatergoing public: "All of France and even its capital know that true taste has one of its premier tribunals in this city, where so many great men are born."[146] On another occasion, the troupe credited Rouen's audiences with playing a central role in forming France's great stage artists. "How many actors—actors famous because you have encouraged them—have embellished the capital with their talents?" an actor asked. "Yes, messieurs, it is nearly to you alone that the capital owes its leading actors, it is by your lessons that they are formed, and it is also thanks to you that every day they enjoy their success."[147] The director in Lyon flattered her subscribers that they possessed one of the premier stages not only in France but in all of Europe. With their support, she explained, it would continue as "the cradle of most of the talents who have enriched the theaters of Paris and those of foreign courts."[148] For the price of a theater ticket or a subscription, directors in these cities and others implied, spectators participated in a theater network that connected them directly with the royal stages of Paris and helped to sustain France's cultural dominance in the theater arts.[149]

Success

Directors' marketing efforts paid off as exceptional numbers of spectators passed through the doors of France's new playhouses. The success of their strategies can be measured in several ways. First, cities began to host longer theater seasons. As long as traveling companies predominated, directors could only entertain a city for as long as the public would make it worthwhile.[150] Early in her career, La Montansier explained the financial limitations under which she operated her traveling troupes. When officials in Amiens requested that she bring her actors to entertain the city for the winter season of 1767, she politely declined: "Charged with an enterprise of at least ninety thousand livres, independently of my earnings for the summer, I need for the winter a city that gives me in five months fifty thousand [livres] to find myself either meeting or a little above my expenses. There is no city that I would prefer to Amiens for the pleasure of being there, but there are those where the profits . . . are regularly more advantageous."[151] Around midcentury, directors (and investors) began to seize on favorable conditions to establish resident theater companies that performed throughout the year, primarily in cities such as provincial capitals, trading centers, and important garrisons. By the early 1760s, Favart scarcely exaggerated when he observed that "each provincial city wants to have a troupe."[152] His point was seconded by a provincial actor who wrote in 1767 of "the indispensible necessity of a resident theater (*un spectacle continuel*) in the principal cities of the provinces."[153] Several cities serve to illustrate the institutionalization of theater during this era. In Nancy, during the late 1750s and early 1760s the theater season ran from November through Easter; in 1767 the troupe began to perform throughout the year. In the 1760s, troupes performed in Rouen for six months of the year. By the late 1780s one of La Montansier's troupes performed there some fifty weeks a year.[154] During the 1780s Montpellier and even Lorient came to boast resident theater troupes. In total, in 1789 no fewer than fourteen provincial cities hosted year-round theatrical entertainment, while dozens of others enjoyed regular seasons of performance each year.[155] The vitality of provincial theater in France becomes clear by comparison with the perform-ing arts culture in England, where as late as the 1770s not a single city out-side of London enjoyed such year-round entertainment. Although English provincial troupes based themselves in cities such as Manchester, Norwich, and Bath, they spent months each year performing on circuits in the smaller towns in the region.[156]

The performance schedules of theater troupes provide a second measure of public theater's growing presence in provincial urban life. Even in cit-ies with established resident companies the pace of performance intensified significantly during the late eighteenth century. With large casts of actors, singers, and dancers hired on salary, directors found it cost effective to per-form more frequently. In Lyon, during the 1761 season the theater company performed an average of four evenings a week. In contrast, by the 1780s the company performed every night of the week. With just thirteen closures for holidays, concerts, and other reasons, the total number of performances that year came to 321 for the regular theater season.[157] Nor was France's second largest city alone in enjoying such an active theater scene. In fact, Bordeaux's troupe began performing seven evenings a week from its debut in 1761, and the Marseille company began to do so in 1779. By the mid-1780s, the Toulouse and Nantes companies adopted a similar performance schedule.[158] For the 1788 season, the director in Montpellier proposed to offer spectators seven evenings a week of entertainment for eight months of the year, and three evenings a week for the remainder of the season.[159] With annual theater seasons that lasted a week longer than in Paris, provincial stages such as these gave substantially more performances than the Paris Opera, and some sur-passed even the number of performances given by the Comédie-Française.[160]

Given more opportunities to attend, provincial audiences turned out in growing numbers. Financial records maintained by two theater companies allow us to document this growth. In Bordeaux, without any increase in ticket prices revenue for the theater company grew from an average of about 180,000 livres a year during the 1760s to almost 270,000 livres a year during the 1770s, an increase of nearly 50 percent in just a decade. By the mid-1780s, following the move into the larger Grand Théâtre and an increase in ticket prices, Bordeaux's theater company more than doubled this income, taking in more than six hundred thousand livres a year.[161] Lyon's records reveal an increase in spectatorship that was almost as dramatic. Whereas the total box office receipts for the 1761–62 season can be estimated at about 122,000 livres, by the mid-1780s annual gross revenues rose to well over three

hundred thousand livres. Income from daily admissions to the Lyon theater—
the tickets purchased by customers who were, on average, less wealthy and
privileged than subscribers—roughly tripled during the final three decades
of the Old Regime.[162]

Performing under Pressure

Over the course of the eighteenth century, entrepreneurs de spectacle developed new approaches to theatrical production that enabled them to tap
more successfully into the growing consumer public. In public theaters from
Nancy to Nantes and from Metz to Montpellier, large and versatile troupes
led by professional directors presented expansive repertories, while forging
closer cultural ties between Parisian and provincial audiences. Yet despite
their success in establishing professional theater in everyday urban life, directors found that even during theater's heyday theatrical production was no
easy business. Like Monnet, directors found that the multivalent approach
came with its own challenges. "One cannot deny that multiplying the genres
of spectacles has multiplied the number of salaried actors for all the troupes,"
one directrice observed. With actors demanding ever-higher salaries, production costs rose sharply. "The disadvantages," she concluded, "are the
same for all the provincial cities where there is a theater."[163] Under pressure
financially and catering to increasingly discriminating audiences, directors
had their work cut out for them.

The experiences of Madame Destouches-Lobreau illuminate the challenges that directors faced as they strove to achieve critical and financial
success, as well as the steps they took to meet these challenges. When she
reassumed the direction of the Lyon stage in 1764 after an interlude of several
years working as an actress, the troupe she inherited was in complete disarray.
On opening night, a "very sad and very unhappy debut," the company, in
her own words, was "found to be dreadful."[164] The evening culminated in
the better part of the audience loudly booing a leading actress who had previously found favor in the city. Destouches-Lobreau agreed with the audience's verdict on the troupe, saying that "it is not possible that the public can
be happy if it is not better composed."[165] In a rare series of letters written
to the *prévôt des marchands*, the chief magistrate of Lyon, during that critical
spring and summer, the directrice described the efforts she made to build up
the troupe's talent and to please her customers. She remained hopeful that
the public would not unjustly blame her for the troupe's failings. "In the
public I hear a general cry," she wrote, "*Md. Lobreau is going to make this troupe*

good, she will not tolerate that it be so bad. I will make sure to respond to the good opinion that the public would want to have of my capacity."[166] Confident in her abilities, she was also fully aware that both her reputation and her finances were at stake. With the troupe in this state, she acknowledged, the theater company could not hope to bring in the same income that it had in earlier years.

Destouches-Lobreau's first step was to recruit new talent, including a leading actress and a female singer from abroad. She had to spend money to make money, a strategy she understood well. As she explained in a letter, "when one works alone, one can make sacrifices to please the public."[167] She claimed that to raise these funds she sold all that she possessed.[168] She hired more musicians and placed them on a strict rehearsal schedule until she judged that they had become quite good. She also started building up a dance corps. Her ability to improve the troupe was limited by the fact that she was unable to fire any actors, who were on contract to her predecessor Rosimon for the remainder of the theater year. So, "to compensate the public," as she put it, she contacted leading Paris actors and singers, inviting them to give guest performances in Lyon during their holidays.[169] She worked tirelessly with her actors to bring out the best of their talents. "I am overcome with exhaustion every night," she wrote, "but at least I have a calm spirit."[170] This resolve came from her conviction that she had done everything within her power to improve the company. "It will not be for lack of care," she asserted, "if I do not make this the best company in the provinces."[171]

By investing in her performers and providing her audience what they most appreciated, Destouches-Lobreau delivered on her promise. Under her direction, the Lyon theater emerged as one of the best in France—and one that made money. During the decade following her retirement, however, Lyon hosted a parade of directors, many losing substantial sums, and even a brief stint without any director at all, during which time the actors ran the company themselves *en société.*[172] On opening night in 1786, an actor speaking on behalf of the troupe told the audience with candor that "a career in theater becomes more difficult every day."[173]

Many provincial directors found that despite growing sales, their expenses grew as fast or faster. Actors' salaries, which comprised well over half of a troupe's operating budget, soared as directors competed with one another to hire top talent for a growing numbers of theaters. In Bordeaux and Lyon, the total cost of salaries for these troupes more than doubled between the early 1760s and the late 1770s. This growth continued in the 1780s, when salaries for the Lyon troupe rose from about two hundred thousand livres a year to more than 250,000 livres.[174] As one director recognized, there seemed no end in sight for this escalation of pay, which "can only increase from year to year."[175] At the same time, directors faced higher expenses in other areas, such as rising rents for larger and more elegant new playhouses. New directors often borrowed large sums of money to acquire the theater privilege, purchase a magasin, and pay salary advances and travel expenses for the cast. In Bordeaux in the late 1780s, the debt carried by the directors had grown to 1.2 million livres.[176] Servicing these debts drained these enterprises. Finally, many of the day-to-day costs associated with running a theater, such as the candles and oil necessary to illuminate these larger playhouses, were calculated on a per-performance basis, rising as the pace of performance increased.[177]

Directors responded to these pressures in various ways. Many, as seen in chapter 3, sought to exploit their privilege to their advantage, collecting payments from any directors or popular performers who sought to work in their territory. Some looked for ways to create additional seating in the playhouse, for example by adding a set of fourth boxes as a means of increasing revenue. Others raised prices for subscriptions, although that risked alienating a crucial customer base.[178] Economizing on production expenses was another option, although that, too, was a risky one. Spectators and local commentators often denounced cutbacks that were believed to diminish the quality or variety of performances. In Lyon a local journal explicitly advised against adopting cost-saving measures: "We must warn the new directors that their economical intention suggests that they would not give actors who are capable of satisfying the parterre salaries that are commensurate with their talent."[179] Consequently, a number of directors adopted the strategy of spending even more to bring in larger crowds. "The public demands the most varied and dazzling spectacles," one Lyon director explained, "and one must neglect nothing in this regard to satisfy it."[180]

Ultimately, theater directors relied on more than their own talent, ingenuity, and hard work to meet payroll and perhaps even make a profit. They could accomplish little without the talents of the actors, singers, and dancers who performed the ever-larger numbers of roles required to maintain public interest. The authority that directors claimed over theatrical production, their increasingly commercial orientation, and their relentless focus on the bottom line created new tensions in the performance industry. In an essay entitled *La Réforme des théâtres* published in 1787, the actor, playwright, and director Jacques-Thomas Mague de Saint-Aubin lamented the existence of a breed of director who "treats the public as his debtor, and the actors as slaves." He warned such a character not to forget that "it is the public that enriches him, and the actors who bring in the revenue."[181] The relationship between theater directors, their actors, and their audiences, Mague de Saint-Aubin recognized, was triangular. It could be mutually beneficial, but it could also become contentious. In the chapters that follow, we turn to these two crucial partners in the enterprise of theater: the actors and singers who did the work of performing and the urban consumers who paid for their performances.

CHAPTER 5

The Work of Acting

By all accounts, Madame Marion's debut at the municipal theater of Lille in the spring of 1774 was a disaster. As the actress acknowledged, while she performed the role of Cleopatra in Pierre Corneille's *Rodogune*, she could barely deliver her lines over heckling from the crowd. Nonetheless, she completed every last syllable: "I don't say perform, this would have been impossible for me."[1] Indeed, one Lille theater enthusiast reported that she "bombed like I've never seen."[2] Her director Raparlier blamed the actress for her inability to win over the audience, and he used the incident to fire her just weeks into her yearlong contract. Marion, in contrast, attributed the crowd's hostility to a cabal on behalf of a rival actress—a woman favored by soldiers of the local garrison—with whom she was double cast. Marion protested that the director had no right to punish her for the caprice of the crowd. "The truth," she argued, "is that I have not broken any of the clauses of my contract," adding that "if it were necessary for him to fire all [the actors] who met with displeasure here without meriting it, I would defy him to run a theater."[3] Who was in the right, the actress performing (if poorly) the roles for which she had been hired, or the director heeding the will of the public? Marion, suddenly finding herself alone and unemployed in a new city, took her case to France's royal dramatic theater, the Comédie–Française.

When Madame Marion signed the contract to work for the director of the Lille troupe, she, like hundreds of other actors and actresses, sought to benefit from the vogue for theater that was taking hold in French cities in the second half of the eighteenth century. By the mid-1770s, we have seen, only a minority of actors and actresses still joined the intimate, collectively run troupes that had defined professional theater in France from the 1580s through the early eighteenth century. Cooperative, profit-sharing companies on the model of the Comédie-Française had already been largely replaced by companies led by directors who took control of administrative and financial affairs. When accepting a position as a *pensionnaire* in such a troupe, Marion agreed, among other things, to perform a set of roles that included queens, noble mothers, and characters as the director required, to attend all rehearsals and meetings on time, and to provide her own costumes for the annual season. For her efforts she was to be paid a salary of two thousand livres a year, an amount that both she and the King's Players felt was rather low for such an important set of supporting roles.

As a new hierarchical division of labor took shape between directors and their actors, disagreements arose concerning the relative rights and responsibilities of the employer and the employee. Under this new labor regime, the traditional means of settling conflicts, through discussion in a company assembly and voting among troupe members, was no longer practical. Since provincial actors and directors lacked the corporate code or jury of masters that guilds typically used to set standards and resolve labor disputes, contentious issues were often brought before the Comédie-Française. As growing numbers of directors and actors presented their questions and disputes to the King's Players, they drew the royal company into an active role overseeing the development of France's theater industry.

In her letter to the royal actors, Madame Marion explained that she had hesitated before taking the step of asking for their intervention: "I have not dared until now to address you to ask you to do for me a service of the greatest importance; but my husband inspires me to be more bold in writing to me from Berlin that I can do so with confidence, and that the pleasure that you take in obliging [actors] would gladly extend even to me."[4] Her husband was correct. Over the course of the eighteenth century, hundreds of performers and directors turned to the King's Players in Paris for information, advice, and arbitration of their conflicts. The Comédie-Française recorded nearly two hundred such petitions from French theater professionals working in the provinces, the colonies, and abroad. Together with the company's responses, these form a unique resource for scholars.[5] To this point, our knowledge of actors and especially actresses has been informed primarily by representations of these men and women by philosophes, critics, novelists, and pornographers, who depicted them as talented celebrities or as libertines, liars, and debt-ridden spendthrifts.[6] The letters of provincial performers and directors, in which they shared concerns about theater work and the ways it shaped their lives, convey a different picture. They allow us to begin to understand this theater subculture not as it was represented (or misrepresented) by Rousseau, Catholic critics, or a sensationalist media, but rather through the voices of the very actors and actresses, who, year after year, brought dramatic literature to life.

Labor history presents a revealing perspective from which to study changes in theatrical production during an era of rapid growth and commercialization. Approaching actors as workers may seem unusual to those accustomed to labor histories that typically focus on bakers, seamstresses, and other guild laborers who worked with their hands. Even contemporaries set acting apart from other livelihoods. Acting did not fit into eighteenth-century categories of skilled labor, yet neither was it accepted among the liberal arts, which included the professions and intellectual and artistic occupations. Unlike most other urban trades, acting was never granted corporate status. The stigma of actors' excommunication from the Gallican Church, alongside their legally and socially marginal existence, denied them such official recognition and protection.[7] Religious and social prejudices against professional performers were compounded by contempt for the very work of acting, which the playwright and critic Charles Collé derided as "a profession or rather a trade in which the man who exercises it is obliged to make me laugh for my money."[8]

Yet making the audience laugh—and return for another performance—was hard work. The poem "Portrait of a Provincial Actor (*Portrait du comédien de province*)" (1779) depicts the challenges facing those trying to make a living in the theater: "To have for sole relaxation / Rehearsals by the dozen / To work conscientiously / This or that role, where frequently / [The actor] collects for only recompense / Whistles unleashed with impunity / By the cabal or out of hatred / Sometimes to have a good contract / Not to have one any more the next season . . . / From city to city constantly . . . "[9] Despite an actor's best efforts, the poet reminded readers, the unexpected bankruptcy of his troupe could send him straight to the poorhouse.

Exchanges between individuals such as Madame Marion and the royal company enable us to trace the quotidian work lives of eighteenth-century actors. Their letters also allow us to examine the evolving and at times contested relationships between directors and their actors. In the place of "rapacious" directors and performers who were "allowed no formal protest," we find that most eighteenth-century actors and actresses in fact enjoyed many recognized rights.[10] These were affirmed through the contract negotiations that employers and employees concluded before the opening of each new theater season. These contracts defined theatrical production in important ways, influencing what was performed, under what circumstances, and by whom. At the same time, the language of contract rights provided actors with a powerful vocabulary with which to articulate and defend their interests. Madame Marion was not alone in believing that her contract, which she assured the royal actors was "well made, well cemented," would prove to be her salvation.[11] The letters and petitions that actors sent to the King's Players and the responses issued by the royal company demonstrate the extensive influence that the Comédie-Française came to exercise over the rapidly developing French theater industry. In their arbitrations, the royal actors weighed the need to allow the industry to respond flexibly to evolving market conditions against the importance of protecting the rights that the men and perhaps especially the women working in theater had traditionally enjoyed in collaborative troupes.

The royal actors' involvement in establishing a foundation for modern commercial theater in France, however, went well beyond arbitration and oversight. Recognizing the opportunities opened up by the growing numbers of provincial stages, Paris celebrities began to market their own talent throughout France. Leading performers such as the tragedian Henri Lekain set up short-term engagements with provincial acting companies to reap the financial benefits of fame. Despite official pressure to remain in Paris and devote their attention to the royal stages, actors and singers found it profitable to cater to an emerging national public. These new commercial relationships challenged the cultural hegemony of the capital, leaving Parisian audiences in the uncomfortable position of competing for the attention of their favorite stars.

Working in the Business

In order to evaluate the labor conflicts that theater professionals brought before the Comédie-Française, it is necessary to understand something of the structure—and everyday realities—of a career in the theater. To work as an actor in the late eighteenth century required no formal schooling, training, or apprenticeship.[12] What one did need, however, was a contract formally extending a position in a theater troupe for the upcoming annual season.[13] This contract, signed by both the actor or singer and the director, specified which roles the performer would play, in what cities, and for what period of time. It typically included clauses in which the actor agreed to assiduously attend all rehearsals and meetings, to be on time for performances, to respect any police regulations for the theater, and to provide all of his or her own costumes. The contract listed the salary, advances, travel reimbursements, and other benefits he or she would receive. Finally, it spelled out the fines, damages, and interest to be paid should either party violate the contract. Most actors and singers, it seems, signed contracts that lasted for a single season. Consequently, the labor market for French theater operated on an annual cycle. Although many actors decided to remain with the same troupe for another year, many others did not. As a result, the season culminated in a great reshuffling of personnel over the two-week Easter holiday.

As the numbers of French theater companies and performers grew, the process of hiring became more anonymous. Collective troupes had traditionally recruited new performers in person, often in Paris. Yet during the late eighteenth century, only the largest and most successful provincial theater companies, like those of Marseille and Bordeaux, could budget tens of thousands of livres a year for "trips to Paris and in the provinces to choose the subjects who might form a good troupe."[14] Most directors could not afford to spend this kind of time and money traveling from city to city. At the same time, as all troupes grew in size, directors found themselves with ever more positions to fill. Increasingly, hiring took place through the mail, with directors and performers negotiating through exchanges of letters. By the 1770s, contracting by mail had become a common method of hiring even for small traveling companies.[15]

Inquiries began long before the opening of the new theater season. Contemporaries maintained that July was the month when actors traditionally began their search for a position to begin the following Easter. It was common practice to sign a contract during the early fall.[16] According to tradition, signed contracts became binding for both parties a full five months before they were to take effect. After this point, actors who received a more attractive offer or directors who found a more talented candidate were required to pay fines and damages to free themselves from the agreement.[17]

When the season came to an end, there were, of course, always actors and actresses—those less accomplished, less talented, or less lucky—who found themselves with no contract in hand, just as there were always directors desperate to fill their remaining vacancies. During the spring recess before the start of the new season, Paris became the hub of a secondary job market. Behind the Comédie-Française, a café on the rue des Boucheries served as the meeting place for the out-of-work actors.[18] During these critical weeks, this café served as a theater marketplace where actors and directors made inquiries, acquired introductions, and conducted informal auditions. A critic of this system complained that in this setting a director was "forced to choose at random in the tumultuous and overzealous crowd of people without jobs: this is how he is almost sure to be deceived." Reliable information, it seems, was difficult to obtain, for "each [actor] dazzles you with pompous displays of his talents, and with lying monologues of his successes."[19] Even the café owner, who dispensed recommendations and acted as a talent agent, could not be trusted. He benefited from placing as many actors and actresses as possible by taking a cut of their salary. For the lucky, contract agreements were hastily concluded and individuals moved immediately to their new theaters. Among the unlucky—those estimated two to three hundred who faced the prospect of unemployment until the next year's season—some might cast their lot together and form a traveling cooperative troupe.[20]

Negotiating Contracts

The theater labor market in France became increasingly competitive during the 1760s, an era when, according to the intendant of the Menus-Plaisirs, "the taste for theater seems to grow from day to day."[21] The growth in the numbers of provincial troupes, which coincided with increased demand for French actors and singers throughout continental Europe, worked to the advantage of actors and actresses. The more talented and better-known performers often received multiple job offers, enabling them to pit eager directors against one another. The bidding wars that ensued not only raised salaries but also drew talent away from France to foreign courts. In October 1763, the king ordered that all French actors, singers, and dancers—but especially the King's Players—obtain explicit permission from the crown before leaving France.[22] Such efforts apparently did little to stem the escalating costs of staffing a troupe. In the early 1770s, the director in Metz complained of the difficulties he faced in hiring at a time when the better actors and singers could almost name their price:

> The superior talents are always destined for the capital, which itself, as we know, doesn't have any more than necessary; as for the actors who try themselves in the provinces, those who are tolerable put themselves at a price so high that the lowest is 4,000 livres, and it is very rare that the richest cities, such as Lyon, Bordeaux, Marseille, etc., let them escape; the others fall back to the second-order cities, [and] demand salaries of 3,000 livres and 2,500 livres.[23]

This director despaired of making the Metz troupe profitable in such circumstances. Actors, he and others found, leveraged rising demand to their own profit, leaving it to directors to balance the books.

The budgets of theater companies confirm the widespread impression, shared by directors as well as other observers, that salaries for provincial performers rose substantially during the latter decades of the Old Regime. Between 1768 and 1788 salaries for those working for eight large and midsized companies performing in cities including Brest, Douai, Pau, Nantes, Lyon, Montpellier, and Rouen averaged more than two thousand four hundred livres a year.[24] Men and women performing leading roles in large cities and in foreign courts could command two or even three times this figure, and their salaries rose rapidly during these decades. For example, in 1767 the highest paid singers and actors in the Bordeaux theater company earned about four thousand livres a year. Twenty years later, the celebrity dancer and choreographer Jean Dauberval and his wife threatened to leave Bordeaux unless they received thirteen thousand livres each, an astonishing sum that they were in fact granted.[25] Salaries also improved, if less dramatically, for the lower ranks of actors. At midcentury, an actor might earn as little as thirty livres a month. By the 1770s and 1780s, the very lowest salaries in most troupes were typically between five hundred and six hundred livres a year for actors and actresses who held annual contracts that specified a salary.[26] In general, provincial actors and actresses were quite well paid in comparison with those working in other occupations. Earning on average four to ten times as much as a provincial journeyman, their salaries compare favorably to those of master surgeons at the Hôtel-Dieu, engineers, and university professors.[27]

Ultimately, rising theater salaries in the provinces led the king's intendant of the Menus-Plaisirs, Papillon de la Ferté, to recommend raising the amount paid to those actors who were ordered to debut in Paris and accepted into the royal dramatic company. For fully vested members in the Comédie-Française, the income they earned from their share in the troupe's profits increased markedly during the later eighteenth century. For eighty years following its founding, a full share of the company, although fluctuating significantly, had brought members an average of roughly three to four thousand livres a year. In the 1760s, however, this income began to climb steadily above ten thousand livres a year. The amount that the King's Players received per share reached a high of twenty-six thousand livres in the mid-1780s.[28] This placed most royal actors in a different league financially than their provincial colleagues. During actors' initial entry into the troupe, however, new members regularly started on a very small salary while waiting for a full share to open up. (Because the total number of shares was fixed, such an opening required the death or retirement of a troupe member.) The honor of such a position and the prospect of future wealth were intended to compensate for initial years of penury. Still, it was not natural, the intendant argued in 1767, "that an actor who earned 7 or 8,000 livres in the provinces could come to Paris for 1,200 livres for a year."[29] The royal theaters, he felt, needed to respond to the new national trends for their own good, in order to promote recruitment and raise morale.

Women working in the theater benefited disproportionately from rising eighteenth-century demand. This is particularly noteworthy because scholars of women's work have characterized the seventeenth and eighteenth centuries as an era in which working women confronted diminishing opportunities and low wages, one in which "women's salaries across all fields of work declined relative to those of men."[30] Yet by the 1770s, actresses and female singers typically started at salaries of no less than six hundred livres a year. This baseline salary was considerably more than most working women could earn: more than four times what a successful lace worker might make in a year, and more than six times the yearly wages of most female servants.[31] Salaries rose as high as six to eight thousand livres a year for actresses performing leading roles in provincial companies. Most significantly, average salaries for actresses working in the eight provincial companies noted above were approximately 2,450 livres a year, while those for the actors in these same companies were only about 2,350 livres a year. Whereas most women in manufacturing and crafts earned between one-third and one-half the income of men in the same occupation, actresses regularly earned as much as or more than actors.[32]

Because experienced and talented women proved the scarcest and therefore the most sought–out performers, actresses and female singers proved particularly adept at working the labor market to their advantage.[33] Charles-Simon Favart recognized as much as he scoured the talent pool of Paris and traveled to audition candidates in the provinces to fill positions for the court theater in Vienna. He explained to the director of the theater, the comte de Durazzo: "I am desperately sorry to still have nothing certain to send you; the subjects that Y[our] E[xcellency] needs almost cannot be found; a trained actress, young, with a pretty face, a good musician, who unites the talents of the voice with those of acting, seems to us a phenomenon, *rara avis in terris* (a rare bird in the lands)."[34] Actresses who possessed these qualities made the most of their bargaining power. One such talent, Mademoiselle Luzy, initially snubbed Favart's advances, having been offered a salary of five thousand livres a year from the theater in Bordeaux. A determined Favart countered by proposing six thousand livres a year to entice her to move to Vienna.[35]

In addition to higher salaries, some successful actresses and singers used this leverage to try to obtain work for their husbands. A set of letters between Madame Montrose, who was then performing with a French theater company in the city of Cádiz in Spain, and the directrice Madame Destouches-Lobreau in Lyon provide one example of how actresses negotiated such matters. Montrose received an attractive offer to perform in the Lyon company. "But," she responded in a letter to the director, "you do not speak of my husband. The step I took in coming to join him in a country mortal for my health should have convinced you that I will not decide to abandon him."[36] The actress then proposed a new joint contract, in which her husband Dalainval, formerly an actor with the Comédie-Française, would perform kings and noble fathers, or tragic leading roles. "My husband [has] good diction, a superb voice, a lot of spirit, here are his qualities and I would not want to mislead you," she wrote, "I think that 12,000 [livres] for us both would not be too much and I think that you will not regret them." Montrose was well positioned to make such a request. She enjoyed a favorable reputation based on previous performances in Paris and Marseille and she had worked for Destouches-Lobreau in the past. Moreover, theater troupes regularly hired almost twice as many men as women to perform the more numerous male roles. Her husband, she concluded, "will go wherever I will go, rather than have us separate he would prefer to perform for nothing, but it is fair that he be paid."[37] Montrose and her husband were not alone in pursuing such a strategy. Other actors followed the careers of their more successful wives. Duverger explained that his wife alone had initially been offered a contract at the theater in Orléans. "However, on the precise observation that I made to [the director] of not wanting to remain with nothing to do," he wrote, "he made me a joint contract with my spouse."[38]

Not only wives, but also sisters and mothers were at the center of negotiations intended to secure positions for their relatives. Favart approached a number of female performers who refused to sign a contract unless other family members were hired into the same company. Mademoiselle Beaupré, then performing in Compiègne, only considered moving to Vienna with her brother and his wife, and she negotiated for all three. Sieur Prin lauded the talents of his two daughters, yet stipulated that the girls would need to be hired together with their older brother, also an actor. The renowned Madame Dugazon proposed to Favart that she, her husband, her son, and her daughter all be hired for Vienna.[39] Such tactics were not always successful. Favart did recommend offering the Prins a contract for five thousand livres a year for all three children. Vienna's stage, however, simply could not accommodate the entire Dugazon family. Likewise, Montrose's attempts to secure a joint contract with her husband for Lyon ultimately failed. Without any position for him, Montrose steeled herself for a long-term separation from her husband. She wrote back to accept Destouches-Lobreau's initial offer, but expressed her frustration: "I confess to you that the impossibility of your giving Dalainval some employment upsets me greatly, but finally, it's a year lost, I must add this sacrifice to all the others."[40]

Careers in Motion

The inauguration of new provincial playhouses and the establishment of more resident theater companies promised actors more than financial benefits. For many it also brought greater stability to the acting life. Those in traveling troupes were required to accompany their director wherever he or she determined to go, in France or abroad.[41] An actress named Lamare described her trials working in one such troupe in the 1770s: "For two or three months [the director] wanted to take us successively to Orléans, to La Rochelle, to Angers. We were every day, he would say, on the eve of departure, and [yet] we never left at a moment when we were expecting it in the least. He sent around a circular notice Sunday morning [ordering] that we prepare our luggage, perform the show, and leave the following day."[42] She wrote that on one occasion, just twelve days after arriving in the town of Niort, "we had to abruptly clear out without having the time to get ourselves together."[43] Throughout these peregrinations, in addition to performing leading female roles, Lamare also looked after her daughter, who performed children's roles in the troupe without being paid. The strain of such frequent travel and the added expense of short-term lodging and food increased the demands of this career. Actors' letters make clear that most preferred a position in a resident theater company. "I make it a principle not to contract with a troupe that travels," actress Rosalie Ganie wrote to a director during contract negotiations; "I like to be in a stable troupe, if your plan is to stay in Valenciennes, in this case I do not ask for any salary increase."[44]Another actor readily agreed to pay one thousand livres to break his contract with one of Mlle Montansier's traveling companies in order to perform at the public theater in Marseille. "I sensed all the advantages," he explained, "preferring a fixed troupe to the wandering, expensive and exhausting life" he had experienced in traveling troupes.[45]

Even as resident public theater companies were established in growing numbers of cities, however, most actors—including those in the top rungs of the profession—did not typically settle permanently in a single city. Instead, they changed the rhythm of their lives, staying one or perhaps several years at a theater before moving on. For example, Berville, a relatively successful actor, performed in ten different cities before he moved to Paris in 1788, entertaining audiences in Lyon, Brussels, Lille, Dijon, Grenoble, Geneva, Montpellier, Toulouse, Vienna, and the city of Versailles.[46] The theater labor market, his career demonstrates, operated on a fully national and even international basis. An actor might seize opportunities for better roles, for a higher salary, or to develop his or her talents before a new audience. According to one commentator, this continuous movement of performers from city to city raised the quality of acting in France: "It is in passing through these different trials . . . that talent is refined, is polished, is strengthened, is resolved."[47]

Of the many changes in the acting profession during the late Old Regime, perhaps the most important for the day-to-day lives of actors and singers was the intensification of the work itself. Directors' emphasis on variety required them to maintain repertories that by contemporary standards seem impossibly large. Even for experienced performers, it was almost impossible to keep many dozens of roles fresh in their minds. For this reason, almost all troupes, including those in Paris, employed a *souffleur*, or prompter.[48] When actors and actresses negotiated for a contract, they submitted a list of the repertory that they knew and would be ready to perform on relatively short notice. An extensive and versatile repertory was so important for actors seeking employment that some even resorted to embellishing their experience and roles, much to the distress of directors attempting to organize an appealing program only to find a key player unable to deliver.[49] For performers, the pressure was undoubtedly intense. De Villeneuve, a professional actor for only two years, described the challenges he faced breaking into the theater. A shaky debut culminated in a crisis when his director scheduled him to perform a role completely new to him, a tragic role that was "long and exacting, of the greatest difficulty, and . . . I played [it] for the first time after only six days of study."[50] Those six days were apparently not enough to satisfy the crowd or his director. The following day the actor's company moved on to a new city, leaving de Villeneuve behind.

Eighteenth-century actors learned the ropes by working at this relentless pace before critical audiences. Mademoiselle Clairon argued that provincial troupes were the only schooling necessary or even possible for would-be actors. Likely recalling her own trial by fire on provincial stages, she emphasized the knowledge and experience gained through those struggles: "the necessity of earning the salary one receives, the vanity of triumphing over one's fellow cast members, the fear of the public, the memory that one develops through working without rest, the confidence and the presence that one acquires by mounting the stage every day."[51] Provincial audiences developed a reputation as particularly demanding, especially "the big cities where the furor for the stage has made the citizens very hard to please and very enlightened about all matters concerning dramatic talent."[52] When audiences turned openly hostile, they could push even the most experienced actors and singers to the edge.[53]

Considering the intense physical and emotional strains experienced by actors, the competitive nature of the career, and the economic pressures felt by directors, it is only to be expected that the theater—like other eighteenth-century workplaces—would experience labor disputes. Conflicts erupted over a wide range of matters from pay to casting to illnesses (feigned as well as real). There were actors who refused to perform or abandoned their troupes in midseason, just as there were directors, like Madame Marion's employer in Lille, who tried to fire actors who were under contract. Although theater contracts laid out the basic rights and responsibilities of each party, they were silent on many matters and left ample room for interpretation—and dispute—on others. Even in cases when one party was clearly at fault, the enforcement of contractual policies could prove a significant challenge. During the late Old Regime, actors and directors alike turned to the Comédie-Française for help in settling their disputes, in righting wrongs, and in protecting both earnings and reputations.

Labor Arbitration and the Comédie-Française

Since at least the early eighteenth century, provincial players had turned to the royal actors for guidance about theater customs and traditions.[54] Already by 1729 internal regulations for the Comédie-Française noted that the responsibility for responding to queries from provincial actors would be given to certain members of the troupe. Only in the middle of the century, however, did provincial theater become a matter of importance to the court. In 1757, in the most significant reform of the Comédie-Française since its founding, the king's advisors formally entrusted the royal actors and actresses with the responsibility of advising on issues and disputes raised by provincial performers and directors.[55] In 1766, new regulations specified that a committee of actors who were charged with a leadership role in the troupe "will be given the responsibility of judging the disputes of the directors and actors of the provinces."[56] The records of the royal theater for the 1770s and 1780s indicate that depending on the matter at stake decisions might entail a simple response from a member of the committee or a discussion and vote by the general assembly of actors and actresses. At times the legal counsel of the royal company responded to matters. In all cases, however, these decisions were issued in the name of the Comédie-Française.[57] The King's Players became known to their colleagues as *"les Juges de la Comédie,"* the acknowledged authorities on French theater traditions.[58] Indeed, an actor working in Grenoble wrote to the royal theater, perhaps with a degree of self-interested obsequiousness:

> There is no actor in the provinces who does not know of the zeal with which you always dispense justice, which each actor has the right to demand when in need, following the traditions of the theater, & of which the royal judges would not begin to know without relying on your decisions.[59]

During the nearly two decades of arbitration for which records have survived, letters arrived from actors and directors in Lyon, Bordeaux, and Marseille, with their large and prestigious public theaters, and from performers with troupes as small as eight entertaining in cities such as Saint-Omer and Pau. By 1789, the Comédie-Française had received queries from actors and directors entertaining in more than fifty French cities.[60]

There is a certain irony in the fact that the King's Players were chosen for this task. Even as these actors busily adjudicated provincial disputes, critics vociferously denied actors' legal status, including their right to hold public office or testify in French courts of law. Prior to 1789, actors were relegated to the same diminished civil status as the executioner.[61] Meanwhile, playwrights such as Louis-Sébastien Mercier and Jean-François Cailhava, frustrated at the manner in which the royal players selected new plays to perform, complained that the troupe had descended into decadence and portrayed the royal actors as vain, petty, selfish, quarrelsome, and even outright dishonorable. Finally, the company's royal overseers repeatedly rebuked members for flouting the troupe's own regulations.[62] Nonetheless, this was the group entrusted with the responsibility of overseeing the practices of French theater—and with good reason. The King's Players were deeply invested in the success of provincial companies, both professionally and, in many cases, personally. Provincial troupes after all were the main arena for recruitment of new members, the "nursery" for the royal theater.[63] Moreover, since nearly all royal actors had begun their own careers in provincial troupes, they understood theater's traditions, as well as the likely transgressions of both actors and directors, better than anyone else.[64]

Through its decisions, the royal company pursued two motives that were at times in conflict. On the one hand, the royal company, by standardizing practices, sought to promote an efficient and competitive labor market that would allow directors to effectively capitalize on France's growing interest in the performing arts. On the other hand, in their oversight of a relatively free trade, the royal actors were influenced by the "corporate idiom" as they sought to ensure not only the profitability of provincial stages for the individuals involved but also the cohesion, professionalism, and dignity of the acting community.[65] Weighing the importance of tradition against the need for change, the King's Players used their regulatory powers to articulate a set of professional policies that governed the French theater industry.

Above all, the Comédie-Française promoted the actor's contract as the key to professional security for the actor himself as well as for his director. Members of the royal theater company closely evaluated the terms of contracts to determine each party's rights and responsibilities. Already in the seventeenth century actors had signed contracts when they joined theater troupes. During the eighteenth century, however, the possibility that these documents would be enforced increased the importance of contracts within the labor market. Contract violations, when verified, allowed the wronged party to sue for damages. Those actors and directors who accepted only verbal commitments left themselves vulnerable to exploitation.[66] Members of the Comédie-Française chastised fellow performers that they "never see except with the greatest chagrin the type of indifference that their provincial comrades place on the accomplishment of their contracts."[67] Contracts, they complained, were "too frequently broken and too little respected, as much by the entrepreneurs and shareholders as by [actors]."[68] Allowing contracts to be easily overturned, they pointed out, was just as dangerous for performers as for directors: "This ease of breaking contracts made on public faith would make none of them valid. . . . The *pensionnaire*, for his part, would believe himself no more tied to his director, or some associate who would have hired him, than the latter with his *pensionnaire*."[69] As desperate letters to the royal actors make clear, a contract that was not honored spelled disaster for the actor who might well have turned down other opportunities only to find himself facing the possibility of an entire year of unemployment. Likewise, a director faced with the defection of a lead actor or actress midseason could find a successful enterprise suddenly on the brink of bankruptcy. When faced with those who tried to escape their responsibilities, whether directors or performers, the Comédie-Française endorsed stiff fines and legal action.[70]

Through their arbitration, members of the Comédie-Française helped to define the rights not only of actors but also of the still evolving position of theater director. The royal theater confirmed directors' authority over all

administrative and artistic matters included in a contract or deemed reasonable for the success of the enterprise. Directors could select the repertory, or,
as one director wrote into his contracts, "all the plays that I will want to have
performed."[71] Contracts specified the various categories of roles that an actor
or actress was hired to perform, but directors had significant latitude in determining which cast members would perform specific parts. This distribution
of roles was so important to actors that this issue prompted the largest number of letters to the royal theater, approximately one in four. Most commonly,
actors, actresses, and singers agreed to perform sets of roles out of a typology
that ranged for men from leading roles to kings and fathers to young lovers,
and for women from leads to queens, mothers, young maids, or love interests,
and various character roles. This practice was endorsed by the Comédie-
Française. Less frequently directors of dramatic troupes issued contracts for
actors or singers to perform all the roles usually performed by one of the
King's Players. For instance, an actor might be hired to perform the roles that
were in the repertory of Monsieur Molé. Since roles were not infrequently
performed by doubles or might be given at some point to another actor, this
system created many potential conflicts and was discouraged by the royal
company. A contract also specified whether the roles would be performed by
the actor alone (*en chef*), in alternation with another actor (*en partage*), or at the
discretion of the director.[72] In consultation with the cast, directors traditionally compiled each week's repertory list a few weeks in advance, giving the
actors an opportunity to refresh their memory or learn roles that were new
to them. Actors were bound to comply, even when this meant learning new
works in French or, more rarely, in another language. Along with performing,
learning and maintaining this repertory of roles represented for professional
actors the core of their work. The roles an actor played, and their successes
or failures in these roles, shaped his or her professional reputation, earning
potential, and opportunities for future employment.

With so much at stake, the casting of shows sparked regular disputes
between performers who were protective of their career interests and jealous
of the opportunities provided to their competitors. For example, an actor
named Delaval had been hired to perform supporting roles including kings,
tyrants, and noble fathers for the theater in Nantes. When his director hired
another actor to perform "leading roles in all genres and noble fathers," a
conflict arose between the two men. Delaval protested that his director was
pushing him out of the parts for which he was hired and was now asking
him to perform small roles that he did not already know. Did he have to
learn roles not specified in his contract, he inquired, or could he insist that
he and his rival divide the contested roles?[73] In another case an actor named

Desroches was certain that his career would be ruined if, instead of his usual older supporting roles such as noble fathers, kings, and peasants, he were required to perform the role of lover. He protested that with "neither the physique, nor the character, nor the lightness that is necessary, I would surely do it very badly. Add to this that the public seeing me play in the first piece a lover and in the second piece a father. . . cannot accustom themselves to it, and this could not but do me a very great wrong."[74] The Comédie-Française determined that the power of the actor over his roles lay only in the negotiation of the contract language, namely what roles were spelled out and whether he or she were hired *en chef*. If this was not the case, the director was free to choose what roles those in the company would perform.

Financial matters constituted another source of conflict. As discussed in chapter 4, directors generally accepted not only administrative and artistic authority but also financial responsibility for the company, which they shared in some cases with shareholders. Directors provided their actors with a salary advance before the season began, travel expenses for the performer to meet the troupe, and transportation for their baggage.[75] Salaries for the cast and crew had to be paid, typically every two weeks, regardless of how much the troupe did or did not earn. When the theaters of France were closed by decree for several weeks to mourn a royal death, the director in Périgueux stopped paying his actors. The troupe, in turn, refused to reopen the theater without their back wages. The assembly of the Comédie-Française decided in favor of the actors in this case and others like it. "The *pensionnaires*," the royal theater announced, "not being destined under any circumstances to share the profits of the direction, cannot be responsible for its losses."[76] They were to be paid in entirety. The extent of the director's financial responsibilities actually increased over the course of the eighteenth century. In an influential action on behalf of provincial performers, the King's Players decided in 1788 that a per diem could be claimed by all traveling performers as an implicit right, even when it was not specified in their contract. As a result, whenever actors stayed in any city less than one month, they could claim a substantial daily allowance of between three and six livres to help cover expenses such as short-term lodging.[77] This financial windfall improved the circumstances of itinerant performers by compensating them for the hardship of their travels.

The decisions of the Comédie-Française ensured that directors continued to respect certain rights that actors in collaborative troupes had traditionally claimed. For example, the royal actors insisted that directors pay those actors who were too sick to perform. (As one might imagine, this sparked accusations that certain performers were simply feigning illness.) Moreover, directors were to continue to pay the ill cast member until his or her contract expired or until the individual in question died.[78] Even the actor who set out to begin a new job in a new city but became too ill to travel and did not reach the destination was to be paid for the duration of his contract. To the director in Lille whose actor was unlikely to perform for the rest of the season, the Comédie-Française insisted: "This incident is without doubt very sad for the directors, but this event is even more unfortunate for the *pensionnaire,* to whom it would be inhuman to deprive of all subsistence in such a case."[79] In these ways, the royal company fostered a sense of community and responsibility among actors and directors.

The King's Players also intervened on behalf of actors and actresses to protect them from brazenly unfair employment practices. Since performers were often hired based on a brief audition or even through the mail based on their reputation alone, this system risked the dissatisfaction of directors when their actors finally arrived for the new season. As Madame Marion learned in her experiences working in Lille, some directors tried to cut their losses by firing those who did not meet their expectations. In the cases brought before them, the Comédie-Française always supported performers if they had indeed fulfilled the obligations of their contracts. "A subject's lack of talent, avowed or not," they determined, "is never a cause for breaking [the contract]." Actors should be paid in these circumstances, they explained, because "the wages of a *pensionnaire* are his whole resource and are only a light weight upon a large enterprise. If the entrepreneur allowed himself to be wronged, this responsibility is the punishment due to his negligence or to his overzealousness."[80] Such was the Comédie-Française's response to a director in Rochefort, who had fired actress Mademoiselle Demeyrant alleging that she was without talent. The royal company informed the director that he was required not only to pay the actress's salary but that by the terms of her contract he should even allow her to perform.[81]

The nature of the authority exercised by the royal actors deserves some explanation. Many cases involved voluntary arbitration between opposing parties. In others, authorities including urban magistrates and local courts were also involved in adjudicating disputes. In a number of cases, such authorities openly acknowledged their own lack of expertise regarding theater practices and traditions, and requested that the Comédie-Française weigh in on a matter.[82] During the Old Regime, such requests from courts for consultation and arbitration were not uncommon. In fact, French merchant courts, which judged contract disputes such as those between employer and employee, regularly enlisted arbiters to try to bring about a reconciliation of the two parties or, when this was not possible, to try to come to an equitable judgment on the matter.[83] The Comédie-Française maintained that it issued its decisions on labor matters "only as opinion."[84] At the same time, however, its members staunchly defended their right to determine theater policy that applied throughout France. By the 1780s, resentment had arisen among some directors and stockholders regarding the responsibilities to which the Comédie-Française held them. Directors in Bordeaux, for example, tried to break from this sphere of influence by including in their contracts a clause specifying that they shielded themselves from the decisions of the royal theater. This incensed the royal actors, who responded by declaring that according to custom and tradition all of the Bordeaux contracts bearing such language were invalid.[85] Given that the decisions of the royal theater were implicitly endorsed by the powerful Gentlemen of the King's Bedchamber and even by the king himself and were used by courts to reach decisions, directors who valued their professional reputation and their privilege had little choice but to submit to the jurisdiction of the Comédie-Française.

Organizing the Profession

This overview of the acting profession allows us to compare the work culture of these performing artists with that of artisans. Readers familiar with the history of manufacturing trades in the eighteenth century may see parallels in the conflicts between directors or masters and their employees, the cooperative nature and intimacy of working conditions, and the geographic mobility of journeymen and actors, many of whom gained experience and skill working in cities throughout France.[86] The differences, however, are even more revealing. As a case of a noncorporate labor community—one that, although structured by local monopolies, required no formal training and allowed actors an uncommon degree of "liberty of placement"—theater can help us to understand the functioning of an exceptionally open labor market in the eighteenth century.[87] Unlike corporate trades, acting—with the exception of the royal theaters—had no established and stable hierarchy. Instead, actors were evaluated professionally based on their talent, experience, reputation, and appeal. Supply and demand for particular parts also played a role. Directors, who as we have seen frequently came from the ranks of actors and singers, sometimes performed roles in their companies. Among their employees, leading actors and actresses might earn more money than they did. In other words, in place of an ordered ranking correlated to age and experience, such as that demonstrated in the corporate world, the theater was deeply marked by its equality of opportunity. Provincial actors contracted on the market and competed among themselves for better roles, higher salaries, and perks such as benefit performances on their behalf. Within theater companies, the differences in roles and salaries that distinguished professional performers from their peers shifted from year to year. Actors and actresses accepted the benefits as well as the risks of this livelihood.

The competition and individualism so evident in the theatrical labor market were mitigated somewhat by theater's legacy of cooperation and a mutual reliance reinforced by actors' status as outsiders. If most actors and actresses welcomed the relative liberty of their occupation, however, they viewed this liberty as functioning within limits: the rights of the individual were weighed against the needs of the community.[88] Whether in hopes of preserving or defying such limits, provincial actors and directors helped to articulate the changing norms of employment and theatrical production by appealing to the royal theater company in their petitions. As the Comédie-Française mediated the process of commercialization for the French stage, the royal company retained a belief in theater as a professional community and sought to define its practices as well as its spirit.

Acting thus challenges the rigid divide historians have drawn between organized and unorganized labor, suggesting that the realities for workers were more complex. Workers without a corporate status have been characterized as having little group solidarity and few opportunities to protect themselves and their labor.[89] Yet actors developed their own means to address their work concerns and establish norms. Even without the corporate and domestic ties that bound masters to apprentices or journeymen to their fellow workers, actors were bound by the work itself, the cooperative effort of performing a play or an opera. The distinctive lifestyle of these social outcasts constituted another bond within this insular community.

The unusual oversight of the Comédie-Française helped acting to maintain its culture of mutuality and relative equality even in the midst of commercialization. The distinctiveness of this path relative to other trades is especially evident in the case of women in the theater. The professionalization of acting did not have the negative impact on women that it often did in other occupations during the early modern era. This fact should be attributed in part to the participation of the royal actors *and actresses* of the Comédie-Française in the decision-making process. When matters of provincial arbitration were brought before the committee or the general assembly, contested issues were discussed and then put to a vote. Submitting disputes to a jury of masters was common practice among the privileged trades of France. The sharing of power between men and women that characterized the royal theater, however, was perhaps without parallel in the corporate world.[90] As a rule, members of the Comédie-Française treated provincial actresses and women directors

like their male counterparts, evaluating contractual obligations without concern for the sex of the individual in question. Although fewer women than
men brought cases before the Comédie-Française, those who did confidently asserted their right to fair treatment on issues ranging from wages to
roles to default of contract.[91]

In those cases when women's status became a point of contention, such
as when directors were faced with a pregnancy that would interfere with
an actress's ability to perform, the King's Players upheld policies generally
favorable to women.[92] This was demonstrated when a director in The Hague
tried to withhold wages from an actress named Madame Mailland when she
became pregnant. He argued that he had hired her as a widow and, although
she had remarried during her three-year contract, he did not feel contractually obligated to pay her during the pregnancy (and period of recovery) that
followed. The Comédie-Française, however, stood firm that "a director cannot under any circumstances be authorized to withhold the pay of a married
woman in the case of pregnancy."[93] Women who became pregnant outside of
marriage did not receive the same consideration, yet they, too, were granted a
certain protection in the theater. Their salary could be withheld later in pregnancy—when it would have been considered indecent for them to perform
in public—and during the period when they were indisposed following the
birth, but they were not, it seems, to be fined or fired.[94]

Following the standards of the Comédie-Française, French theater
companies held men and women to the same professional and contractual
obligations. In doing so, they not only resisted the gender hierarchy that
characterized mixed-sex work in other sectors of the economy. Their actions
also refuted Rousseauist notions of gender complementarity that were used
to silence women's voices, restrict women from leadership, or impose a different moral standard on women than on men.[95] Unlike women prominent
in other trades, such as the mistresses of the all-female Paris seamstresses'
guild, actresses and other female performers did not need to legitimate their
status on the basis of a sexual division of labor, feminine vulnerability, or
other justifications rooted in difference.[96] In the theater, it had long been
openly acknowledged that women were "as useful [to the company] or
more so than the men."[97] Although a sexual double standard that would
hold actresses (but not actors) accountable for their personal as well as their
professional actions had been promoted by critics such as Louis Riccoboni
of the Comédie-Italienne as the key to restoring the morality of the stage,
the Comédie-Française actively resisted such changes.[98]

Ultimately, the royal players used their authority to do more than simply
arbitrate individual conflicts brought to their attention. As word of specific

decisions spread within the French theater community, often with surprising speed, the King's Players helped to articulate the labor practices that would define the developing industry. In the process, they mediated between theater's traditional practices, often established to protect the individual at the expense of the troupe, and the commercial pressures facing directors who were responsible for making these companies profitable. They sought to define equitable contractual standards (if not standards of talent) that could be agreed on by actors as well as directors. Working to maintain the functioning of an open yet integrated labor market, the royal actors and actresses also valued—and sought to enforce—common, uniform policies, most apparently through the language of the decisions they issued bearing on the rights and responsibilities of various parties. They encouraged actors and directors to look out for their own best interests, chastising not only those who attempted to evade their responsibilities, but also those who allowed themselves to be victimized. Still, they remained sensitive to the humane treatment of performers. In this way, the Comédie-Française's endorsement of innovation and commercial necessity was tempered by a corporate vision that, despite the absence of formal corporate status for actors, recognized the importance of tradition, community, and good faith in the success of France's theaters.

Fame and Fortune on the National Stage

As the members of the Comédie-Française consulted on growing numbers of arbitration cases, they found themselves enjoying a unique vantage point from which to appreciate the commercial vitality of France's growing theater industry. With playhouses opening their doors in more than seventy provincial cities during the prerevolutionary era and numerous year-round troupes taking up residence, the royal players looked for ways to get in on the action. Even as the prestigious royal company profitably entertained Parisian audiences, individual members engaged in innovative collaborations with provincial troupes to take advantage of these new markets. From the time that Louis XIV founded the royal company in 1680, the King's Players had performed almost exclusively for audiences in Paris and at court.[99] Around the middle of the eighteenth century, however, royal actors began to capitalize on their talent and prestige by making highly remunerated special appearances on stages throughout France.

The career of the most famous tragic actor of the era, Henri-Louis Cain, known to contemporaries as Henri Lekain, demonstrates the developing interdependence between Paris performers and provincial theaters, one forged through mutual profit.[100] In journals, Lekain recorded every role that he performed between his acceptance as a member of the Comédie-Française in 1752 and 1777, shortly before his death early the following year. These journals also included the city where he performed it.[101] His itinerary can be reconstructed as he moved back and forth between Paris and provincial cities as well as foreign courts, to take advantage of the financial opportunities they offered. It was money that first motivated Lekain to seek opportunities outside of the capital. Like other aspiring members of the Comédie-Française, Lekain was initially hired in a trial capacity and placed on a very modest salary of one hundred livres a month, plus one livre for each performance. In 1752, he received a partial, three-eighths share in the company. Only in 1758 did he finally receive a full share. During these intervening years, although he was earning only a few thousand livres a year, Lekain was responsible for providing his own costumes and paying other significant expenses associated with membership.[102] During these years, money concerns weighed heavily on the actor. Voltaire, a friend and mentor, tried to intervene with the Gentlemen of the King's Bedchamber on Lekain's behalf to obtain a larger share and improve his financial situation, but without success.[103] During Lekain's second year with the royal company Voltaire advised him to give several performances at the theater in Dijon to benefit his fame but also his fortune.[104]

In his first provincial appearances in the spring of 1753, Lekain starred in seven different tragedies over the course of a week, including *Oedipe*, *Mahomet*, and several others by Voltaire. Lekain, although still a relative novice with the royal company, was advertised as the "famous actor of the Comédie-Française."[105] Prices for the stage seats and the boxes were raised by a third and those for the parterre by a fifth for the occasion, but Dijon crowds were undeterred. For his debut in the role of Tydée in Crébillon's *Électre*, according to reports in the local newspaper, "the whole room was full." The audience was "extremely happy," the editor noted, as the director must have been when the box office took in more than eight hundred livres. The successful week culminated in Lekain's performance of Orosmane in *Zaïre*, when excitement rose to a new pitch: "There was such a crowd that there has never been anything like it at the theater." Lekain apparently charmed Dijon society, for the newspaper noted that "this famous actor was exceedingly fêted in Dijon; everyone was eager to make polite gestures to him and he received many gifts."[106]

Drawn by the financial benefits, the enthusiastic crowds, and his love of travel, Lekain established a pattern of provincial touring that he would maintain throughout his lifetime. During his career with the Comédie-Française, Lekain gave an average of twelve performances a year outside of

The royal actor Henri-Louis Lekain depicted in the role of Genghis Khan in Voltaire's *L'Orphelin de la Chine*. Courtesy of the Bibliothèque nationale de France.

Paris and the court.[107] During the 1750s and '60s, these engagements comprised about one-tenth of his annual stage performances. Later in his career, these performances came to represent one-quarter or more of Lekain's public theater appearances. As Lekain's reputation grew, so did demand to see him. "There really is more than one province in France where le Kain is adored," the *Almanach des gens d'esprit* informed readers, "and they desire his return there like that of a comet whose appearance assured an abundant year."[108] This leading royal actor performed widely in France's largest cities, but he also appeared in more modest provincial venues such as La Rochelle, Rennes, Toulon, and Dunkerque. During his lifetime, he entertained audiences on thirty different provincial stages.[109]

Guest performances such as these proved lucrative for royal actors and local directors alike. For actors and actresses whose share in the Comédie-Française resulted in equal rewards for all the fully vested members, the opportunity to enhance their income based on their talents and reputation in a freer market was appealing. The celebrity and publicity they had achieved by performing on the royal stages, many found, was a highly marketable commodity. During the early days of such tours, in the 1750s, Paris actors and actresses often requested two hundred to three hundred livres per provincial performance. Three decades later, directors complained that the cost of booking *any* performers from the royal stages started at around five hundred livres per evening, to which the director needed to add travel and other expenses, and rose to six hundred to seven hundred livres and even higher.[110] France's most celebrated talents, such as Lekain, earned as much as six thousand livres for ten days of performances, a sum that even top provincial performers might aspire to earn in a year.[111] At rates such as these, on a per performance basis royal actors were much more highly remunerated for their work outside of Paris, even during the 1780s when company profits soared.[112]

Directors, for their part, also profited from these special events. Such guest appearances required a high initial investment. Directors more than recuperated these costs, however, by suspending monthly and annual subscriptions and selling tickets at higher than normal prices. Typically ticket prices were raised by a third, but on occasion they were as much as doubled.[113] Some directors also sold multiple appearances as a single package deal.[114] Yet in spite of higher prices, in city after city audiences packed the house, turning out in greater numbers for Paris celebrities than for any other performances. According to one contemporary, when Lekain performed in Montpellier, spectators literally fought with one another over seats, all of which had been claimed by two in the afternoon for a performance that would start hours later. More than six hundred spectators were turned away. For this series of performances by the famed actor, even after all extraordinary expenses were paid the Montpellier directors cleared between eight thousand and nine thousand livres.[115] During the 1787–88 season in Lyon, the ten most profitable evenings of the year—those that brought in two thousand livres or more—all featured such star power. Together, that season's extraordinary guest performances, sixteen in all, grossed nearly thirty-two thousand livres, almost 10 percent of the theater's revenue for the entire year. Royal actors and singers typically drew such crowds by re-creating roles that had made them famous in the capital.[116] Local directors used new marketing techniques to promote excitement, bringing attention to the reputations these individuals had already established in Paris and in the press. For example, as early as 1759 an advertisement informed the Lille public that Lekain would be arriving soon "to give five performances of only his best roles." The poster encouraged spectators to purchase tickets in advance, before he arrived, so as to assure themselves seats in the likely event that the shows sold out.[117]

In the 1760s, provincial directors began to orchestrate such events on a more regular basis. A Rouennais boasted in 1763 in a letter to the *Mercure de France* that "it is customary for the directors of our theater to attract the leading subjects of the theaters of Paris to perform here during the last week of Lent."[118] Because the royal theaters closed one week earlier for the Easter recess than theaters elsewhere in France, royal actors were free to cultivate such engagements, and many did. In Rouen, the singers Sieur Larrivée and his wife Demoiselle Lemière had used their vacation to perform a series of seven operas.[119] Another correspondent informed readers in 1765 that Lyon, too, was an attractive performance venue for Paris artists. Mademoiselle Dumesnil of the Comédie-Française had performed for three weeks in the beautiful municipal playhouse.[120] By the 1780s, such performances had become de rigueur for any respectable provincial stage. They also became more frequent. During a single annual season the Toulouse theater hosted touring guest artists, mainly from Paris, for six weeks and Bordeaux's Grand Théâtre did so for nearly twelve weeks.[121]

In sum, provincial cities together constituted a significant market that royal actors and singers eagerly tapped into. Some proved particularly gifted at such entrepreneurial self-promotion. After Mademoiselle Sainval aînée was forced out of the Comédie-Française in 1779 following an ugly public battle with a colleague over roles, she made a successful career of touring provincial stages, spending weeks and even months at a time performing in Lyon, Toulouse, and elsewhere. Her success was such that it encouraged her younger sister to follow her example.[122] The diva of the Paris Opera, Anne-Antoinette-Cécile Clavel, known as Madame Saint-Huberty, sang regularly for fans in cities such as Lyon, Marseille, Toulouse, and Bordeaux on tour circuits that lasted for weeks at a time. When Saint-Huberty threatened to retire from the Opera in 1783 because she was not paid enough, the king granted her not only a raise but also, upon her demand, two months of annual leave so that she could accept short-term engagements in the provinces. Her earnings from these tours constituted the basis for her considerable fortune.[123] The economic opportunities that could be generated by Parisian fame proved so enticing that in early 1789 a society of men of talent including "the principal subjects of the three royal theaters of the capital" approached the municipal government in Lyon with the goal of securing the privilege for the city's stage.[124] Fages, an experienced provincial director, would manage operations in Lyon. His Parisian partners (who regrettably remain unnamed) "unanimously vowed to devote the time of their vacations in alternation to the prosperity of the Lyon theater."[125] Their offer was accepted.[126]

These performances, according to contemporary accounts, left deep impressions on audiences. One letter to Lekain described the effect his visit provoked in the writer—and others—when he performed in Lyon:

> Do you remember your passage to Lyon, in 1767? Your constant success in Paris could well have made you forget your success in the provinces: as for me, I will never in my life forget the state of drunkenness into which you threw the city of Lyon; that you gave two tragedies in one evening; that you made more than two thousand Lyonnais have supper in the playhouse; and that with your great . . . reputation, to guard my seat and see *Mahomet*, I ran the risk of not supping until two o'clock in the morning, if *Monsieur le Commandant* had not had the extreme goodness to send me food.[127]

Several decades later, the *Journal de Lyon* suggested similar reactions among the many admirers who flocked to hear Saint-Huberty sing: "A crowd without precedent, verses, crowns [thrown on stage], cheers were the signs of the approval that the spectators gave each day to this inimitable actress, and they only saw her leave with the keenest regret."[128] Such visits, moreover, engaged those beyond the paying spectators who attended performances. When Saint-Huberty arrived in Marseille in the summer of 1785, for example, the city organized elaborate public festivities that one participant and ardent fan described as "worthy of a sovereign."[129] The daylong celebration included cannon salutes, a parade involving an estimated two hundred boats, which the singer enjoyed from her own luxury gondola, and aquatic contests in her honor. When Saint-Huberty returned to the harbor, the quays were crowded with excited onlookers. In an outdoor theater, she was crowned by "Apollo" as a tenth muse. A ball and extravagant supper followed, during which the crowds approaching her were so numerous that onlookers worried that Saint-Huberty and her party risked being suffocated. When she left the city, after giving twenty-three performances, it was reported that she took with her more than one hundred crowns that had been presented to this queen of the stage as gifts by her fans.[130] As urban crowds thronged to performances and other events to celebrate a star such as Lekain or Saint-Huberty, they took part in a veritable cultural phenomenon. Spectators experienced what contemporaries described as the "delirium" and "frenzy" inspired by these immortals, a sense of communal transport that, such terms suggest, was felt viscerally. This sensation, moreover, was one they shared with fans not only locally but in cities throughout France.[131]

As early as the late 1760s, the increasing absences of leading performers of the Comédie-Française became a source of conflict between members and their royal supervisors. One of the royal advisors most closely involved with the company, the duc de Richelieu, decried the practice of granting leaves for such performances, which he felt was "very harmful to the interests of the Comédie and very detrimental to the service of the public."[132] The number of permissions for leave was reduced, and at times foreign visas were refused. Nonetheless, actors and actresses found ways to arrange these matters through the intercession of influential individuals, an extended sick leave, brief engagements closer to Paris, or, most commonly, performances during the royal theater's extended spring holiday.[133] Lekain, for one, was especially adroit at arranging such leaves. The actor struggled in his lifetime with chronic poor health, and his ailments were well known. His habit of using his illnesses as an opportunity to reach new publics, however, generated frustration among Parisian audiences, critics, and even his royal overseers. "Sir Lekain leaves to take the waters," the intendant of the Menus-Plaisirs noted sarcastically, "all the while feeling well enough to detour more than one hundred leagues from his route to go earn a thousand écus in Brittany."[134] "I saw him declare himself sick after he had performed seven or eight times in a winter," one critic remembered. "He abandoned the capital, got in a carriage, and went to see if he did not get on better in the provinces performing two times a day."[135]

The responsibilities of the King's Players to the crown and to their audiences in Paris, and the personal opportunities that came from cultivating a growing national public, were fundamentally in conflict. The more famous royal performers became increasingly conspicuous in their absences, leaving their understudies in the company to entertain audiences in the capital while they embellished their personal careers. This behavior by members of the reigning French theater troupe drew critical commentary from those who felt that these appearances detracted from their commitment to the Paris public. "Messieurs the *Comédiens français* went as usual to make their harvests in the provinces during the week of the Passion," Charles Collé grumbled: "On their return, they retired to their country houses; they prepared nothing new for opening night, but they conducted their business well and amused themselves, and the public is supposed to be content."[136] Such complaints suggested that catering to this wider public sapped Paris's cultural life, characterized by fewer new performances at the Comédie-Française and perhaps less incentive to respond to the demands of the Paris public. Disregarding such protests, growing numbers of royal actors successfully worked the system both ways, collecting their shares or salaries as members of a protected royal company while also filling their own purses through private engagements.[137]

During the late eighteenth century, the monarchy's concerted efforts to appropriate all the best talent in France for the royal stages in Paris, a cultural policy set in motion a century earlier, fell short as the King's Players concocted excuses to leave the capital to pursue opportunities for enrichment. Provincial cities, with their playhouses filled to capacity with adoring crowds, festivities and gifts presented in honor of visiting celebrities, and generous pay, held out advantages that the capital did not. Ultimately, Paris's loss was France's benefit. As leading actors and singers pursued a new kind of commercial fame that became possible only in the late Old Regime, they ceased in effect to think of themselves as Paris performers or royal players in the service of the king. By cultivating broad audiences of devoted fans, Lekain, Saint-Huberty, and others made themselves into France's first national stars.

Work, Rights, and the Production of Culture

When Rousseau announced disapprovingly that "the theatre has rules, principles, and a morality apart," contemporaries may well have perceived this as referring to the personal and sexual lives of actors—especially the women of the stage—rather than to their work.[138] Indeed, according to Lenard Berlanstein, actresses and female singers and dancers emerged during the eighteenth century as the most desirable mistresses for highborn men, the central female participants in aristocratic libertinism. A substantial number of actresses—although by no means all—welcomed the publicity (as well as the extravagant gifts and gratuities) that they could generate through their sexual conquests. The renown achieved by these women shaped the ways that all theater professionals were perceived during this era.[139] To Rousseau, who believed that "women must be relegated to the domestic sphere for society to function properly," actresses were dangerously unnatural women whose brazen disregard for feminine virtues such as chastity and modesty threatened to unman men.[140] Yet even as he took actresses to task for their "dissoluteness," Rousseau also recognized that the practices and values of theater professionals stood at odds with those of traditional Old Regime society in other fundamental ways.[141]

Labor history illuminates one such area of difference. In the French theater industry of the late eighteenth century, the relationships between directors and the actors and actresses in their employ differed substantially from the corporate and hierarchical ideal promoted by guilds. Nor did they resemble the patriarchal and paternalistic relationships grounded in deference and loyalty that masters traditionally forged with their servants.[142] The authority of the director was real, to be sure, yet both the longstanding traditions of the theater itself and the contractual nature of theater work established the relationship between director and actor in more egalitarian terms, based on the exchange of pay for specific services, with each party free to negotiate more beneficial terms of employment. (The director must regard his *pensionnaires* "as his equals," the director and actor Mague de Saint-Aubin argued on the eve of the Revolution, "because they are.")[143] In a theatrical labor marketplace marked by a remarkable equality of opportunity for novices and experienced players and for men and women alike, professional actors and singers understood that their abilities would be evaluated, above all, according to their profit potential and market value. The stage offered a career in which actresses, like their male colleagues, were rewarded not for their feminine virtue and modesty, but for their ability to master roles quickly, execute them well, and to fill the house again and again. One savvy actress expressed her abilities and merit in these terms, writing that "my talents have been approved of by the public in such a way as to increase the director's income."[144]

Under the new organizational structure that came to predominate in the French theater industry in the eighteenth century, theater professionals increasingly conceived of their employment using the language of rights.[145] Mademoiselle Duclos, who wrote to the Comédie-Française in 1774, provides just one example among many. Although she was hired to perform the lead soubrettes *en chef*, her director hired a second actress to alternate the parts with her. She invoked her contract to oppose what amounted to a demotion. "Don't I have the right to refuse to share [these roles]?" she inquired of the King's Players, "or to force my Director to pay me my salary without doing anything, if he insists on wanting this new arrival to play the soubrettes?"

Another actress, writing in 1789, used similar language when arguing that her director should allow her to perform lead roles: "I think . . . that he doesn't have the right to deprive me of playing a part that I have held everywhere and that is mentioned in my contract."[146]

The rights that actors and directors invoked in such circumstances were not the universal natural rights or rights of man that were beginning to enter French philosophical and political discourse at this time.[147] Nor were they the traditional communal rights long claimed by peasants. Rather, the rights invoked by actors were individual and negotiable, grounded in labor traditions specific to the theater and also in consent. The language of contract rights used by actors and directors needs to be understood within the context of contemporary commercial discourse. During the eighteenth century many French men and women signed contracts, whether for the sale of goods or land, for employment, or for marriage. Disputes over these contracts were often brought before merchant courts, which were located in cities throughout France. According to the legal historian Amalia Kessler, during the late Old Regime these commercial courts promoted a new conception of commerce as a necessary and virtuous social function, one that was not the domain of merchants alone but was open to all. By assuming a certain legal equality among the parties to a contract, their approach to commercial law—and to commerce more broadly—had the largely unintended effect of eroding "both the logic and the institutional structure of corporatism."[148] When the King's Players utilized a similar framework for assessing precedent, contractual responsibility, and individual rights in their arbitrations, they, too, can be seen as implicitly accepting and promoting a new understanding of the social order, one grounded in greater openness and individualism.

Ultimately, the changes that marked the work of acting during this era have broad implications for the ways that we think about cultural production in prerevolutionary France. Two matters deserve particular consideration. First, it is worth emphasizing that the Comédie-Française's leadership in negotiating this transition and defining the emergent industry by standardizing labor and hiring practices—perhaps the most influential means by which the state shaped the developing theater industry outside of Paris—did not originate in official decrees issued by the court. Rather, the Comédie-Française was drawn into its critical advisory role from below, by the provincial actors and directors who persistently requested the opinion of their respected and influential colleagues in Paris on matters regarding the customs and practices of the theater business. By formally recognizing the royal players' authority to define theater policy, however, the royal government did encourage the development of uniform commercial policies that facilitated the integration of the emerging theater industry and, consequently, of cultural life throughout urban France.

Second, a better understanding of the labor conditions under which theater was produced forces us to reconsider the ways we understand the authority of the theater public at this time. Scholars working within the Habermasian framework have tended to highlight the influence wielded by the eighteenth-century public, which has been characterized as "independent, critical, and the ultimate arbiter of cultural . . . matters."[149] Yet focusing too narrowly on the authority of the public simplifies what were in fact complex interactions among producers, consumers, and the providers of cultural goods and services. The intervention of the Comédie-Française demonstrates that in the eighteenth century the business of performing did not involve serving the whims of the public at any cost. In fact, directors and their companies were expected to meet labor standards upheld by the Comédie-Française and to respect employment traditions and contractual obligations that influenced what audiences saw and in what forms. Having taken her case to the royal troupe following her fiasco of a debut in Lille, the actress Madame Marion was vindicated in her conviction that by performing her roles to the best of her ability she had done nothing to warrant being fired. The troupe affirmed that "a director must be entirely responsible for the choice he makes of his employee." Moreover, in this particular case, they added, the nature of the roles assigned to Marion and the below-average salary she was to be paid "prove that the director did not count on talents of the first order." Regardless of audience displeasure, the King's Players supported the actress's demand for the full execution of her contract.[150]

Decisions such as these provided professional actors with a significant measure of employment protection in the short term. In the longer run, however, there was no substitute for popular success. As directors and actors undertook the work of theatrical production, neither group could afford to ignore the sentiments of their increasingly vocal and demanding customers. Year-round theater companies like this one in Lille were more dependent than ever on the patronage of the local public, whose opinions—whatever their merit—did impact the bottom line. Both employers and their employees worried over the reception of the works they produced. They learned to be wary of a mercurial public that could offer up adulation but also vicious criticism. For it was not only actors who staked claims to rights: spectators, too, increasingly proclaimed and demanded their own rights—as consumers.

CHAPTER 6

Consumers of Culture

During his travels in the south of France in the late 1780s Johann Georg Fisch made a point to attend the theater in every city that boasted a playhouse. At the theater, he explained, "in one evening one can learn so much more about the nature, the character, the taste of a public than one could collect in weeks of arduous observations" in the streets among the people, in narrow social circles, or in coffeehouses, where everyone is looking for distractions.[1] While attending performances in cities such as Montpellier, Aix, Marseille, Nîmes, and Toulon, Fisch proved as interested in the drama taking place in the parterre and boxes around him as in the works produced onstage. In Toulon, where he attended a "very mediocre" performance of the comedies *La Fausse Agnès* and *Le Fou raisonnable*, he moved from box to box "in order to see the people." Toulon's theater audience, he was told, drew more heavily from wealthy elites, with men and women of the middling classes attending less often than in other cities. Those from "common bourgeois households" may well have been put off by the particularly reprehensible behavior of about half a dozen young military officers, whom he observed shamelessly propositioning prostitutes in language that Fisch suggested would make any respectable person blush.[2] (Elsewhere, he found, theater audiences generally behaved with greater decorum.) Yet, from his perspective, the most important factor shaping the social composition of a theater audience was money. "In the long run," he wrote, "it will be decided by who can pay the expenses."[3]

163

During the late Old Regime, keen social observers like Fisch turned to theater spectators and the ways they acted and interacted to obtain a unique perspective on urban societies in the midst of economic growth and cultural change. As dedicated playhouses opened their doors in more than seventy cities across metropolitan France, urban consumers claimed their places within these new institutions. From Metz to Marseille, even as royal authorities and city magistrates vied for seats that conferred honor and distinction, an array of other urban elites, including aristocrats, *parlementaires*, tax farmers, lawyers, négociants, bankers, and manufacturers, paid dearly for the privilege of sitting in a prominent first box or on benches on the stage itself.[4] Meanwhile, low-end tickets were priced to sell, and sell they did. In the relatively inexpensive, standing-room-only parterre, contemporaries encountered a wide array of men from the working and middling classes, ranging from university students, shopkeepers, watchmakers, painters, chefs, clerks, secretaries, tailors, wigmakers, and domestic servants, to doctors, lawyers, city magistrates, local *bourgeois*, and foreign travelers.[5] Women, too, turned out in significant numbers. Aristocratic ladies and bourgeois wives (and widows) attended performances with their husbands, daughters, and friends. These women sat apart

SALLE DE LA RUE DE TALLEYRAND EN 1785.   B... .
                                            REIMS

In this contemporary representation of the interior of the Reims playhouse, a sizable number of women appear in the boxes and also in the amphitheater at the rear of the playhouse. "Salle de la rue Talleyrand en 1785," by permission Reims, Bibliothèque municipale, LCII C 26.

from the female servants, shopgirls, and courtesans who also came to the theater.[6] In ports, we have seen, captains and their sailors attended shows, whereas in garrisons army officers and common soldiers rubbed shoulders (and sometimes exchanged blows) with civilians.[7] With tickets priced to accommodate a range of incomes and tastes, provincial theaters attracted a public that was even broader and more heterogeneous than that of the royal theaters in Paris. By drawing support across traditional social divides, the provincial public theater, according to one urban historian, stood out as "perhaps the sole marker of cultural union in the city."[8]

For spectators, a theater ticket offered for sale was no ordinary commodity. Theater companies offered unprecedented access to performing arts culture, enabling theatergoers to choose among the rich and diverse offerings. Audience members bought the opportunity to experience these performances— but also much more. Contemporaries turned to these new public spaces to meet friends and acquaintances, conduct business, enjoy refreshments, display fashionable clothing and accessories, flirt, people-watch, make mischief, and stage demonstrations, among other things, all before a crowd of onlookers. A traveler attending a performance in Lyon undoubtedly spoke for many when he found that "the least interesting part of the spectacle was the actors."[9]

At the same time that theaters offered up possibilities for a new kind of public sociability, they also promoted cultural criticism. Audiences seized the opportunity to express their opinion of the performance and the actors. Eighteenth-century theater audiences were lively and outspoken participants in the evening's entertainment.[10] Not just parterre audiences, but those in the boxes, too, delighted in offering loud ovations to signal their pleasure, and in unleashing the whistles, hisses, and other indignations known as *le sifflet* to express their disdain.

Scholars such as Daniel Roche and Colin Jones have suggested that a new, more egalitarian consumer sensibility emerged in the eighteenth century, fostered by the new practices of consumption and commercial exchange that were becoming a more prominent aspect of everyday life, particularly in France's cities.[11] Approaching the spectators who flocked to France's new stages as cultural consumers allows us to expand on these arguments by examining changes in consumer behaviors over time, the attitudes underlying audience practices, and the responses of the authorities to an increasingly empowered theater public.

Directors and urban magistrates alike found that bringing large, high-spirited and opinionated crowds into close quarters on a regular basis was not without its challenges. In 1780, an ardent supporter of the Bordeaux stage recognized the cultural authority that could be had for the price of a theater ticket:

> Look at me! For my money
> Established a competent judge
> Of the great Corneille and of Voltaire
> Proud republican of the parterre
> For a purchase of twenty sous on entering
> The right to whistle at [actress] La Clément
> [Actors] Granger; Romainville; Teisseire;
> It is assuredly a beautiful reign
> This ephemeral despotism.[12]

Many spectators believed, like this individual, that along with their ticket they bought the "right" to condemn or applaud a play or an actor. The municipal or military authorities responsible for maintaining public order and safety in France's playhouses disagreed. From their perspective, the sifflet and other audience interventions threatened public order by generating tumult that could result in riots. Moreover, the absolutist state forbade public protest, which was considered an affront to the authority of the king and even an act of sedition. Charged with reining in audience excesses and establishing a more respectful and civilized atmosphere in France's new civic playhouses, authorities therefore took steps to regulate and police audience behaviors in an attempt to impose order on the provincial public.

Yet in city after city, those responsible for maintaining order in public theaters proved unable to master crowds of spectators who asserted their will to shape local cultural offerings more confidently than ever. Those attending the theater effectively harnessed the power of the consumer to make even bolder demands on directors and authorities alike. This is especially striking in the theater boycotts staged in Rouen and several other cities in the 1780s, in which spectators took their cause out of the playhouse and into the streets. When confronting audience demands, both the directors of these public theaters and political authorities found themselves torn between the desire to discipline upstart spectators and the pragmatic recognition that placating audiences would allow them to avoid clashes that threatened to alienate the theater's consumer base, inflame the populace, and perhaps even incite violence. Both parties also understood that for these valued civic and cultural institutions to thrive, theater companies needed more than the governor, the garrison, or the city magistrates were willing to provide. Facing these dilemmas, even agents of the crown conceded that directors needed their customers—and every sou they brought in.

Consuming Culture

In the case of theater, studying patterns of cultural consumption, including audiences' social makeup, is particularly challenging because of the ephemeral nature of the experience.[13] Unlike clothing, furniture, books, and other material objects, tickets and subscriptions did not make their way into post-mortem inventories, scholars' primary source of information regarding consumer behavior in the eighteenth century. Theater companies did not keep records of the hundreds of individuals who paid cash at the box office to purchase tickets to a given performance. To my knowledge only a single complete list of provincial season ticket subscribers has survived.[14] Yet glimpses of these elusive spectators, as well as their practices and attitudes toward the theater, can be caught in travelers' memoirs, police reports, theater regulations, newspapers, and other sources. Drawing on these resources, we can begin to compose a sketch of this nascent provincial theater public.

As a general rule, in order to attend a performance of a show in a provincial theater one needed to buy a ticket. There were, of course, exceptions. According to tradition, political authorities such as the mayor or the royal governor claimed the prerogative to grant free entry to theatrical performances to themselves, members of the city council, and other high-ranking and well-connected individuals at their discretion. These tickets were given as "an honorable distinction to persons of dignity or those who occupy eminent positions."[15] Much to directors' chagrin, this policy was often subject to abuse as growing numbers of individuals demanded free entry for themselves and others and directors dared not contradict them. In response to protests, attempts were made to delimit these free entries by compiling formal lists of those who qualified. Still, when everyone from the mayor to the city treasurer and the city architect was included, the number enjoying this privilege could reach as high as several dozen.[16] Mayors and royal governors were even known to extend this prerogative to their household staff, a practice that was deeply resented by those who paid to sit in an expensive area of the playhouse and therefore expected to find themselves surrounded by a distinguished clientele.[17] One Rouennais complained that "if [the director] is forced to grant free entry to . . . the valets of the leaders of the city, he should not let them indiscriminately occupy the best seats. It is disagreeable for a man who has paid his écu to find himself in the parquet next to a Swiss [guard], a cook . . . the washerwoman of the house from which he has just left and where he dined, to be importuned by their bizarre reflections, their stupid admiration, their unrestrained bravos, and their tiring familiarity. A corner in the thirds [third boxes] ought to suffice for these people."[18]

The great majority of spectators, however, purchased their ticket at the box office. The cost varied widely depending on where in the theater a spectator wanted to sit or stand. Most directors offered at least three different price categories for tickets, although those operating in more elaborate houses featured as many as six.[19] In the majority of provincial cities, the least expensive entrance tickets cost about twelve sous, although in some cases they cost as little as six sous. This was roughly equivalent to the cost of attending the popular boulevard theaters in Paris. Only in Bordeaux, Lyon, and a few other cities did the theaters charge spectators a minimum of twenty sous, which, for most of the century, was equivalent in price to the cheapest tickets for the Comédie-Française in Paris.[20] Such a ticket usually granted a spectator entry to the parterre or highest balcony or paradis. The men and women buying these inexpensive tickets typically made up half or more of the total theater public.[21] For about twenty-four to thirty-six sous a ticket, men of greater means and their wives might choose to sit in a second box, in the amphitheater, or in the parquet. The most expensive tickets in the house, those for seating in the prominent first boxes, in balconies overlooking the stage, or even on the stage itself, often cost two to three livres or more. At times, elites in Bordeaux paid up to five livres for stage seating for an opera; in Lyon a seat in one of the balconies adjacent to the stage could cost as much a six livres.[22] (Wealthy Parisians might well have seen even these prices as a bargain, given that equivalent seats at the Paris Opera went for as much as forty-eight livres.[23]) Over the course of the eighteenth century, the price of tickets remained remarkably stable. In several cities, the price of the least expensive tickets actually dropped following the inauguration of a significantly larger new playhouse as the director set out to expand the audience base and fill the house.[24]

To put these prices in perspective, a twelve-sou ticket cost more than a cup of coffee at a café or a rice cream at one of Paris's new restaurants (2–3 sous and ten sous respectively). It cost less, however, than a cheap edition of a popular "philosophical" book sold on the black market or a rather old, worn waistcoat sold on the secondhand clothes market (both starting around seventeen sous), and less than half as much as a meal at a Parisian table d'hôte (26–40 sous).[25] Costing about half of the daily wage of a journeyman in a provincial city, the threshold for attending a local public theater was set fairly low.[26] At this price, the theater was accessible not only to professionals, shopkeepers, university students and the sons of local bourgeois but also to artisans, clerks, and assistants to local merchants. In some audiences we find manufacturing workers and even the odd spectator who was unemployed.[27] Occasional spectatorship in the parterre or paradis, and even in the second or third boxes, might therefore be placed in the same category of consumption as the "populuxe" commodities, or inexpensive copies of aristocratic luxury goods, that were purchased by so many middling and working-class households during this era.[28]

For men and women of greater means, a three-livre ticket for a first box cost about as much as an engraved print of a contemporary painting or a modest restaurant dinner.[29] Still, this indulgence cost contemporaries less than the cost of an annual subscription to a local newspaper (about six to ten livres) or a philosophical journal (twenty to forty livres), or an annual membership in a reading club (twenty livres or more).[30] Meanwhile, a season subscription to the theater in Bordeaux, Lyon, or Lille, which granted entry to all regular performances for the full theater year, was in league with a complete outfit of brand-new clothes (around one hundred livres).[31] Such a subscription, in sum, represented a genuine luxury.

An account book recording the names of customers purchasing subscriptions to the Lyon theater for the 1787–88 season provides the only detailed portrait we have of this elite tier of spectators.[32] In this important center for banking and silk manufacturing, those purchasing subscriptions came predominantly from the commercial elite. Among those who could be identified, spectators who were prominent in banking, wholesale trade, the silk industry, and the "bourgeoisie" together purchased nearly 60 percent of subscriptions. The remaining subscribers included nobles, lawyers and other professionals, and royal office holders. Among the seven men who paid as much as 576 livres to reserve an entire box for the year we find the military commander of the province, the marquis de Scepeaux, three bankers, a royal solicitor (*procureur du roi*), a royal tax-collecting officer (*receveur des aides*), and a "bourgeois."[33] The composition of elites in a theater audience, we can be sure, differed from city to city. As one actor acknowledged regarding theater audiences, "There exists, as everyone knows, a striking difference between the cities of parlements and nobility, and the cities of commerce."[34] In cities which were home to provincial parlements the nobility of the robe comprised a much more important sector of the audience than in primarily commercial cities such as Lyon or Nantes, while in garrisons, as we have seen, the nobility of the sword constituted a defining elite presence. Yet in cities throughout France the urban elites who came to patronize new public theaters also included substantial numbers of prosperous and aspiring commoners from the upper and middling ranks. Contemporary accounts of spectatorship in the late eighteenth century suggest important changes under way in how the social order was represented in France's playhouses.

As public, commercial institutions, theaters operated according to different principles than the other leading provincial cultural institution, the academy of arts and sciences, which was long dominated by the nobility and clergy.[35] Spectatorship was not a matter of selective membership, but one of consumption. Contemporaries provocatively proclaimed the theater "a place where money alone placed at the same level the nobility and the commoners [*la roture*], in according them an equal right."[36] Strikingly, the Parlement of Paris, France's most powerful high court of law, gave this interpretation the weight of legal authority. In 1782, when ruling on an incident in which an aristocratic army officer publicly forced a lawyer to surrender his seat in a balcony at the Comédie-Française, the court affirmed that commoners did not need to defer to aristocrats in the playhouse. An individual's estate or social status was not to determine his or her access to theater seating available for public purchase.[37] Theater attendance, the Parlement of Paris agreed, was a commercial transaction, and seats were to be claimed on a per ticket and first-come basis.

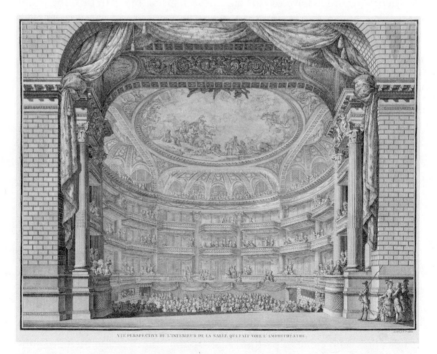

VUE PERSPECTIVE DE L'INTÉRIEUR DE LA SALLE, QUI FAIT VOIR L'AMPHITHÉÂTRE.

The social and political hierarchy of spectatorship was put on display in playhouses such as the Grand Théâtre of Bordeaux, as seen in this representation of the theater's interior. "Perspective View of the Bordeaux Theater showing the Auditorium," from Victor Louis, *Salle de spectacle de Bordeaux* (Paris, 1782). Courtesy of the Billy Rose Theatre Division, The New York Public Library for the Performing Arts, Astor, Lenox and Tilden Foundations.

Such commercial equality of access was all the more significant because during the Old Regime the consumption of luxury commodities such as theater subscriptions did more than simply reflect one's status in the social and political hierarchy. Luxury consumption, John Shovlin has argued, actually "served to *produce* social distinctions and a hierarchy of power."[38] Although cities continued to enjoy traditional means of ordering their populations through public ceremonies such as citywide processions, these officially organized expressions of hierarchy based on birth, privilege, and one's status in the corporate order were less frequent and less prominent than in earlier eras.[39] In the eighteenth century, public playhouses emerged as the premier urban sites for personal display, and thus served as central arenas in which residents negotiated claims to status. And in these venues, as Fisch noted, money—and decisions about how it should be spent—came to play the determining role in constituting the hierarchy of spectators.

Spectatorship among Elites

Although travelers and others who chronicled their experiences attending provincial theaters often have little to say of middling spectators and the anonymous "young men" of the parterre, they vividly convey the remarkable success with which public theaters won the patronage of an array of urban elites. Theaters, their accounts make clear, fulfilled a critical social as well as cultural purpose in cities that enjoyed many fewer entertainment and leisure options than the capital. As one Bordeaux commentator explained, "To act [in society plays] or to go to the theater, these are the two amusements that we have to choose from during winter or else we are condemned to die of boredom, and to pass for misanthropes."[40] When chronicling Lyon in 1786, the writer and theater critic Grimod de La Reynière described the theater as "the principal and almost the only amusement; it is the daily rendezvous of all busy people; it is there that they come to relax [*se délasser l'esprit*] and to arrange for the evening a few enjoyable suppers."[41] Even in a midsized city such as Limoges, a resident observed that "the theater has become, for most of us, a need; it's the rendezvous of the businessmen on the one hand, of the men of leisure on the other."[42] In commercial cities, in particular, during evening performances business was often mixed with pleasure. In Marseille, an observer went so far as to assert that "négociants do more business at the theater than at the stock exchange."[43]

During the 1770s and 1780s, competition for seats in status-conferring boxes became more intense. Urban prosperity, growing consumerism, and the rising popularity of theater meant that more people were spending more money on tickets and subscriptions. Playhouses in France, unlike their English counterparts, allowed no reserved seating unless an individual rented an entire box for the full season.[44] Nor were servants allowed to reserve seats on behalf of their masters.[45] Subscribers and daily ticket holders alike needed to arrive early enough to secure a desirable seat. Among distinguished spectators in Marseille, late arrivals at the playhouse preferred to crowd into the corridors outside the first boxes, rather than compromising themselves by sitting in less prestigious second boxes. According to observers, significant numbers of elites were turned away from that theater each night because their needs could not be accommodated. In 1785, the investors in the city's new playhouse and their favored architect, Claude-Nicolas Ledoux, recommended sharply increasing the number of the most distinguished seats in the house, those occupied by the city's commercial, administrative, and noble elites, from 450 to eight hundred seats. In addition, this plan would have added three hundred more seats destined specifically for the "bourgeoisie."[46] Elsewhere, too, there were complaints that there were not enough places in the playhouse for elite spectators. In Bordeaux, the governor complained of the frequent disputes that broke out over seating in the boxes. In Toulon, proposals were put forth to build parquet seating in the front portion of the parterre for "the officers, ladies, and residents not finding space elsewhere."[47]

Women featured prominently among the elites who turned out to attend performances. During her extensive travels in France, Anna Francesca Cradock, an English traveler of status and means, went to the theater in nearly every city she visited, including in Marseille, Montpellier, Toulouse, Nantes, Bordeaux, Rochefort, Saumur, and Lyon. She often attended with her husband, Joseph Cradock, but also went in the company of female and male companions.[48] Cradock was far from alone in her enthusiasm for music, dance, and drama, and for the social opportunities that these playhouses offered to upper-class women. In Lyon, by the late 1780s the number of women purchasing expensive annual subscriptions had risen to over one hundred and sixty.[49] Meanwhile, a list of individuals permitted to sit in the box reserved by the commander of the city included thirty-one women from the highest ranks of society.[50] With the presence of so many women, the boxes of the Lyon theater, in the words of one spectator, were decorated "with an undulating sash of hats, of bonnets, of plumes, and of ribbons."[51] Playhouses, in fact, emerged as important sites of female sociability. When visiting Rouen, the English writer Hester Thrale was invited to go to the theater by her friend Mrs. Strickland "less for the Pleasure of the Representation, than for the Sake of getting acquainted with . . . Madame

Du Perron—a Lady of Rank and Fashion."[52] Her rendezvous with Madame Du Perron proved a success. During the course of the evening, "some civil things passed between us, & she invited all our Society to sup with her on Sunday Night next."[53] Even in a small city such as Nevers, society women came out to patronize the theater. When Mlle Tonton, the sister of the playwright Beaumarchais, stopped there with her father while en route to take the waters in Pougues, she attended the theater primarily, it seems, to show off her latest Parisian fashions and to upstage those around her. In a letter to her sister describing the evening, even as Tonton ridiculed provincial social and cultural life, she conveyed the importance of this theater for women such as "madame la Baillive, madame l'Élue, and others, who honored with their presence the pitiful playhouse which they are, parenthetically, only too happy to have."[54]

Theater directors, as seen in chapter 4, specifically courted female spectators, seeking to draw them in with flattering advertisements and discounted subscription prices. Women were valued for more than the fact that they adorned the hall with their gowns and coiffures, although contemporaries did consider "the ladies who fill the boxes" to be "the principal ornament of a salle de spectacle."[55] Women were also believed to foster politeness and civility in the theater, as elsewhere in French society.[56] Contemporaries praised women's ability to draw men around them, soothe male egos, and harmonize their often opposing viewpoints. According to the French writer and economist Morellet, "The free commerce of the two sexes [is] one of the most powerful principles of civilization and of the improvement of sociability."[57] For directors, the fact that women rarely attended the theater alone may have been an even more important consideration. Both directly and indirectly, female spectators helped to draw in additional customers, especially men. Women's presence in the playhouse proved so significant that some considered the number of female spectators to be an indicator of a play's success. This was the case in Dijon, where the editor of the *Mercure dijonnais* shared with his readers the number of women at performances as a means of gauging the size of the crowd. When the royal actor Lekain gave his series of special guest performances in the city in 1753, the editor contrasted the fifty-seven women who attended his performance of Rhadamiste in *Rhadamiste et Zénobie* with the more modest number of women at *Gustave*, only about twenty-five. In terms of female attendance, the final performance was a particular triumph. "We counted there more than 110 ladies," the editor noted, a number of whom had arrived more than four hours in advance to secure their seats.[58]

Women traditionally took seats in the front row of the boxes or balconies. In Lyon, as one spectator noted, "No man would dare take a seat there in the front: the parterre, very boisterous and unrestrained in other respects, would take its revenge."[59] Women might also sit in the parquet, in the amphitheater, and in some cities even on the stage itself. But in keeping with tradition, women never attended performances in the boisterous parterre, where they might be jostled, harassed, or otherwise compromised by the all-male crowd. As a rule, prominent and wealthy women sat in first boxes, bourgeois wives sat with their husbands in the second boxes, and working girls climbed the stairs to the third boxes or the paradis.[60] Yet such rules were not hard and fast. In Orléans, for instance, the widow of a printer and the wife of an apothecary could be found sitting with royal officers and nobles in the "queen's box."[61]

Women paid for more expensive theater seats at least in part because the distinctions that came with theater seating held greater social significance for women than for men. Whereas elite male spectators were relatively free to move throughout the playhouse and even to stand in the parterre if they chose, women faced more constraints. Mrs. Cradock, for example, hardly considered sitting anywhere but in the first boxes. One evening in Montpellier, however, she and two companions could only get seats in the amphitheater, "where society ladies never go except on Sunday nights when the house is generally full."[62] Because the night in question was a Sunday and the tickets she would normally have bought were already sold out, she felt that she could accept this seat, which she found to be excellent. In Reims, seating for women within the proposed new playhouse proved a significant concern for the members of the joint-stock society. Members feared that with just two rows of boxes seating the playhouse would be insufficiently stratified: "our respectable bourgeois ladies would be mixed up (*confondues*) with ladies' maids."[63]

For elite women, getting mixed up—literally and figuratively—with their social inferiors threatened more than their social standing. Social boundaries also served to protect women's moral respectability in a space where not all were, in fact, respectable. Prostitutes displayed themselves provocatively before the crowd in public theaters in Bordeaux, Toulouse, and Marseille, among other cities. When the famed womanizer Giovanni Giacomo Casanova traveled to Marseille in 1760, he puzzled over the fact that four of the first boxes on either side of the playhouse were filled with pretty and well-dressed women without a single man among them. Then, during the first entr'acte, this mystery was solved as "*messieurs* of all classes approached these boxes with familiarity" to set up sexual rendezvous. He soon seized the opportunity to invite one of these women to "sup" with him, an engagement that was sealed when he paid her a gold Louis in advance for the pleasure of her company.[64] In the view of one chronicler of theatrical life in Bordeaux, the presence of these prostitutes effectively threatened the virtue of all women in the playhouse:

> It is humiliating for virtuous *citoyennes* to compromise themselves next to these courtesans; they do not even dare to present themselves in the boxes, for fear of blushing before strangers who, by mistake, insult their modesty. Always attached to their household, they must deprive them- selves of innocent pleasures to protect the integrity of their reputation; because a respectable woman who, out of inclination and taste, would follow the theater, and who would not enjoy a distinguished fortune, would authorize a critic to doubt her morals.[65]

In an attempt to prevent this kind of harassment and disorder, Bordeaux restricted prostitutes to certain boxes in the house, and forbade men from sitting in these boxes or talking lewdly with these women. Men apparently arranged meetings in the warming room (*chauffoir*) instead.[66]

Concerns about the company respectable women might be forced to keep at the theater may well have suppressed women's overall rates of theater attendance. While attending a performance in Toulouse, even the intrepid Mrs. Cradock was "chased" from the playhouse before the end of the per- formance by the heat and tumult of the crowd, but above all by "the cava- lier behavior of a woman occupying our box."[67] The theater's reputation as a space of libertinism, contemporaries found, was not without merit. This made it all the easier for Rousseau and other influential moralists of the era to trumpet the dangers that theatrical attendance posed to girls and women and, by extension, to the family and society as a whole.[68] The rowdiness of fellow spectators proved another source of concern. In Poitiers, for instance, accord- ing to one resident, "Many women, especially of high society, absented them- selves from this type of amusement, some from scruple, the others because of the private scenes that often came to trouble the order [of the playhouse]. It was above all to the theater that officers and students took their quarrels."[69]

In spite of such concerns, however, women did participate regularly as spectators in provincial playhouses. Indeed, public theaters offered women spectators new opportunities for cultural consumption and for participa- tion in urban public life at a time when institutions of the public sphere such as provincial academies and Masonic lodges typically remained closed to them.[70] By actively recruiting women and openly facilitating sociability between men and women, theaters provide an important example of an institution of the public sphere that was neither premised on the exclusion of women nor inherently masculine. In fact, evidence suggests that during the final decades of the Old Regime women's theater spectatorship grew substantially.[71]

At the same time, it is undeniable that a significant majority of spectators in all provincial playhouses were male. Men rented boxes and purchased subscriptions at much higher rates than women.[72] Military subscriptions added to this gender imbalance, as did the hundreds of tickets dedicated for men alone in the parterre. At the theater, if women's presence provided a gauge of the success of an evening this was precisely because women constituted a visible minority. In other words, the remarkable expansion of performing arts culture in urban France was paid for primarily by an increase in cultural consumption by men—elites as well as those of the middling and the more prosperous working classes. If, as scholars have argued, material consumption during the late Old Regime was increasingly associated with women, cultural consumption—at the theater and perhaps elsewhere—presents a noteworthy exception to this emerging gender norm.[73] These predominantly male customers, moreover, approached a night at the theater as much more than a spectator sport.

The Show Begins

What did customers experience when they came to the theater for an evening of entertainment? During the late eighteenth century, public theaters provided the setting for an experience that, in spite its differences, took on similar contours throughout France. As showtime neared, carriages and sedan chairs crowded the entrances and the side streets of provincial playhouses, delivering elegantly dressed passengers.[74] Audience members of more modest means arrived on foot, attempting not to sully their theater attire and shoes as they carefully picked their way through streets that were often muddy and foul. On especially popular evenings, such as the opening and closing nights of the season, Sundays, and performances by visiting actors or singers, finding a seat could present a challenge and spectators did well to arrive in advance. For typical performances, however, those with subscriptions frequently came and went at their leisure over the course of the evening.

In most houses, the curtain rose promptly at 5:30 p.m. Directors made sure of this, for when a performance was delayed, the police might be called to investigate and whoever was responsible for the delay would be fined.[75] As spectators found their places, candles and oil lamps illuminated the house. The auditorium typically remained lighted during the show. This meant that theatergoers could observe the performance onstage as well as one another, a key interest of contemporaries.[76]

Investors, architects, and urban authorities, this book has shown, put great efforts into the design and decoration of playhouses, often deliberately setting out to achieve a new elegance through brightly painted interiors and stage curtains, as well as sculptures and other adornments. Even for those theatergoers who set out to purchase a luxury commodity, however, they did not necessarily buy comfort. A significant portion of the audience, namely the men in the parterre, stood on their feet for the three to four hours that performances typically lasted. Spectators—even those in the boxes—could find themselves uncomfortably crowded, jostling for space. The temperature was another challenge. In the winter, playhouses could be drafty and cold.[77] Yet perhaps worse than the cold was the heat: a playhouse packed with hundreds of spectators could become stiflingly hot, likely due to a combination of poor ventilation and excess body heat. During a performance in Marseille at which not a single seat was free, Mrs. Cradock described the heat as intolerable, so much so that she and her companions left before the end of the performance.[78] A spectator in Montpellier noted in his journal that "the heat was so strong at the theater that a fellow found fourteen candies melted in his candy box. I saw it."[79]

When the performance began, the quality and range of the performers and the sophistication of sets, costumes, and machinery varied significantly from city to city. Within the contested cultural hierarchy of the late eighteenth century, Lyon, Bordeaux, and Marseille consistently came out on top. These cities featured talent of the highest caliber as well as great diversity in offerings. After these three, larger cities with regular theater companies and wealthier publics fared better, generally speaking, than small cities with traveling troupes. Such differences can be gauged in the diaries of travelers. When in Montpellier, Mrs. Cradock praised the quality of the musical concerts and greatly admired a ballet that was well conducted and majestically executed, concluding that she had not seen anything better in the genre.[80] In Saumur, in contrast, she found nothing good to say about the performance she attended in what she described as an old barn made of planks, lit by chandeliers with just three tallow candles and lamps stinking of fat. (The playhouse, built by the joint-stock society, would not open for several years.) The orchestra consisted of one miserable musician playing a violin with three strings. Of the performance itself, her notes are terse: "A bad play, and all the actors, excepting one, even worse."[81] Arthur Young, too, had very different experiences at the theaters that he attended while traveling in France. He gave very high praise to the Rouen theater company and in particular admired the talents of an actress named Madame de Fresne. In fact, this troupe impressed him so greatly that he came away convinced of the superiority of French theater to that of his native England "in the number of good performers, and in the paucity of bad ones; and in the quantity of dancers, singers, and persons on whom the business of the theatre depends, all established on a great scale."[82] Yet in Besançon, the "miserable performers" gave him cause to qualify his enthusiasm for the French stage. Displeased with the city in general and in a bad mood, he found that the "bawling, and squeaking of *l'Épreuve Villageoise* . . . had no power to put [him] in better humour."[83]

During performances such as these, the stage itself was often crowded with spectators. Although stage seating was banned at the Comédie-Française in 1759, this practice continued elsewhere in France. At times, the presence of too many well-to-do customers made it difficult to place the scenery and props and left too little room for the actors to perform. During an oversold performance benefiting a particularly popular actress in Nantes, the police estimated that sixty *additional* people had crowded onto the stage, leaving us to wonder what the total number seated there might have been.[84] Such crowds blocked the view of those in the parterre, at times sparking cries of protest. Contemporaries also complained that these audience members distracted from the focus on the performance. This was particularly true when they made themselves part of the entertainment. During a performance of the opéra-comique *Le Tonnelier* in Nantes, for example, a ship captain named Carret was seated on one of the front rows of benches on the stage. During a scene in which an actress set down a basket and delivered the line "Look, here is a cake and a bottle of wine . . . let's have our snack," Carret reached out, lifted the basket's lid, and helped himself to a brioche. Those in the parterre responded by clapping, whistling, and shouting "O the glutton!"[85]

Such active engagement in the performance and lively commentary by spectators appears widely in contemporary accounts. Police reports, journals, and other sources document a wide array of audience behaviors and misbehaviors. Rather than sitting quietly during the performance, spectators often talked loudly. According to one contemporary, in the south of France, a theater was considered "a public space" in which "everyone talks, sings, and cries as freely as on a large street." Spectators with subscriptions turned their boxes into "salons," while women and girls sitting in the orchestra gossiped about who had delivered a baby, who had sent away a servant, and who had lost their dog.[86] Everywhere, spectators interrupted shows freely by clapping and with laughter, shouts, boos, catcalls, insults, chants, and whistles. At times, spectators stood on the benches and used them to jump from one area to another, threw fruit at performers and spectators alike, pushed, shoved, danced, took seats among the musicians, and deliberately tried to make the performers and stage spectators laugh.[87] They heckled performers, as when a spectator loudly accused an actor of skipping lines and then shouted "if you don't know your role, take up a book." Members of the audience disrupted performances by pounding canes. On one occasion, they even blasted away on toy trumpets that the offenders had bought at the fair.[88]

Spectators drew on this extensive repertoire of responses—and added to it—not only to amuse themselves by making mischief, although this was apparently one common motivation.[89] They also did so to influence theatrical production. Audience members rewarded their favorites with thunderous applause, cheers, and demands for good roles, encore performances, and even benefit performances in their favor. At the theater in Rouen, Mrs. Thrale was greatly amused by "a Riot" in favor of an actress. In her mind, the fervor displayed that evening topped even that of the notoriously uproarious London crowds: "I never heard so much Violence expressed on any Occasion during my twenty Years acquaintance with the Stage."[90]

Spectators seem to have been even more inclined to shout down actors or plays that were not to their liking. In large cities with resident troupes, cabals in which spectators organized in advance to celebrate or criticize a play or performer were not uncommon.[91] Typically the cabalists, often drawing on support from others in the house, used the sifflet to try to prevent an actor from performing or a play from beginning. Actresses and actors might appear before the crowd multiple times, but each time they would be "obliged to retire by the cries, boos, and whistles of the parterre."[92] Audiences also creatively varied their signs of disapproval. During one cabal in Bordeaux, when the targeted actor first appeared on the stage, "there arose a surprising noise that was made by dint of coughing, spitting, or blowing noses, which lasted during all the time that he remained on the stage, with the result that one could not hear one word of his role."[93] In Rouen, cabals disrupted performances so frequently that authorities implemented guidelines for how to respond. Actors were instructed to continue the performance "regardless of the noise that the parterre could make; however, if the tumult becomes too loud, they will retire in the hallways until it has calmed down. They will reappear then up to three times, and if silence has not been reestablished, the actors and actresses will retire definitively," and the curtain would come down.[94]

Theater customers cared a great deal about what was performed and who performed it. When performers canceled unexpectedly due to illness, crowds protested vehemently—so much so that police were known to go to the homes of performers to verify that they were in fact too sick to perform or, if not, to escort them back to the playhouse.[95] Last-minute changes in repertory, usually due to the illness of a cast member, almost invariably elicited unrest and protests. This was true even when changes were relatively small. During a performance of *La Rosière* in Bordeaux, for example, when a dance number that typically concluded the work was omitted, angry spectators hurled apples at the troupe's dance master. The crowd remained in the playhouse for several hours, and in the tumult several chairs were broken.[96] Spectators expected that they would get what they paid for. When they felt the contract between director and spectator had been broken, they did not hesitate to express their displeasure. To minimize such events, local authorities pressured directors and actors to deliver precisely what they advertised or else face fines or even imprisonment.[97]

Interestingly, police reports demonstrate that audiences used the sifflet for more than targeting performers or particular works. It was also directed toward fellow spectators. Parterre audiences in particular took it upon themselves to call out those who disturbed the show or their fellow spectators. When a spectator wore his hat during the show, for example, an act that was prohibited by theater regulations as well as by tradition, the audience invariably took notice. Hats blocked the view of other spectators; removing one's hat was also a sign of respect.[98] From Beauvais to Bayonne, audiences joined in calling for the removal of hats, shouting chants such as "Hat off [*Bas le chapeau*]!" or even "Hat off or they will not perform [*Chapeau bas, ou l'on ne jouera pas*]!"[99] Another frequently chanted refrain, "Make room on the stage [*Place au théâtre*]!," called upon stage spectators to stop crowding the actors.[100] The repertory of cries employed by theater audiences included many others directed at fellow spectators, including: Quiet there! Silence! Get down! Make way for the ladies! and others.[101] Such public reprimands frequently proved effective. At times, however, they merely generated hostility. Young military officers in particular resented being told what to do by a crowd of civilians and commoners. In Clermont-Ferrand, a cavalry officer sitting in one of the first boxes was talking so loudly with his neighbor that the two disrupted the actors. One of the guards at the theater asked him repeatedly to quiet down, and the parterre spectators eventually added their own calls for silence. The officer yelled back, "Go f . . . yourself, parterre!"[102] The parterre erupted in such a fury that the police worried that a riot might ensue. Such fears of rioting crowds were realized in Marseille during the spring of 1766. When, despite repeated calls to make space for the actors, spectators sitting on the stage, including several army officers, refused to move, parterre spectators began to throw oranges and apples at them. The officers responded by throwing the fruit back at the parterre spectators. They followed this up with chairs, candles, and stage lamps. A general melee ensued.[103]

Recent scholarship has argued that during the late Old Regime a cultural shift was already under way in French playhouses that would transform these passionate, loud, and frequently disorderly early modern audiences into the silent, respectful observers and listeners of the modern era.[104] Such work points to a series of innovations in theatrical production in the capital as contributing to this process of pacifying spectators. The removal of stage seating from the Paris playhouses at midcentury rendered the stage the domain of the performers alone, creating a greater physical and psychological separation between actors and audience. Technological advances enabled the royal theaters to illuminate the stage more brightly and the auditorium more dimly. Benches were installed to seat (and calm) rowdy parterre audiences. Together, scholars argue, measures such as these helped to establish a conceptual "fourth wall" between actors and spectators—and new expectations regarding the relationship between the audience and the performers on stage.

As late as the 1780s, however, the vast majority of spectators in France appear to have been untouched by such reforms. They were hardly content to sit quietly and "gaze in rapt attention at the actors who ignore them."[105] In fact, more strongly than ever, the members of the rapidly growing provincial public conceived of themselves as actors with a legitimate role to play, if not in the performance itself then in the business of theater as it was more broadly conceived.[106] According to a widely shared consensus, praising or condemning a performance and even reprimanding fellow spectators constituted customary responses to which all customers were entitled. Contemporaries recognized this commercial logic, even when they did not approve: "It is an old prejudice that each parterre spectator for his twelve sous acquires upon entering [the playhouse] the right to dispense justice, either to the actors who displease him, or to the spectators whom he does not believe to behave there with a tolerable decency. The boos, the whistles, the throwing of an orange or an apple are the sentences that this judge issues."[107] Directors, urban magistrates, and even military commanders would find it difficult indeed to challenge the moral economy of the playhouse.[108]

The Problem of Discipline

Both local and royal authorities, this book has shown, found many reasons to embrace the institutionalization of theater in French cities. An important element of theater's appeal rested in the potential for displays of authority, which made it an ideal terrain in which to perform political power.[109] The theater, in fact, has proved a popular metaphor for historians describing the political culture of the absolutist Old Regime, an era when royal power, at least in theory, "was acted out before a passive audience."[110]

The problem of discipline in France's playhouses stemmed from the fact that even when confronted with ritual displays of authority—and indeed even when in the presence of armed guards—theater audiences were far from passive. In France, the political and social challenges posed by unruly theater crowds date back at least as far as the sixteenth century, when urban authorities began to crack down on the student and festive societies that performed farces, citing the dangers of urban strife and even violence.[111] In the eighteenth century, disciplining theater audiences once again emerged as a significant concern. In these more formal playhouses, with hundreds and even thousands in attendance, acts such as the sifflet that had been largely tolerated began to appear as dangerous license that threatened public order. What audiences perceived as legitimate forms of protest, representatives of royal authority castigated as insubordination that, in the words of one governor, "greatly resembles a type of sedition."[112]

In most cities the responsibility for maintaining public order during performances, and therefore for disciplining theater patrons, fell to the municipality. Local police and bourgeois militias in France were charged with more than preventing and investigating crime. They also assumed responsibility for prohibiting unlawful assemblies and for upholding "the obedience due to His Majesty," both of which informed their approaches to policing public playhouses.[113] In cities with large garrisons the city shared with the army the duty to maintain public order. Due to the large numbers of soldiers and officers who held subscriptions for theaters, the king instructed garrison commanders to take measures to ensure that officers observe "the greatest propriety" in the playhouse and that order be maintained.[114] To the consternation of certain municipal authorities, this at times provided an excuse for the military to take theater policing into its own hands.[115] For the most part, however, policies regarding inappropriate audience behaviors and decisions concerning their enforcement were determined locally.

The first step when confronting disorderly audiences was to issue formal regulations prohibiting inappropriate behaviors in the playhouse. Outside of Paris, where the policing of the royal theaters became a priority of the court in the 1690s, the earliest theater ordinances appeared in cities such as Marseille and Bordeaux in the 1720s.[116] It was only in the second half of the century, however, coinciding with the widespread establishment of public theaters in the provinces, that formal regulations became common for almost every public theater. These were often issued or revised at the inauguration of a new playhouse.[117] Initially most regulations stressed the common theme of preventing the disruption of the performance. For example, in an early regulation for the Bordeaux theater from 1745, the city forbade spectators "to commit any violence, indecency, or other disorder on entering or leaving, to shout and make noise before the show begins, to whistle and boo during the intermission, and to interrupt the actors during the performances, in whatever manner and under whatever pretext it might be" on penalty of the very substantial fine of five hundred livres.[118] Expectations governing audience behavior evolved over the course of the century. By the late 1750s, Bordelais faced prohibitions that extended to more minor misdeeds that might trouble the performance, such as wearing hats after the curtain was raised, standing in the amphitheater, sitting in stage seats in indecent postures, crowding the hallways, or crossing the stage during the performance.[119] In subsequent decades regulations continued to grow more detailed. By the late 1780s some provincial theater regulations specified as many as fifty or more articles concerning the actions of spectators as well as those of the actors and musicians in the troupe.[120] These regulations, moreover, often gave local police or guards considerable discretion, even more than that granted to the soldiers who policed the royal playhouses in Paris.[121]

Although the policing of France's theaters has usually been characterized as a state concern, royal authorities and municipal officials were not the only ones invested in defining standards of acceptable behavior.[122] Directors and investors, too, had a stake in clarifying policies for their patrons. Disorder and rowdiness could drive away clientele. Cabals could demoralize actors and add burdensome expenses when directors were deprived of using actors they had already hired, or when audiences demanded that new talent be added to the theater troupe. In Nantes, the shareholders who financed the local theater company actually drafted the city's first theater ordinance themselves and presented the regulations to the city, requesting that they be enacted and posted. The city complied, making only minimal changes.[123] In Valenciennes, the city consulted the shareholders of the theater troupe in the process of drafting regulations.[124] In Nîmes, in an unusual arrangement, the shareholders, through their representatives, participated directly in maintaining order and safeguarding their new playhouse.[125]

When surveying provincial theater regulations, two developments from the 1770s and 1780s stand out as meriting closer attention. First, we see greater attention to explaining the reciprocal rights and responsibilities of the administration and the patron. Regulations defined the traditional relationship between actors and audiences in increasingly contractual language. Spectators were often informed that they would not be allowed to move to more expensive seats without paying an additional fee and that they needed a countermark to leave the theater and reenter during the same evening. Some regulations also specified the circumstances under which customers might demand a refund. In some cities, customers were assured that they would be treated fairly and equally for their money, as in Lille, where new regulations guaranteed that "no subscription in the terms and at the price and conditions fixed above can be refused."[126]

Second, ordinances increasingly reached beyond disruptive acts to address behaviors that offended sensibilities. This can be seen as an attempt to establish a higher level of decorum within cultivated surroundings that were central to elite sociability and also reflective of the cultural status of a city. When the lavish new Grand Théâtre opened in Bordeaux, the city articulated its own ideal social geography, while promoting luxury and display as integral to the theatergoing experience. The implementation of a dress code was central to this effort. It seems that those who could afford to attend the theater, including even those sitting in the most prominent and expensive seats, were not always dressing the part. "The porters and interior sentinels," new regulations proclaimed, "will see to it that no one enters who is not decently dressed, each relative to the seat that they propose to occupy." "As a consequence," they continued, "it is expressly forbidden to all people to present themselves in a *redingote* [a fitted frock coat] or *manteau* [an outdoor coat] anywhere other than the parterre, upper balcony, or second boxes." Those sitting in more illustrious seats were instructed to check these outer garments.[127] Boots were to be permitted only in the parterre and second boxes, and to military men in uniform in other restricted areas, "but never," the regulations emphasized, "in the galleries, balconies, or first boxes."[128] In 1783, the Swiss guard in Bordeaux was instructed that all women, even mothers, were to be denied entry to the theater if they were not wearing the formal dress known as a *robe*.[129] In Orléans, as well, the city complained of "abuses" taking place during performances, with people sitting on stage and in the boxes wearing clothing that "is not decent there."[130] We see concerns for civility expressed in the regulations for the new Nantes playhouse, inaugurated in 1788, which specifically prohibited spectators from relieving their bodily needs anywhere except in the toilets. In provincial cities, those responsible for policing were instructed to remove not only spectators "who would disturb [*troubleraient*] the performance" but also those "who will not comport themselves with the appropriate decency [*la décence convenable*]."[131]

Authorities who held out hopes of subduing and civilizing theater audiences soon found that regulations alone did not effectively change audience behaviors. Already in the 1740s, the city council and police of Bordeaux expressed their frustration that "although many regulations have been made that establish good order in the theater, as much for the actors and actresses as for the spectators, still it remains . . . that many people give themselves license to interrupt the actors and actresses, and to trouble the performances."[132] Similar concerns were echoed in Nantes in the 1770s. In spite of existing theater regulations local authorities complained that "for some time disorder and license have been introduced in the theater, and have been taken to such a point that something that should be an object of honest recreation and peaceful amusement has become an occasion of indecency and tumult."[133] The sheer frequency with which theater ordinances were reissued—no fewer than thirty appeared in Bordeaux between 1720 and 1789—speaks to the persistent difficulties in enforcing them.[134]

Around midcentury, urban authorities began to adopt the step of heightened policing. This escalation of force in the provincial playhouse began in the 1750s, after the king stationed armed soldiers inside the royal playhouses of Paris. Over the next few decades the practice of placing militia or guards in theaters was widely adopted throughout France. But whereas the royal stages typically employed a minimum of forty to sixty soldiers to accomplish their policing duties, a number that might be increased to two hundred or more for special performances, in Bordeaux, the site of one of the largest provincial playhouses, the theater was frequently policed with as few as six guards.[135] If even in Paris, the most heavily policed city in France, the king struggled to restrain theater audiences, in provincial cities authorities encountered challenges that were in some ways even more daunting.

To begin with, policing a theater was no easy task. Audiences nearly doubled in size in France's largest cities between the 1760s and the 1780s, making for larger and more anonymous crowds. The police in Nantes repeatedly acknowledged the difficulties they faced in identifying those who were responsible for disrupting a performance, particularly when a large number of individuals joined in.[136] Further, it was one matter to discipline an individual and quite another to bring to order several hundred or more. As a rule, police or soldiers typically resorted to picking out one or a small handful of the principal troublemakers and making arrests.[137] Usually, such a restrained show of force brought order to the crowd, allowing the performance to continue. The individuals who were arrested might be fined, or, less frequently, imprisoned.[138] In cases when police could find no ringleaders or when they felt complaints to be justified, authorities either addressed the cause for the disruption—for example, by arresting an individual who provoked the audience by refusing to quiet down or to remove his hat—or they simply waited for the crowd to quiet down.[139] For the public, this policing strategy had the consequence that the majority of those who whistled, shouted, or otherwise expressed their opinions seem to have faced no disciplinary action at all.

In fact, for theater crowds, the sifflet and the cabal proved quite effective tools. Directors understood all too well that they ignored audience sentiment at their own peril. They also faced pressure from local authorities to keep their customers happy.[140] When directors responded to audience demands for specific shows or favorite actresses, spectators found their efforts validated. Meanwhile, spectators developed creative ways to assert their right to critically engage in the performance that kept them one step ahead of the authorities. In the 1780s, for example, spectators who were officially prohibited from using the sifflet began throwing verses and letters onto the stage and demanding that the actors read them aloud.[141] These missives literally gave a voice to the public, as recognized in Lyon where the authorities complained that "everyone [wants] to make use of this to make his opinion known."[142] The problem was that although some notes praised actors or actresses, others "contained mortifying criticisms."[143] In cities such as Lyon, Metz, Lille, Bordeaux, Nantes, and Brest, this practice was condoned—in some cases for a number of years—before it was eventually prohibited.[144]

By tacitly acknowledging the right to commentary and tolerating a variety of forms of expression, authorities sent their audiences mixed messages. The duc de Richelieu made this point when he repeatedly reprimanded the municipal officers of Bordeaux for what he saw as laxity in enforcing the very laws that they themselves had established. "On many occasions," he admonished, "you have been so weak of spirit and of means that you have allowed scandalous tumults to continue with impunity, in the theater in particular."[145] He asked them to consider the effect it had on the public when the city permitted spectators to transgress the theater regulations so publicly.[146]

Although royal officers frequently shared Richelieu's contempt for the alleged inability of municipal forces to master turbulent theater crowds, the military proved no more effective at maintaining public peace in the theaters under its jurisdiction.[147] On those exceptional occasions when armed soldiers did attempt to restrain a theater crowd through the use of force, the results were often disastrous. As was the case with other eighteenth-century crowds, when policing actions violated audiences' sense of their customary rights, they were much more likely to resist.[148] In the 1770s and 1780s, attempts by royal soldiers to stop spectators from engaging in such traditional behaviors as demanding the performance of a different work, tapping their feet to music and playing games, and calling for a hat to be taken off provoked bloody skirmishes in playhouses in Marseille, Angers, and Beauvais.[149] Scholars such as Jeffrey Ravel have drawn attention to these violent encounters, in which the very soldiers entrusted with maintaining order in playhouses aggressively attacked spectators, striking them with bayonets and even discharging their weapons. In two such cases, Marseille and Angers, military authorities claimed perhaps disingenuously that tense confrontations escalated unexpectedly when soldiers mistakenly believed they had encountered armed resistance from men in the parterre. The same could not be said for the incident in Beauvais, where a young army officer who felt that he had been insulted by the crowd leapt into the parterre with several companions to seek revenge.[150] In each of these cases, significant numbers of spectators sustained serious injuries. In Marseille and Beauvais spectators died from their injuries. The outcry from local citizens was fierce and immediate. As Ravel has shown, criticism was cast in a politicized language that decried such tactics as "armed tyranny."[151]

When word of these tragically mishandled affairs reached Versailles, the crown was not pleased. The king sought order in French playhouses, not incompetence resulting in bloodshed. Investigations were launched. In Marseille and Angers, the military was stripped of policing duties in the playhouse, which were restored to municipal authorities. The officers responsible for a spectator's death in Beauvais were imprisoned and the theater there was closed.[152] Such catastrophic failures constituted object lessons in the dangers of using violent force to confront theater audiences, mistakes that municipal and royal officials in these cities and others sought to avoid in the future.[153]

Such incidents of violent repression are best understood, in a new light, not as representative of the French state's relationship with the provincial theater public, but rather as exceptions that prove the rule of the guarded permissiveness of these new cultural arenas.[154] After years and in some cases decades of loosely enforced ordinances, spectators in these cities believed themselves to be exercising their legitimate authority, and the community supported them. As late as the 1780s, the problem of order and discipline remained unresolved. There was widespread acknowledgement that spectators in France's large cities were "naturally lively, impatient, and sometimes undisciplined, and as a consequence difficult to contain without a vigilant and even severe police."[155] Yet when the very individuals who policed provincial theaters complained that "for some time these sorts of indecencies are committed in almost all the performances, which bothers the actors and prevents the fans from enjoying the beauty of the performance," they implicitly recognized the ineffectiveness of the strategies they employed.[156] To successfully contest spectators' deeply held commercial values, authorities needed to be both able and willing to dominate theater audiences. During the final years of the Old Regime, as we will see, they often proved themselves to be neither.

Commercial Protest and the Rights of the Public

Nowhere is the confident and shared consumerist sensibility of provincial theater spectators more evident than in the strikes and boycotts staged by ardent and angry spectators in the 1780s. In these cases, when theater patrons felt that police unduly restricted their critical expression, they expanded their repertoire of protest to apply pressure on directors where it most hurt—the bottom line. Daily ticket sales, after all, remained the primary source of income for theater companies. Organized strikes effectively captured the attention of directors and authorities alike. The best documented and most successful of these strikes took place in Rouen in 1787. This episode sheds light on the motivations and convictions of those involved in the protest as well as the ways in which they leveraged their authority as consumers to shape local cultural offerings. Remarkably, the Rouen strike also demonstrates the extent to which local and even royal officials proved willing to tolerate organized protests by the theater public rather than risking a violent clash that might further alienate the public and even threaten the theater with bankruptcy.

On the opening night of the new theater season in Rouen in 1787, a group of theater devotees who were frustrated with the management's unresponsiveness and dissatisfied with the overall quality of the entertainment provided by the city's resident theater troupe threw a letter onto the stage and demanded that it be read aloud. An actor named Bérard, undoubtedly unaware of the contents, complied. "To the public," the missive began, "Messieurs, the moment, the circumstances, all is favorable, all leads us to explain ourselves freely. This statement does not include the ideas of a single individual; they are those of many people who dare to flatter themselves that these same ideas will be indebted to yours. With this supposition, permit us, messieurs, to use the collective word *we*."[157] In deliberately provocative and often offensive language, the letter laid out an extensive agenda of reform for the troupe, one of many that were under the direction of Mademoiselle Montansier and her partner Neuville. The crowd listened as the actor read harsh criticisms of the cast members, including demands "that this pretty boy, so vain, so proud, so insolent, and with so little merit, that the other [actor] so inclined to drink, so disgusting for those with whom he is on stage, so tattered and so indecent, never again perform before our eyes." With regard to several younger players in the troupe, the statement proclaimed that the

public would no longer tolerate "children," adding, "we demand professionals *(sujets)* and not students."[158] Among the demands presented, the call for
a ballet corps featured prominently.[159] Because neither La Montansier nor
Neuville resided in Rouen, the excited crowd demanded a response from the
troupe's manager Walleville. The president of the parlement, however, prohibited Walleville from appearing before the public. Instead, guards moved
in to break up the protest, arresting one troublemaker, a candymaker who
was sentenced to serve eight days in jail and pay a fine of twenty livres, and
fining several others ten livres apiece.[160]

Two days later, with no official response from the directors, these frustrated theater critics unveiled a new and more ambitious plan. They decided
to place economic pressure on the theater's management, calling for a boycott
of the theater until their demands were addressed. They produced handwritten notices, songs, and other materials to publicize their cause. One such
notice, entitled "Decision of the Parterre," announced: "Seeing the unjust
pretensions of the police, given the lack of capacity of the actors who make
up the troupe of this city, the young people are asked to abstain from going to
the theater until the manager has satisfied the will of the public. Deliberated
18 April 1787."[161] Another piece proclaimed that the "good citizen" and
the "true patriot" would not go to the theater until the public had received
its due.[162] These announcements and others clearly expressed anger at La
Montansier and Neuville for their apparent disregard for their customers'
opinions and for what was deemed the inadequate quality of the entertainment they provided. Yet they also lashed out at the city magistrates and
parlementary authorities for what was widely perceived as oppressive action
that violated audience rights.[163]

To enforce the strike, the protesters organized demonstrations outside of
the playhouse, using personal intimidation to turn back potential customers. When the police forbade the blocking of access to the theater, a small
number lingered nearby, quietly taking note of all who went in. Anonymous
pamphlets then attacked those who did not honor the boycott, ridiculing
them as spies or whores. Songs set to popular tunes mocked the theater
manager, various actors, and the police lieutenant, while celebrating the boycott.[164] The strike proved devastatingly effective. The vicomte Dulau, the
military commander in Rouen, estimated that within a few days fewer than
fifty spectators, including the soldiers of the garrison, had attended the performance. Not long after, this number had dropped to fewer than twenty.[165]
More than two weeks into the strike, the editor of the *Journal de Normandie*
noted "the ennui that seems to reign over this great city since the theater is
deserted."[166] Such widespread adherence to this prohibition was motivated

by more than intimidation. Authorities acknowledged that the cause was "tacitly approved by the vast majority of people of the city, who would like to have a better theater."[167] Municipal and royal officers, as well as the theater's directors, watched anxiously as a relatively minor incident in the playhouse escalated into a public protest that threatened to severely damage the finances of the resident theater troupe and that flouted their authority.

Dulau reproached the municipality for allowing the situation to escalate and reminded local authorities that public protests could not be tolerated under any circumstances.[168] This makes it all the more remarkable that he deliberately refrained from using force.[169] In fact, he recommended that the demands of the protesters should be met. He explained in a letter to the royal governor, the duc d'Harcourt, "I believe that if Madame Montancier [*sic*] would come to Rouen (not however with her associate who is infinitely hated), that she bring with her a good tenor and a good female singer, which is very necessary here, these two roles being very badly filled, that she say some respectable things to the public, and that she promise to look for ways to please [the public] and to do even better, that all would end advantageously for her, and for the tranquility of all." He assured Versailles that a company of grenadiers was ready nightly to march on the theater, yet remained firm that a direct confrontation with the crowd should be avoided: "I would really rather not be obliged to make too much use of force, and I believe that it is easy for Madame Montancier to calm everything by taking the simplest means and those that for her will surely be the most lucrative. I really fear that, without this step, she will see her revenue diminish considerably and that all this will give us trouble."[170] Montansier was indeed losing hundreds of livres or more each day. If the public were further incited, bankruptcy would only be a matter of time. Winning back spectators' approval through gestures of goodwill seemed to this commander the most effective way to restore order while also supporting theater in the city.

In the event, Montansier and the authorities saw eye to eye. Walleville informed the directrice, then in Versailles, of these events, sending on a copy of the petition that had been thrown on the stage. (At the same time, she also received orders from the authorities, presumably demanding that she do whatever was necessary to resolve the conflict quickly, that she "hastened to execute.")[171] Montansier made her plan of action clear in a contrite public letter that was published in the *Journal de Normandie*. She responded point by point to the demands presented on opening night. Because Mademoiselle Montansier had numerous actors and singers already in her employ in the various companies that she directed, she could relocate talent quickly and with relatively little cost. Several new performers, she wrote, were already on their way to Rouen, including two female leading singers, Mademoiselle Verdelet and Mademoiselle Guérin, as well as a male lead, Sieur Paulin. Most of those who had been targeted for removal would no longer appear in Rouen. She requested that the public give one singer a second chance, explaining, "Talent is *rare, very rare*, and above all with tenors; one does not find them." If the public would allow this individual to remain, she wrote, the management would ensure that he always appeared on stage in proper attire. She made no promises regarding ballet, however, which she described as "an object of excessive expense" that require her to raise ticket prices.[172] In this letter, La Montansier pointedly and repeatedly bowed to the authority of "le Public," assuring readers that she and Neuville were ready "to do everything to give [the public] new proof of our zeal and of our submission to its will."[173]

Controversy continued in Rouen for several weeks. The editors of the *Journal de Normandie* received a "substantial number" of letters responding to that of Mademoiselle Montansier, most of which sounded similar notes.[174] In one of those chosen for publication, a subscriber noted approvingly that he had seen "with the greatest surprise the tone that reigned in said letter" and Montansier's desire "to reconcile with the public." The letter continued, however, by pointing to those demands that La Montansier had not met, such as hiring dancers. This anonymous subscriber (*abonné*) ended the letter by offering a veiled threat. The director, following her own pecuniary interests, would surely decide to meet these demands and likely increase her income, "rather than expose herself to not having any spectators."[175] (After reading this letter, Montansier in fact requested official approval to raise ticket prices so as to pay for a ballet troupe.[176]) As the promised new actors and singers began to arrive, spectators returned to the Rouen playhouse bolstered by their success, so much so that Montansier and Neuville would face a second such protest just over a year later![177]

Both economically and politically, the theater boycott proved a clever strategy for provincial audiences. In the capital, scholars have argued, the establishment of royal theaters patronized and administered by the monarchy curtailed the economic authority of Parisian audiences over the actors and performances they attended. The King's Players, after all, served not only the public, they also served the crown.[178] In provincial cities, in contrast, the establishment of resident commercial theater companies can be seen as enhancing the economic authority of spectators vis-à-vis actors. In the era of traveling troupes, an audience's refusal to attend performances would have sent the actors packing, probably in short order. Further, small, collectively operated companies were limited in their ability to respond to consumer demands for different works or for new actors and singers. With the advent of large year-round troupes dependent almost entirely on box office revenue and subscriptions, spectators from Lille to Lyon found directors eager to listen to their suggestions and complaints, and often quick to respond. Directors, as we have seen, could not afford not to do so. In the 1780s, when audiences introduced the boycott as a tactic, they explicitly did so as "a punishment" against directors who resisted the will of the public.[179]

The boycott was politically savvy because, unlike the use of the sifflet or demonstrations in the playhouse itself, there was nothing technically illegal in refusing to attend theatrical performances. As the commander in Brest observed in the midst of a theatergoers' boycott during the spring of 1789, "the theater [is] still on the same footing as it had been since its creation; . . . the citizens [are] still their own masters, to come or not to come" to performances.[180] Even royal officials accepted the logic of the marketplace. At the same time, when spectators urged others to refrain from attending the theater until amends were made and reforms were undertaken to restore audience rights, it was clear to all that their message was more than economic and cultural—it was also political.

In Brest, where the navy still owned the Théâtre de la Marine and oversaw the policing of the audience, the politics of the boycott became especially evident.[181] Civilian outrage was sparked when naval authorities sought to ban the practice of throwing verses on stage, which they had previously allowed. On the closing night of the season, in early April 1789, the reading of such a verse was not permitted despite the enthusiasm of many young men from the town. When naval guards stepped in to arrest a man sitting in the parquet for calling out "the verses!" the audience rose up in support. A military officer responded by calling the guard to arms. The indignant spectators quickly emptied the theater. Crowds gathered in the streets, but were forced back. The individual who had been arrested was released just half an hour later. It seemed that order had been restored.[182] At this time, however, the assembly of the Third Estate was meeting in Brest to draw up their lists of grievances (*cahiers de doléances*) to submit to the king, and its representatives took up the cause. They demanded that civilians no longer be subjected to policing by the navy—what one petition denounced as the "humiliations" of "military despotism."[183]

Alienated by heavy-handed military policing techniques that seemed to infringe on spectators' right to express their opinions, the young citizens of the Third Estate led the public in launching a strike. The leaders of this action declared their refusal to return to the playhouse until policing policies were changed and their rights were ensured. Moreover, they prohibited other city residents from attending the theater. When the theater reopened in late April (following the annual closure), the urban community supported the protest, including even the municipal authorities. According to one observer, only a single townsman was noticed in the audience, and he was booed when he left.[184] The boycott lasted several weeks. In the midst of the strike, in negotiations intended to resolve the conflict, the city magistrates presented additional demands to the naval commander. Most sought greater sharing of authority over the public playhouse between the municipality and the navy. Yet, seeking to bring theater practices in the Brest in line with those else-where in France, they also demanded that the first boxes should be open on a first-come basis to any customer who was appropriately dressed and that such customers should not be displaced by anyone (presumably by aristocratic military officers).[185] Civilian audiences returned to the theater only after the naval commander offered conciliatory gestures to the municipal officers by pledging to review policing policies and to follow more closely the royal regulations applicable to public theaters in all French garrisons.[186] In this case, the consumer boycott provided a means to assert popular and municipal sovereignty over the performances taking place within the provincial theater that was most closely affiliated with the absolutist state.

The establishment of a French theater industry profoundly shaped con-sumer sensibilities in urban France. In flagrant violation of official prohibi-tions, a generation and more of theater customers loudly and confidently engaged actors, directors, fellow spectators, and even local and royal authori-ties—or watched as others did so. They set out to shape the performing arts locally and invoked consumer "rights" to legitimate their actions. The boycotts, demonstrations, and other audience actions staged during the 1780s in cities such as Bordeaux, Rouen, Brest, and even, as we will see, in the colo-nies, reveal an erosion of royal authority in France, particularly following the announcement that the Estates-General would be convened. Contempo-raries noted that the police were relaxing their severity, and the public took full advantage of this freer rein. "Never has the parterre enjoyed such a great license," a theater enthusiast in Bordeaux observed in the fall of 1788. "The [theater] public," he explained, "is in such an effervescence of patrio-tism, it would be dangerous to contradict it."[187] Municipal authorities in Marseille apparently agreed. During the spring of 1789, when an exhilarated public demanded that the city officers appear in their box for a performance of *La Partie de chasse d'Henri IV*, listen to patriotic speeches, and display a gift of a tapestry bearing the arms of the city and the crown, the local magistrates entertained serious misgivings. In particular, they worried about the unpre-dictable outcomes of a politicized event gathering crushing crowds, and the precedent that might be established in expecting the city officers to do the bidding of the people.[188] In spite of their unease, however, they felt they had little choice but to comply. The region, agitated by France's revolutionary political situation and in the midst of economic crisis, was being wracked by violent disturbances.[189] They justified this concession to the public by explaining that "the theater, forming a sizeable meeting, requires the greatest care to stop it from becoming a hotbed of fermentation and of disorder."[190]

The monarchy, for its part, endorsed such accommodations. Royal ministers urged local authorities to resolve boycotts and other audience protests quickly, and in such a way as to bring spectators back into the playhouse. In May of 1789, even as representatives to the Estates-General gathered in Versailles, the king's reform-minded finance minister, Jacques Necker, applauded Marseille's actions, which he characterized as politically advantageous given the turbulent circumstances. Cultivating the good will of the public, he wrote, would give the local authorities "more power to dissipate this spirit of insurrection that today is mixed with almost everything that is done in the name of the people." Necker went so far as to explicitly embrace a policy of acceding to audience demands that were deemed to be "well-founded." This was, he explained, "one of the best means of preventing unfounded demands and unjust resistance."[191] The voice of the theater public had been heard—and heeded—at the highest levels.

CHAPTER 7

The Production of Theater in the Colonies

In April 1766, the *Affiches Américaines* pub-
lished an article that celebrated the inauguration of a new public theater
in the city of Cap Français, Saint-Domingue, describing the playhouse in
detail. Although local residents had founded a private, amateur theater society more than twenty years earlier, and a professional theater troupe had
taken up residence two years prior, only at this point did Le Cap, as it was
known, come to enjoy a playhouse befitting its stature as the largest and
wealthiest of French colonial cities. On the interior, the theater, built by
a local entrepreneur named Arthaud, seems to have adhered closely to the
designs becoming popular in France. To gather the audience more closely
around the stage, the auditorium was laid out in an oval design reminiscent
of the Lyon playhouse. On each side of the playhouse ten first and second
boxes overlooked the stage, the orchestra, and parterre, and, at the rear of
the house, the amphitheater. The "king's box," used by the royal governor
general of the colony, boasted the arms of France and Navarre painted in
gold, as well as two tapestries embroidered with gold fleurs-de-lis, while the
intendant's box, located on the opposite side of the house, featured naval
themes. The blue stage curtain featured four genies: two represented comedy and tragedy, while two others held up a Latin legend declaring that
comedy corrects morals through the use of humor. The article enthusiastically announced that the Le Cap theater "more than fulfilled the idea that

one could have of what a theater should be"—an idea that was defined above all in reference to the metropole.[1]

In fact, Saint-Domingue's local newspaper might well have been describing one of the many new provincial playhouses opening at this time were it not for the final line of the article. The colonial nature of the Le Cap theater was betrayed with the announcement that "the rear amphitheater will be only for mulattoes and mulatresses."[2] Whereas in metropolitan France, new public theaters offered spectators of different ranks a remarkable equality of access, in every public playhouse in Saint-Domingue the *gens de couleur*—free people of color, often of mixed European and African ancestry—were officially denied entry to the "white" sections of the playhouse. Rather, they attended theatrical performances in areas set aside for people of color.[3] Although slave owners rented out their slave musicians to perform in the orchestra, those in bondage—who numbered nearly half a million by 1789— were not permitted to attend the theaters as spectators.[4]

To this point, this book has analyzed the development of new practices of theatrical production and consumption in the cities of France. Yet French plays and operas, designs for sets and costumes, and actors and directors were not constrained by the boundaries of the Hexagon. Nor were the new institutional models for funding and operating theaters—or the cultural habits and attitudes that they fostered. Indeed, when this new playhouse opened in Le Cap, the vogue for theater was already spreading quickly in France's most valuable colony. The cities of Port-au-Prince, Les Cayes, and even Léogane had recently welcomed professional theater companies, and a troupe would soon be established in Saint Marc.[5] Professional theater would be introduced in Martinique in 1771 and in Guadeloupe in 1772. By 1789, at least eleven cities in France's Caribbean and Indian Ocean colonies enjoyed dedicated public theaters.[6] Before the end of the colonial Old Regime, the *Affiches Américaines* would advertise more than two thousand dramatic productions performed in Saint-Domingue alone.[7] In fact, the French colonies at this time boasted the most extensive theater network in the Americas, with theatrical production surpassing that of the nascent troupes in the United States and rivaling even the well-established theaters in New Spain (modern-day Mexico).[8]

The rich terrain of colonial theater, explored by scholars such as Jean Fouchard, Bernard Camier, and Laurent Dubois, is particularly relevant for the study of the commercialization of the French stage and the role of the state in that process.[9] By comparing colonial institutional approaches and economic and cultural practices with those in the provinces, we can deepen our understanding of the new cultural economy emerging in the eighteenth

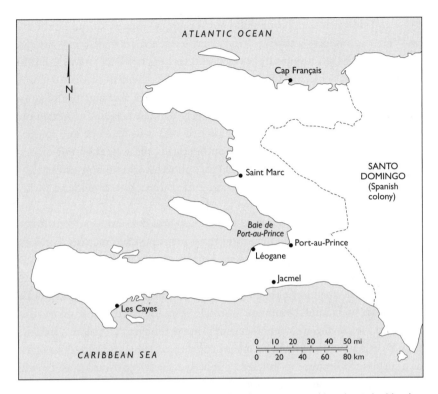

In Saint-Domingue, France's wealthiest colony, public theaters operated in at least six cities during the late Old Regime.

century and its influence on contemporary society.[10] Moreover, studying metropolitan and colonial theater practices in the same analytical frame casts new light on both the cultural continuities that drew the French empire closer together in the decades preceding the Revolution, and the cleavages that marked the colonies as a world apart.[11]

New colonial stages, as we will see, paralleled their provincial counterparts closely in many respects. In the cities of Saint-Domingue, as in most cities in France, it was local entrepreneurs, shareholders, directors, and actors who took the initiative in establishing and producing professional entertainment. From its origins, the commercial theater industry in the French Caribbean operated as an extension of metropolitan theater networks, a point that the press self-consciously emphasized. Nonetheless, important differences marked the cultural and social experience of theatergoing in Saint-Domingue. This chapter focuses on two distinctive aspects of colonial theater. First, for expatriates living thousands of miles away from France, as well as for Creoles born and raised in the colonies, the remarkable popularity of public theater was not expressed as a matter of civic pride or a marker of a city's status. Rather, theater was vaunted as a vital connection with the cultural life of France around which the colony's diverse—and divided—residents could rally. Although the Creole language, black characters, and specifically colonial themes did occasionally make their way to these stages, directors more often made a point of selling their audiences access to dramatic and musical performances that were presented as authentically metropolitan. For spectators living on the peripheries of the Francophone world, anxious about their own cultural and racial identity, attending the theater thus provided a means to affirm their Frenchness.[12]

The racial politics of theatrical production and consumption constituted a second and more striking departure from metropolitan practices. For even the most earnest attempts to re-create French theater in this Caribbean setting faltered when confronted with the racial hierarchy that defined so much of colonial life during the final decades of the Old Regime. To readers who are familiar with Saint-Domingue's brutal yet intensely profitable slave economy and the racialized society that supported it, the fact that colonial theaters would deliberately segregate people of color from whites is unlikely to come as a surprise. Theaters—politicized public spaces that gathered large crowds on a regular basis—in this way reinforced the predominant order of this plantation colony, one that increasingly distinguished free from unfree, and white from nonwhite. To borrow from Frederick Cooper and Ann Laura Stoler, the public theater provided an institution through which European colonists "fashioned their distinctions" and "conjured up their 'whiteness.'"[13] This formal hierarchy of race contrasts with the more fluid and contested hierarchies of status and wealth that predominated in most French provincial playhouses. Colonial theaters, in other words, offered customers a spectacle in which spectators of color participated as marginalized, second-class citizens.

What is surprising, given the increasingly exclusionary racial climate in Saint-Domingue during this era, is that gens de couleur were allowed into these playhouses at all. According to the most important chronicler of life in colonial Saint-Domingue, Médéric-Louis-Élie Moreau de Saint-Méry, the separate seating for mulattoes in the new Le Cap playhouse, which was mentioned almost casually at the close of the article in the *Affiches Américaines*, marked a turning point. This was the first time that the lighter-skinned gens de couleur were explicitly authorized to attend the theater in the city.[14]

Curiously, theaters did not follow the pattern of other leading colonial social and cultural institutions in their approach to racial difference. Even as the gens de couleur began to confront what the historian Stewart King has called a "dizzying variety of discriminatory regulations" imposed by whites "in an attempt to discourage or punish free colored social advancement," free people of color were reserved a place in the theaters, one that became increasingly important over the next two decades.[15] Colonial theaters became open to gens de couleur and free blacks in ways that other leading institutions of the colonial public sphere such as Masonic lodges, chambers of agriculture and of commerce, and the Cercle des Philadelphes (the academy of arts and sciences) were not.[16]

During this period of escalating racial tensions, why did colonial theaters follow a different path? This chapter argues that the answer lies in the fact that—unlike royal academies, secret societies, or honorific groups—colonial theaters operated commercially, subject to market pressures. In the colonial setting, this marriage of culture and commerce would have unexpected outcomes, ultimately enabling gens de couleur in cities such as Port-au-Prince, Les Cayes, and Léogane to come to the stage not only as spectators but as musicians, directors, and even singers and actors. Remarkably, in the early 1780s the Port-au-Prince theater director broke the colonial tradition of maintaining all-white casts and hired a young singer of color to take on leading roles in his company. In colonial playhouses, on the eve of the Revolution, performances given by multiracial casts offered a competing spectacle to that of the segregated audience. They depicted a more inclusive French community made possible through the representation of fiction, yet one that implicitly called into question the racial hierarchies and exclusive white privilege upon which the colonial political economy was founded.

Establishing Public Theaters in the Colonies

Those seeking to establish professional public theaters in France's colonies faced rather daunting challenges. Simply recruiting professional actors and actresses of some talent to the Caribbean was expensive and logistically complicated. Then, "when a happy chance brings them," one observer noted, "they are extremely difficult to keep there."[17] Performers demanded significantly higher salaries in Saint-Domingue than on the mainland. The costs involved in mounting a troupe, therefore, were exceptionally high. Although the resident theater company in Le Cap featured a small cast of just twenty actors and actresses, during the 1770s and early 1780s it had an annual operating budget of roughly 235,000 colonial livres, equivalent to about 156,000 livres tournois or French livres.[18] By the late 1780s, the theater company in Port-au-Prince had a budget of 280,000 colonial livres for a troupe of just sixteen. These budgets were larger than those for provincial companies that had nearly twice as many performers.[19] In addition to personnel challenges, natural disaster posed a significant threat. Earthquakes damaged and even destroyed colonial playhouses, in one case sending spectators fleeing a performance in a panic.[20] Finally—and perhaps most critically for those financially responsible for these enterprises—the potential pool of spectators in many colonial cities was quite small to support professional theater. Saint-Domingue experienced rapid population growth during the later eighteenth century, yet as late as 1789 there were only about sixty thousand free inhabitants, roughly thirty-two thousand whites and twenty-eight thousand free people of color living in the entire colony. Although Le Cap's population was about 18,500 in 1789, making it slightly smaller than a provincial city such as Valenciennes, Port-au-Prince was only about half that large, with a population of ninety-four hundred. Moreover, half or more of the urban residents in Saint-Domingue were slaves. In a city such as Les Cayes, with a population of about 5,650, and even more so in those considered to be second- and third-tier cities, such as Saint Marc or Léogane, the potential audience base was small indeed.[21] Nonetheless, local individuals and groups including entrepreneurs, civic leaders, and theater professionals repeatedly came forward to build and replace playhouses, and to establish new troupes and revive failing ones.

Professional theater in the colonies grew out of interest within the local community, promoted by entrepreneurialism and arts investment. This is particularly clear in the case of Le Cap, where public theater had its roots in an amateur theater society, a pastime for colonists that provided a creative outlet and fostered social community.[22] For more than two decades, a group of about sixty residents supported monthly performances for families and friends. Then in 1764, in the midst of the prosperity that followed the Seven Years' War, theater in Le Cap was reestablished as a professional, commercial venture. The social and cultural role of the theater in urban life, as well as the magnitude of its influence, changed. No longer limited to spectators with personal ties to the patrons and performers, the theater opened to a paying public.[23] Henceforth, those who purchased annual subscriptions could attend the theater two or more evenings a week.[24] Despite periods of financial difficulty, a resident theater company offered year-round performances in Le Cap until 1791, when the slave uprising and Revolution closed the stage.

In 1771, when the theater's director, a man named Chinon, decided that he could no longer afford to continue the enterprise alone, colonists came together to support the resident theater company. Likely borrowing a page from the theater society in Bordeaux, which was almost undoubtedly familiar to merchants engaged in the Atlantic trade, wealthy colonists created a joint-stock company "to run and administer the said theater of the city of Le Cap."[25] They set out to raise 150,000 colonial livres by selling fifty shares at three thousand livres each. Chinon himself bought a share and offered his expertise. The joint-stock company purchased his sets, props, and costumes for the tidy sum of seventy thousand colonial livres and paid to take over his privilege.[26] As with provincial joint-stock theater companies, this new institution was organized democratically. The forty-nine members were invited to gather regularly to discuss business matters and vote on important issues in meetings that were advertised in the local newspaper, the *Affiches Américaines*. Rather than relegating the day-to-day artistic and administrative business to a paid manager or director, they elected representatives from among the shareholders to undertake these responsibilities, aided by several actors.[27] At least every three months, these representative directors were instructed to report to the general assembly of shareholders on "all that will be interesting and advantageous to undertake for the utility, embellishment, and attractiveness of the spectacle."[28] In this way, the Le Cap shareholders took collective responsibility for hiring, determining the repertory, and making policy for the theater.

For twelve years, this group financed and ran the Le Cap theater company.[29] In a 1774 petition seeking royal financial support for the theater company, these investors stated that personal interest and profit were not their motivations in supporting the theater. They "had no other objectives in making their enterprise," they argued, "than the entertainment of their fellow citizens and the public good." They added that "only the general good and patriotic spirit inspired them" to repeatedly intervene by contributing additional funds and contracting new debts on behalf of the theater.[30] Yet, as in cities such as Lorient, members shared the conviction—at least initially—that they could and should make money on their investment in the arts. The bylaws anticipated that shareholders would receive a 10 percent annual return.[31] These aspirations were not realized. During the first seven years of its existence the enterprise struggled with mounting debt, and additional funds needed to be raised to keep the enterprise afloat.[32] Business picked up significantly in the late 1770s and early 1780s as more French and Spanish sailors and soldiers began to pass through the port. Nonetheless, by the time the company finally dissolved in 1783, turning the privilege over to an independent director, the shareholders had lost an estimated 3,434 colonial livres per share.[33] (Still, it is important to consider that those shareholders who attended performances during those twelve years did so for free. With annual subscriptions for white men selling for 360 livres, shareholders who followed the stage regularly during those twelve years would have come out ahead.)

Despite this lackluster economic performance, the Le Cap theater society achieved its goal of maintaining a quality residential theater troupe in the city. The society proved particularly influential and was emulated elsewhere in the colony and in the French Caribbean. According to the playwright Paul-Ulrich Du Buisson, who resided in Saint-Domingue in the 1770s, "the only way to support Theater in the Islands is to make a company of shareholders, modeling itself on that of Le Cap."[34]

Although Le Cap boasted the most active public theater in the colony, other cities in Saint-Domingue also patronized professional dramatic and lyric entertainment. A Creole director, actor, and playwright named Claude Clément first established a professional theater company in the capital of the colony, Port-au-Prince, in 1762.[35] The troupe struggled, however, and broke up within a few years. The converted playhouse where performances took place ultimately closed in 1767. It was not until nearly a decade later that the colonial administration succeeded in enticing two local businessmen, the Mesplès brothers, to build a new public theater with the hope of reviving regular performances in the city. The playhouse was inaugurated in October 1777 and a theater troupe began giving performances three evenings a week. Even in this larger new building accommodating 750 spectators, it proved a challenge for the directors to put on performances profitably. According to Moreau de Saint-Méry, the theater finally stabilized under the direction of M. Acquaire, whose entrepreneurial efforts were supported by urban growth, rising prosperity, and the city's growing military presence. By the late 1780s, the troupe, which consisted of eight actors, eight actresses, and eleven musicians, supported by a prompter (*souffleur*), a machinist, a painter, a tailor, a hairdresser, and several other workers, was making money.[36]

Not long after theater first came to Port-au-Prince and Le Cap, colonists in Les Cayes also expressed interest in establishing a theater. In March 1765, inhabitants of the city and plain of Les Cayes petitioned the colonial authorities for permission to establish a theater to be administered by two prominent residents. The playhouse opened within a year. Before the end of the colonial Old Regime, there were at least ten changes of administration, with each successive director attempting to make professional theater sustainable in this small city. The local community was apparently not daunted by repeated setbacks. In 1788, spectators in Les Cayes celebrated the inauguration of a new public playhouse costing an estimated 120,000 colonial livres, roughly equivalent to the cost of the playhouse in Saint-Quentin.[37]

Finally, actors and actresses, too, played a role in promoting the growth of colonial theater by forming cooperative troupes and cultivating new audiences. In 1767, performers from the recently shuttered theater in Port-au-

Prince, joined by several others from Le Cap, gathered in Saint Marc, the third largest city in Saint-Domingue.[38] There they found enough enthusiasm to put on several weeks of performances. When this initial venture succeeded, they added several more performers to their ranks and converted a hall into a theater capable of entertaining four hundred. In 1769, the troupe introduced opéra-comique and set about recruiting additional actors from France. Shortly after two local women had taken over the direction, disaster struck in the form of an earthquake that damaged the building. Attendance declined due to fears about security, and the Saint Marc theater was forced to close in 1771. At this point, local investors raised funds to build a new, safer theater, constructed under the supervision of M. de Villeneuve, a local businessman. In 1773, this new theater, which accommodated five hundred people, opened to the public. De Villeneuve maintained a close association with the theater as various companies went in and out of business during these decades. He even established a group of shareholders in 1778 to finance the resident theater troupe.[39]

In addition to these four cities, an intermittent theater was signaled by Moreau de Saint-Méry and in the *Affiches Américaines* in Léogane, a city tied to the cultural sphere of nearby Port-au-Prince, in the 1760s. The theater then closed for two decades, it seems. During the late 1780s, a wealthy free man of color reestablished a playhouse and founded a theater company there that performed for several years, as we will discuss later in this chapter.[40] Finally, the towns of Petit-Goâve and Jacmel, according to advertisements in the *Affiches Américaines*, also at least occasionally welcomed theater companies. In Jacmel, such performances took place in a playhouse built in 1785 by an entrepreneur named Galois.[41]

The directors and shareholders who ran the theater companies in Saint-Domingue recruited most of their performers from France, working through agents in Paris and major port cities. To encourage actors and singers to move to the colonies, directors offered salaries that were higher on average than those in most provincial troupes, along with multiyear contracts. One contemporary explained that "no good performer would want to leave France without guarantees for several years."[42] Colonial theater entrepreneurs attributed the high cost of theatrical production not only to salaries but also to recruitment costs and retention challenges that were unique to the colonial setting. A joint-stock company proposing to establish a theater company in Martinique noted in particular "the very expensive transport of a troupe that we are forced to make that much more numerous, because the place being far away, we would find it impossible to replace those subjects whom we would be deprived of by death or by the illnesses to which these

Europeans are exposed in a climate so different from their own."[43] Once in Saint-Domingue, actors and actresses earned as much as eight thousand to twelve thousand colonial livres (about fifty-three hundred to eight thousand *livres tournois*) for leading roles, salaries that were competitive with those for the theaters of Lyon and Bordeaux. For supporting roles, those performing in Le Cap earned between three thousand to eight thousand colonial livres (about two thousand to fifty-three hundred *livres tournois*) annually, salaries that were on the whole considerably higher than average salaries in provincial troupes. In addition, directors guaranteed most players performances for their benefit that could bring them hundreds more. In these troupes, as in the provincial theater companies, women were typically the highest paid performers.[44] Because talent was scarce relative to rising demand, when their initial contract expired those actors who remained usually negotiated one-year contracts. Many moved from company to company.[45] As the number of theater troupes grew, competition for actors prompted the colonial government to issue legislation specifically prohibiting directors from hiring away performers currently under contract to a director elsewhere in the colony.[46]

The case of the Devals, a married theater couple who moved between provincial and colonial stages, sheds light on the process by which actors were recruited to the colonies from France. In 1774, Joseph Deval and his wife, Sophie, left Arles, where both were presumably performing, to venture across the Atlantic. Having concluded negotiations by mail with a theater agent in Paris, they traveled to Marseille to sign a joint three-year contract to perform for the Spectacle de Fort Saint-Pierre in Martinique.[47] Joseph took a position as the music director of the Martinique theater, responsible for staging comic operas and other musical works, for conducting the orchestra, and for playing the violin when not conducting. Sophie sang and acted leading and supporting roles including soubrettes and young lovers. Their combined salary of six thousand French livres a year plus an annual performance or concert in their benefit was higher than average salaries for provincial performers during that era, and was almost certainly more than they would have been earning working for a traveling company performing in Arles. In addition to these forms of remuneration, their new employers provided Madame Deval with a hairdresser and lighting for her dressing room at the theater. When the troupe traveled to another city in Martinique for a period of less than three months, both performers were to be reimbursed for travel, lodging, and food. The shareholders also agreed to pay for their travel, food, and lodging en route to their port of embarkation and then on to Saint-Pierre, and supplied them with a fifteen-hundred-livre advance on their wages. The financial opportunity, when combined with the attractive positions they were offered, seem to have proven powerful incentives to relocate to the colonies. The theater in Martinique was still quite new, but the Devals may well have known others who had left France to perform in Saint-Domingue. The risks were lessened, moreover, because the treasurer general of the colony guaranteed their contracts, which also included return travel to a French port. The Devals performed at the theater in Martinique for about two years. When they left the troupe in 1776, they brought a complaint against the theater society that hired them to the Comédie-Française, demanding payment equivalent to the cost of their return voyage to France despite their intention to remain in the colony. This dispute, which led to the preservation of a transcription of their contract, demonstrates that the jurisdiction of the King's Players over labor disputes extended beyond mainland France to the colonies, which fostered continuities in theater practices that helped the industry remain united throughout the empire.[48]

Provincial Theaters, Colonial Theaters, and the State

As this brief overview demonstrates, the theater industry that was constituted in the colonies beginning in the 1760s closely paralleled the organizational patterns that characterized the theater industry in provincial France. All six of the public playhouses in Saint-Domingue, like the majority in the metropole, were constructed and operated, at least initially, by private businessmen, directors, actors, or investors.[49] (The lack of involvement by local authorities, which in provincial France paid to build a substantial minority of the new playhouses and in some cities provided subsidies to theater companies, is noteworthy.) These entrepreneurs, as in France, rented these commercial public spaces for substantial sums. In Le Cap, Arthaud charged fifteen thousand colonial livres annually for use of the playhouse, while the theater's café brought him an additional six thousand colonial livres. In Port-au-Prince, the Mesplès brothers charged six thousand colonial livres a year for their smaller theater.[50] As was increasingly common in France, in Saint-Domingue directors and directrices—for there were several women among their ranks—obtained privileges from the royal governor granting them sole performance rights in their city.[51] The twenty-year concession for the theater in Le Cap cost twenty thousand colonial livres.[52] Like their provincial counterparts, colonial directors embraced variety in their repertory offerings as an essential selling point, one that was perhaps even more critical overseas. As Du Buisson explained, "The public that goes to performances is always about the same. One must frequently give them new [works], or else they get bored and desert. The best plays can barely be performed three times in six months, even in Le Cap where you find the most foreigners, which makes this work laborious."[53]

This is not to say that the state was not invested in the establishment and maintenance of a network of colonial stages that offered, among many other things, a prominent means to showcase royal authority. Governors provided incentives to promote theater-building and even offered emergency funds to shore up struggling troupes. They almost always did so, however, by encouraging the efforts of local entrepreneurs and joint-stock societies. When the Le Cap theater society nearly closed in 1775 due to financial problems, royal colonial authorities responded to a call for assistance. "Gifts" from the government totaling some 163,000 colonial livres—roughly 10 percent of operating expenses between 1775 and 1783—kept the society in business and the stage from going dark.[54] In Port-au-Prince, royal authorities laid the groundwork for the construction of the new playhouse built in 1777.[55] Frustrated at the lack of an active stage in the colony's capital, the governor of Saint-Domingue, the comte d'Ennery, encouraged local elites to build a playhouse at their own expense, but without success. Next, he pinned his hopes on François Mesplès and his brother, even paying a personal visit to their home to offer them a generous land concession on the centrally located Place Vallière. In exchange for building a respectable playhouse, the two businessmen would receive adjacent land to develop that they would own in perpetuity. D'Ennery died before the deal was completed, but his successor renegotiated on similar terms.[56] These governors' belief that a new playhouse would draw actors to Port-au-Prince and spark the formation of a local public was borne out as Port-au-Prince emerged in the 1780s as Saint-Domingue's second stage.

Later, when this same playhouse fell into a dangerous state of disrepair and the entrepreneurs refused to renovate, royal authorities became more directly involved in the local cultural economy. Prompted by concerns about public safety, the governor exercised an option in the original concession to purchase the Port-au-Prince playhouse back from the builders. After acquiring the stage in 1786, colonial administrators made essential repairs. They continued renting out "the King's theater," applying the eight thousand colonial livres of income this generated toward the support of a new poorhouse in the city.[57] In this way, during the late Old Regime, the monarchy joined, somewhat reluctantly, the ranks of theater owners in Saint-Domingue.

The state's strategic investments in the performing arts can be seen as reflecting the desire to deepen French sovereignty over the colony. Saint-Domingue was one of only a few colonial possessions that remained in France's overseas empire following its defeat by Britain in the Seven Years'

War, and it was by far the most lucrative. Troublingly, from the perspective of royal officials, the relationship between colonists and officers of the crown was contested, marked by hostile resistance to the assertion of royal authority over local affairs, by separatist rhetoric, and even by episodes of open rebellion.[58] The presence of substantial numbers of French troops stationed in the colony and passing through during the era of the American War of Independence, may well have provided an additional rationale for a move that echoed, although without replicating, the navy's interventions in theatrical life in Brest.

Ultimately, it was not only the structures of theatrical production that were shared between colony and metropole. So, too, were some of the fundamental practices and outlooks of the spectators who paid to attend professional theatrical performances. Metropolitan critics, it is true, described colonists as fundamentally uncritical spectators. One theater almanac declared that "the inhabitants of Le Cap are so avid for comedy that as long as they have any actors at all in front of their eyes, they spare them the rest, because one must be content with what one has, for want of anything better."[59] Yet colonial authorities, like those in France, found audiences to be outspoken and difficult to control. Spectators, eager to voice their opinions, shouted and called out during performances, unleashed the whistles of the sifflet, and pounded canes on the floors and benches of playhouses. They demanded that authors and performers appear on stage to be honored or attacked, they hectored actors, and they formed cabals to shout down performances. Members of the audience threw verses onto the stage and demanded that they be read, practices similar to those seen in contemporary provincial playhouses.[60] As in the metropole, police intervention in the colonies did little to change practices that theater spectators considered to be appropriate expressions of public opinion that were fully within their rights.

Strikingly, colonial audiences even made use of the boycott to assert their cultural authority and to protect what they perceived as their consumer rights. In Le Cap, where royal soldiers guarded the playhouse, the lieutenant du roi had already earned the animosity of the public during the early 1780s by the severity of his policing. On various occasions, he refused to allow the actors to accede to audience demands that a monologue be repeated, and refused to permit the reading of a letter that had been thrown on stage. This animosity turned to enmity during a performance on 26 May 1785. When a soldier in the Le Cap regiment attempted to silence a particularly noisy spectator, a fellow patron spoke out in this young man's defense. The lieutenant du roi then ordered that both of these men be ejected. As soldiers seized the two spectators, their fellow audience members rebelled. The crowd came to their rescue, violently overwhelming the soldiers and managing to set one of the men free. Both were later prosecuted in court for their actions that evening (one for having disrupted the performance and the second for having bitten a soldier). Angered by what were perceived as excessive policing tactics that impinged on spectators' traditional liberties, vocal members of the colonial public demanded of the governor that royal soldiers no longer be allowed to police performances. They called for the director to refund subscription fees to all who desired refunds. To give these demands weight, the protesters announced that no one would go to the theater until their demands had been met. According to Moreau de Saint-Méry, this boycott lasted for over a month. Only after a new interim colonial governor offered concessions that changed the ways the theater would be policed did the public finally begin returning to the Le Cap playhouse.[61]

French Identity on the Margins

Although those establishing professional theaters thousands of miles from the metropole faced considerable challenges, they also enjoyed remarkable success. Colonists actually outstripped spectators in France in their support for the stage. Comparing the number of seats offered in public theaters with the size of the urban population provides a means to gauge enthusiasm for professional public theater.[62] During the late 1780s all of the Parisian public playhouses collectively held about thirteen thousand spectators for a city with a population of roughly six hundred thousand, or one entry for every forty-six residents. In Bordeaux, the new Grand Théâtre that opened in 1780 offered roughly one ticket for every forty-eight residents, while the public theater in Le Mans held one seat or place in the parterre for every twenty-three residents.[63] In comparison, at this time the five public playhouses that were regularly active in Saint-Domingue collectively held just over thirty-four hundred seats, or one for every seventeen free colonists—including whites and free people of color—residing in the entire colony. These colonial audiences, moreover, were willing to pay substantially higher prices than their provincial counterparts to attend theatrical performances. For a single ticket for an evening's performance, white parterre spectators in Saint-Domingue typically paid more than five times what they would have paid at most playhouses in metropolitan France. Spectators of color paid more than twice what they would have paid for comparable seats in provincial cities.[64] Why did colonial society demonstrate this level of engagement with professional public theater? To answer this question, it is necessary to explore the role that theater played in promoting a sense of French identity and cultural community among those living thousands of miles from the metropole.

Historians often emphasize the cosmopolitan nature of life in late-eighteenth-century Saint-Domingue, particularly in Le Cap, known to contemporaries as "the pearl of the Antilles."[65] Contemporaries, in contrast, were more apt to characterize colonial life as life on the margins.[66] The colonies had long been regarded as "the sewer of Europe," and many still believed them to be populated "by the dregs of the metropoles," reflecting the earlier days when Saint-Domingue had in fact been populated by pirates, buccaneers, and outlaws.[67] During the late eighteenth century, the Caribbean colonies occupied what was at best an ambiguous space in the French imagination. The high profits of the sugar and coffee trade attracted growing numbers of nobles and bourgeois to the expanding Atlantic trade and sparked a rise in immigration to the colony from France.[68] Yet, among these new arrivals many, it was believed, privileged their personal advancement above all else. "Who are those who go to Saint-Domingue?" one critic asked, before responding: "in large part young men without principles, lazy and libertine, escaping from paternal authority . . . others are rogues and villains who have found the means to avoid the severity of justice: a few are honest men."[69] Self-interest and greed were believed to dominate colonial life, which was widely criticized as crassly materialistic.

If one came to the colonies to make one's fortune, it was not without paying a price. Although luxury goods, liquor, mistresses, and domestic slaves were all readily available to those who could afford to pay, contemporaries also confronted the oppressive heat, chronic illness, urban filth, brutality, and, in the minds of many colonists, cultural backwardness that characterized everyday life in this tropical frontier society.[70] "Since I have been here," the baron Wimpffen noted, "I have not yet found anyone, not a single one, whom I did not hear curse both Saint-Domingue and the obstacles that keep cropping up that from one year to the next prolonged his stay in this hell." And to make matters worse, Wimpffen acidly observed, one was surrounded by bad taste: "Taste is still quite Creole in Saint-Domingue, and Creole taste is not le bon goût: it still smells a bit of the buccaneer."[71] Don Ignacio Gala described the toll taken by chronic dissatisfaction with everyday life: "The desire to return to Europe agitates them continually: the image of Paris . . . represented in their imagination with all the attractions of its public pleasures, social delights, and the superficialities of refined luxury, continually disturbs their domestic repose, and makes them see this mantle of riches with such great disaffection that they believe they can only recover the happiness that they have lost when the desired day arrives of their return to France."[72] Those who could return to the metropole increasingly did so. Absenteeism rose in the late eighteenth century until approximately 40 percent of sugar plantation owners managed their estates from France.[73] "The general mania in Saint-Domingue," Moreau de Saint-Méry affirmed, "is to speak of return or of a visit to France. Everyone repeats that he will leave next year, and they only consider themselves as travelers."[74]

Visitors encountered colonists gripped by an obsession with France, one shared even among white Creoles born in the colonies. Many wealthy Creoles cultivated close ties with the metropole, sending their sons to France at a young age to obtain the education that was not available locally. Individuals such as Moreau de Saint-Méry, a native of Martinique, spent considerable time studying and living in France. Creoles' relationship with French culture was complicated, however, by a widely shared prejudice that stigmatized those born and raised outside of France. Indeed, the inhabitants of Saint-Domingue were urged to "cure themselves" of various customs "that still distinguish them to their disadvantage from the French of Europe."[75] Such attitudes proved common not only among royal administrators, known for treating Creoles as their inferiors.[76] They were also apparently internalized by Creoles themselves. *Les Veuves créoles* (The Creole Widows), one of the earliest comedies written and performed in the colonies, plays on such themes. The three wealthy widows of the title compete for the affections of a French chevalier living in Martinique, a false suitor interested only in their money, but one who holds out the promise of marrying these women and taking them to live in France.[77] One widow, Madame Sirotin, expresses her desire to stop living "in the country" and makes plans to sell her property and move to France, a dream shared by her sister, the widow Madame Grapin.[78] The third and youngest widow, Mélite, is ridiculed for believing that her earlier visit to France had refined her and elevated her against her competition. "For having lived in France, where her husband, by paying, made himself pass for a man of quality," the chevalier mocks, "she imagines herself to have more depth, more merit than those who have never left here. But she took nothing from this voyage but several additional degrees of impertinence."[79] The comedy sets the audience up to laugh at Creole manners in a way that deliberately emphasizes the social and cultural gulf separating metropole and colony. One of the title widows, known for wearing humorously idiosyncratic clothing that she maintains is high fashion, is drawn in by the Frenchman's false flattery. In her ridiculous garb, she wonders aloud: "You believe then that I would be neither out of place nor embarrassed if I found myself all of a sudden in the middle of Paris, in the highest society [*le plus grand monde*]?"[80]

For homesick expatriates anxiously waiting their moment to return to France, as well as for Creole colonists concerned about their marginal cultural status, new public theaters provided a means to embrace and assert their Frenchness. For transatlantic merchants as for the military officers and soldiers stationed in the colony, theaters provided continuity with their previous lives by extending many of the same leisure and social opportunities available in ports and garrisons on the mainland. For Creoles seeking to assimilate more fully into French culture, colonial theaters offered unique opportunities. The fact that the language spoken on stage was almost exclusively French—rather than the Creole commonly spoken in everyday interactions—set theaters apart. Moreau de Saint-Méry, in fact, explicitly recommended that individuals could take language lessons at the theater.[81] Occasionally directors did stage works in which characters spoke Creole. Two such works, authored by the Creole actor Clément, are *Jeannot et Thérèse*, a Creole adaptation of Rousseau's *Devin du village*, and *Julien et Susette*, described as a "Negro translation [*traduction nègre*]" of the popular comic opera *Blaise et Babet*.[82] Such works, Bernard Camier has argued, signify the birth of an authentic local cultural production, one that mixes colonial and metropolitan idioms in "creolized" works.[83] Yet plays and comic operas such as these constituted only a small fraction of the repertory performed in the colony. As in most French cities, directors staged works drawn overwhelmingly from the theaters of Paris.[84]

From the beginnings of professional theater in Saint-Domingue, connections with the metropole were advertised explicitly. The director Chinon rooted the new Le Cap theater firmly in the French dramatic tradition by presenting *Le Misanthrope*, perhaps the most famous comedy by France's most renowned playwright, Molière, for the city's first public performance.[85] Publicity drew in audiences by focusing self-consciously on the "Frenchness" of the repertory and performers. In fact, one of the very first newspaper advertisements for theater in the colony promoted the comic opera *Le Cadi dupé* as "generally applauded in France."[86] References to France quickly became a staple of advertising copy for theatrical performances in both the Port-au-Prince and Le Cap editions of the newspaper, increasing in frequency between the 1760s and the 1780s. Advertisements regularly celebrated the Parisian success of a new play in the repertory, sometimes including the number of performances a work had been given at one of the three royal stages. Plays performed at court were singled out, as well as those that had enjoyed successful runs in provincial cities. Jean-Marie Collot d'Herbois's *François à la Grenade*, for example, was advertised as having been performed in Lille and Douai, and "successively on all the stages of the provinces."[87] Beyond producing a French repertory, colonial theater companies claimed to closely emulate French stages in costuming, set design, staging, and effects. For example, the local newspaper announced that for an upcoming performance of Thomas Corneille's *Le Festin de Pierre*, "all will be carried out and performed like in Paris."[88] For a performance of *La Belle Arsène*, all would "be executed as it was at the Italiens in Paris in the previous January."[89] For another production, an actor boasted of having gathered the advice of "enlightened connoisseurs who have seen this work in France," including advice on acting strategies for certain roles and on set decorations.[90] Actors and actresses were promoted in a similar fashion. When Madame Mourel added her talents to the theater company in Le Cap, she was vaunted as "newly arrived" from France.[91] Occasionally, the *Affiches Américaines* also featured articles on the happenings of the royal stages, which served to further stimulate interest in metropolitan theater culture while also enhancing its prestige.[92] Colonists seem to have followed the Paris theater scene with avid interest. According to one visitor, upon his arrival in the colony he was barraged with questions about "which were the latest theatrical novelties" in the capital.[93]

The cultural connections and immediacy to France that colonial theaters offered their audiences deepened in the 1780s when prominent performers from Paris began to embark on colonial tours. The distance between France and the Caribbean (and perhaps the cost) was too great for these stages to entice the stars of the Comédie-Française and the Paris Opera. Yet Saint-Domingue theaters did draw several Parisian performers. The most famous of these was Louis-François Ribié, a celebrity from Nicolet's Théâtre des Grands Danseurs du Roi on the Boulevard du Temple. Ribié toured the colony with his "Troupe of Parisian Actors" in 1787–88, and later returned to Martinique and Saint-Domingue in 1791 for several additional months of performances.[94] Such tours established greater immediacy with contemporary Parisian culture. They also demonstrate the extent of Saint-Domingue's integration into French commercial and cultural networks. Indeed, in a new national theater directory published in 1791, the Le Cap theater company was listed alongside those of Paris, Bordeaux, Lyon, and other provincial cities.[95]

To understand colonists' heightened commitment to public theater, the access that theaters provided to the language, literature, and cultural trends of the metropole constitutes one essential part of the explanation. The unique social role fulfilled by these institutions constitutes a second. In a colonial society marked by division and conflict, theaters fostered a sense of community by providing a public space where mutually hostile groups could come together, if only to enjoy the same entertainment or to indulge in a collective longing for France. This was no small feat, for the whites of the colony were united in the benefits of racial privilege but, rather notoriously, in little else.[96] *Grand blancs*, including white planters and other wealthy colonial elites, had little common cause with the *petits blancs*, a broad social category that included white artisans, small farmers, workers, and the poor. Planters traditionally harbored little affection for the négociants who, protected by trade monopolies, made their fortunes provisioning colonists with goods from France and buying colonists' sugar, coffee, indigo, and other commodities only to resell them for a higher price once they had returned to ports such as Nantes, Bordeaux, and Marseille. In addition to these groups, the cities of Saint-Domingue were also home to sizable numbers of French soldiers and sailors, royal administrators, clergy, and foreigners. Colonial society was further strained by a significant gender gap: women made up less than 20 percent of the white population. Meanwhile, occupying an increasingly contested terrain in contemporary society were the gens de couleur, whose rapidly growing population and wealth threatened to undermine the racial basis of colonial slavery.[97]

With relatively few social and entertainment alternatives available even in the colony's largest cities, theaters quickly became leading institutions in colonial society. Shareholders in the Le Cap theater society explained the importance of the theater's contribution in these terms: "If theater is useful in Europe, where there are many other types of leisure and relaxation, one can say that it is even more indispensable in the colonies where there is only this one establishment."[98] These investors exaggerated less than one might imagine when they claimed that "all orders of citizens go to [the theater] quite commonly."[99] According to some, the performance was only a pretext for the opportunity to gather socially and converse.[100] Especially in larger port cities such as Le Cap and Port-au-Prince, the theater successfully brought together expatriates and Creoles, planters and French traders, and soldiers and royal administrators into a space where they could put aside their differences. Indeed, one contemporary explained that those living in the colonies "only find themselves really together at the Comedy."[101] The diverse membership in the Le Cap theater society itself—which included aristocratic military officers, plantation owners, wholesale merchants, and lawyers, among others—lends support to such claims.[102] By gathering heterogeneous audiences, the theater in Le Cap, according to shareholders, fostered "a harmony of spirit and an agreeable willingness to do business. The habit of seeing one another and talking," they argued, "diffuses personality conflicts, and often brings about new projects and new business which contribute to the growth of the land, and to the advantage of its inhabitants."[103] Moreau de Saint-Méry concurred. He described the theater as a habitual business rendezvous, with negotiations conducted during the shows, making for noisy hallways. In addition, as in garrison cities in France, the colony's sizable population of French sailors and soldiers was kept busy in the evenings at the theater. For white women, too, we are told, attending the theater provided a welcome social diversion and an opportunity for personal display. Using women's attendance as a measure of theater's popularity in Le Cap, Moreau de Saint-Méry noted as many as 130 female spectators at a performance; another commentator noted more than twice this number. "It would be impossible to do without a theater in Le Cap," Moreau de Saint-Méry concluded. "We have little society in this city, and there we are at least gathered if we are not united."[104]

Finally, for at least some of those who resided on the peripheries of the Francophone world, the theater proved attractive for a third reason: because it provided a means to counter the threat of degeneration that in the minds of contemporaries loomed frighteningly over all those who lived in the tropics. According to the leading scientific theories of the eighteenth century, climate directly influenced many aspects of the human condition, including the mores, work habits, and even the skin color of individuals and their descendents. Race, in other words, was widely viewed as inherently unstable. Naturalists such as the comte de Buffon, the abbé Prévost, and Cornélius de Pauw argued explicitly that Europeans who lived in hot, sunny climates for long periods of time would inevitably begin to transform from white to black, a devastating prognosis for colonists and especially Creoles.[105] This possibility of lapsing into blackness and barbarism, known as the "law of regression" or "reversion," as scholars have noted, was among colonists' greatest fears.[106] According to these theories, cultural practices such as attending the theater constituted some of the only means to actively combat degeneration by providing a means to "civilize" the colonial population. When a theater director and several leading négociants proposed to reintroduce professional theater in Saint-Pierre, Martinique, they employed this discourse of climate to argue that the civilizing effect of a theater was desperately needed. "The inhabitants of Martinique," they wrote, "just as those of [all] colonies placed under a burning sun, are drawn irresistibly towards inaction." For amusement, locals turned to gambling and other pastimes, with serious consequences: "Commerce languishes, public confidence deteriorates. But, the theater could stave off these terrible inconveniences." When the previous public theater had been active in Martinique, they explained, "the Creoles, who were degenerating markedly each day, drew from it all of a sudden the energy, taste, and ardor to educate themselves, so much so that many today distinguish themselves with advantage among their fellow citizens."[107] Nor was this salutary civilizing influence of the stage reserved for whites alone. Because of theater, they wrote, the "free men of color have lost the barbarism of their origins, refine themselves, and take up manners." These changes could only be attributed to the theater, they maintained, because "before its existence, despite the forms of instruction that we had, minds did not stupefy less rapidly." The bankruptcy of the theater troupe had placed colonial society at risk. Once a successful public theater was reestablished under their plan, however, they were confident that within a few years "the people of Martinique will no longer differ from Europeans except owing to the climate."[108]

Scholars such as Cooper and Stoler have argued that in the imperial context differences, especially racial differences, needed to be continually "defined and maintained."[109] Colonial theaters certainly provided a prominent site where racial differences could be articulated and reified. The striking success of colonial theaters among French and Creole spectators alike, however, suggests the extent to which the corollary was also true. In the colonial context, samenesses—in the sense of cultural similarities and a shared French identity—also needed to be actively cultivated and self-consciously asserted. In Saint-Domingue, the practice of attending theatrical performances served to emphasize all that was shared among the diverse and typically divided populations of whites, including the privilege that distinguished them as a caste from slaves as well as from spectators of color. It is not insignificant that although Moreau de Saint-Méry recorded in detail the racial hierarchies imposed in each colonial playhouse, he had relatively little to say about the hierarchical distribution of white spectators by estate, social status, wealth, or appearance within the playhouse, matters of significant interest to provincial commentators and French authorities. He, like so many other colonial commentators, chose to celebrate the fragile sense of community grounded in sociability and shared French cultural practices that predominantly white colonial audiences cultivated at the theater.[110]

Race and the Colonial Playhouse

Dramatic changes in the demography of the colony helped to fuel the "new racism" that came to define everyday interactions in the colony during the final decades of the Old Regime.[111] During the 1750s and 1760s, as the numbers, wealth, and prominence of gens de couleur in colonial society grew rapidly, whites began to stake new claims to racial difference. They did so in an attempt to stabilize the colony's fluid racial terrain.[112] For generations it had been common practice for European men living in Saint-Domingue to take women of African and mixed-racial heritage, slave as well as free, as *ménagères* who would manage their household and in many cases share their bed. When children resulted from these unions (and other couplings), fathers often freed those who were born into slavery as well as their mothers. As a result, by the late eighteenth century Saint-Domingue came to feature one of the largest populations of free people of African descent in the Americas, one that by 1789 approximately equaled the number of white colonists. It was also one of the wealthiest such populations, with free people of color enjoying very substantial holdings in land and slaves. Early in the century, French and colonial authorities had often included the African or mulatto wives, mistresses, and children of white male colonists within the category of "white" society. As rapid mulatto advancement fueled discontent and fear among whites, however, perceptions changed. Restrictive new forms of racial legislation, originating both in the colony and in France, were introduced that limited the rights of the gens de couleur with the intent of establishing a distinct intermediary caste between slaves and whites.[113]

As a result, beginning around the 1760s even prominent, educated, land- and slave-owning individuals who had formerly lived as "white" colonial elites found themselves increasingly disenfranchised within colonial society. Gens de couleur were disqualified from holding public office and from holding noble titles. They could no longer become commissioned officers in the militia or enter into most professions. Sumptuary laws regulated what mulatto men and women were permitted to wear and own in order to establish a more visible distance between castes. Although not all of these laws were effectively enforced, the divisions between whites and nonwhites, both symbolic and real, intensified.[114]

As particularly prominent cultural institutions, the new public theaters of Saint-Domingue played an important role in elaborating and reinforcing these new conceptions of racial difference. Colonial playhouses, like those in metropolitan France, featured hierarchical interior designs that ordered and displayed the urban community. Within these playhouses, as we have seen, spectators were segregated by race. In Port-au-Prince, free people of color sat in the second boxes. In Léogane they took seats in the amphitheater. In Saint Marc, they initially watched from the highest balcony before they were moved to the rear of the parterre. In Le Cap, when a third row of boxes was added to the theater in 1784, the gens de couleur mounted a separate staircase to seats there.[115] Whereas in most cities all spectators of color sat together regardless of the "nuances" of their skin, in Le Cap racial distinctions were further elaborated. From the time that darker skinned freed blacks (*nègres*) finally gained admittance to the playhouse in 1776, they sat separately from mulattoes. In the words of Moreau de Saint-Méry, "when a *négresse* and her mulatto daughter come to the comedy, they separate; the ebony to the left, the copper to the right."[116] Although free people of color could attend masked balls and dances in certain colonial playhouses, they were only permitted, at least in theory, to sit in the boxes and watch as the white attendees danced and socialized. Elsewhere such dances were segregated more fully. The proposal for a new playhouse in Saint Marc prohibited gens de couleur from subscribing to the balls that whites attended, but noted parenthetically that if there were balls specifically for the free coloreds, these individuals would pay at the entrance.[117] Such restrictions could apply to joint-stock societies as well. In Le Cap, shareholders established racial restrictions on membership intended to exclude nonwhites. Bylaws mandated that shareholders could not sell their shares to gens de couleur or even to *mesalliés*, those who married across colonial racial boundaries. If such individuals did somehow obtain shares, such as through a bequest, the society claimed the right to purchase them back.[118]

The ways in which theater tickets were sold to the public both reflected and reinforced this deepening concern with racial difference. Individual tickets and subscriptions were priced differently for whites and for free people of color. White men paid the most for annual subscriptions, which in the 1780s cost 360 colonial livres for the Le Cap theater. For yearly subscriptions, white women paid about two-thirds as much. In some cases, subscriptions were offered for white children at a still lower price. In contrast, free people of color—male and female alike, and of all ages—constituted a third price category. In most cases, gens de couleur paid only half as much for their theater tickets as the least expensive parterre tickets for whites. To attend performances at the theater in Saint Marc for a year, a person of color would have paid slightly more than a white child.[119]

Documenting the widespread adoption of policies that established free colored spectators as a separate and inferior class within theater audiences does not solve the problem of why they were permitted to attend in the first place. To address this issue, the origins and evolution of these policies requires closer attention. Rather than reflecting a coherent policy imposed by royal or colonial authorities, theater admissions policies were created by the entrepreneurs and shareholders who ran colonial theaters. Moreover, they evolved in an ad hoc manner, with market factors almost undoubtedly playing a large role. It seems hardly coincidental that free people of color were first officially permitted to attend the theater in Le Cap not when it first became public, in a space seating just a few hundred, but rather when the theater company moved into a large new public playhouse in which well over a thousand seats needed to be filled. For the director and, later, the theater's shareholders, opening the playhouse to free people of color, especially women, was a shrewd business strategy. This produced as many as eighty additional paying audience members nightly.[120] It also had a second—and likely even more important—benefit: the presence of mulatto women, and particularly the prostitutes among them, attracted many other spectators into the playhouse, namely the white men who constituted the majority of colonial audiences. In Le Cap, it was well known that male colonists and soldiers alike went to the theater specifically to seek out the companionship of women of color. Contemporaries describe men crowding into the seats in the amphitheater directly below the boxes of particularly attractive young courtesans. Entr'actes and intermissions rang out with calls between these male spectators and the women above, who flirted and arranged rendezvous, purportedly to take the fresh air outside.[121] The contingent nature of these policies is highlighted by the fact that they were altered a decade later when the *négresses* of Le Cap, through the intermediary of Moreau de Saint-Méry himself, petitioned the shareholders for the right to attend the theater "with their daughters."[122] The decision to accommodate their request by expanding admissions took place at a time when shareholders were under extreme financial pressure. Just two months earlier, the Le Cap theater society, bankrupt, had announced that it was closing. Only an infusion of financial support from a dedicated core of shareholders and, according to Moreau de Saint-Méry, contributions from the royal government, kept the theater in play.[123] As the institution reorganized to emerge from this crisis, shareholders made two substantial changes in the administration of the theater. They expanded the number of performances from two to three evenings a week and they expanded admission to include free blacks.[124]

This policy, introduced at a time when more restrictive racialist legislation was the order of the day, stirred public controversy because it was perceived as dangerously inclusive. According to one outspoken critic, Michel-Réné Hilliard d'Auberteuil, of the many "great prerogatives" claimed by the shareholders of the Le Cap theater society, "the most dangerous" was "that of making the laws" regarding the color line.[125] Colonists, he wrote, had protested in vain against allowing free blacks (*nègres*) into the theater, arguing that "if it is a privilege for [the gens de couleur] to enjoy performances put on for whites, it must be restricted instead of extended."[126] Hilliard d'Auberteuil argued that the shareholders should have continued to admit mulattoes only because, he claimed, they were fewer in number, closer to whites, wealthier, and generally better mannered than manumitted blacks. He went so far as to assert provocatively that the Le Cap shareholders even allowed slaves to attend the theater as paying spectators, a claim that others disputed.[127] Such an allegation served as more than simple hyperbole. It laid bare the pragmatic difficulties of policing the colonial racial order in an institution open to a consumer public. Could white spectators really be certain, he implied, that every spectator with a dark complexion was in fact free? His ardent opposition to the new policy of allowing blacks into the playhouse was also rooted in widely shared fears that expanding the rights of nonwhites, even such seemingly inconsequential ones such as the right to attend the theater, constituted a slippery slope that would ultimately threaten the racial hierarchy on which the colonial political economy was founded. Indeed, Hilliard d'Auberteuil argued explicitly that allowing free blacks to attend performances would have dire consequences, upsetting the social order by giving them dreams that were beyond their ability and station, whetting their appetite for luxury—and by implication their desire to have what whites had. Blacks, he wrote, would soon imagine themselves dressed in imported fabric and lace, enjoying a life of privilege that they could not afford. To realize these dreams they would turn to crime.[128]

A decade later, members of the Chamber of Agriculture in Martinique voiced similar fears about the presence of free people of color in the newly rebuilt playhouse in Saint-Pierre "because the theater draws them as well, and the ordinances admit them." Adapting elements of Rousseau's antitheater rhetoric to the colonial racial context, they complained that permitting gens de couleur to attend theatrical performances promoted luxury consumption among nonwhites by providing them a venue to flaunt their wealth. This disrupted the social order, they argued, and brought about a collapse of morality. "This luxury of the free people of color has been taken to its fullest development," they argued. "Theft has become necessary to supply it."[129] To critics such as these, discriminatory seating policies could not erase the profound significance of the presence of free people of color and free blacks as cultural consumers at the playhouse. The consequences, they suggest, were real for both the people of color whose imaginations they believed to be fired with inappropriate desires for equality, and for the white spectators, who were forced to witness impressively staged displays of personal luxury by free people of color that implicitly challenged white supremacy.[130]

Whites were not alone in resisting changes to the complexion of the colonial audience. In Le Cap, when mulatto women spectators learned of the aspiration of free *négresses* to join them in the playhouse, they rejected the plan. In fact, they threatened the shareholders that they would stop attending the theater if this "*confusion*" took place.[131] Their threat proved an effective tactic. To avoid alienating this important clientele, the shareholders decided that a compromise was in order: blacks would attend, but they would sit separately from mulattoes, creating a further distinction based on color.[132]

By leveraging their economic influence, these women of color were able to participate in negotiating and policing racial distinctions in the playhouse.[133]

Rather than thinking of the gens de couleur as a minority whose presence in the playhouse was grudgingly tolerated, it is perhaps more accurate to think of them—as Hilliard d'Auberteuil did—as having been invited in by the entrepreneurs and shareholders who operated these stages.[134] Indeed, as Camier and Dubois have shown, the numbers of gens de couleur invited into colonial public theaters grew over time, in keeping with their growing population and wealth. Only slightly more than 5 percent of seats in the 1766 playhouse in Le Cap, the colony's most populous city, were initially allocated for people of color. When the new playhouse opened in Port-au-Prince in 1778, this rose to 15 percent of the seats, a number that may have increased in the 1780s. In the Léogane playhouse that opened around 1786, nearly 18 percent of seats were reserved for spectators of color. In the playhouse constructed in Fort Royal, Martinique, gens de couleur occupied 40 percent of theater seats.[135] Questions remain as to whether segregationist policies were rigorously enforced, especially when the *Affiches Américaines* ran a short piece in 1784 mentioning the presence of blacks ("*nègres*") in the first boxes at the Le Cap playhouse.[136] What is clear is that at a time when other leading institutions of culture and sociability had closed their doors to non-whites, the commercial sector proved an important exception, with growing numbers of women and men of color attending professional theaters where they took in performances of French dramatic literature, music, and dance, and participated actively in colonial public life.

At the same time, colonial theaters also constituted a field of opportunity for people of color who were professional musicians as well as directors and patrons of the arts. By the late 1770s and 1780s, gens de couleur began to be celebrated as instrumental soloists in newspaper advertisements with growing frequency. A musician named Rivière was the first to receive such acclaim for concertos that he performed on the violin and mandolin at the theater in Port-au-Prince. A number of other violinists of color followed in his footsteps, performing solos at the theaters of Port-au-Prince and Le Cap in the 1780s.[137] Even more remarkably, as we have seen, a prominent free colored man named Jean-Louis Labbé established a theater troupe in Léogane in 1786. His troupe performed with an orchestra in a house that he converted into a playhouse that could accommodate an audience of four hundred. Labbé not only financed, administered, and directed the troupe: as the sergeant of the local militia, he also supervised the policing of performances. Labbé's efforts lasted for only two years before he sold the playhouse. Yet during his relatively brief tenure, his patronage of the arts increased Labbé's esteem in colonial society. Moreau de Saint-Méry extolled Labbé's efforts: "I wish that the theater of Léogane will last, above all when I consider that its director does not seek gain; and his motive is too generous for me not to hasten to praise him."[138] Labbé's prominent accomplishments in the cultural sphere, through which he sought to prove his virtue, could not erase the deep racial prejudices he confronted in daily life. In the advertisement for the sale of the theater, he signified his status as a person of color by referring to himself as "le nommé Labbé," noting with some bitterness that "in spite of everything, no one in the colony [would consent] to address him as Monsieur," a title of respect reserved for whites.[139] Yet this very statement suggests that by establishing this theater Labbé affirmed his belief in his own merit and abilities. It also reveals the growing intolerance for colonial racism harbored by ambitious gens de couleur such as himself.[140]

Integrating the Colonial Stage

Most striking of all were the claims that performers of color staked on colonial stages during the 1780s. For most of the colonial Old Regime, it seems that racial segregation on Saint-Domingue stages was even more complete than that in the auditorium. Colonial theaters maintained white casts, hiring actors and actresses from France or of white Creole background.[141] Several times a week, these acting companies represented the fictions of a white French community: comedies and dramas for the most part set in Europe, along with tragedies located in Greek or Roman antiquity or in exotic faraway locales. In the occasional works that did feature explicitly black characters—often local creations—whites performed these roles. For the performance of one such work, the newspaper advertised to readers that an actor "known for perfectly imitating the gestures and languages of the Blacks, will play the role of Figaro, with the costume of a black valet."[142]

This tradition was challenged in 1781 when a young mixed-race singer known as Minette debuted with the Port-au-Prince theater company at the age of fourteen. She grew up in Port-au-Prince, the daughter of a mulatto woman and a prominent white colonist. A gifted musician, Minette was taken under the wing of a local singer, Madame Acquaire, who helped her prepare for a career on the stage. Following several successful concert performances in late 1780 and early 1781, she appeared as Isabelle in the opéra-comique *Isabelle et Gertrude* on 13 February 1781. Crossing the color barrier, Minette won over crowds and quickly became a youthful favorite on the Saint-Domingue stage.[143]

In addition to her evident talent, several factors likely encouraged the director of the Port-au-Prince theater company, François Saint-Martin, to hire Minette, eventually as a principal in his troupe. First, French military involvement in the War of American Independence beginning in 1778 had disrupted transportation between France and the colony. This made it difficult to recruit performers from France, so much so that the theater in Saint Marc closed for lack of actors. In 1780, a critic warned Saint-Martin that without the addition of talented performers from France his theater troupe would certainly go bankrupt.[144] It was in the midst of this personnel crisis that Minette's precocious abilities drew her to the attention of Saint-Martin. Second, Saint-Martin may have seen in Minette's youth and charm a means to attract the patronage of the thousands of soldiers and sailors passing through the port, and perhaps that of the substantial community of gens de couleur in and around Port-au-Prince.[145] Finally, Minette's youth and racial status seem to have made her vulnerable to exploitation. Minette proved a less expensive hire than a white singer because, at least initially, she was not paid. Three years after she debuted in his troupe, Saint-Martin confessed on his deathbed that he had never given her the salary of eight thousand livres per year indicated in her contract. Yet the director's final wishes, as recorded by the local notary, reveal his desire to fulfill his obligation to a young woman whose success almost undoubtedly exceeded his expectations: "I did not pay her one sou . . . from her salary which is due to her from me in its entirety. For this reason I want that this sum be taken from . . . my estate and paid by my executor to the D[emoiselle] Minette upon my death."[146]

In spite of such obstacles, Minette succeeded in building for herself a very successful career. One of the stars of the colonial stage, she continued to star in operas and comic operas until 1789, when she moved to New Orleans. Between 1780 and 1789, Minette was mentioned in the press more than forty times, making her the second most celebrated performer in Saint-Domingue during this era.[147] As a pioneer, she took care in developing her professional reputation, refusing to perform works she perceived as Creole productions, and accepting only those with European pedigrees. In an advertisement for a benefit performance of *L'Infante de Zamora* on her behalf, she introduced the opera she had chosen by establishing, in her words, that "this is not one of those ephemeral productions that bastardize and degrade the lyric stage, which are only local and which very often only address the everyday events of private society; it is an opera approved by good taste, and fans of beauty will always see it with pleasure."[148] To assert her legitimacy as a musician and rising star, Minette, too, leveraged the prestige of metropolitan culture.

Minette's success opened the door for other actors and actresses of color. Most notably, her sister Lise began performing at the theater in Les Cayes in 1784. She was later hired by Labbé to perform in Léogane, and also appeared in Saint Marc and Port-au-Prince.[149] Taking into account the careers of both sisters, all of the leading professional theater companies in Saint-Domingue with the exception of the Le Cap theater company hired performers of color during the 1780s. Evidence concerning other contemporary actors and actresses of color is extremely scarce, yet the indications that we do have suggest that these two women were not alone. According to a newspaper advertisement, during Ribié's first tour of the colony in 1788 he shared the stage with a "black Creole" actor who performed the role of a prince. A visitor to the colony who attended a performance in Port-au-Prince in the mid-1780s described actors and a chorus of singers that included blacks, mulattos, and whites, "a mixture of color."[150]

The integration of colonial theater companies at this time seems all the more remarkable—and paradoxical—given that as Minette and her sister drew devoted followings, outside of the playhouse antagonism between whites and people of color was reaching new heights.[151] Given the social stigma attached to actresses as a social group, hiring an actress of color was unlikely to be perceived as an attack on the colonial social order. Nonetheless, contemporaries certainly took note of the significance of Minette's career. Moreau de Saint-Méry recognized Minette's extraordinary talent, but also gave credit to her director for what he characterized as the risky move of introducing her on the stage. Saint-Martin, he wrote, "agreed to see prejudice put to battle with pleasure." Hiring Minette, "against colonial prejudices," he argued, was a praiseworthy example of politics conceding to art.[152]

Implicitly or explicitly, the introduction of people of color into colonial troupes must have raised the issue of how to cast these actors and singers in the works that constituted the theatrical repertory, almost all of which were imported from France. Advertisements in the *Affiches Américaines* reveal that Minette quickly took on leading roles in *L'Amoureux de quinze ans*, *Toinon et Toinette*, and *Zémire et Azore*, to name just a few.[153] In these works and others, she represented women from an array of social positions, geographic locales, and historical eras, including the daughter of an innkeeper in a Flemish port city, the daughter of a wealthy French family, a young French noblewoman, the daughter of a Middle Eastern merchant, and even a Spanish princess.[154] By contemporary colonial standards, Minette's performance of many of these roles constituted cross-racial casting. In contrast with the segregated audience beyond the curtain, the characters that she, her sister, and others performed on stage were integrated into fictional worlds brought to life several evenings

a week. In their performances, actors of color such as Minette helped to create an imaginary that represented the ideal that leaders in the free colored
community would set out to claim for themselves in 1789: a world in which
skin color and family lineage were not the defining characteristics shaping
one's legal, social, or professional status, a world in which free people of color
could be fully and equally French.

It would be fascinating to know if the effect of integrated performances
was as powerful for other spectators as it was for Alexandre de Laujon, who
attended the theater in Port-au-Prince on his arrival in Saint-Domingue.
At first, de Laujon was surprised by the segregation of audiences, with black
spectators above and whites below. Then the play began. "The actors made
me laugh a lot," he remembered; "a mistress was yellow, a lover white, and
several blacks played the role of courtiers. It was necessary to report to the
theater not to hear talk of prejudices." By the time the multiracial chorus
appeared, he could hardly contain his astonishment. "What is more, I heard
many voices that surprised me," de Laujon concluded, "and I did not find
that the piece was badly performed."[155]

The initial hiring of an actress of color in Port-au-Prince may well have
resulted from the convergence of unusual circumstances. Colonial audiences,
however, proved more than willing to appreciate the talents of Minette and
Lise, just as they were willing to support violin concerts by the virtuoso
Rivière and performances staged by the troupe of Jean-Louis Labbé. As a
number of theater companies began to present French works of fiction with
a mixed-race cast, they suggested different ways in which a multiracial community might be imagined. Performances at the Port-au-Prince theater,
among others, challenged audiences either to blind themselves to the well-
publicized racial identity of its popular leading singer or to accept it and
contemplate the representation of a mixed-race society that was not constituted in hierarchical, racialist terms. In this way, theaters proposed a means
to address issues of integration and assimilation that were too fraught and
controversial to be directly addressed elsewhere in colonial society.[156] What
could be achieved in performance would prove much harder to achieve in
political battles in which the fate of France's most profitable colony and its
half million slaves were held in the balance. It would take revolution—in
France and in Saint-Domingue—before all of the residents of the colony
would successfully claim their freedom and political rights as citizens. Yet in
the 1780s, in the colony's theaters, directors, performers, and audiences had
already begun to entertain the vision of a changed society.

Epilogue

Culture, Commerce, and the State

In 2009, the French Ministry of Culture and Communication celebrated its fiftieth anniversary. This branch of government, created by Charles de Gaulle in 1959, advances a mandate "to make accessible the capital works of humanity and above all of France to the greatest possible number of French citizens, to assure the widest audience for our cultural patrimony, and to promote the creation of the works of art and the spirit that enrich it."[1] Today's ministry employs much of its multi-billion euro budget to sustain and encourage the arts and humanities, with a primary emphasis on French culture construed in the broadest terms.[2] Theater has long enjoyed a place of prominence in the ministry's agenda.[3] Former minister Christine Albanel praised France's performing arts industry as "the premier network in Europe, and probably in the entire world," one that included no fewer than 1,235 ensembles and companies devoted to the performance of theater, opera, music, and dance.[4]

The French state, rather than the public, is the primary source of support for many of these performing arts institutions. For a national theater company such as the Comédie-Française, the government provides substantial subsidies that in recent years have exceeded 70 percent of the troupe's annual operating budget. This level of state funding is well over twice what non-commercial English theaters receive from the British state and more than ten times the proportion of direct federal funding enjoyed by a premier

American performing arts institution such as New York's Lincoln Center.[5] Indeed, the French state's especially prominent role in the nation's cultural production, embraced as an integral aspect of French exceptionalism, is without parallel elsewhere in the West.[6]

The high-profile cultural interventions through which the government has sought to engineer the cultural marketplace in the performing arts have drawn praise both domestically and abroad from those who admire the ministry's initiative and deep financial commitment to promoting French culture. "What money can buy, culturally speaking, the French have bought," one commentator observed.[7] Yet these policies have also sparked controversy, as demonstrated by the heated debates that erupted in the 1980s and 1990s. Critics have taken issue with the limited agency accorded to local and regional authorities in determining cultural policies, as well as the disproportionate scale at which Parisian institutions are funded, prompting repeated calls and initiatives for decentralization. They have questioned the effectiveness of the state's policies in achieving its stated goals of fostering cultural creation and democratizing participation in cultural institutions. Others have turned a spotlight on the sensitive issue of just what constitutes "French" culture worthy of public support.[8]

During these modern-day culture wars, politicians and scholars alike have identified deep historical roots for France's distinctive state-driven cultural agenda, often tracing its origins back to France's absolute monarchs. There is little doubt that the policies of Louis XIV and his Bourbon heirs deeply marked the cultural landscape in Paris and, through the preeminent royal institutions that Old Regime kings established and patronized, the nation as a whole. Yet viewing the cultural policies of the Old Regime court as a precursor for the current-day relationship between the state and cultural production, I suggest, obscures more than it illuminates. The evidence presented in this book throws the limits of such a genealogy into relief, with the relationship between the state and the stage in eighteenth-century France emerging as considerably more complex than the myth of a nascent absolutist cultural state would seem to allow. When the history of the French theater industry is reframed to take into account the experiences of the vast majority of French playhouses, actors, and spectators—namely, those in provincial cities located throughout the Hexagon as well as in France's colonial possessions—the cultural ambitions of Old Regime monarchs appear considerably more limited in scope than those of postrevolutionary regimes. Aimed at promoting theater and opera that would glorify the monarchy and establish the cultural supremacy of France, the royal policies established in the late seventeenth and eighteenth centuries focus almost exclusively on the capital and the court.

What is perhaps most remarkable is their lack of concern with theatrical life elsewhere in the kingdom. Even as patronage, privilege, and direct royal oversight came to define theatrical production in Paris, the emergent French theater industry as a whole developed very different strategies, operating according to models that were fundamentally commercial.

In fact, extensive state intervention in the theater industry on a national scale was largely a nineteenth-century innovation. In contrast with the court- and Paris-focused policies of earlier French kings, Napoleon Bonaparte inaugurated a centralized, coordinated policy for theatrical entertainment that encompassed urban France as a whole. Napoleon's assertion of author- ity over French theater in the early nineteenth century, as scholars point out, involved reinstating certain Old Regime practices that had been abolished during the French Revolution. He reimposed censorship and reestablished state subsidies and exclusive privileges for the three leading Paris stages, which were reclaimed as "national" theaters. Yet Napoleon's decree of 1806 and subsequent regulations also harbored greater ambitions. For the first time he expanded systematic state oversight to *all* public theaters in metropolitan France. Napoleon determined the number of public playhouses that would operate in each city: eight in Paris, two in Bordeaux, Lyon, Marseille, and Nantes, and one everywhere else. His minister of the interior designated which of these cities would entertain a sedentary municipal company, and he established twenty-five traveling circuits to be used by itinerant theater troupes to entertain audiences in smaller locales.[9] (The colonies, of which the recently independent Haiti was no longer part, were not addressed in this legislation.[10]) Moreover, Napoleon established a state licensing system for theater directors and their troupes that would define the French theater industry until 1864, a system that "made the government ultimately respon- sible for all theatres through its appointed delegates."[11] During the Restora- tion, King Louis XVIII built on these Napoleonic initiatives and even pushed them a step further when he directed municipal governments to build their own public theaters or to purchase them from their private owners whenever possible, in an effort to bring the theater arts more definitively under state authority.[12]

Even as these mechanisms of state oversight were being put into place, some contemporaries remained skeptical about the benefits of such policies for the theater business. "The best regulations in the world do not provide spectators," one critic cautioned, "and without spectators, no actors."[13] Most eighteenth-century theater companies, this author likely knew, had received little or nothing in the way of subsidies. They succeeded or failed based on their ability to marshal the patronage of enough paying customers. Yet he need not have worried about the financial implications of this new system. When nineteenth-century provincial theater companies experienced financial difficulties, municipal authorities across France felt compelled to step in to shore up their city's premier theater or opera company with subsidies that only grew over time. In fact, after 1824 the state permitted resident theater troupes to be established only in provincial cities that agreed that if necessary they would subsidize the director of the theater.[14] By the end of the nineteenth century, some city governments paid out as much as a quarter million francs annually to keep prestigious yet unprofitable stages in business.[15]

This nineteenth-century agenda of state intervention in the performing arts would have significant implications for the theater industry, not least by distancing these subsidized theater companies from their entrepreneurial and commercial roots, and from their intimate reliance on an expanding, socially diverse, and critical consumer public. On the production side, theater became more hierarchical. The authority of the licensed directors over their actors grew, even as directors working within this system found themselves with less real freedom and autonomy. Napoleon restricted the opportunities available to women in the theater profession. Despite the successes of eighteenth-century directrices such as Madame Destouches-Lobreau and Mademoiselle Montansier, his administration deemed women morally unfit to direct theater companies, an exclusionary practice that became law in 1824.[16] State regulation and licensing also curtailed local agency and innovation. Public theaters, to be sure, remained especially prominent social and political institutions, as well as symbols of civic pride and a source for urban rivalry.[17] But whereas eighteenth-century cities such as Lyon and Bordeaux, through the beautiful and influential public playhouses they constructed, found a means to contest Parisian cultural hegemony and to lead the nation, nineteenth-century regimes officially consolidated a tiered cultural framework within which the predominance of the national theaters of Paris would prove unassailable.

To understand how France's theater industry became so extensive and influential in the first place, I argue, it is necessary to recast the Old Regime state in a supporting rather than a leading role. Theaters, to be sure, commanded the attention of various royal authorities. This was particularly true after midcentury, as dozens of new playhouses were inaugurated and year-round performance companies began to take up residence in a significant number of cities, catering to their stagestruck residents. We should not discount the intervention of military commanders, royal governors, and intendants in the construction and renovation of certain playhouses, most notably the Théâtre de la Marine in Brest, and in the development of provincial theater privileges that opened new possibilities for directors to expand their operations. Yet, as a rule, the royal government was not interested in funding or managing theatrical production on the local level. Indeed, it is telling that in contemporary treatises calling for the reform of the French stage, those familiar with the business of theater complained above all about the *lack* of government intervention in theatrical production outside of Paris. These reformist actors and directors proposed a variety of strategies to achieve greater uniformity, centralization, order, and control within a field of enterprise that they characterized as sprawling and underregulated.[18]

Approaching the making of a French theater industry through the study of local practices not only recasts the nature of the absolute monarchy's engagement in French cultural life. It also deepens our knowledge of the new practices of cultural production and consumption that came to mark France during the final decades of the Old Regime—and of their influence on French society. Three points merit particular attention. First, local agency and innovation proved essential to the establishment of this vast cultural network. Rather than being imposed from above by a centralizing state, theatrical life in France was built up in provincial and colonial "peripheries." When it came to the everyday work of constructing playhouses, establishing theater companies, and staging productions, local entrepreneurs, investors, and theater professionals emerge as the crucial agents of cultural, social, and economic change.

Second, by the 1780s the French theater industry operated as an influential national and imperial media. Even a brief account of the performance history of Beaumarchais's influential blockbuster *The Marriage of Figaro* conveys this point clearly. When this controversial play finally received the approval of the censor and began its unprecedented run of performances at the Comédie-Française in late April of 1784, urban audiences elsewhere in France and the empire did not have long to wait until they, too, would have an opportunity to laugh at this risqué comedy and listen to the spirited valet's antiaristocratic monologue. Within months of the play's publication in 1785, acting companies staged the much-anticipated work in Lyon, Nantes, Rouen, Nancy, and Lille, as well as in the principal cities of Saint-Domingue. During the next few years directors in Bordeaux, Toulouse, Valenciennes, and undoubtedly many other cities presented *The Marriage of Figaro* to audiences eager to experience this cultural phenomenon for themselves.[19] As this example of diffusion suggests, spectators in far-flung cities flocked to performances featuring broadly similar repertories of French literature and music, performed at times by the same national stars in performances that may even have evoked similar sensibilities. By providing a framework for formative collective experiences, France's extensive commercial theater industry provided a powerful means for building cultural community and a sense of national identity. To paraphrase the historian William McNeill, theaters helped to keep French city dwellers together by enabling them to become culturally synchronized in time and across substantial geographic distance.[20] Yet, far from presenting spectators with a uniform or static spectacle of what it meant to be French, local public playhouses became forums for debate on how the nation should be defined, ordered, and even ruled.

Third, the history of France's theater industry broadens our understanding of France's expanding and increasingly commercialized public sphere. This is true not only because theaters were perhaps the most prominent and widespread institutions of the public sphere. Theaters also provide a rare window into the ways that public opinion was generated, wielded, and contested by groups of individuals in face-to-face social encounters, as opposed to through the more extensively studied medium of print.[21] The emergence of theatrical public opinion as a powerful public force was inextricably intertwined with the new egalitarian consumerist sensibility that emerged in France at this time.[22] Over the course of the eighteenth century, both theatrical production and consumption came to be defined by contractual relations that, in specifying payment for services, assumed a certain a priori equality among the parties. Indeed, by the 1780s professional theaters operated according to commercial principles that included according customers—noble as well as commoner—"an equal right" for their money.[23]

This is not to say that all would-be shareholders, actors, and customers were, in fact, equal. But even as some theater joint-stock companies, such as those in Bordeaux and Lorient, recruited only among wealthy and powerful notables, others deliberately reached out to potential investors across a broad social spectrum, and to men as well as women. In cities such as Le Mans and Saumur, the only criteria to become a shareholder were that an individual have the funds to contribute to the venture and perhaps a desire to participate in administering it. Even in Saint-Domingue, where the elite white members of the theater society of Le Cap expressly prohibited gens de couleur and those who married across the color line from participating as shareholders, elsewhere in the colony Jean-Louis Labbé, a prominent individual of mixed racial heritage, founded a playhouse and directed a theater company. Among theater professionals, it is true, salaries and opportunities varied widely. Yet this was because the terms of employment were negotiated on an individual, competitive basis in a national job market. Actors and actresses alike earned their living according to their talents and abilities as valued by market forces, a striking contrast with the structures of most guild-based work. Finally, for spectators, the status hierarchies embodied in theater seating in France's playhouses became increasingly complex and stratified over the course of the century. Women were everywhere excluded from standing in the parterre, while in the colonies the gens de couleur were relegated to segregated seating. Yet even taking into account these and other exceptions, such as the honorific seats accorded to ruling authorities and the subscriptions of military personnel, most theater spectators chose which performances to attend and which category of seating to occupy, making these decisions according to personal taste, evolving cultural and social expectations, and their ability and willingness to pay. Public theaters, in other words, offered opportunities that many other contemporary institutions of the public sphere did not.

Indeed, despite the political claims staked by local and royal authorities, in practice the business of theater in France operated according to what contemporaries recognized as a distinctly individualistic and egalitarian ethos. In this book I have suggested that this was neither accidental nor incidental, but embedded in theater's commercial foundations. Furthermore, if we take theater as our guide, the commercial public sphere, although not blind to gender or skin color, was neither essentially "masculinst" nor essentially racist.[24] Rather, it proved to be remarkably flexible, adaptive, and open to talent. Indeed, for those living in some eighty French and French colonial cities, the experience of attending performances in their local playhouse offered up striking counterexamples to the formal hierarchies of estate, gender, and race that implicitly and explicitly structured so much of everyday life.

The experience of spectatorship may have been ephemeral when compared with the consumer goods whose purchase transformed contemporaries' wardrobes, home environments, and domestic rituals. Its influence, however, was felt far beyond spectators' purses. Rather like the department stores of the late nineteenth century, the dedicated public playhouses and resident theater companies established during the eighteenth century can be seen as helping to introduce hundreds of thousands of urban customers to a new regime of consumption—in this case, the consumption of culture.[25] Public theaters offered their customers more than an evening of dramatic entertainment. As members of the professional and commercial bourgeoisie took seats next to aristocrats in prestigious first boxes, the theater also invited spectators to participate in a prominent and officially sanctioned social gathering that demonstrated the possibilities of social change.

Perhaps most significantly, theater spectatorship during this era was premised on a cultural consumption that was not passive, but rather was engaged and critical. Cultural criticism, along with arts patronage and self-conscious displays of luxury, ceased to be the domain of an exclusive aristocratic or courtly elite. Spectators—who purchased their tickets for fixed prices rather than bargaining as customers still did in most commercial transactions—by and large refused to subscribe to a mentality of caveat emptor that would have absolved the director and actors of responsibility for the quality of the evening's performances. Rather, audience members expressed their opinions loudly and cast their claims in the language of commercial rights. In 1787, one contemporary summed up this prevailing consumerist spirit as: "*I paid to enter the theater . . . so I acquired the right to state my way of thinking and to reject what displeases me.*"[26]

With their large crowds of enthusiastic and demanding spectators, France's theaters stood out to authorities and intellectuals alike as uniquely influential institutions. On this point, Jean-Jacques Rousseau's assessment of theater in his *Letter to M. d'Alembert on the Theatre* resounded broadly. The playwright and social commentator Louis-Sébastien Mercier observed: "A salle de spectacle is among us the only meeting point which gathers men; and where their voice can be raised in concert. It is there that this intimate feeling that penetrates the soul triumphs . . . and alerts it to its divinity. The Dramatic Art becomes in this way more important, more majestic, more worthwhile, and, from this point of view, one could call the theater the *chef-d'oeuvre* of society."[27] When the playwright Marie-Joseph Chénier compared the influence of reading a book with that of attending a theatrical performance, he placed much greater emphasis on the latter. "A book scattered in studies slowly manages to make a multitude of different impressions, but isolated ones, almost always without enthusiasm," he explained. In contrast, he argued: "The sensation that the performance of an excellent dramatic work makes upon two thousand people gathered at the Théâtre-Français is quick, passionate, unanimous. It is renewed twenty times a year in all the cities of France."[28]

When these theater spectators felt—and acted—passionately and in concert, they became much more than a "blind and noisy multitude" to be disdained or dismissed. They made themselves into a public.[29] Unlike the literary public, these theater publics were not brought into being by writers "claiming to speak in their readers' name."[30] For the many spectators who—despite official prohibitions—cheered or jeered a performance or watched others do so, theatrical public opinion was much more than a discursive construct. By the 1780s, it had emerged as a very real force that all directors, actors, and authorities had to reckon with. French political writers may have theorized that public opinion was essentially "rational, universal, impersonal, [and] unitary."[31] Theater directors, whose very livelihood required them to be particularly attuned to the vagaries of public opinion, knew better. On any given evening, their spectators might prove sober or whimsical, bored or impassioned, harmonious or violently at odds. Some nights a cabal attempted to dictate audience responses. Yet, as travelers and other contemporaries observed, an excellent performance of an excellent work indeed held the potential to unite and transport a rapturous public.

The members of these theater publics did more than speak a language of commercial rights. As we have seen, they vigorously applied and defended these concepts. In the 1780s, as royal authority waned, spectators in cities from Rouen to Bordeaux to Le Cap, Saint-Domingue, moved well beyond the use of the sifflet. Crowds organized protests, public demonstrations, and boycotts in the name of the public that gave them practice in "techniques of disobedience" directed against municipal and even royal authorities.[32] Ironically, the very playhouses and theater troupes that agents of the royal government had welcomed as a means to publicly assert their political authority and privileged status served to erode the hierarchical conception of the body politic upon which that authority and privilege were founded, one that was manifested in legal inequalities and, at least in theory, a royal monopoly on political authority. The royal government, as we have seen, proved neither willing nor able to effectively discipline spectators who had become convinced of the legitimacy of their actions. When royal authorities condoned protests and boycotts, and even at times privately endorsed them, they allowed theater spectators to gain powerful experience in wielding public opinion successfully to bring about change.

The Revolution quickly brought the commercialization of France's theater industry—a process that had been under way for decades—to its culmination. As early as mid-October of 1789 the Comédie-Française found itself abandoned by the crown when the Gentlemen of the King's Bedchamber instructed the troupe's members not to address future concerns to the royal household, but rather to the new mayor of Paris. Over a century of royal patronage and protection of the royal theaters soon came to a close.[33] Just fifteen months later, in January 1791, the National Assembly voted to abolish theatrical privilege throughout France, dismantling the system of monopoly concessions that had formed the basis upon which almost all French playhouses had been constructed and most theater troupes assembled. The Le Chapelier law, as it was known, permitted any individual to build and operate a playhouse, to establish and direct a theater troupe, and to perform any repertory. France's theater industry became a field of free competition. This legislation ushered in "a period of frantic dramatic activity" that proved both exhilarating and painful as dozens of new theaters opened—and, in many cases, closed—in the capital as well as in other cities throughout France.[34]

Early in the Revolution, actors demanded an end to the civil and political reprobation that had for so long marked their profession. In late 1789, they received recognition of their rights as citizens. Audiences, for their part, lost no time in claiming theaters as key spaces of revolutionary sociability and political contestation.[35]

Yet even in the midst of such changes, much of the day-to-day business of theater remained the same. Although directors of commercial theater troupes now competed openly with one another for paying spectators, they still hired actors, actresses, and singers to work for them on contract for a salary. Most still performed in playhouses built during the previous four decades. The troupes they assembled still staged varied repertories that were comprised substantially of traditional Old Regime favorites, complemented by contemporary revolutionary novelties.[36] As they struggled to stay in business, directors adapted the structures of commercial theatrical production that they had developed over the course of the eighteenth century to the new circumstances of the Revolution.[37]

According to the literary scholar Susan Maslan, revolutionary theater served as "perhaps the most significant crucible for the formation and expression of public opinion," playing a crucial role in "the creation of modern French democratic culture and democratic subjectivity."[38] This was possible, I argue, because during the late Old Regime, in France and in colonies such as Saint-Domingue, commercial theaters had already begun to rehearse these very roles. During the decades leading up to 1789, France's theater professionals and their spectators developed a repertory of cultural practices and convictions that they drew upon as royal authority collapsed and the nation embarked on the process of forging a new social and political order.[39]

Timeline of Inaugurations and Significant Renovations of Dedicated Public Theaters in France and the French Colonies, 1671–1789

Each entry in this timeline, unless otherwise noted, refers to the inauguration of a playhouse that was open to the public and dedicated for the purposes of theatrical entertainment. These buildings may have been newly constructed or converted from an earlier purpose. When a city appears more than once on the timeline, this typically indicates that a new theater has replaced an earlier one that was damaged, destroyed, closed, or simply deemed inadequate. Because of the substantial number of public theaters in the capital, additional information has been provided about Parisian playhouses to allow readers to distinguish among them. This timeline was compiled from a large number of sources, which are provided in the notes.[1]

1671	Toulouse
1685	Marseille
1688	Lyon
1690	Lyon (new theater replaced playhouse destroyed in fire)
1689	Paris, Comédie-Française moved to the rue des Fossés-Saint-Germain-des-Près
1692	Montpellier
1695	Marseille
1699	Lille
1701	Strasbourg

1702	Lille (new theater replaced theater destroyed in fire in 1700)
1712	Metz
1719	Dijon
1720	Bordeaux
1728	Lyon
1729	Metz (theater improved)
1732	Bordeaux
1733	Marseille
1734	Avignon
1737	Rennes
	Rouen
	Toulouse
1739	Bordeaux
	Nîmes
1740	Brest (date uncertain, 1740s)
1742	La Rochelle
1743	Dijon (theater renovated and improved)
1745	Nantes (date uncertain, by 1745)
1748	Nancy (former court theater opened to public)
1749	Amiens
1750	Angoulême
1752	Arras
	Metz
	Paris, Opéra-Comique in the Saint-Laurent Fairground
	Perpignan
1754	Troyes
1755	Bordeaux
	Carpentras
	Montpellier
	Nancy
1756	Lyon
1757	Versailles
1758	Aix-en-Provence
	Douai
1759	Clermont-Ferrand
	Paris, Théâtre de Nicolet (Théâtre des Grands Danseurs du Roi) on the Boulevard du Temple
1760	Montauban
1761	Auch
	Tours

1762	Limoges (theater located in Hôtel de Ville also held meetings of merchant court)
	Port-au-Prince, Saint-Domingue
1763	Angers
	Dieppe
1764	Cap Français, Saint-Domingue (private society theater opened to public)
	Paris, Paris Opera moved to the renovated Salle des Machines in the Tuileries Palace
1765	Caen
	Nevers
1766	Brest
	Cap Français, Saint-Domingue (new, larger theater inaugurated)
	Les Cayes, Saint-Domingue
	Lunéville (court theater became public)
	Poitiers
	Toulon
	Toulouse (theater expanded, renovated)
1768	Agen
	Colmar
	Grenoble
	Paris, Théâtre des Associés on the Boulevard du Temple
1769	Paris, Théâtre d'Audinot (later Théâtre de l'Ambigu-Comique) on the Boulevard du Temple
	Rochefort
	Saint Marc, Saint-Domingue
1770	Abbeville
	Bastia, Corsica (date uncertain, early 1770s)
	Port Louis, Île de France (present-day Mauritius, date uncertain, before 1773)
	Paris, Paris Opera relocated to the Palais-Royal
1771	Châlons-sur-Marne (city now named Châlons-en-Champagne)
	Limoges (existing stage was dedicated exclusively for performance)
	Saint-Pierre, Martinique
1772	Basse-Terre, Guadeloupe
	Mâcon
1773	Cambrai

Le Havre

Saint Marc, Saint-Domingue (new theater replaced theater
  destroyed in earthquake)

1774   Bayonne

Beauvais

Paris, Théâtre des Associés on the Boulevard du Temple (new
  theater was built)

Saint-Quentin

1775   Le Puy

1776   Le Mans

Rouen

1777   Dunkerque

Langres

Reims

Troyes

Versailles

1778   Alençon

Port-au-Prince, Saint-Domingue

Soissons

1779   Chalon-sur-Saône

Lorient

Paris, Théâtre des Variétés-Amusantes (later known as the
  Théâtre des Élèves de l'Opéra) on the Boulevard du Temple

1780   Amiens

Angoulême

Bordeaux

Laval (date uncertain, theater inaugurated c. 1780)

1781   Paris, Paris Opera moved to the Boulevard Saint-Martin

Valenciennes

1782   Paris, Comédie-Française moved to the Théâtre-Français (now
  the Théâtre de l'Odéon)

Pointe-à-Pitre, Guadeloupe

Vienne

1783   Paris, Comédie-Italienne moved to the Théâtre des Italiens
  (also known as the Opéra-Comique; remodeled just one
  year later)

1784   Besançon

Nancy (theater extensively renovated)

Paris, Théâtre de Beaujolais in the Palais-Royal

Quimper

1785	Arras

1785   Arras
Douai
Compiègne
Jacmel, Saint-Domingue
Périgueux (date uncertain, theater inaugurated c. 1785)
Léogane, Saint-Domingue
Pau
Saintes
1786   Paris, Théâtre de l'Ambigu-Comique (theater renovated)
1787   Lille
Marseille
Montpellier (theater rebuilt after fire)
Saint-Étienne
Saint-Pierre, Martinique (new theater built)
1788   Les Cayes, Saint-Domingue
Nantes
Saumur
1789   Fort-Royal, Martinique (date uncertain, opened by 1789)
Nîmes

NOTES

The following abbreviations are used in the notes.

Archives and Libraries

AD	Archives départementales
AM	Archives municipales de
AN	Archives nationales, Paris
ARS	Bibliothèque de l'Arsenal, Paris
AV	Archives de la Ville et de la Communauté urbaine de
BM	Bibliothèque municipale de
BMCF	Bibliothèque-Musée de la Comédie-Française, Paris
BNF	Bibliothèque nationale de France, Paris
CAOM	Centre des Archives d'Outre-Mer, Aix-en-Provence
NL	Newberry Library, Chicago
SHD	Service historique de la Défense, Vincennes

Journals

AESC	*Annales: Économies. Sociétés. Civilisations*
AHR	*American Historical Review*
FHS	*French Historical Studies*
JMH	*Journal of Modern History*
RHMC	*Revue d'histoire moderne et contemporaine*
RHT	*Revue d'histoire du théâtre*
RSBAD	*Réunion des sociétés des beaux-arts des départements*

Introduction

1. Charles-Simon Favart, *Mémoires et correspondance littéraires, dramatiques et anec-dotiques, de C.S. Favart*, 3 vols. (Geneva: Slatkine Reprints, 1970), II: 45, Favart to M. le comte de Durazzo, 28 December 1762.

2. Ibid., "to need and to rarity" and "multiply . . . to infinity," II: 133, Favart to Durazzo, 29 July 1763; "each provincial city," II: 45, Favart to Durazzo, 28 December 1762.

3. Bertrand de La Tour, *Réflexions morales, politiques, historiques, et littéraires, sur le théâtre*, 10 vols. (Avignon: Marc Chave, 1763-66), I:1–2.

4. Ibid., 2–3; Charles Desprez de Boissy, *Lettres sur les spectacles: Avec une histoire des ouvrages pour & contre les théâtres*, 6th ed., 2 vols. (Paris: Boudet, 1777), I: 601.

5. On the origins of professional theater in France and the establishment of regular public theater in Paris, see W. L. Wiley, *The Early Public Theatre in France*

(Cambridge: Harvard University Press, 1960). On theater in provincial cities during the sixteenth and seventeenth centuries, including the marginal status of seventeenth-century professional public theater when compared with Jesuit theater, see Sara Beam, *Laughing Matters: Farce and the Making of Absolutism in France* (Ithaca: Cornell University Press, 2007).

6. For the locations of the new public theaters inaugurated in French and French colonial cities between the 1670s and 1789, the dates of their inauguration, and the citations for this evidence, see the appendix.

7. Roger Chartier, Dominique Julia, and Marie-Madeleine Compère, *L'Éducation en France du XVI au XVIIIe siècle* (Paris: Société d'édition d'enseignement supérieur, 1976) 249–50; "*chambre de commerce,*" in Jacques Savary des Bruslons, *Dictionnaire universel de commerce, d'histoire naturelle, et des arts et métiers*, 4 vols. (Paris: Veuve Estienne, 1750), I: 797–809; Daniel Roche, *Le Siècle des lumières en province: Académies et académiciens provinciaux, 1680–1789*, 2 vols. (Paris: Mouton, 1978), I: 15–74; and Gilles Feyel, "La Presse provinciale française dans la seconde moitié du 18e siècle: Géographie d'une nouvelle fonction urbaine," in *La Ville et l'innovation: Relais et réseaux de diffusion en Europe, 14e–19e siècles*, ed. Bernard Lepetit and Jochen Hoock (Paris: Éditions de l'École des hautes études en sciences sociales, 1987), 89–111, esp. 93. According to Ran Halévi, Masonic lodges, which numbered at least 650 by the Revolution, did outnumber theaters: *Les Loges maçonniques dans la France d'Ancien Régime: Aux origines de la sociabilité démocratique* (Paris: A. Colin, 1984), 19.

8. Of the playhouses operating in French domains as of 1789, the largest accommodated more than a thousand spectators, including those of Lyon (2,000), Bordeaux (1,726), Rouen (1,450), Metz (1,400), and Le Cap Français, Saint-Domingue (1,500). The smallest public theaters, such as those in Avignon and Vienne, held only a few hundred. Here, I take the audience capacity of the theaters of middling cities such as Arras (550), Montauban (500), Le Mans (600), Pau (800), Dunkerque (984) and Cambrai (900–1,000) as more broadly representative. Therefore, I base this estimate on seven hundred spectators per theater for the eighty-two public theaters in the provincial and colonial cities listed in the appendix. Most of these theaters, it should be noted, did not host resident theater companies. They would have offered performances several evenings a week, for only part of the year. Pierre Frantz and Michèle Sajous-d'Oria, with Giuseppe Radicchio, *Le Siècle des théâtres: Salles et scènes en France, 1748–1807* (Paris: Bibliothèque historique de la Ville de Paris, 1999), 94, 100, 138, 154, 158–159, 167, 175, 181–182, 184, 187; Henri Lagrave, "Le dix-huitième siècle (1715-1789): Le 'siècle d'or bordelais'," in Henri Lagrave, Charles Mazouer, and Marc Regaldo, *La Vie théâtrale à Bordeaux des origines à nos jours. Tome 1: Des origines à 1799* (Paris: Éditions du CNRS, 1985) [henceforth cited as Lagrave, *La Vie théâtrale à Bordeaux*], 233; Henri Tribout de Morembert, *Le Théâtre à Metz*: Tome 1, Du Moyen Age à la Revolution (Metz: Éditions Le Lorrain, 1952), 1:65; M. L. E. Moreau de Saint-Méry, *Description topographique, physique, civile, politique et historique de la partie française de l'isle Saint-Domingue*, ed. Blanche Maurel and Etienne Taillemite, 3 vols. (Paris: Société française d'histoire d'outre-mer, 1984), I: 358; Robert Deschamps La Rivière, *Le Théâtre au Mans au XVIIIe siècle* (Mamers: Fleury et Dangin, 1900), 33. The Paris theater audience estimate is taken from Martine

de Rougemont, *La Vie théâtrale en France au XVIIIe siècle* (Paris: Honoré Champion, 1988), 223.

9. The concept of England as Europe's leader in commercial culture was articulated forcefully in Neil McKendrick, John Brewer, and J. H. Plumb, *The Birth of a Consumer Society: The Commercialization of Eighteenth-Century England* (Bloomington: Indiana University Press, 1982), and it continues to inform works such as John Brewer's *Pleasures of the Imagination: English Culture in the Eighteenth Century* (New York: Farrar, Straus and Giroux, 1997), xxiii–xxv. On the playhouses and touring acting troupes of provincial England, see Sybil Rosenfeld, *Strolling Players and Drama in the Provinces, 1660–1765* (New York: Octagon Books, 1970), and Peter Borsay, *The English Urban Renaissance: Culture and Society in the Provincial Town 1660–1770* (Oxford: Clarendon Press, 1989), 117–122, 329–31.

10. In approaching theater as a business enterprise of remarkable cultural influence, I have been inspired by Robert Darnton's *The Business of the Enlightenment: A Publishing History of the* Encyclopédie, *1775–1800* (Cambridge: Harvard University Press, 1979).

11. Perhaps the paradigmatic expression of cultural change driven by the French state can be found in Eugen Weber's *Peasants into Frenchmen: The Modernization of Rural France* (Palo Alto: Stanford University Press, 1976). On twentieth-century state interventionism in the cultural sphere, see Philippe Poirrier, *L'État et la culture en France au XXe siècle* (Paris: Le Livre de Poche, 2000), and especially Marc Fumaroli, *L'État culturel: Une religion moderne* (Paris: Flammarion, 1991). On the state and the performing arts, see F. W. J. Hemmings, *Theatre and State in France, 1760–1905* (Cambridge: Cambridge University Press, 1994).

12. Pierre Nora, volume introduction to Pierre Nora, ed., *Rethinking France: Les lieux de mémoire*, vol. 1, *The State*, trans. Mary Trouille under the direction of David P. Jordan (Chicago: University of Chicago Press, 2001), 1: xxxvi.

13. Quote from Roger Chartier, "Trajectoires et tensions culturelles de l'Ancien Régime," in André Burguière, ed., *Les Formes de la culture* (Paris: Édition de Seuil, 1993), 307–92, 345 (quote). On this process of cultural centralization, see esp. Peter Burke, *The Fabrication of Louis XIV* (New Haven: Yale University Press, 1992).

14. François Hédelin, abbé d'Aubignac, *La Pratique du théâtre par l'abbé d'Aubignac* (Amsterdam: Jean Frédéric Bernard, 1715), 7.

15. Robert Isherwood, *Music in the Service of the King: France in the Seventeenth Century* (Ithaca: Cornell University Press, 1973); Jean-Marie Apostolidès, *Le Roi-machine: Spectacle et politique au temps de Louis XIV* (Paris: Les Éditions de Minuit, 1981); and Georgia Cowart, *The Triumph of Pleasure: Louis XIV and the Politics of Spectacle* (Chicago: University of Chicago Press, 2008). On the establishment of the royal theaters, see Rougemont, *La Vie théâtrale en France*, 213–60; Émile Campardon, *Les Comédiens du roi de la troupe italienne pendant les deux derniers siècles* (Paris: Berger-Levrault et Cie, 1880), xvii; and Victoria Johnson, *Backstage at the Revolution: How the Royal Paris Opera Survived the End of the Old Regime* (Chicago: University of Chicago Press, 2008), 83–147. On theater as "royal spectacle," see James Johnson, *Listening in Paris: A Cultural History* (Berkeley: University of California Press, 1995), 9–34.

16. Max Fuchs makes this argument in *La Vie théâtrale en province au XVIIIe siècle* (Paris: E. Droz, 1933), esp. 44 and 53. Although Fuchs privileges the heavy hand of the royal government, he does acknowledge that theater's expansion entailed "the capitalist transformation of the acting profession" (7). Subsequent historians have relied extensively on Fuchs's work, as in Hemmings, *Theatre and State in France*, 3, 137–42. Daniel Rabreau likewise emphasizes the role of the royal government in theater building and design during this era in his beautifully illustrated *Apollon dans la ville: Le Théâtre et l'urbanisme en France au XVIIIe siècle* (Paris: Éditions du Patrimoine, 2008), 9, 30 and 206. Rougemont, in contrast, suggests somewhat ambiguously that theater was imposed on the provinces by Paris, in *La Vie théâtrale en France*, 17.

17. I borrow this phrase from Isherwood, *Music in the Service of the King*.

18. The urban populations cited in this book are taken from Bernard Lepetit, *The Pre-industrial Urban System: France, 1740–1840* (Cambridge: Cambridge University Press, 1994), appendix B.

19. McKendrick, Brewer, and Plumb sparked intense—and intensely productive—scholarly debate following the publication of *The Birth of a Consumer Society*. Daniel Roche deserves credit for pioneering scholarship on the consumer revolution in France in *The People of Paris: An Essay in Popular Culture in the 18th Century*, trans. Marie Evans and Gwynne Lewis (Berkeley: University of California Press, 1987); idem., *The Culture of Clothing: Dress and Fashion in the Ancien Régime*, trans. Jean Birrell (Cambridge: Cambridge University Press, 1994); and idem., *A History of Everyday Things: The Birth of Consumption in France, 1600–1800*, trans. Brian Pearce (Cambridge: Cambridge University Press, 2000). Scholarship in this field is too extensive to survey here, but notable works include Cissie Fairchilds, "The Production and Marketing of Populuxe Goods in Eighteenth-Century Paris," in *Consumption and the World of Goods*, ed. Roy Porter and John Brewer (New York: Routledge, 1993), 228–48; Annik Pardailhé-Galabrun, *The Birth of Intimacy: Privacy and Domestic Life in Early Modern Paris*, trans. Joyce Jocelyn Phelps (Philadelphia: University of Pennsylvania Press, 1991); and Jennifer M. Jones, *Sexing La Mode: Gender, Fashion and Commercial Culture in Old Regime France* (Oxford: Berg, 2004). Many studies focus on Paris, but scholars have confirmed that the provinces also experienced a surge in consumption and consumerism in the eighteenth century: Michel Figeac, *La Douceur des Lumières: Noblesse et art de vivre en Guyenne au XVIII siècle* (Bordeaux: Mollat, 2001), and Colin Jones, "The Great Chain of Buying: Medical Advertisement, the Bourgeois Public Sphere, and the Origins of the French Revolution," *AHR* 101 (February 1996): 13–40.

20. Colin Jones, *The Great Nation: France from Louis XV to Napoleon* (London: Penguin, 2002), 358; Louis-Sébastien Mercier observed that "you can no longer guess a man's profession from his dress or circumstances" in *Panorama of Paris: Selections from "Le Tableau de Paris," by Louis-Sébastien Mercier*, ed. Jeremy D. Popkin, trans. Helen Simpson and Jeremy D. Popkin (University Park: Penn State Univ. Press, 1999), 54.

21. Lepetit emphasizes the importance of networks of exchange among French cities during this era in *The Pre-industrial Urban System*.

22. Jürgen Habermas, *The Structural Transformation of the Public Sphere: An Inquiry into a Category of Bourgeois Society*, trans. Thomas Burger (Cambridge: MIT Press, 1989). For a further discussion of Habermas's theory, see Craig Calhoun, ed., *Habermas and the Public Sphere* (Cambridge: MIT Press, 1992); Jones, "Great Chain of Buying," 16.

23. Jeffrey S. Ravel, "The Coachman's Bare Rump: An Eighteenth-Century French Cover-Up," *Eighteenth-Century Studies* 40:2 (2007): 279–308, quote from 281.

24. Jeffrey S. Ravel, *The Contested Parterre: Public Theater and French Political Culture, 1680–1791* (Ithaca: Cornell University Press, 1999), esp. 3–7. In contrast, scholars such as Keith Michael Baker have defined the public sphere as "the literary public sphere." See "Defining the Public Sphere in Eighteenth-Century France: Variations on a Theme by Habermas," in *Habermas and the Public Sphere*, ed. Calhoun, 181–211, esp. 184–85; and, more broadly, Baker's essays in *Inventing the French Revolution: Essays on French Political Culture in the Eighteenth Century* (Cambridge: Cambridge University Press, 1990).

25. These quotes are from Jones, "Great Chain of Buying," 16, and Habermas, *Structural Transformation*, 38, who also writes of this process on 21, 35, and 164. For Jones's arguments linking commercialization to the making of a revolutionary bourgeoisie, see "Great Chain of Buying" as well as "Bourgeois Revolution Revivified: 1789 and Social Change," in *Rewriting the French Revolution*, ed. Colin Lucas (Oxford: Clarendon Press, 1991), 69–118.

26. Thierry Rigogne similarly seeks to reframe our understanding of cultural production by considering the kingdom as a whole, although excluding the colonies, in *Between State and Market: Printing and Bookselling in Eighteenth-Century France* (Oxford: Voltaire Foundation, 2007).

27. Benedict Anderson, *Imagined Communities: Reflections on the Origin and Spread of Nationalism* (London: Verso, 1991), 5–7.

28. Nicolas Bricaire de la Dixmerie, *Lettres sur l'état présent de nos spectacles, avec des vues nouvelles sur chacun d'eux, particulièrement sur la Comédie Françoise & l'Opéra* (Amsterdam: Duchesne, 1765), 6–8; Nicolaï Karamzine, *Lettres d'un voyageur russe*, trans. Wladimir Berelowitch (Paris: Quai Voltaire, [1792] 1991), 158. Karamzine's letters in this collection are dated from 1789 and 1790.

29. Anderson credits print-capitalism in general, and newspapers in particular, with establishing the foundations for a national consciousness during the early modern era. They forged community in part by establishing a new sense of simultaneity among readers, who became conscious that they were reading the same news at the same time. *Imagined Communities*, 22–46.

30. My thanks to David Bell for suggesting this approach.

31. My thinking on this subject has been influenced by Stéphane Gerson's *The Pride of Place: Local Memories and Political Culture in Nineteenth-Century France* (Ithaca: Cornell University Press, 2003), esp. 278. On the problems with a diffusion model of culture, see also Peter Borsay, "The London Connection: Cultural Diffusion and the Eighteenth-Century Provincial Town," *London Journal* 19: 1 (1994): 21–35.

32. According to Daniel Roche, Paris represented 7.6 percent of the urban population of metropolitan France in 1750 and only 6.5 percent in 1790. *France in the Enlightenment*, trans. Arthur Goldhammer (Cambridge: Harvard University Press, 1998), 180.

33. By way of comparison, at any one time total membership in provincial academies came to approximately twenty-five hundred members, although these academies also held events and contests that were open to the public. Membership in French Masonic lodges at this time has been estimated variously at around thirty-five thousand and between fifty thousand and one hundred thousand. Given source

limitations, it would be difficult to hazard a guess as to the total size of the theater-going public in eighteenth-century France. It does seem clear, however, that public theater audiences during the Old Regime rivaled and probably even exceeded in size the readership of the periodic press, which at its peak featured more than eighty different newspapers and journals that together sold upwards of sixty thousand copies a year. Roche, *Le Siècle des lumières*, I: 189, 192; Jeremy Caradonna, *The Enlightenment in Practice: Academic Prize Contests and Intellectual Culture in France, 1670-1794* (Ithaca: Cornell University Press, 2012); Halévi, *Les Loges maçonniques*, 43; Roche, *France in the Enlightenment*, 436; Jack Censer, *The French Press in the Age of Enlightenment* (London: Routledge, 1994), 12, 184; Jones, "Great Chain of Buying," 18.

34. Among the numerous studies of the theaters of Paris, the works they performed, and the importance of the stage more broadly in the social, intellectual, and political life of this era, see especially Marvin A. Carlson, *The Theatre of the French Revolution* (Ithaca: Cornell University Press, 1966); William Weber, "L'Institution et son public: L'Opéra à Paris et à Londres au XVIIIe siècle," *AESC* 48 no. 6 (November-December 1993): 1519–40; Johnson, *Listening in Paris*; Ravel, *Contested Parterre*; David Trott, *Théâtre du XVIIIe siècle: Jeux, écritures, regards* (Montpellier: Éditions Espaces 34, 2000); Paul Friedland, *Political Actors: Representative Bodies and Theatricality in the Age of the French Revolution* (Ithaca: Cornell University Press, 2002); Gregory S. Brown, *A Field of Honor: Writers, Court Culture and Public Theater in French Literary Life from Racine to the Revolution* (New York: Columbia University Press, 2005); and Susan Maslan, *Revolutionary Acts: Theater, Democracy, and the French Revolution* (Baltimore: Johns Hopkins University Press, 2005). Scholars such as Marie-Emmanuelle Plagnol-Diéval and Dominique Quéro have only recently begun to study the private theatricals that were so popular in France during this era. See their edited volume, *Les Théâtres de société au XVIIIe siècle* (Brussels: Éditions de l'Université de Bruxelles, 2005).

35. Max Fuchs's *La Vie théâtrale en province au XVIIIe siècle* appeared in 1933. Fuchs continued this project in *Lexique des troupes de comédiens au XVIIIe siècle* (Paris: Librairie E. Droz, 1944), and the posthumously published *La Vie théâtrale en province au XVIIIe siècle: Personnel et répertoire* (Paris: Éditions du CNRS, 1986). Rabreau recently noted that since 1933, in this field "knowledge has progressed relatively little," despite mounting evidence that does not fit Fuchs's chronology and interpretation (*Apollon dans la ville*, 23). Architectural studies such as Rabreau's are noteworthy exceptions to the general neglect of theater beyond Paris. See also Frantz and Sajous d'Oria, *Le Siècle des théâtres*, and Michèle Sajous d'Oria, *Bleu et or: La scène et la salle en France au temps des Lumières, 1748–1807* (Paris: CNRS Éditions, 2007). With regards to colonial theater, Jean Fouchard produced the classic studies *Le Théâtre à Saint-Domingue* (Port-au-Prince: Imprimerie de l'État, 1955) and *Artistes et repertoire des scènes de Saint-Domingue* (Port-au-Prince: Imprimerie de l'État, 1955). Interest in colonial stages has been recently revived in works such as Laurent Dubois and Bernard Camier, "Voltaire et Zaïre, ou le théâtre des Lumières dans l'aire atlantique française," *RHMC* 54:4 (December 2007): 39–69.

36. One particularly valuable example of this body of work is Lagrave, *La Vie théâtrale à Bordeaux*.

37. On trends in cultural pessimism in the twentieth century, see Tyler Cowen, *In Praise of Commercial Culture* (Cambridge: Harvard University Press, 1998), esp. 9–14, 181–210. Noteworthy French critiques of commercial culture include Guy Debord,

The Society of the Spectacle, trans. Donald Nicholson-Smith (New York: Zone Books, 1994), and Jean Baudrillard, *The Consumer Society: Myths and Structures*, trans. Chris Turner (London: Sage, 1998).

38. Jean-Jacques Rousseau, *Politics and the Arts: Letter to M. d'Alembert on the Theatre*, trans. Allan Bloom (Ithaca: Cornell University Press, 1960), 26, 100.

39. John McManners, *Church and Society in Eighteenth-Century France: Volume 2, The Religion of the People and the Politics of Religion* (Oxford: Clarendon Press, 1998), 312–42.

40. Rousseau, *Politics and the Arts: Letter to M. d'Alembert*, 62–63, 73–74, 119.

41. Ibid., 98. In using a longer version of this quote as an epigraph for this book, I took the liberty of changing the translation of the French term *moeurs* from Bloom's "manners [morals]" to "mores," which I consider to be truer to the original.

42. Roger Chartier, *The Cultural Origins of the French Revolution*, trans. Lydia G. Cochrane (Durham: Duke University Press, 1991), 2.

43. See, for example, Baker, *Inventing the French Revolution*; Robert Darnton, *The Forbidden Best-Sellers of Pre-Revolutionary France* (New York, W. W. Norton, 1996); Sarah Maza, *Private Lives and Public Affairs: The Causes Célèbres of Prerevolutionary France* (Berkeley: University of California Press, 1993); Jones, "Great Chain of Buying."

1. Investing in the Arts

1. *Affiches du Mans*, 12 December 1774, p. 199.

2. AD de la Sarthe 111 AC 611, "Extrait des registres du Bureau de l'hôtel de ville du Mans." On the history of theater in Le Mans before the new theater was inaugurated, see Deschamps La Rivière, *Le Théâtre au Mans*, esp. 6–24; and L. H.[ublin], *Notice sur le théâtre et sur les anciennes salles de spectacle du Mans* (Le Mans: Pellechat, 1885).

3. *Affiches du Mans*, 12 December 1774, p. 199. The subscription, initially estimated at one hundred shares to raise fifteen thousand livres, was later expanded to 120 shares. AD de la Sarthe 111 AC 611, "Tableau de la société d'actionnaires." On Chesneau-Desportes, the society and the playhouse, see Deschamps La Rivière, *Le Théâtre au Mans*, 24–74.

4. *Affiches du Mans*, 2 January 1775, p. 3; 23 January 1775, p. 15; 6 February 1775, p, 22-23; 13 February 1775, p. 28; AD de la Sarthe 111 AC 611 "Arrest du conseil du Monsieur, frère du roi," 20 May 1775.

5. AD de la Sarthe 111 AC 611; Sylvie Granger, "Il était une fois une salle de spectacle," *La Vie mancelle et Sarthoise* 42 (April 2001): 6–7, esp. 7.

6. Gustave Cohen, *Le Théâtre en France au Moyen Âge*, 2 vols. (Paris: Rieder, 1928); Carol Symes, *A Common Stage: Theater and Public Life in Medieval Arras* (Ithaca: Cornell University Press, 2007); Beam, *Laughing Matters*.

7. Paul Scarron, *Le Roman comique, par M. Scarron*, new ed., 4 vols. (London: n.p., 1781) 1: 21–30. Scarron published the first installment of the work in 1651.

8. Robert Mesuret, *Le Théâtre à Toulouse, de 1561 à 1914* (Toulouse: Musée Paul Dupuy, 1972), 10–17; Georges Mongrédien and Jean Robert, *Les Comédiens français du XVIIe siècle: Dictionnaire biographique, suivi d'un inventaire des troupes, 1590–1710, d'après des documents inédits* (Paris: Éditions du CNRS, 1981), 309–26.

9. See the appendix.

10. Ibid. In this book, the city of Bastia, Corsica, is included as part of metropolitan France. These numbers include the first playhouses deliberately renovated or built new and dedicated exclusively for the purpose of theatrical performance, as well as later theaters built to replace these earlier structures. The evidence presented here differs significantly from that presented by Fuchs, which is commonly cited by scholars. Fuchs argued that theater declined in popularity and theater-building slowed precipitously during the last fifteen years of the Old Regime: Fuchs, *La Vie théâtrale en province au XVIIIe siècle*, 53, 105–7.

11. Fuchs, *La Vie théâtrale en province au XVIIIe siècle*; Hemmings, *Theatre and State*, 3; Dominique Leroy, *Histoire des arts du spectacle en France* (Paris: L'Harmattan, 1990), esp. 79 and 81; Rabreau, *Apollon dans la ville*, 9 and 30; Rougemont, *La Vie théâtrale en France*, 17.

12. The theater that Mademoiselle Montansier constructed in Le Havre is included here because it was already under way in 1789, although it was not inaugurated until the following year. A list of these playhouses, along with bibliographical references on the individuals or groups building them, is presented in Lauren Clay, "Patronage, Profits, and Public Theaters: Rethinking Cultural Unification in Ancien Régime France," *JMH* 79 (December 2007): 729–71, 741–42, 771. To those, I am adding the privately built theaters in Toulouse (1671) and Bordeaux (1732). (The privately built theater in Amiens (1780), included in this data, was inadvertently omitted from the timeline of that article.) Because the construction of the Besançon theater was supported by both the municipality and the royal government, that playhouse is included in both of these categories. Mesuret, *Théâtre à Toulouse*, 10–17; Lagrave, *La Vie théâtrale à Bordeaux,* 172.

13. Quoted from AN T 210, 3, Papiers la Ferronnays. Petition from the shareholders of the theater in Cap-François, Saint-Domingue, 1774. A similar sentiment was conveyed in a report on the theater of Marseille arguing that "almost all the playhouses of the kingdom belong to cities": AN H 1359, n. 81, "Observations sur les projets de construction d'une salle de spectacle à Marseille."

14. See note 12. These fifty-six theaters (which do not include the three theaters built through aristocratic patronage) were located in forty-five cities.

15. Georges Mongrédien provides a list of acting companies "protected" by members of the royal family as well as other eminent noble families in *Dictionnaire biographique des comédiens français du XVIIe siècle* (Paris: Éditions du CNRS, 1972), 173–97. Detailed financial discussions between the directors of the theater companies in Marseille and Lyon make no mention of financial patronage from the royal governors whose names they bear. AM Lyon 3 GG 98 and 99.

16. On the development of the provincial privilege, see Max Fuchs, "Recherches sur les origines au privilège provincial des theaters," *RHMC* 26 (1930): 81–100; AM Nantes GG 676, n. 10; and chapter 3 of this book.

17. Armand-Paul Vogt, *Le Théâtre à Nancy depuis ses origines jusqu'en 1919* (Nancy: Impr. Grandeville, Beigue et Cie, 1921), 4–6.

18. On the Theatres Royal established by the British Parliament, see Rosenfeld, *Strolling Players*, 2, and Allardyce Nicoll, *The Garrick Stage: Theatres and Audience in the Eighteenth Century* (Athens: University of Georgia Press, 1980), 64–66. The

closest French case was the establishment of the naval theater in Brest where the performers were known, at least briefly, as the *Comédiens du roi au port de Brest.* Prosper Levot, *Histoire de la ville et du port de Brest*, 3 vols. (Brest: l'auteur, 1864–66), II: 273–86.

19. Such requests were explicitly denied to both Grenoble and Arras. AN H 39 IV, n. 52, "Arras, 1783: Amortissement d'une salle de spectacle."

20. On the involvement of intendants with urban building projects, see Jean-Louis Harouel, *L'Embellissement des villes: L'urbanisme français au XVIIIe siècle* (Paris: Picard, 1993), and Richard Cleary, *The Place Royale and Urban Design in the Ancien Régime* (Cambridge: Cambridge University Press, 1999), 13.

21. Frantz and Sajous d'Oria, *Le Siècle des théâtres*, 122, 136, 177, 179, 181, 188; Pierre Jourda, *Le Théâtre à Montpellier: 1755–1851* (Oxford: Voltaire Foundation, 2001), 13.

22. Cleary, *Place Royale and Urban Design*, 12–14; Gail Bossenga, *The Politics of Privilege: Old Regime and Revolution in Lille* (Cambridge: Cambridge University Press, 1991), 39.

23. Lagrave, *La Vie théâtrale à Bordeaux*, 196.

24. Cleary makes this point in *Place Royale and Urban Design*, 14, 47.

25. On the drawbacks of these seats even at the Paris Opera, see Johnson, *Listening in Paris*, 16–17.

26. France's intendancies are listed in Léon Mirot and Albert Mirot, *Manuel de géographie historique de la France* (Paris: Picard, 1979), 315–24 and 349–95.

27. On municipal authority over performance in the seventeenth century and earlier, see Beam, *Laughing Matters*; on the eighteenth century, see Fuchs, *La Vie théâtrale en province au XVIIIe siècle*, 115–26.

28. Clay, "Patronage, Profits, and Public Theaters," 741–42 and 771.

29. Robert Mesuret, *Le Théâtre à Toulouse*, 16–18; Emmanuel Vingtrinier, *Le Théâtre à Lyon au XVIIIe siècle* (Lyon: Metton, 1879), 11; Pantaléon Deck, *Histoire du théâtre français à Strasbourg (1681–1830)* (Strasbourg: F. X. Le Roux & Cie, 1948), 20–21.

30. On the costs of these new public playhouses, see *Trois siècles d'opéra à Lyon: De l'Académie royale de musique à l'opéra-nouveau* (Lyon: Association des amis de la Bibliothèque municipale de Lyon, 1982), 52; Lagrave, *La Vie théâtrale à Bordeaux*, 180; Etienne Destranges, *Le Théâtre à Nantes depuis ses origines jusqu'à nos jours, 1430?–1893* (Paris: Librairie Fischbacher, 1893), 32–37.

31. On municipal motivations for building a theater, see esp. "Déclaration de l'assemblée des notables autorisant les consuls à transférer la salle de spectacle dans l'ancien local de l'élection," 9 December 1767, reprinted in Francisque Habasque, *Documents sur le théâtre à Agen, 1585–1788* (Agen: Imprimerie Veuve Lamy, 1893), 14–15; *Délibération du conseil de ville tenu pour la construction de la salle de spectacle* issued in 1759, reproduced in André Bossuat, "Le Théâtre à Clermont-Ferrand aux XVIIe et XVIIIe siècles," *RHT* 13 (1961): 105–71, esp. 146; Jules-Édouard Bouteiller, *Histoire complète et méthodique des théâtres de Rouen: Depuis leur foundation jusqu'à nos jours*, 4 vols. (Rouen: Giroux et Rénaux, 1860), I: 24.

32. Nicholas Papayanis, *Planning Paris before Haussmann* (Baltimore: Johns Hopkins University Press, 2004), 17.

33. Quoted in G. Musset, "Le Théâtre à La Rochelle avant la Révolution de 1789," *RSBAD* (1889): 649–58, 656 (quote).

34. Until 1769, Lorient served as the headquarters to the French East India Company. The company's recent bankruptcy may have cast uncertainty on the city's fortunes. Quoted in J. L. Debauve, *Théâtre et spectacles à Lorient au XVIIIe siècle* (Paris: chez l'auteur, 1966), 28.

35. "Histoire des salles: Documents inédits, XVIIIe siècle. Jeux de Paume, Marchés d'aménagement en théâtres," *RHT* 4 (1948–49): 271–72.

36. Ibid.

37. Tribout de Morembert, *Le Théâtre à Metz*, 1: 33.

38. This painting, created c. 1716, is reproduced in Frantz and Sajous d'Oria, *Le Siècle des théâtres*, 9.

39. On the spaces where performances took place in French cities during the late seventeenth century, see Mongrédien and Robert, *Les Comédiens français du XVIIe siècle*, 309–26; Albert de Luze, *La Magnifique histoire du jeu de paume* (Paris: Delmas, 1933), 88–117; and "Histoire des salles: Jeux de paume, Marchés d'aménagement en théâtres," 271–72. Léon Lefebvre, *Histoire du théâtre de Lille de ses origines à nos jours*, 5 vols. (Lille: Lefebvre-Ducrocq, 1901–07), I: 175; André Segond and Eric Arrouas, *L'Opéra de Marseille, 1787–1987* ([Marseille]: Jeanne Lafitte, 1987), 9, 63; *Trois siècles d'opéra à Lyon*, 50–53; Mesuret, *Théâtre à Toulouse*, 10–17.

40. Jourda, *Théâtre à Montpellier*, 12.

41. Tribout de Morembert, *Le Théâtre à Metz*, 34.

42. Ibid., 47–65; Lucien Decombe, *Recherches d'histoire locale: notes et souvenirs. Le Théâtre à Rennes* (Rennes: F. Simon, 1899), 44; Gustave Lhotte, *Le Théâtre à Douai avant la Révolution* (Douai: L. Crépin, 1881), 50–51; É. G. de Clerambault, "Le Théâtre à Tours à l'époque de la Révolution," *Bulletin trimestriel de la Société archéologique de Touraine* 20 (1916): 81–91, esp. 82–83; Frantz and Sajous d'Oria, *Le Siècle des théâtres*, 143, 165, 191, 192.

43. Destranges, *Le Théâtre à Nantes*, 20–21; Frantz and Sajous d'Oria, *Le Siècle des théâtres*, 160; Danielle Teil and Roger Heyraud, *Saint-Étienne et le théâtre: Du vaudeville à la comédie, 1650/1990* (Paris: Éditions Xavier Lejeune, 1990), 10–12.

44. Segond and Arrouas, *L'Opéra de Marseille*, 9; Lagrave, *La Vie théâtrale à Bordeaux*, 172; Édouard-Hippolyte Gosselin, *Recherches sur les anciens théâtres du Havre et d'Yvetot* (Rouen: C.-F. Lapierre, 1875), 16–33; Jacques Villard, *Le Théâtre Montansier à Versailles: De la Montansier à Francis Perrin* (Marly-le-Roi: Éditions Champflour, 1998), 15–16.

45. For an overview of the Parisian theater system and its restrictive monopolies, see Rougemont, *La Vie théâtrale en France*, 235–78.

46. For an example of such a theater privilege, see AN H 1359 n. 74.

47. Quoted in Frantz and Sajous d'Oria, *Le Siècle des théâtres*, 160.

48. Quoted in Frédérique Pitou, "Les Pratiques de divertissement à Laval au XVIIIè siècle," *Histoire urbaine* 1 (June 2000): 87–104, 96 (quote).

49. AD de la Loire-Atlantique C 392, n. 73, 74, 78, and 46, contracts from 4 April 1755, 17 April 1756, 10 April 1747, and statement from the intendant from 10 November 1771.

50. AN H 1359, n. 92.

51. AN H 1359, n. 122. Chomel to Monseigneur de Calonne, 13 February 1784. When the Beauvais playhouse was ordered closed in 1786, the owner protested, echoing Chomel's despair at the loss of his livelihood. Ernest Charvet, *Recherches sur le anciens théâtres de Beauvais* (Beauvais: Imprimerie D. Père, 1881), 143–44.

52. Marseille conducted this investigation in 1739. AN H 1359, n. 92, 95, 96.

53. Villard, *Le Théâtre Montansier*, 33–35.

54. Roche, *History of Everyday Things*, 42.

55. These included playhouses and/or theater companies in Bordeaux, Marseille, Nantes, Montpellier, Limoges, Reims, Rouen, Le Havre, Nîmes, Rochefort, Toulon, Toulouse, Lille, Lorient, Le Mans, Lyon, Nancy, Perpignan, Valenciennes, and Saumur. AM Bordeaux GG 1004 b, letter to Bordeaux from Marseille on behalf of the theater shareholders, 1783; Destranges, *Le Théâtre à Nantes*, 41–42; AD de la Loire-Atlantique C 321 n. 45; SHD A^1 3677, p. 140, "Arrest du conseil d'état du roi, Conçernant des actionnaires du spectacle de Nancy," and A^1 3694 f. 223; BMCF 2 ATO Carton 198, Province 1776, Laurent [to CF], 9 April 1776; Province 1774, [Anon. to CF] 17 October 1774, and Comédiens divers, hors Comédie-Français [henceforth Com. div.], "Directrice Destouches Lobreau," Montrose Dalainval to Destouches-Lobreau, 1779; Léon Vallas, *Un Siècle de musique et de théâtre à Lyon 1688–1789* (Lyon: P. Masson, 1932), 224–25, 403, 425–26; AD de la Sarthe 111 AC 611; Robert Clément, *Les Théâtres de Nîmes au cours des siècles* (Nîmes: Lacour, 1986), 12–13; Monique Moulin, *L'Architecture civile et militaire au XVIIIe siècle en Aunis et Saintonge* (La Rochelle: Quartier Latin, 1972), 73–75: Louis Paris, *Le Théâtre à Reims depuis les Romains jusqu'à nos jours* (Reims: F. Michaud, 1885), 259–60 and 154; BNF Ms. Nouvelles acquisitions françaises (hereafter Naf) 9411 f. 284; *Mercure de France*, September 1769, pp. 174–75; *Affiches du Mans*, 30 September 1776, p. 157; Bouteiller, *Histoire . . . des théâtres de Rouen*, 1: 24; A.-Jacques Parès, *Aperçu sur les spectacles de Toulon avant la Révolution* (Toulon: Soc. Nouv. des Imprimeries Toulonnaises, 1936), 14–15; Segond and Arrouas, *L'Opéra de Marseille*, 9; Debauve, *Théâtre et spectacles à Lorient*, 29; René Maurice, *La Création du théâtre à Lorient au XVIIIe siècle* (Lorient: Impr. du Nouvelliste de Morbihan, 1941), 7–8. The joint-stock societies of Le Mans, Saumur, and Lille are discussed at length below.

56. Henri Lévy-Bruhl, *Histoire juridique des sociétés de commerce en France aux XVIIe et XVIIIe siècles* (Paris: F. Loviton & Cie., 1938), 42–53, 180–273.

57. The dates listed parenthetically indicate the year when these theaters were inaugurated.

58. A. Durieux, *Le Théâtre à Cambrai avant et depuis 1789* (Cambrai: J. Renaut, 1883), 50; René Ancely, *Histoire du théâtre et du spectacle à Pau sous l'ancien régime* (Pau: Impr. commerciale des Pyrénées, 1955), 22–23; A. Fray-Fournier, *Le Théâtre à Limoges avant, pendant & après la Révolution* (Limoges: Ussel Frères, 1900), 113–15; Deck, *Histoire du théâtre français à Strasbourg*, 26; Émile Quéruau-Lamerie, *Notice sur le théâtre d'Angers (1755–1825)* (Angers: Germain et G. Grassin, 1889), 72; AD de la Loire-Atlantique C 321 nos. 3, 10, and 13.

59. Moulin, *L'Architecture civile et militaire*, 73–75; Henry Rousset, *Le Théâtre à Grenoble: Histoire et physionomie 1500–1890* (Grenoble: Imprimerie Dauphinoise, 1891), 7–9; Bouteiller, *Histoire . . . des théâtres de Rouen*, I: 24; Debauve, *Théâtre et spectacles à Lorient*, 29; Paris, *Le Théâtre à Reims*, 259–60 and 154; Maurice, *La Création du*

théâtre à Lorient, 7–8; Lefebvre, *Histoire du théâtre de Lille*, II: annexe II, 406–18; AM Saumur 4M93, *Tableau général de messieurs les actionaires des halles et salle de spectacle, construites à Saumur par forme de tontine* (Saumur: Dominique-Michel de Gouy, 1789); AN H 1359; and Parès, *Aperçu sur les spectacles de Toulon*, 15.

60. These investors were aided by the prince de Guéméné, who was alleged to have paid an additional one hundred thousand livres for decorations for the playhouse. Debauve, *Théâtre et spectacles à Lorient*, 24–29 and 33; Maurice, *La Création du théâtre à Lorient*, 7–8.

61. On the development of the tontine, see Robert M. Jennings and Andrew P. Trout, *The Tontine: From the Reign of Louis XIV to the French Revolutionary Era* (Philadelphia: S. S. Huebner Foundation for Insurance Education, University of Pennsylvania, 1982). The inspiration for this form of funding a theater may have come from Britain, where theaters were built by selling shares in the enterprise in cities including Bristol (1729), Bath (1750), Sheffield (1762), and Liverpool (1772). Borsay, *English Urban Renaissance*, 329–31. The fact that the earliest theater joint-stock companies were located in Atlantic port cities such as Bordeaux (1760) and Rochefort (1766) suggests that investors may also have been inspired by French commercial investment models.

62. Lefebvre, *Histoire du théâtre de Lille*, 2: v; and Paris, *Le Théâtre à Reims*, 155.

63. On gambling in the eighteenth century, see Francis Freundlich, *Le Monde du jeu à Paris, 1715–1800* (Paris: Albin Michel, 1995), and John Dunkley, *Gambling: A Social and Moral Problem in France, 1685–1792* (Oxford: Voltaire Foundation, 1985).

64. Lefebvre, *Histoire du théâtre de Lille*, 2: xxi–xxiv.

65. Sources enabled me to reconstruct the social background of ninety-nine of the 108 shareholders in the case of Le Mans, seventy-two of seventy-six in the case of Lille, and one hundred out of 116 in the case of Saumur. For each of these societies, a female investor who did not have a noble title or occupation listed was associated, wherever possible, with the social group representative of her husband or family. This analysis is based on AD de la Sarthe 111 AC 611, *Tableau de la société d'actionnaires, Autorisée par Monsieur, frère du roi, suivant ses lettres-patentes du 20 mai 1775, pour la construction d'une sale de spectacle dans la Ville du Mans, Conforme au registre journal de Mr. Rey, Trésorier de ladite société* (Le Mans: Charles Monnoyer, 1777), and information from the register of the theater society kept by M. Rey; AM Saumur 4M93, *Tableau général*; "Arrest du conseil d'état du roi, Qui approuve & autorise la construction d'une salle de spectacles en la ville de Lille, Du 26 janvier 1785," *Recueil des édits, arrêts, lettres-patentes, déclarations, règlemens et ordonnances, Imprimés & mis à exécution par ordre de M. l'intendant ou par les différens tribunaux de la ville de Lille* (Lille: N.-J.-B. Peterinck-Cramé, Imprimeur ordinaire du Roi, 1785); and Lefebvre, *Histoire du théâtre de Lille*, 2: Annexe II, 406–18. Lists of these investors are reproduced in Lauren Clay, "Theater and the Commercialization of Culture in Eighteenth-Century France" (PhD diss., University of Pennsylvania, 2003), 339–46.

66. According to William Doyle, of the more than fifty thousand venal offices in France, commoners held the vast majority. Only about thirty-seven hundred offices conferred nobility directly on their owners. *The Oxford History of the French Revolution* (New York: Oxford University Press, 1989), 25–26. Unless noble status is otherwise indicated in the records, these individuals have been considered members of the Third Estate.

67. AD de la Sarthe 111 AC 611, *Tableau de la société d'actionnaires* and register.

68. Lefebvre, *Histoire du théâtre de Lille*, 2: 406–18.

69. AM Saumur 4M93, *Tableau général*, and 4M92, "Extrait du registre des délibérations des actionnaires pour la construction de la salle de spectacle, et des halles, à Saumur."

70. Jean-Baptiste Cassin, "prêtre," purchased two shares in the society, as did Honoré Bauné, "prêtre, prieur." AM Saumur 4M93, *Tableau général*.

71. *Affiches du Mans*, 12 December 1774; 2 January 1775; 23 January 1775; 13 February 1775.

72. AM Saumur 4M92, "Extrait du registre."

73. Ibid.

74. The only exceptions were the initial two investors in the Saumur project, who purchased eighteen shares and twelve shares, respectively, in the endeavor.

75. AM Saumur 4M92, "Extrait du register," "Ordonnance de police, 29 avril 1788."

76. Daniel Roche has documented that the majority of the members of provincial academies (57 percent) were nobles or clergy. The remaining minority included lawyers and other professionals, as well as officeholders, but few individuals engaged in commerce, trade, or manufacturing. The election of women to academies, he notes, was extremely rare: Roche, *Le Siècle des lumières en province*, I: 99–105, 193, 197. Although women were typically excluded from Masonic lodges, Margaret Jacob notes that some Continental lodges did in fact begin to admit women in the later eighteenth century, including several in France: *Living the Enlightenment: Freemasonry and Politics in Eighteenth-Century Europe* (Oxford: Oxford University Press, 1991), 69, 120–42. Among these theater societies, ten women owned shares in Le Mans. Five women in Lille owned shares on their own accord, a sixth woman was a co-owner of two shares with her husband, and a share was purchased by a man on behalf of seventh woman or girl. Women in Saumur were clearly identified as owners of five shares, including one share that was collectively owned by four women or girls with the same family name, presumably sisters. For Saumur, I also include an additional five shareholders not listed as madame, mademoiselle, or widow, but who have traditionally female names. For sources, see note 65.

77. AM Saumur 4M92, "Extrait du registre."

78. According to theater records, the society began reimbursing shareholders in 1788. Cited in Paris, *Le Théâtre à Reims*, 261 and 269.

79. Similarly, investors in Nancy created a joint-stock company to support a resident theater company "in the view of public utility and with the specific renunciation of all profit." SHD A^1 3677, p. 140. "Arrest du conseil d'état du roi, Concernant des actionnaires du spectacle de Nancy."

80. For investors inspired by "the general good" and by a "patriotic zeal," see AD de la Loire-Atlantique C 321, n. 45, 22 July 1770; and *Affiches du Mans*, 6 March 1775, p. 39. On the centrality of utility in Enlightenment discourse, see Jones, *Great Nation*, 171–225, esp. 174–78, 191; on professionals, see Jones, "Bourgeois Revolution Revivified," esp. 98–99, 107–12.

81. Michel Taillefer, "L'échec d'une tentative de réforme académique: Le Musée de Toulouse (1784–1788)," *Annales du Midi* 89, no. 134 (1977): 405–18; John Iverson, "Forum: Emulation in France, 1750-1800, Introduction," *Eighteenth-Century Studies*

36 (2003): 217–23; Catherine Duprat, *"Pour l'amour de l'humanité"*: *Le temps des philanthropes; La philanthropie parisienne des Lumières à la Monarchie de Juillet*, 2 vols. (Paris: Éd. du C.T.H.S., 1993), 1:59.

82. On the concept of cultural capital, see Pierre Bourdieu, *Distinction: A Social Critique of the Judgment of Taste*, trans. Richard Nice (Cambridge: Harvard University Press, 1984), esp. 1–96, 112–14.

83. "Actionnaires du théâtre de Rochefort, en 1766," *Recueil de la Commission des arts et monuments historiques de la Charente-Inférieure et Société d'archéologie de Saintes* 7 (1884): 326–29. This was also the case with joint-stock companies supporting resident theater troupes. In Bordeaux, we have seen, the duc de Richelieu founded that society in 1760. In Nantes, a society to establish a resident theater company recruited the support of the duc de Duras, one of the king's closest advisors, as well as the marquis de Brancas, governor of the city. AN H 1359 n. 81 and n. 156; AD de la Loire-Atlantique, C 321, n. 45.

84. Roche, *Le Siècle des lumières en province*; Guy Chaussinand-Nogaret, *The French Nobility in the Eighteenth Century: From Feudalism to Enlightenment*, trans. William Doyle (Cambridge: Cambridge University Press, 1985), 33–35.

85. Christine Adams, *A Taste for Comfort and Status: A Bourgeois Family in Eighteenth-Century France* (University Park: Pennsylvania State University Press, 2000), 189, and also 194.

86. Daniel Roche notes that of the six thousand members of France's academies during the Old Regime, fewer than 160 were traders and manufacturers. "Négoce et culture dans la France du XVIIIe siècle," *RHMC* 25 (1978): 375–95, esp. 376–77, 381.

87. Jones, "Bourgeois Revolution Revivified," 104–10.

88. Maurice, *La Création du théâtre à Lorient*, 7; Debauve, *Théâtre et spectacles à Lorient*, 29.

89. Debauve, ibid.

90. Philip T. Hoffman, Gilles Postel-Vinay, and Jean-Laurent Rosenthal, *Priceless Markets: The Political Economy of Credit in Paris, 1660–1870* (Chicago: University of Chicago Press, 2000), 62, 66–67, 160–61, 164–65.

91. On noble investment in joint-stock companies, see Guy Richard, "La Noblesse de France et les sociétés par actions à la fin du XVIIIe siècle," *Revue d'histoire économique et sociale* 40 (1962): 485–523.

92. Maurice, *La Création du théâtre à Lorient*, 7–8; Fernand Braudel and Ernest Labrousse, eds., *Histoire économique et sociale de la France. Tome II: Des derniers temps de l'âge seigneurial aux préludes de l'âge industriel (1660–1789)* (Paris: Presses universitaires de France, 1970), 616, 632–41.

93. AM Saumur 4M93, *Tableau général*. In provincial Britain, a significant number of theaters were built through investment by subscriptions, with subscribers often earning a profit. Evidence suggests, however, that these English theaters drew support almost exclusively from elites, resulting in a less socially diverse group of investors than theaters in France. Helen Berry, "Creating Polite Space: The Organization and Social Function of the Newcastle Assembly Rooms," in *Creating and Consuming Culture in North-East England, 1660–1830*, ed. Helen Berry and Jeremy Gregory (Aldershot: Ashgate, 2004), 120–40, esp. 133.

94. AD de la Sarthe 111 AC 611, Pinchinat to Chesneau Desportes, 18 February 1776.

95. Extensive records about rentals of the theater are available from 1776 until 1784. A payment of twelve livres was made in 1778. Thereafter, payments of between two livres ten sous and fifteen livres, averaging about ten livres, were made to shareholder each year until at least 1793. Sources regarding these payments are not available after this point. AD de la Sarthe 111 AC 611. The rental arrangement in Le Mans differed from the strategy employed by the theater society in Reims, which instead took one-seventh of the profits earned by performers, as well as income from balls and dances held in the theater. The investors aimed to host troupes for six months of the year, and to use the space for balls and dances during the other six months. Paris, *Théâtre à Reims*, 268–69.

96. Many documents related to the building of the Marseille theater can be found in AN H 1359, esp. nos. 90-185.

97. AN H 1359, n. 113 and n. 74, "Lettres-Patentes du Roi." On Ledoux's design for this Marseille playhouse, which arrived too late to be included in the competition, see Anthony Vidler, *Claude-Nicolas Ledoux: Architecture and Social Reform at the End of the Ancien Régime* (Cambridge: MIT Press, 1990), 185–90.

98. AN H 1359, n. 103, letter from Rebuffet to M. Harivel, 13 April 1785.

99. AN H 1359, n. 73. Letter from Rebuffet and associates to Mgr. Necker, Ministre d'État, 19 November 1788.

100. AM Lyon 3 GG 101, n. 220, 4 September 1787, letter from Bonneville to M. les Prevôt des marchandes et échevins; AM Lyon 3 GG 99, November 1787, "Questions relatives à l'entreprise des spectacles de Marseille."

101. Even after this point, the former theater served as a dance hall, concert hall, and meeting space until it was demolished in 1986. Granger, "Il était une fois," 7.

102. Lefebvre, *Histoire du théâtre de Lille*, 2: xx–xxi.

103. AM Saumur 4M92, "Extrait du register des délibérations."

104. Segond and Arrouas, *L'Opéra de Marseille*, 69; William B. Cohen, *Urban Government and the Rise of the French City: Five Municipalities in the Nineteenth Century* (New York: St. Martin's Press, 1998), 129.

105. Jones, "Bourgeois Revolution Revivified," 109.

106. *Affiches du Mans*, 12 December 1774, p. 200.

107. *Affiches du Mans*, 23 January 1775, p. 15.

108. Those elected were the marquis de Vennevelles, M. de Vandy (*directeur général des fermes du roi*), M. de Fondville (*receveur des tailles*), and M. Chesneau-Desportes. *Affiches du Mans*, 13 February 1775, p. 28.

109. *Affiches du Mans*, 24 November 1777, p. 186.

110. For example, see *Affiches du Mans*, 13 February 1775, p. 28; 17 July 1775, p. 29; 27 November 1775, p. 190; 20 May 1776, p. 83; 3 March 1777, p. 34; 24 November 1777, p. 186; 24 March 1783, p. 47; 14 April 1788, p. 58.

111. In Reims, too, the general assembly of shareholders met repeatedly and established regulations for the theater, and the society elected directors as well as a treasurer. The records of the theater society in Saumur demonstrate that as early as the preliminary meeting, decisions would be made according to majority rule (*à la pluralité des voix*). Although a commission of six was entrusted to make certain

decisions, such as determining the placement of the new theater, important decisions were regularly reserved for a meeting of the general assembly of the shareholders. Paris, *Le Théâtre à Reims*, 262; AM Saumur 4M92, "Extrait du registre"; "Actionnaires du théâtre de Rochefort, en 1766," 328.

112. Lévy-Bruhl, *Histoire juridique des sociétés de commerce*, 192–99.

113. *Affiches du Mans*, 13 February 1775, p. 28. In a sample contract for the Lille tontine, five representatives are listed, of whom four were noble. Lefebvre, *Histoire du théâtre de Lille*, II: 419.

114. Nineteenth-century private organizations of arts patronage include the art associations discussed in Sherman's *Worthy Monuments: Art Museums and the Politics of Culture in Nineteenth-Century France* (Cambridge: Harvard University Press, 1989), 132–53; and the music patrons and concert societies discussed in William Weber, *Music and the Middle Class: The Social Structure of Concert Life in London, Paris, and Vienna between 1830 and 1848*, 2nd ed. (Burlington: Ashgate, 2004), 61–98.

115. Although the Comédie-Française and the Comédie-Italienne were administered through the King's Household throughout the Old Regime, after 1749 responsibility for the Paris Opera shifted between the city and the royal government. Rougemont, *La Vie théâtrale en France*, 235–60, esp. 254; Weber, "L'Institution et son public," 1528–33; Claude Alasseur, *La Comédie-Française au 18e siècle: Étude économique* (Paris: Mouton, 1967), 45, 72.

116. On the chronic insolvency of the Paris Opera and need for subsidies for its survival during the Old Regime and Revolution, see Johnson, *Backstage at the Revolution*, 41–42, 161–78, 194.

117. Alasseur, *La Comédie-Française au 18e siècle*, 9, 37–41.

118. Monique Mosser and Daniel Rabreau, eds., *Charles de Wailly, peintre architecte dans l'Europe des Lumières* (Paris: Caisse nationale des monuments historiques et des sites, 1979), 65–67.

119. BMCF 2 ATO Province 1774, Lamare [to CF], 7 February 1774.

120. AD de la Sarthe 111 AC 611. This comment, made considerably earlier, was relayed in a letter by Delinière, 2 April 1776.

121. See *Affiches du Mans*, 25 March 1776, p. 50, and 13 May 1776, p. 78.

122. *Affiches du Mans*, 13 May 1776, p. 78.

123. *Affiches du Mans*, 20 May 1776, p. 82. See also AD de la Sarthe 111 AC 611, "Dévis éstimatif de la dépense à faire pour construire un batiment de 80 pieds de longueur sur 40 de largeur."

124. *Affiches du Mans*, 20 May 1776, p. 81.

2. Designing the Civic Playhouse

1. AM Nantes BB 105, f. 30v-31, 15 March 1777. On the history of this playhouse, including the groups urging the construction of a new playhouse, see Alain Delaval's *Le Théâtre Graslin à Nantes* (Nantes: Joca Seria, 2004), esp. 13–78.

2. BM Nantes 50103, "Remarques sur la nécessité de construire une salle provisionnelle de spectacles à Nantes, Par une société d'amateurs," 2.

3. As seen in chapter 1, similar land development strategies involving public theaters were employed in Marseille and Paris. In Lyon, the impact that the new the-

ater was likely to have on property values in the city stirred controversy over where it should be located. See BM de Lyon, Fonds Coste 50 (1462), "Réclamations contre le choix de l'emplacement pour la construction d'une salle de spectacle"; as well as AD du Rhône 1C 202, "Projet de bâtir une nouvelle salle dans le jardin de l'hôtel de ville" and "Opposition de plusieurs habitants."

4. BM Nantes 50106, "Observations de M. Graslin, Sur les additions très-importantes à faire au quartier neuf de Nantes," 44.

5. These cost estimates were provided in AM Nantes GG 289, parish register by Father Le Feuvre, rector at St. Nicolas, in notes 1 and 2 at end of register. They are confirmed in Destranges, *Le Théâtre à Nantes*, 34–40.

6. Arthur Young, *Travels in France During the Years 1787, 1788 & 1789*, ed. Constantia Maxwell (Cambridge: Cambridge University Press, 1950), 115.

7. On developments in theater architecture during this period, including discussions of the theaters of Lyon and Bordeaux, see especially Daniel Rabreau's *Apollon dans la ville* and Frantz and Sajous d'Oria's well-illustrated exhibition catalogue, *Le Siècle des théâtres*, which features brief discussions of the new theaters built in Paris as well as in dozens of provincial cities during this era. On the influence of theater architecture and its place within the context of French architecture more generally, see Louis Hautecoeur's classic *Histoire de l'architecture classique en France*, 7 vols. (Paris: Picard, 1943–57), vol. 4, esp. 160–61 and 430–51; and Wend von Kalnein's *Architecture in France in the Eighteenth Century*, trans. David Britt (New Haven: Yale University Press, 1995), 85, 166–67, 184–87, 228–29, 235–36.

8. J. F. Blondel, *Cours d'architecture, ou Traité de la décoration, distribution & construction des bâtiments; Contenant les leçons données en 1750, & les années suivantes*, 6 vols. (Paris: Desaint, 1771–77), II: 263–64.

9. *Trois siècles d'opéra à Lyon*, 52; Lagrave, *La Vie théâtrale à Bordeaux*, 180; Destranges, *Le Théâtre à Nantes*, 32–37.

10. On eighteenth-century urban development, see Harouel, *L'Embellissement des villes*. Here I borrow from Daniel Sherman's *Worthy Monuments*.

11. Rabreau, for example, emphasizes intendants and governors as the primary agents in eighteenth-century theater building, which he describes as characteristic of French centralization. Although he acknowledges that others participated in building and designing theaters, their roles, he argues, were "distributed from Paris" (*Apollon dans la ville*, both quotes from 30). In this, he follows scholarship on seventeenth- and eighteenth-century France that traditionally depicts the expanding monarchic state—through its royal governors and especially its intendants—as the force behind eighteenth-century urbanization. In this literature, municipal authorities often appear as passive participants and even as coerced victims of political centralization. Pierre Lavedan, *Les Villes françaises* (Paris: Vincent, Fréal, & Cie., 1960), 147; Emmanuel Le Roy Ladurie with Bernard Quilliet, "Baroque et lumières," in *Histoire de la France urbaine: Tome 3, La ville classique de la Renaissance aux Révolutions*, ed. Georges Duby (Paris: Seuil, 1981), 287–535, esp. 439–81, 485–88; and Nora Temple, "Control and Exploitation of French Towns during the Ancien Regime," in *State and Society in Seventeenth-Century France*, ed. Raymond Kierstead (New York: New Viewpoints, 1975), 67–87. For more balanced accounts of the roles played by local authorities in urban building and cultural affairs, see Harouel, *L'Embellissement des villes*, and Cleary, *Place Royale and Urban Design*.

12. Voltaire (François-Marie Arouet), "Dissertation sur la tragédie ancienne et moderne," preface to "Sémiramis" (1748) in *Oeuvres complètes de Voltaire*, 70 vols. (Paris: Impr. de la Société littéraire-typographique, 1785–89), III: 340–41.

13. Mongrédien and Robert, *Les Comédiens français du XVIIe siècle*, 309–26; T. E. Lawrenson, *The French Stage and Playhouse in the XVIIth Century: A Study in the Advent of the Italian Order*, 2nd ed. (New York: AMS Press, 1986); Frantz and Sajous d'Oria, *Le Siècle des théâtres*.

14. André-Jacob Roubo, *Traité de la construction des théâtres et des machines théâtrales* (Paris: Cellot & Jombert, 1777), 27; Frantz and Sajous d'Oria, *Le Siècle des théâtres*, 10, 47–59.

15. David Garrick, *The Diary of David Garrick, Being a Record of His Memorable Trip to Paris in 1751*, ed. Ryllis Clair Alexander (New York: Benjamin Blom, 1971), 5.

16. David Garrick, *The Journal of David Garrick Describing His Visit to France and Italy in 1763*, ed. George Winchester Stone Jr. (New York: Modern Language Association of America, 1939), 6–7.

17. Denis-Pierre-Jean Papillon de la Ferté, *Journal de Papillon de la Ferté, intendant et contrôleur de l'argenterie, menus-plaisirs, et affaires de la chambre du roi (1756–1780)*, ed. Ernest Boysse (Paris: Paul Ollendorff, 1887), 198. See entry for 16 February 1767.

18. Hester Lynch (Thrale) Piozzi and Samuel Johnson, *The French Journals of Mrs. Thrale and Doctor Johnson*, ed. Moses Tyson and Henry Guppy (Manchester: Manchester University Press, 1932), quotes from 98, 96, 98, emphasis in original.

19. Jacques-François Blondel, *Architecture françoise*, 4 vols. (Paris: Charles-Antoine Jombert, 1752), II: 14–15.

20. Roubo, *Traité de la construction des théâtres*, 3.

21. Pierre Patte, *Essai sur l'architecture théâtrale: ou, De l'ordonnance la plus avantageuse à une salle de spectacles, relativement aux principes de l'optique & de l'acoustique* (Paris: Moutard, 1782), 105.

22. On the construction and design of the theaters of Montpellier and Metz, see Jourda, *Le Théâtre à Montpellier*, 11–19; Tribout de Morembert, *Le Théâtre à Metz*, 47–65; Rabreau, *Apollon dans la ville*, 34–39. The plans for these influential theaters were reproduced, along with those of Lyon, Paris, and several other European cities, in the plates of the *Encyclopédie* under the heading "Théâtres," *Recueil de planches, sur les sciences, les arts libéraux, et les arts méchaniques, avec leur explication*, 11 vols. (Paris: Briasson, 1762–72), vol. 10. They also appear in Gabriel Pierre Martin Dumont, *Parallèle de plans de plus belles salles de spectacles d'Italie et de France, avec des détails de machines théâtrales* (New York: B. Blom, 1968), originally published in 1774.

23. Rabreau discusses this trend in *Apollon dans la ville*, 42–71. See also Lagrave, *La Vie théâtrale à Bordeaux*, 175–80; Dumont, *Parallèle de plans*; and Frantz and Sajous d'Oria, *Le Siècle des théâtres*, 55–60, 101–6, 110, 113, 128–29, 143, 186–87.

24. Vingtrinier, *Le Théâtre à Lyon*, 11.

25. AD du Rhône 1 C 202, Letter to M. le comte de Saint-Florentin, 25 June 1754.

26. AM Lyon BB 321 f. 35 bis-36.

27. The Lyon theater was the most expensive public theater constructed in France to that point, far exceeding the costs of the theater of Metz (about 250,000 livres), as well as the theater for the Comédie-Française (about 200,000 livres). Pierre

Claude Reynard estimates that the cost to the city was even higher: over one million livres. Tribout de Morembert, *Le Théâtre à Metz*, 51–52; *Trois siècles d'opéra à Lyon*, 52; Alasseur, *La Comédie-Française au 18e siècle*, 9, 37–41; Reynard, *Ambitions Tamed: Urban Expansion in Pre-revolutionary Lyon* (Montreal: McGill-Queen's University Press, 2009), 20.

28. J. G. Soufflot, *L'Oeuvre de Soufflot à Lyon: Études et documents* (Lyon: Presses universitaires de Lyon, 1982), esp. 221–22. On Soufflot and the Lyon theater, see also Allan Braham, *Architecture of the French Enlightenment* (London: Thames and Hudson, 1980), 19–82, esp. 30.

29. The theaters of Metz (inaugurated 1752) and Montpellier (inaugurated 1755) also appeared as monumental buildings set off on plazas. The Montpellier theater was freestanding, while the Metz playhouse would be flanked by other buildings through arches. Rabreau, *Apollon dans la ville*, 34–37; Donald C. Mullin, *The Development of the Playhouse: A Survey of Theatre Architecture from the Renaissance to the Present*, (Berkeley: University of California Press, 1980), 87, 89–90.

30. On two different occasions earlier theaters in Lyon had burned down, just a few of the many such incidents in France over the course of the century. A convent located near the site of the earlier theater had opposed rebuilding because of the threat of future fires. *Trois siècles d'opéra à Lyon*, 31–32; Vingtrinier, *Le Théâtre à Lyon*, 8. On fears of theaters as fire traps, recall BM Nantes 50103, "Remarques sur la nécessité de construire une salle."

31. Hautecoeur, *Histoire de l'architecture classique en France*, vols. II–IV. In this, Soufflot participated in broader trends evidenced in Metz and Montpellier.

32. Compare the architectural designs for these auditoriums in *Recueil de planches*, vol. 10.

33. Braham, *Architecture of the French Enlightenment*, 30.

34. *Pace* Rabreau, *Apollon dans la ville*, 107–10.

35. Jean Le Rond d'Alembert, who had described Lyon's earlier jeu de paume theater as "detestable," wrote, "The new [theater] is very beautiful and very worthy of Soufflot." (Quoted in Vallas, *Un Siècle de musique et de théâtre à Lyon*, 292.)

36. The influence of the Lyon style can also be detected in the façades of the theaters of Aix-en-Provence, Amiens, Châlons-sur-Marne, and others. Bossuat, "Le Théâtre à Clermont-Ferrand," 129; *L'Art du théâtre à Valenciennes au XVIIIe siècle* (Valenciennes: BM de Valenciennes, 1989), 24; Frantz and Sajous d'Oria, *Le Siècle des théâtres*, 123–24, 135, 149, 162; Delaval, *Le Théâtre Graslin*, 47. Charles Marionneau, *Victor Louis, architecte du théâtre de Bordeaux: Sa vie, ses travaux et sa correspondance, 1731-1800* (Bordeaux: Impr. de G. Gounouilhou, 1881), 127–31.

37. The most important of these works include Dumont, *Parallèle de plans*; Ch. N. Cochin, *Projet d'une salle de spectacle pour un théâtre de comédie* (Paris: Jombert, 1765); Chevalier de Chaumont, *Exposition des principes qu'on doit suivre dans l'ordonnance des théâtres modernes* (Paris: Jombert, 1769); Roubo, *Traité de la construction des théâtres*; Patte, *Essai sur l'architecture théâtrale*; and Victor Louis, *Salle de spectacle de Bordeaux* (Paris: Esprit, Libraire, 1782). In the contemporary periodical press, see the extensive discussions regarding the new Besançon theater designed by Claude-Nicolas Ledoux in the *Journal de Paris* during March and April of 1783.

38. Quoted in Jean-Marie Pérouse de Montclos, *Les Prix de Rome: Concours de l'Académie royale d'architecture au XVIIIe siècle* (Paris: Berger-Levrault, 1984), 94, 251.

39. Cochin, *Projet d'une salle de spectacle*, 2. See also Chaumont's *Exposition des principes* where he discusses the new theaters of Lyon, Brest, and Versailles, as well as the principal theaters of Paris.

40. On the primacy of the royal stages of Paris for aspiring playwrights seeking to make their reputations as men of letters, see Brown, *A Field of Honor*, 35–75.

41. This and the following discussion of the architecture of Bordeaux's Grand Théâtre are informed by Kalnein, *Architecture in France*, 184–87; Lagrave, *La Vie théâtrale à Bordeaux*; and Charles Marionneau, who conveniently assembled much of the documentary evidence concerning the construction of the Grand Théâtre in the volume *Victor Louis*.

42. AM de Bordeaux GG 1004 a, Letter from shareholders, Bordeaux, 8 April 1780.

43. AM de Bordeaux DD 37, "Salle de spectacle de l'hôtel de ville"; Lagrave, *La Vie théâtrale à Bordeaux*, 170–74.

44. Lagrave, *La Vie théâtrale à Bordeaux*, 174, 230–32.

45. Rabreau makes this case in *Apollon dans la ville*, 168–79.

46. Lagrave, *La Vie théâtrale à Bordeaux*, 177; Louis, *Salle de spectacle de Bordeaux*, 1–2.

47. Marionneau, *Victor Louis*, 110–12, 113, 115; on a second offer made by private investors in 1778, 380–83; on the theater as the most extensive building project, 240 and 379; on money for the city hall from Genoa, 226; Lagrave, *La Vie théâtrale à Bordeaux*, 177.

48. Marionneau, *Victor Louis,* 206.

49. Rabreau quoted in Lagrave, *La Vie théâtrale à Bordeaux*, 196.

50. Ibid., 196.

51. Dupré de Saint-Maur quoted in Marionneau, *Victor Louis*, on 379 and 382.

52. Diary entry from 26 August 1787 in Young, *Travels in France*, 59–60.

53. AN H 1359, n. 133, Mémoire by de Rapalli, 5 May 1783.

54. J.-J. Duthoy, "A Lille, à la fin du XVIIIe siècle. Documents inédits concernant Michel Lequeux, les artisans-sculpteurs lillois, le plan d'urbanisme de l'Intendant Calonne," *Revue du Nord* 65 (1983): 507–14; 512–13, quoting intendant Charles Alexandre de Calonne, emphasis in original.

55. In Nîmes, for example, the city council in 1778 expressed the desire "to build a playhouse, such as those one sees in the principal cities of the kingdom and of the province." Quoted in Frantz and Sajous d'Oria, *Le Siècle des théâtres*, 125.

56. Georges Lecocq, *Histoire du théâtre de St.-Quentin* (Paris: Raphael Simon, 1878), 15–17, quote on 17.

57. Roubo, *Traité de la construction des théâtres*, 25.

58. Lepetit, *Pre-industrial Urban System*, appendix B, 449–50.

59. This is based on conservative estimates of population in 1750. Jan de Vries, *European Urbanization, 1500-1800* (Cambridge: Harvard University Press, 1984), 30, 269–78. Jones also stresses France's strong population growth, particularly in the provinces, in *Great Nation*, 161–68, 182.

60. Colin Jones writes that France's colonial trade increased tenfold during the eighteenth century in *Great Nation*, 163–67 and 354–56. See also Le Roy Ladurie, *Histoire de la France urbaine*, 3: 366–83.

61. Lepetit, *Pre-industrial Urban System*, appendix B, 449–50; Jones, *Great Nation*, 166; Le Roy Ladurie, *Histoire de la France urbaine*, 366–67.

62. This is evident in Jean-Pierre Bardet's study of Rouen, in which he traces the declining image and status of the city in the eighteenth century. *Rouen aux XVIIe et XVIIIe siècles: Les mutations d'un espace social* (Paris: Société de l'édition d'enseignement supérieur, 1983), 2 vols., I: 53–98. Michel Vovelle suggests that Aix entered a period of crisis and decline in the later eighteenth century in "Apogée ou déclin d'une capitale provinciale: Le XVIIIe siècle," in Marcel Bernos et al., *Histoire d'Aix-en-Provence*, ed. Michel Vovelle (Aix: Édisud, 1977), 179–82, 208–19.

63. Lepetit, *Pre-industrial Urban System*, 69.

64. Quoted in ibid., 68.

65. Quoted in Rousseau, *Politics and the Arts: Letter to M. d'Alembert*, 4. D'Alembert's article "Genève" originally appeared in the *Encyclopédie ou Dictionnaire raisonné des sciences, des arts et des métiers*, ed. Denis Diderot and Jean Le Rond d'Alembert, 28 vols. (Paris: Briasson, 1751–72), 7: 578.

66. On negative attitudes toward commerce and commercial elites in France, see Sarah Maza, *The Myth of the French Bourgeoisie: An Essay on the Social Imaginary, 1750–1850* (Cambridge: Harvard University Press, 2003), 24–26.

67. AD de la Loire-Atlantique C 323, n. 30.

68. The ceiling allegory is described and reproduced in Louis, *Salle de spectacle de Bordeaux*, plate 23. This original ceiling was restored and can be viewed today.

69. Inaugural performances celebrating commerce and the arts include *Le Réveil d'Apollon, Prologue en vers libres, Représenté à l'ouverture de la nouvelle salle de spectacle de Lyon* (n.pl.: n.p., 1756); and Auguste Rondel, *Quelques renseignements sur la construction de l'Opéra de Marseille et sur son inauguration, le 31 octobre 1787. Suivis de* L'Union du commerce et des arts, *Prologue composé pour l'ouverture du nouveau théâtre de Marseille et représenté pour la première fois le 31 octobre 1787 par M. Ponteuil, Comédien du Roi* (Marseille: Imprimerie provençale Guiraud, 1924). The inaugural prologue for Bordeaux has unfortunately been lost, but its title, *Le Jugement d'Apollon*, suggests that it too may have sounded similar themes. Lagrave, *La Vie théâtrale à Bordeaux*, 251.

70. On the low rates of participation of commercial traders in academies, see Daniel Roche, *Les Républicains des lettres: Gens de culture et Lumières au XVIIIe siècle* (Paris: Fayard, 1988), 289–93.

71. P. F., "Lettre au sujet du nouveau théâtre de Bordeaux," *Mercure de France* 27 May 1780, 181–89, quote from 189.

72. James Johnson discusses the hierarchical relationship between seating at the Paris Opera and political and social status in *Listening in Paris*, 16–19.

73. Even in a small city such as Saint-Quentin, spectators chose from seven different seating categories with three price ranges. Lecocq, *Histoire du théâtre de St.-Quentin*, 74, 108. The only significant exception to the prevailing approach to theater seating was the controversial Besançon theater designed by Claude-Nicholas Ledoux. See Vidler, *Claude-Nicolas Ledoux*, 162–88; Jacques Rittaud-Hutinet, *La Vision d'un futur: Ledoux et ses théâtres* (Lyon: Presses Universitaires de Lyon, 1982), 70–79, 137–68.

74. Deck, *Histoire du théâtre français à Strasbourg*, 22–24.

75. Compare interior designs of the Montpellier, Metz, and Lyon playhouses in "Théâtres," *Recueil de planches*, vol. 10.

76. Louis, *Salle de spectacle de Bordeaux*, plate 5; also Young, *Travels in France*, 59–60.

77. Young, *Travels in France*, 59–60.

78. AM Bordeaux GG 1004 a, Letter from shareholders dated 12 August 1780.

79. Ibid.

80. In addition to the Café de la Comédie, which rented for more than thirty-three hundred livres in the late 1770s, the city estimated the revenues from renting these spaces at no less than nine thousand livres a year. AM Lyon 3 GG 98 "Extrait des régistres du Conseil d'Etat," 22 January 1777; and AM Lyon 3 GG 100 "Spectacles de Lyon, année 1782 à 1783." Marseille investors responsible for building the new public theater strongly favored a design by Ledoux that would have integrated such commercial outlets. They protested that the design chosen by the Royal Academy of Architecture would result in a neighborhood that was less economically vital and that it would also deprive the investors of the extra rental income. See AN H 1359, n. 113, and Claude-Nicolas Ledoux, *L'Architecture considérée sous le rapport de l'art, des moeurs et de la legislation,* 2 vols. (Paris: F. de Nobele, 1961), II: 196, "Théâtre de Marseille, Projet, Plan du rez-de-chausée de la salle des spectacles."

81. AM Lyon BB 336 f. 112–13.

82. Lefebvre, *Histoire du théâtre de Lille,* II: v. In Nantes, the new municipal theater was originally designed to include six shops that opened directly onto the side streets that bordered the freestanding theater, although these do not appear to have been included. Delaval, *Le Théâtre Graslin à Nantes,* 53.

83. Lagrave, *La Vie théâtrale à Bordeaux,* 235; according to the theater's directors, these spaces rented for about twenty-four thousand livres a year. AM Lyon 3 GG 99, "Questions relatives à l'entreprise des spectacles de Bordeaux," December 1787.

84. François de La Rochefoucauld, *Voyages en France de François de la Rochefoucauld (1781-1783),* ed. Jean Marchand, 2 vols. (Paris: Champion, 1938), II: 116.

85. Pierre Peyronnet, *La Mise en scène au XVIIIe siècle* (Paris: A.-G. Nizet, 1974); Fuchs, *La Vie théâtrale en province au XVIIIe siècle,* 54–74.

86. BM Nantes 50103, "Remarques sur la nécessité de construire une salle," 2.

87. An array of contemporary theater machines providing special effects are reproduced in "Machines de théâtre," *Encylopédie,* 27: 5; Delaval, *Le Théâtre Graslin à Nantes,* 64–70.

88. See inventory from 1778 in Lecocq, *Histoire du théâtre de St.-Quentin,* 44–50.

89. P. F., "Lettre," 184.

90. AM Besançon DD 35, "Observations relatives aux ancienne et nouvelle salles," cited full text in Rittaud-Hutinet, *La Vision d'un futur,* 134.

91. For an overview of antitheater sentiment in the West, see Jonas Barish, *The Anti-theatrical Prejudice* (Berkeley: University of California Press, 1981). On religious and civil sanctions in France, see Sylviane Léoni, *Le Poison et le remède: Théâtre, morale, et rhétorique en France et en Italie, 1694-1758* (Oxford: Voltaire Foundation, 1998); Louis Bourquin, "La Controverse sur la comédie au XVIIIe siècle et la Lettre à d'Alembert sur les spectacles," *Revue d'histoire littéraire de la France* 26 (1919): 43–87, 555–76; 27 (1920): 548–70; 28 (1921): 549–74; and John McManners, *Abbés and Actresses: The Church and the Theatrical Profession in Eighteenth-Century France* (Oxford: Clarendon Press, 1986).

92. Quoted in Léonie, *Poison et remède,* 52.

93. In Paris, the King's Players had trouble finding a placement for their new theater in 1689 because of protests from a number of clergy and religious organizations. Theater projects met significant religious resistance in cities such as Carpentras and Saint-Omer. Jules Bonnassies, *La Comédie-française: Histoire administrative (1658–1757)* (Paris: Didier et Cie, 1874), 92–93; Robert Caillet and René Duplan, *Spectacles à Car-*

pentras (Valence: Imprimeries Réunis, 1942), 31–32; Max Fuchs, "Notes et documents: Le Théâtre à Saint-Omer," *Bulletin de la Société d'histoire du théâtre* (1935): 53–56.

94. AM Nantes GG 289, note 2 at the end of register.

95. [Anon], *Lettre d'un citoyen de la ville de Saint-Quentin, à M**, Sur l'établissement d'une salle de spectacles dans la même ville* (Saint-Quentin: n.p., 1774), 17. For more on this, see 21–24.

96. Ibid, 10–14, 17–18, quotes from 17–18.

97. Ibid, 15–16.

98. AM Bordeaux GG 1004 a, Grand Théâtre misc., and AM Lyon 3 GG 99, "Questions relatives à l'entreprise des spectacles de Bordeaux," December 1787; and 3 GG 100, "Spectacles de Lyon, année 1782 à 1783"; AD de la Loire-Atlantique C 392, n. 73, 74, 78, and 46.

99. Quoted in Albert Babeau, *Les Voyageurs en France depuis la Renaissance jusqu'à la Révolution* (Paris: Firmin-Didot et Cie., 1885), 323. For other travelers' impressions of provincial playhouses, see, for example, Babeau, 186, 278, 322, and La Rochefoucauld, *Voyages en France*, 116–18 and 163–64.

100. For impressions of French theaters by other travelers, see Anna Francesca Cradock, *La Vie française à la veille de la Révolution (1783–1786). Journal inédit de Madame Cradock*, trans. O. Delphin Balleyguier (Paris: Perrin, 1911), 5, 38, 46, 99, 110, 117, 119, 122, 124–25, 128, 143, 153, 158–60, 176, 186, 190, 205, 207, 209, 230, 247, 280; Young, *Travels in France*, 58–59, 115–16, 124–25, 190, 229, 242.

101. Piozzi and Johnson, *French Journals of Mrs. Thrale*, 78; Cradock, *La Vie française*, 117, 247.

102. Cradock, *La Vie française*, 256.

103. Denis Diderot, "Entretiens sur Le Fils naturel" (1757), in *Oeuvres esthétiques*, ed. Paul Vernière (Paris: Éditions Garnier Frères, 1965), 113.

104. Quoted in Babeau, *Les Voyageurs en France*, 285.

105. "Lettre à M. de la Garde, Pensionnaire adjoint au privilège du Mercure pour la partie des spectacles," *Mercure de France* (June 1765), 179.

106. Bricaire de la Dixmerie, *Lettres sur l'état présent de nos spectacles*, 35.

107. ARS Mss 6394 Henri-Louis Lekain, "Description, par lettre alphabétique, de toutes les villes que j'ai parcourues dans mes différents voyages."

108. On this theater, see Daniel Rabreau, *Le Théâtre de l'Odéon: Du monument de la nation au théâtre de l'Europe: Naissance du monument de loisir urbain au XVIIIe siècle* (Paris: Belin, 2007).

109. Bernard Camier, "Les spectacles musicaux en Martinique, en Guadeloupe et en Dominique dans la seconde moitié du XVIIIème," *Bulletin de la Société d'histoire de la Guadeloupe* 130 (2001): 3–25.

110. Friedrich Melchior Grimm et al., *Correspondance littéraire, philosophique, et critique* (Paris: Garnier frères, 1877–82), 16 vols., 13: 112–14.

111. See, for example, the impressions of the new theater provided by Baronne d'Oberkirch, who visited two months after its opening, in Henriette Louise von Waldner Oberkirch, *Mémoires de la baronne d'Oberkirch sur la cour de Louis XVI et la société française avant 1789*, ed. Suzanne Burkard (Paris: Mercure de France, 1989), 171.

112. Kalnein, *Architecture in France*, 185–87.

113. Controller-General of Finance Louis-Gabriel Taboureau des Reaux, quoted in Marionneau, *Victor Louis*, 354.

114. Louis, *Salle de spectacle de Bordeaux*, 9.

115. Ibid., 1.

116. La Rochefoucauld, *Voyages en France*, 116–18.

117. Patte, *Essai sur l'architecture théâtrale*, 115. Patte's essay, published the very year that the new Comédie-Française theater was inaugurated, makes no mention of that playhouse.

118. The powerful trope of Paris-*province* and its lasting influence in the French imagination are explored in Alain Corbin, "Paris-Province," in *Realms of Memory: Rethinking the French Past*, ed. Pierre Nora, trans. Arthur Goldhammer, 3 vols. (New York: Columbia University Press, 1996–1998), I: 427–64. Hemmings, for example, suggests that eighteenth-century cities developed "a provincial cultural inferiority complex"; even Daniel Roche has argued that the establishment of academies and learned societies may indicate, paradoxically, "the slowing of a provincial dynamism." (Quotes from Hemmings, *Theatre and State*, 143, and Corbin, "Paris-Province," 431.)

3. The Extent and Limits of State Intervention

1. See letters dated 13 June and 24 September 1764, in A. Kernéis, "Contribution à l'histoire de la ville et du port de Brest: L'hôtel Saint-Pierre, actuellement la Préfecture Maritime. Le Spectacle de la Marine," *Bulletin de la société académique de Brest* 36 (1911–12): 97–258, esp. 109–12. The navy itself provided this warehouse in 1761, in which a stage was constructed at the expense of the acting company. The permission was granted with the provision that the materials that the navy kept in the warehouse would be moved, stored, and later replaced by the actors, "without costing the navy anything." AN Marine (henceforth Mar.) B² 367, f. 130, 26 June 1761.

2. Letter from Aymar Joseph de Roquefeuil to César Gabriel de Choiseul-Chevigny, duc de Praslin, 16 May 1766, quoted in Kernéis, "Contribution à l'histoire de la ville et du port de Brest," 123. On the approval for the Théâtre de la Marine by the royal government in 1765–66, see AN Mar. B² 381, fols. 18, 20, 45, 87, 89, 107.

3. Lepetit lists the population of Brest as twenty thousand in 1750 and thirty thousand in 1780 in *Pre-industrial Urban System*, 449–50.

4. For a detailed history of the construction of this theater, on which this chapter draws, see Kernéis, "Contribution à l'histoire de la ville et du port de Brest," 108–29, and Prosper Jean Levot, *Histoire de la ville et du port de Brest*, 3 vols. (Brest: l'Auteur, 1865), II: 273–81.

5. This theater, referred to by Kernéis as the Spectacle de la Marine, is more commonly known as the Théâtre de la Marine.

6. The funds to pay for construction came out of the navy budget. AN Mar. B² 381, fols. 18 and 20.

7. The British military, too, had a close relationship with professional theater in the eighteenth century. See Gillian Russell, *The Theatres of War: Performance, Politics, and Society, 1793–1815* (Oxford: Clarendon Press, 1995).

8. For this traditional interpretation highlighting the power of the intendant in the urban context, see Ernest Lavisse, *Louis XIV* (Paris: J. Tallandier, 1978), 168; Pierre Lavedan, *Les Villes françaises* (Paris: Fréal, 1960), 146–74; and Le Roy Ladurie, *Histoire de la France urbaine*, 3: 439–81. The centrality of the military in shaping

European state-building in the early modern era was brought to the fore in the 1980s in works such as Geoffrey Parker, *The Military Revolution: Military Innovation and the Rise of the West* (Cambridge: Cambridge University Press, 1988), and John Brewer, *The Sinews of Power: War, Money, and the English State, 1688–1783* (New York: Knopf, 1989). On the French army during the Old Regime, see especially John Lynn, *Giant of the Grand Siècle: The French Army 1610–1715* (Cambridge: Cambridge University Press, 1997), and Rafe Blaufarb, *The French Army, 1750–1820: Careers, Talent, Merit* (Manchester: Manchester University Press, 2002).

9. Lynn, *Giant of the Grand Siècle*, ix, 61–64; Blaufarb, *French Army*, 7.

10. Blaufarb, *French Army*, quote 7, 12. On the relationship between France's aristocracy and the military, see Jay M. Smith, *The Culture of Merit: Nobility, Royal Service, and the Making of Absolute Monarchy in France, 1600–1789* (Ann Arbor: University of Michigan Press, 1996), 46–49, 191–262.

11. Royal governors, typically chosen from among princes and the very highest aristocratic families, represented royal military authority in France's frontier provinces. Governors were therefore the highest authority in the province. Jean Duquesne, *Dictionnaire des gouverneurs de province sous l'Ancien Régime: Novembre 1315–20 février 1791* (Paris: Christian, 2002).

12. A second French playhouse, the theater in Port-au-Prince, Saint-Domingue, was purchased by the colonial administration in the late 1780s under quite different circumstances. The government's involvement in that case is discussed in chapter 7.

13. This attitude is implicit in the initial contract allowing use of the navy's warehouse in Brest as a theater, discussed in note 1, as well as in a letter from an entrepreneur in Dunkerque, a city with an important garrison, who proposed to build a playhouse in that city that would "cost nothing to the state or to the administration." SHD A¹ 3687 f. 117.

14. On the centrality of public theater in the political culture of Old Regime France, see Beam, *Laughing Matters*, and Ravel, *Contested Parterre*.

15. Burke, *Fabrication of Louis XIV*, 2–3.

16. Apostolidès, *Le Roi-machine*, 33–34; Burke, *Fabrication of Louis XIV*, 49–59.

17. Henri IV first granted the title "King's Players" to a troupe of actors led by Valleran le Conte in 1598. Louis XIII continued to patronize several companies. Wiley, *Early Public Theatre*, 48.

18. On playwrights, see Brown, *Field of Honor*; on the recruitment of singers and musicians for the Paris Opera, see AN AJ¹³ 2: I; and AJ¹³ 18: IX.

19. Apostolidès, *Le Roi-machine*, 8.

20. Burke, *Fabrication of Louis XIV*, 7–9.

21. Isherwood, *Music in the Service of the King*, 114–49; Apostolidès, *Le Roi-machine*, 63–65.

22. On the relationship between ritualized display and political power in absolutist France, see Norbert Elias, *The Court Society*, trans. Edmund Jephcott (New York: Pantheon Books, 1983), esp. 41–65 and 78–116, quote 64; and Emmanuel Le Roy Ladurie with Jean-François Fitou, *Saint-Simon and the Court of Louis XIV*, trans. Arthur Goldhammer (Chicago: University of Chicago, 2001), esp. 23–61.

23. On the social importance of attending the Paris Opera for the king's most powerful subjects in the eighteenth century, see Johnson, *Listening in Paris*, 8–34.

24. Isherwood, *Music in the Service of the King*, 175–76.

25. Carl B. Schmidt, "The Geographical Spread of Lully's Operas during the Late Seventeenth and Early Eighteenth Centuries: New Evidence from the *Livrets*," in *Jean-Baptiste Lully and the Music of the French Baroque*, ed. John Hajdu Heyer (Cambridge: Cambridge University Press, 1989), 183–211, 185–99. On the enforcement of the Opera's privilege outside of Paris, see also AN AJ¹³ 2: I and AJ¹³ 13: III and IV.

26. On sixteenth-century theater regulation, see Beam, *Laughing Matters*, esp. 44–76.

27. An overview of the extensive historiography on the politics of absolutism can be found in William Beik, "The Absolutism of Louis XIV as Social Collaboration," *Past and Present* 188 (2005): 195–224. For a classic interpretation of the relationship of provincial municipalities to the crown in the seventeenth century, see Temple, "Control and Exploitation of French Towns." More recent revisionist interpretations include William Beik, "Louis XIV and the Cities," in *Edo and Paris: Urban Life and the State in the Early Modern Era*, ed. James McClain, John Merriman, and Ugawa Kaoru (Ithaca: Cornell University Press, 1994), 68–85, and Beam, *Laughing Matters*.

28. Beik, "Louis XIV and the Cities," 83.

29. For the sites of France's most significant garrisons in 1789, see Rafe Blaufarb, "Aristocratic Professionalism in the Age of Democratic Revolution: The French Officer Corps, 1750–1815" (PhD diss., University of Michigan, 1996), 117. Compare with the cities inaugurating new playhouses in the timeline in the appendix to this book.

30. Debauve, *Théâtre et spectacles à Lorient*, 19.

31. Of the shareholders in the Saumur theater tontine, a substantial number were cavalry officers known as *carabiniers*. AM Saumur 4M93, *Tableau général*.

32. "Lettre de M. le marquis de Monteynard à tous les commandants des provinces frontières du 13 janvier 1772," *RHT* 13 (1961): 48; AM Lyon 3 GG 99. Twenty sous constituted one livre; twelve deniers made up one sous.

33. SHD A¹ 1391, f. 77–80. Memoir signed by the comte d'Artagnan on 13 September 1697.

34. Ibid., 79.

35. SHD A¹ 1395, 13 September 1697. It was clarified that the order to retain a portion of military salaries for theater for the troops in garrison could only come from the king, while the order for armies at war must come from the commander.

36. SHD A¹ 3147, f. 85. When left to their own devices, officers on campaign engaged in disruptive and dangerous games that caused a significant number of injuries. Ibid., f. 98.

37. D. D. Brouwers, "Le Théâtre à Namur au XVIIIe siècle," *Annales de la société archéologique de Namur* 32 (1913): 169–206, esp. 182–84.

38. SHD A² 20 fols. 95, 98, 99, 100.

39. Favart, *Mémoires et correspondance*, 1: xxiv.

40. Quoted in ibid., 1: xxii.

41. Ibid., 1: xxii–xxiv. The use of plays to boost morale and cultivate patriotism was adopted more broadly following the defeat of the French at the hands of the British in the Seven Years' War. In 1765, military commanders used Pierre-Laurent Buirette de Belloy's patriotic hit *The Siege of Calais* to raise the spirits of the troops. In addition to offering free performances for soldiers as well as for local residents, colo-

nels distributed free copies of the play to companies under their command. In Arras, these were inscribed "To inspire in new soldiers the sentiments of the ancients." Margaret M. Moffat, "'Le Siège de Calais' et l'opinion publique en 1765," *Revue d'histoire littéraire de la France* 39 (1932): 339–54; *Les Spectacles de Paris, ou Calendrier historique & chronologique des théâtres; pour l'année 1766* (Paris: Veuve Duchesne, 1766), 37.

42. The maréchal de Saxe quoted in Blaufarb, *French Army*, 18.

43. Fuchs, *La Vie théâtrale en province au XVIIIe siècle*, 208. The impact of this policy was felt in Perpignan, where subscribers to the new theater inaugurated in 1753 included "all the officers of the garrison, by order of the comte de Mailly." Quoted in Henry Aragon, *Les Monuments et les rues de Perpignan* (Marseille: Laffitte Reprints, 1977), 517, see also 33–34.

44. Tribout de Morembert, *Le Théâtre à Metz*, 75–77, 79, quotation from 75. The Metz troupe performed in the nearby military installations at Sarrrelouis and Richemont.

45. Tribout de Morembert, *Le Théâtre à Metz*, 79.

46. André Corvisier, "Quelques réflexions sur les relations entre armée et marine," in *État, marine et société: Hommage à Jean Meyer*, ed. Martine Acerra, Jean-Pierre Poussou, Michel Vergé-Franceschi, and André Zysberg (Paris: Presses de l'Université de Paris-Sorbonne, 1995), 123–34, 132; Jean Chagniot, "Les Rapports entre l'armée et la société à la fin de l'ancien régime," in *Histoire militaire de la France: 2, De 1715 à 1871*, ed. André Corvisier (Paris: Presses Universitaires de France, 1992), 103–28, esp. 107, 110.

47. On Choiseuil's reforms, see Jean Meyer and Martine Acerra, *Histoire de la marine française: Des origines à nos jours* (Rennes: Éditions Ouest-France, 1994), 115; Jean Meyer, "La Marine française au XVIIIe siècle," in *Histoire militaire de la France*, ed. Corvisier, 2: 151-194, esp. 187-89; G. Lacour-Gayet, *La Marine militaire de la France sous le règne de Louis XV*, 2nd ed. (Paris: H. Champion, 1910), 413–14.

48. Jean Chagniot, "Les Rapports entre l'armée et la société," 104–5; Blaufarb, *French Army*, 16–20.

49. Blaufarb, *French Army*, 18–19, quote from 18.

50. *Histoire de l'École navale et des institutions qui l'ont précédée par un ancien officier* (Paris: Maison Quantin, 1889), 107–15.

51. Chagniot, "Les Rapports entre l'armée et la société," 107.

52. Erica-Marie Benabou discusses the dangers posed by venereal disease, especially syphilis, and contemporary fears that the disease was rapidly spreading in *La Prostitution et la police des moeurs au XVIIIe siècle* (Paris: Librairie Académique Perrin, 1987), 26 and 407–30. See also Susan Connor, "The Pox in Eighteenth-Century France," in *The Secret Malady: Venereal Disease in Eighteenth-Century Britain and France*, ed. Linda Merians (Lexington: University Press of Kentucky, 1996), 15–33. On gambling, see Dunkley, *Gambling*.

53. BNF Ms. Naf 9411, f. 284. Letter from Bompard, the commander at Toulon, to the duc de Praslin, 25 January 1767.

54. This point was made in Bayonne, where it was argued that the city needed "a comedy troupe for the amusement of the citizens and the garrison, who could certainly not find there pleasures, authorized by the laws and the police regulations, that would be more pleasant, more decent, and less expensive." Quoted in E. Ducéré,

"Le Théâtre bayonnais sous l'ancien régime," *Revue de Béarn, Navarre et Lannes, partie historique de la Revue des Basses-Pyrénées et des Landes* 1 (1883): 116–29, 160–62, 186–91, 226–30, 272–80, 320–30, 366–74, 414–23, p. 161 (quote).

55. Meyer, "La Marine française au XVIIIe siècle," 188; AN Mar. B² 367, f. 130, 26 June 1761.

56. Kernéis, "Contribution à l'histoire de la ville et du port de Brest," 108. Letter from Roquefeuil to the duc de Choiseul, 3 December 1762.

57. Ibid., 112 and 124, and Levot, *Histoire de la ville et du port de Brest,* II: 274.

58. Letter from Roquefeuil to Choiseul, 2 August 1765, quoted in Kernéis, "Contribution à l'histoire de la ville et du port de Brest," 118. Many philosophes, including Diderot and Voltaire, promoted theater as an educational force. Marie-Claude Canova-Green, "Le XVIIIe siècle: Un siècle du théâtre," in *Le Théâtre en France des origines à nos jours,* ed. Alain Viala (Paris: Presses universitaires de France, 1997), 233–301, esp. 239.

59. BNF Ms Naf 9411, f. 292–93, 10 August 1768, Roquefeuil to Praslin.

60. See especially Roquefeuil's letter of 16 May 1766 in Kernéis, "Contribution à l'histoire de la ville et du port de Brest," 123.

61. The subscription was restricted to men in the department. Those absent for more than a year would not be included.

62. Kernéis, "Contribution à l'histoire de la ville et du port de Brest," 116–17.

63. Maurice Bernard, *La Municipalité de Brest de 1750 à 1790* (Paris: E. Champion, 1915), 346.

64. AN Mar. B³ 598, 18.

65. BNF Ms. Naf 9411, f. 292, 10 August 1768, Roquefeuil to Praslin.

66. The following incident is described in Lefebvre, *Histoire du théâtre de Lille,* I: 267–68.

67. Quote from ibid.

68. Quoted in John Lough, *France on the Eve of the Revolution: British Travellers' Observations, 1763–1788* (Chicago: Dorsey Press, 1987), 211.

69. On conflicts in Toulon and Calais, see "Affaire de la Comédie de Calais en 1762," in SHD Yᵃ 255; and AN Mar. B³ 540, fols. 120, 137, 168–77, 181, 185–88. Violent theater riots involving royal soldiers in Angers, Bordeaux, and Beauvais that took place later in the century are discussed in Ravel, *Contested Parterre,* 161–90, and in chapter 6 of this book.

70. The circumstances surrounding the demonstrations on behalf of Demoiselle Dezy are related in Louis Petit de Bachaumont et al., *Mémoires secrets pour servir à l'histoire de la république des lettres en France,* 36 vols. (London: John Adamson, 1780–89), 5: 46–47.

71. For example, according to a letter by the new intendant of the navy, Charles-Claude de Ruis-Embito, those leading the different corps in Brest attested in 1772 that the theater accomplished three-quarters of their policing, and he affirmed that its advantages were notable. AN Mar. B³ 598, fols. 169–78, 11 March 1772.

72. *Ordonnance du roi pour régler le service dans les places et dans les quartiers. Du 1er mars 1768; suivi du décret impérial du 24 décembre 1811, relatif à l'organisation et au service des états-majors des places, et annotée des lois, décrets, ordonnances, arrêtés, règlements et autres dispositions qui ont modifié la matière jusqu'à ce jour* (Paris: Librarie militaire J. Dumaine, 1855), 178.

73. For example, in Toulon entrepreneurs approached the commander of the navy to receive his commitment to purchase subscriptions before investing in building a new theater. See BNF Ms. Naf 9411, f. 284.

74. *Ordonnance du roi pour régler le service*, 178.

75. AN Mar. B³ 577, fols. 266 and 269. From Roquefeuil and the naval intendant, de Clugny, August 1768.

76. AN Mar. B³ 592, f. 218, 14 October 1771.

77. Ibid., f. 215.

78. Ibid.

79. Ibid., 218. See also BNF Ms Naf 9411, f. 311, 14 October 1771. Two hundred twenty-one signed the poll. Roquefeuil noted that some officers were out at sea, and that others abstained from the vote.

80. AN Mar. B³ 592, f. 215–16, Letter from Roquefeuil, 11 October 1771.

81. AN Mar. B³ 592, f. 215–16; and Kernéis, "Contribution à l'histoire de la ville et du port de Brest," 172–73, 177.

82. Quoted in Kernéis, "Contribution à l'histoire de la ville et du port de Brest," 121. This was the first authorization, by Secretary of State Choiseul.

83. See, for example, Louis de Gouvenain, *Le Théâtre à Dijon, 1422–1790* (Dijon: E. Jobard, 1888), 69; Mesuret, *Le Théâtre à Toulouse*, 10–17.

84. This episode was symptomatic of the broader political conflict between the parlements and the crown, including representatives of royal authority such as intendants, taking place during the later 1750s, discussed in Julian Swann's *Politics and the Parlement of Paris under Louis XIV, 1754–1774* (Cambridge: Cambridge University Press, 1995), esp. 26, 45–192.

85. This language is from de Montholon's second letter of complaint, in SHD A¹ 3396, f. 296. Letter from M. de Montholon, *premier président* of the Parlement of Metz to the maréchal de Belle-Isle, the governor of the province, 24 February 1752. See also f. 293, Letter from Montholon to Belle-Isle from 9 February 1752, and the response by Jean-François de Creil to Belle-Isle, f. 295, 25 February 1752. On the history of public theater in Metz during this era, including a discussion of this episode, see Tribout de Morembert, *Le Théâtre à Metz*, 47–77.

86. SHD A¹ 3396, f. 293.

87. Ibid., f. 293, 296.

88. Ibid., f. 296.

89. A compromise favoring the *président* and his wife is suggested in both f. 296 and f. 295. The presence of the intendant in the governor's box is indicated in f. 480 in a letter from the subsequent intendant Caumartin to Belle-Isle, 20 December 1754.

90. Ibid., f. 480. On Caumartin himself and his political shortcomings at a subsequent posting, see René Grevet, "L'Absolutisme en province: L'échec de l'intendant Caumartin en Artois (1759–1773)," *RHMC* 44 (1997): 213–27.

91. SHD A¹ 3396, f. 480.

92. Ibid., f. 484. Caumartin to Belle-Isle, December 1754.

93. Ibid., f. 485.

94. Ibid., f. 480.

95. On this dispute, which continued for several months, see AM Nantes GG 678, n. 13–25. Quote from n. 24, 10 April 1788. On the city arms painted in the old

theater, see AM Nantes CC 218, n. 110. In Bordeaux, too, the municipality enjoyed a dedicated first box, marked with the coat of arms of the city. In 1763, however, the mayor and city council of Bordeaux expressed frustration that since the arrival of the governor Richelieu in the city, "our box has become his." Quoted in Lagrave, *La Vie théâtrale à Bordeaux,* 192.

96. See the exchange of letters regarding theater seating for the new commander of the navy stationed in Marseille, AN Mar. B³ 483, f. 70, 26 February 1749, and response AN Mar. B² 338, f. 88, 10 March 1749, quote from latter.

97. BNF Ms Naf 9411, f. 284–85, quote from 285.

98. For examples of specific military seating in playhouses, see *L'Art du théâtre à Valenciennes,* 49; Lefebvre, *Histoire du théâtre de Lille,* II: 24; Tribout de Morembert, *Le Théâtre à Metz,* 76. These benches were usually located in the parquet or orchestra, an area located between the stage and the parterre.

99. SHD A¹ 3699, f. 65–65 bis, 12 December 1776.

100. Ibid. On the matter of reserving benches, a practice that had become widespread by the 1770s, see also f. 10. Letter from the secretary of state for war, Claude Louis, comte de Saint-Germain, to the municipal officers of Valenciennes, 18 February 1776.

101. Quoted in Fuchs, *La Vie théâtrale en province au XVIIIe siècle,* 206.

102. In 1758, young regimental officers and naval guards exchanged insults, drew swords, and even come to blows with *écrivains du roi,* naval supply officers, over rights to honorific seats on the stage of the Toulon theater. AN Mar. B³ 540, fols. 120, 137, 168–77, 181, 185–88.

103. SHD Yᵃ 255, Mousquetaires, 1ère compagnie sur les côtes de Flandres, 1762.

104. The municipal authorities in Lille noted that for special performances "all the officers of the garrison whatsoever have the right to place themselves where they judge à propos for a cost of 24 sols de France." See letter from 1 October 1781 in Fuchs, *La Vie théâtrale en province au XVIIIe siècle,* appendix III, 207.

105. On this conflict in Valenciennes, see SHD A¹ 3699, f. 10, 18 February 1776, and especially f. 65–65 bis, 12 December 1776.

106. See letter from the magistrates of Valenciennes of 6 October 1781, reprinted in Fuchs, *La Vie théâtrale en province au XVIIIe siècle,* 207–8.

107. See also discussions in Douai, Lille, and Cambrai. Ibid., 205–10.

108. Quoted in Adolphe de Cardevacque, *Le Théâtre à Arras avant et après la Révolution* (Arras: Typographie de Sède et Cie., 1884), 78.

109. Ibid.

110. Ibid., 102–3.

111. Lagrave, *La Vie théâtrale à Bordeaux,* 135–37.

112. Max Fuchs, "Recherches sur les origines du privilège provincial." One director wrote to a colleague in 1756 that the privilege to perform in Rouen during one winter would cost him five thousand livres, while the privileges for Reims and Saint-Germain and permission to perform in Amiens could apparently be obtained without payment. ARS Archives de la Bastille (AB) Ms 11921, "Baugran," 102.

113. This list includes several provinces beyond those noted by Fuchs, "Recherches sur les origines du privilège provincial," 84. Specifically, on Anjou, see AM Bordeaux FF 70 (Police des spectacles, Théatres-Bals-Fêtes), Letter from the lieutenant-général of police in Angers to Messieurs the officers of the police of Bordeaux,

20 May 1766; on Picardy, see Pierre Leroy, *Les Comédiens de province en Picardie au XVIIIe siècle* (Amiens: Imprimerie Ansel, 1997), 22; on Bayonne, Ducéré, "Le Théâtre bayonnais sous l'ancien régime," 418–19. At the BMCF, the dossier Com. div. "Saint-Gérand" includes a transcription of this director's exclusive privilege for the "province of Bourgogne, Pays de Bresse, Bugey, Valromey and [Pays de] Gex" for the 1781–82 season.

114. Fuchs, "Recherches sur les origines du privilège provincial." See also the attitude of the royal governor regarding the "pretentions" of the magistrates of Cambrai, who protested when the privilege was instituted there in the 1780s. Durieux, *Le Théâtre à Cambrai*, 66.

115. AM Bordeaux FF 70, 20 May 1766. On theater in Angers, see Jacques Maillard, "Le Théâtre à Angers au XVIIIe siècle," *RHT* 169–70 (1991): 107–18.

116. John Shovlin, *The Political Economy of Virtue: Luxury, Patriotism, and the Origins of the French Revolution* (Ithaca: Cornell University Press, 2006), 10.

117. Fairchilds, "The Production and Marketing of Populuxe Goods," 231.

118. Rigogne, *Between State and Market*; Censer, *French Press in the Age of Enlightenment*, 134, 144, 148.

119. Lefebvre, *Histoire du théâtre de Lille*, I: 361.

120. Again, this practice seems to have originated under Richelieu, who established a privilege in 1745 to shore up the struggling opera company that performed for half of the year in Bordeaux, seemingly at the expense of the comedy troupe that performed during the other half of the year. Lagrave, *La Vie théâtrale à Bordeaux*, 139. Such payments to privileged provincial theater directors are very similar to the payments made to the Paris Opera during the eighteenth century by fairground and boulevard directors and even the Comédie-Italienne for permission to perform music. Collectively, annual payments to the Opera by these theaters rose from forty thousand livres in 1784 to 150,000 in 1788. Robert Isherwood, *Farce and Fantasy: Popular Entertainment in Eighteenth-Century Paris* (New York: Oxford University Press, 1986), 190; Michèle Root-Bernstein, *Boulevard Theater and Revolution in Eighteenth-Century Paris* (Ann Arbor: UMI Research Press, 1984), 41–75.

121. Quoted in Claudine Roubaud, *L'Opéra de Marseille: Recueil de documents d'archives* (Marseille: Service éducatif des archives municipales, 1987), n.p.

122. See agreements between various performers and entrepreneurs and the directrice Destouches cadette in which they agree to pay the "quart franc." AM Lyon 3 GG 99. In Arras, in the early 1780s, the director levied the quart des spectacles on entrepreneurs who displayed other people (i.e., individuals who were biological rarities), savage beasts, and marionettes, and on those who demonstrated feats of strength. Cardevacque, *Le Théâtre à Arras*, 77.

123. In 1787, the Lyon theater received almost twenty-eight hundred livres from the more than eighty performances given by such "petits spectacles." AM Lyon 3 GG 100.

124. AM Nantes GG 676, n. 10.

125. Habasque, *Documents sur le théâtre à Agen*, 29–30.

126. BMCF 2ATO Province 1788. Response from CF, 5 May 1788.

127. The establishment of secondary popular theaters was contested in cities such as Lyon, Nantes, and Bordeaux in the 1780s. Such theaters were usually prohibited from directly competing with the more prestigious elite stages by scheduling

performances at the same times. Most also buoyed up the privileged theater troupe by making payments. See AM Lyon 3GG 99, "Observation sur le nouvel établissement de la petite comédie dans la ville de Lyon"; AD de la Loire-Atlantique C 392, p. 1, Letter from M. le baron de Breteuil, 11 November 1785; AM Bordeaux, R 12 liasse fol. 13.

128. According to de Hautemer, an eighteenth-century citizen of Strasbourg who chronicled the city's history, French players came to Strasbourg nearly as soon as the French arrived in the city. AV Strasbourg, Ms 6 R 26, *Histoire de la ville de Strasbourg*, c. 1780, IV: 103. On the history of French-language theater in the city and its rivalry with the German-language troupes, see Deck, *Histoire du théâtre français à Strasbourg*, esp. 19–50.

129. Deck, *Histoire du théâtre français à Strasbourg*, 39 and 49.

130. AV Strasbourg AA 2161, 29 April 1723.

131. AV Strasbourg AA 2162, Mgr. le marquis de Paulmy to M. de Lucé, intendant, 25 February 1756.

132. ARS AB 11921, "Baugran," f. 106, 28 February 1756. (This director was also known variously as Baugran and Beaugrand.)

133. See ibid., f. 114–15, letter from Beaugrand, 5 March 1756.

134. Ibid., f. 106. Beaugrand was in prison for several weeks before a Strasbourg merchant came forward to secure his debts, allowing him to reassume responsibility for the troupe for at least a short time. Fuchs, *Lexique de troupes*, 12.

135. AV Strasbourg AA 2161, 1 December 1750, "Note et fait sommaire concernant l'opéra-italienne qui représent à Strasbourg depuis quelque têms." The prescribed amount that foreign language actors and singers and popular entertainers paid varied between one-sixth and one-fourth of their gross revenues. AV Strasbourg AA 2162, Mémoire 1782.

136. AV Strasbourg AA 2161, 10 December 1749, "Note."

137. Ibid., "Copie de la lettre de M. Bernard, premier sécretaire de M. le maréchal duc de Coigny à M. de Klinglin Conseiller d'état, Préteur royal de la ville de Strasbourg. À Paris le 21 janvier 1750."

138. See AV Strasbourg, AA 2161 and 2162, esp. February 1786.

139. AV Strasbourg AA 2162, letter from MM. les Preteur, Consuls, et Magistrats de la Ville de Strasbourg to de Contades, February 1786.

140. Ibid.

141. AA 2162, letter from same to de Contades, 4 March 1786.

142. The maréchal de Contades made an exception for songs that were already part of the German troupes' repertories prior to this decision. AV Strasbourg AA 2162, letter from de Contades to the magistrates of Strasbourg, 13 May 1786.

143. Ibid. On the history of the city of Strasbourg under French governance more broadly during the Old Regime, see Franklin Ford, *Strasbourg in Transition, 1648–1789* (New York: W. W. Norton, 1966).

144. This sense of injustice is evident in protests voiced by the magistrates of Dijon, who demanded to know why military commanders denied them the right to publicly authorize theater performances and to appear listed on advertising posters, when their counterparts in Besançon, home to a much larger garrison, enjoyed these prerogatives. According to Gouvenain, this conflict between the municipal authorities in Dijon and the lieutenant general of the province lasted for nearly three years and constituted one of the most serious conflicts between local and royal authority during the entire eighteenth century. *Le Théâtre à Dijon*, 117–22.

145. Although Roquefeuil claimed that the theater company's debts only amounted to fifty-three thousand livres, the intendant de Ruis-Embito calculated that between 1767 and 1772 the sum illicitly advanced by the treasurer to support the Brest theater amounted to 79,788 livres, thirteen sous, nine deniers. AN Mar. B³ 598, fols. 16 and 169–78. On discipline problems related to this theater, see Bachaumont et al., *Mémoires secrets*, 5: 46–47, and AN Mar. B³ 599, fols. 227–28. On tensions with the local community, see Levot, *Histoire de la ville et du port de Brest*, II: 280–81; AN Mar. B³ 577, fols. 269–70, 227–28; Kernéis, "Contribution à l'histoire de la ville et du port de Brest," 134, 183; BNF Ms Naf 9411, f. 289.

146. AN Mar. B³ 598, fols. 169–78, 11 March 1772.

147. Quote is from the response to Roquefeuil's petition in the fall of 1771, noted in the margin, AN Mar. B³ 592, f. 217. This further states that the "total interruption of theater" is necessary until the king's debts have been paid. See also ibid., f. 228, 30 October 1771. On no director risking a contract, BNF Ms. Naf 9411, f. 316, 6 April 1772. On bankruptcy and the order to close the stage in the fall of 1772, anger among the officers, and the eventual termination of these subscriptions in the spring of 1773, AN Mar. B³ 599, fols. 250, 251, 253–56, 267, 295.

148. Quoted in Kernéis, "Contribution à l'histoire de la ville et du port de Brest," 197. Subsequent commanders, fully aware of the shame brought upon their predecessor for financial misappropriations related to the theater, accorded the privilege to independent directors. Nonetheless, it came to light in 1789 and 1790 that the navy was indirectly subsidizing the theater by providing candles and oil, providing the director with workers, and assisting with the theater's upkeep and decorations, contributions that may have amounted to twenty-two to twenty-three thousand livres a year. The king again expressly forbade using navy funds for such purposes (228, 238–39).

4. Directors and the Business of Performing

1. Jean Monnet, *Supplément au Roman comique*, 2 vols. (London: n.p., 1772), 1: 71–75. Victoria Johnson emphasizes the luxury and expense of opera compared to all other forms of entertainment in France in *Backstage at the Revolution*, 3–4. On the history of the Lyon stage during the eighteenth century, see Vallas, *Un Siècle de musique et de théâtre à Lyon*. The financial struggles of earlier directors are recounted in AM Lyon 3 GG 98.

2. Monnet, *Supplément au Roman comique*, 73.

3. The reasons for which Monnet gave up the direction of the Lyon stage are disputed, and include allegations that he lost the privilege for Lyon or left due to financial difficulties. Monnet himself wrote that he left to pursue his ambitions elsewhere. Ibid., 76–117, quote from 100; Vallas, *Un Siècle de musique et de théâtre à Lyon*, 242–44.

4. On the itineraries of French opera troupes in the 1740s, see AN AJ¹³ 13: III. On the alternation of troupes in Lyon, Bordeaux, and Marseille, see Vallas, *Un Siècle de musique et de théâtre à Lyon*, 95, 115, 217; Lagrave, *La Vie théâtrale à Bordeaux*, 133–40; Robert Ambard, *La Comédie en Provence au XVIIIe siècle* (Aix-en-Provence: La Pensée universitaire, 1956), 94.

5. Mongrédien and Robert, *Les Comédiens français*, 10–12 and 236–58; Georges Mongrédien, *La Vie quotidienne des comédiens au temps de Molière* (Paris: Hachette, 1966), 205.

6. Samuel Chappuzeau, *Le Théâtre françois, Accompagné d'une préface et de notes par Georges Monval* (Paris: J. Bonnassies, 1876), 96–104, quotes from 97 and 102. Mongrédien notes as an exception that women were occasionally excluded from meetings of finance. On seventeenth-century acting companies, see also Mongrédien, *La Vie quotidienne des comédiens*, 183–266, and Wiley, *Early Public Theatre*, esp. 80–116.

7. Mongrédien and Robert, *Les Comédiens français*, 10–12 and 236–58; Mongrédien, *La Vie quotidienne des comédiens*, 205.

8. Bonnassies, *La Comédie-française*, 1–175; and Simon Siaud, *La Comédie française: Son histoire—son statut* (Paris: Librairie générale de droit & de jurisprudence, 1936), 39–42.

9. Tellingly, Jean-Baptiste Lully's contract specified that he was "sole master of his royal academy." Isherwood, *Music in the Service of the King*, 150–203; Johnson, *Backstage at the Revolution*, 83–147; Jérôme de la Gorce, *L'Opéra à Paris au temps de Louis XIV: L'histoire d'un théâtre* (Paris: Éditions Desjonquères, 1992), 9–79, quote on 42.

10. Gorce, *L'Opéra à Paris*, 71–72, 88–89, 104–5.

11. Lefebvre, *Histoire du théâtre de Lille*, 1: 205.

12. See correspondence in AN AJ^{13} 13: III.

13. For an early use of this term, see Sieur Boon, "entrepreneur de comédie," whose troupe performed in Lille in 1720. Lefebvre, *Histoire du théâtre de Lille*, 1: 212.

14. This was the case unless shareholders or, very exceptionally, the city government itself held the privilege, in which case these parties usually took responsibility for financial losses and gains, and hired the director on salary to operate the troupe. On directors' financial responsibilities, see BMCF 2 ATO Province 1774, decision by CF, 25 July 1774. The opportunities and risks associated with directing are conveyed in a particularly poignant letter to the royal theater company written by a director named Deletre whose theater company performed in Avignon, Nîmes, and Aix for over twenty years. He writes that he had built up "a fairly considerable fortune" directing in these cities until the Revolution robbed him of all of this, leaving him with losses of two hundred thousand livres, unable to feed his own children. BMCF Com. div. "Deletre, Directeur de Spectacle de Aix, Nismes, Avignon. 1791."

15. Eighteenth-century directors anticipated spending thousands of livres a year maintaining and expanding the magasin. See AM Lyon 3 GG 99, "Projet [pour] l'Etablissment du Spectacle de Lyon." According to M. Frossard, the director of a children's theater troupe performing in Lyon, his entire fortune—well over forty thousand livres—was invested in salary advances and other start-up costs and especially in his magasin. AM Lyon 3 GG 101, n. 179. Destouches-Lobreau's magasin, "the sole fruit of forty years of work," was purportedly "as well furnished as those of the Opera and the Comédie françoise." She estimated its worth at two hundred thousand livres: AM Lyon 3 GG 98, n. 13. "Mémoire signifié Pour Michelle Poncet Destouches," 18.

16. Provincial contracts typically began the second Monday after Easter and concluded on the Saturday before Palm Sunday. See, for example, Madame Marion's contract, BMCF 2 ATO Province 1774. Mme Marion [to CF], 25 July 1774.

17. For example, the term *chef de troupe* appeared in records in Amiens through the 1740s, when it began to be replaced by the term *entrepreneur*. Leroy, *Les Comédiens de province en Picardie*, 5–16.

18. Based on correspondence in BMCF register; 2 ATO Dossiers Province 1774–89, and dossiers in Com. div.

19. NL Case folio FRC 9730, "Dernière Réponse des auteurs dramatiques aux derniers écrits des entrepreneurs de spectacles de départemens; notamment à ceux qui portent pour titre 'Observations sommaires, etc.' et 'Pétition présentée à la Convention Nationale.'"

20. AN AJ¹³ 13: III, Prévot and Échevins of Paris to Sieur Louis d'Hieres, 29 December 1750.

21. Johnson, *Backstage at the Revolution*, 2.

22. AN AJ¹³. III, Prévot to d'Hieres, 29 December 1750.

23. AM Lyon 3 GG 99, "Projet [pour] l'Etablissement du Spectacle de Lyon."

24. Ibid.

25. Ibid.

26. This description draws on Isherwood, *Farce and Fantasy*, 60–80.

27. Ibid., 101–30.

28. Ancely, *Histoire du théâtre et du spectacle à Pau*, 67–68; Leroy, *Les Comédiens de province en Picardie*, 54–55. Lagrave calculates that in 1768–69 the Bordeaux theater hired thirty-seven actors and singers, twenty-eight dancers, and twenty-four musicians, at least 137 people in all. Lagrave, *La Vie théâtrale à Bordeaux*, 313. The "Tableau de la troupe du spectacle de Lyon pour l'année 1787 à 88" listed 177 employees on the theater's payroll, in AM Lyon 3 GG 100.

29. Jourda, *Le Théâtre à Montpellier*, 34–35. A "Projet [pour] l'Etablissment du Spectacle de Lyon" from the early 1760s estimated expenses at 114,500 livres for the year. AM Lyon 3 GG 99.

30. Johnson, *Backstage at the Revolution*, 183.

31. Lagrave, *La Vie théâtrale à Bordeaux*, 141–44, 191–92. In 1770, shareholders increased the amount of capital in the enterprise to one hundred thousand livres. The intendant, too, later invested in the company.

32. [M. Corbun], *Le Voeu de l'humanité, ou Lettres sur le spectacle de Bordeaux* (Bordeaux: Pallandre aîné, 1778), 42–43. By this, Corbun means the traditional military aristocracy, the judicial nobility, and members of the business elite.

33. Ibid., 43.

34. Lagrave, *La Vie théâtrale a Bordeaux*, 221.

35. Ibid., 141–46, 174–80, 190–93.

36. AD de la Loire-Atlantique C 321, n. 34, 16 July 1770.

37. AM Lyon 3 GG 99, "Questions relatives à l'entreprise des spectacles de Marseille," Nov. 1787. In addition to the ninety thousand livres the society paid for the privilege for the theater of Marseille, it also paid three thousand livres a year to the secretary of the government.

38. AD de la Haute-Garonne, 1 C 311, n. 1.

39. Lefebvre, *Histoire du théâtre de Lille*, 1: 386–87; SHD A¹ 3677, fols. 130 and 140. "Arrest du conseil d'état du roi, Concernant des actionnaires du spectacle de Nancy," 3 February 1769; A¹ 3694 f. 5–6 and 39–41; AD de la Loire-Atlantique C 321, n. 45. The Lille shareholders, these sources indicate, were facing difficulties in 1770, but they continued to play a role in the theater at least until 1779.

40. SHD A¹ 3694, f. 223; AD de la Sarthe, 111 AC 611, Renaut to Chesneau-Desportes, 7 July 1776.

41. BMCF 2 ATO Province 1776, Laurent [to CF], 9 April 1776; Province 1774, [Anon. to CF] concerning Dlle Duloir, 17 October 1774; *Affiches du Mans*, 30 September 1776, p. 157.

42. Lefebvre, *Histoire du théâtre de Lille*, 1: 258, 386–88, annex Vbis.

43. SHD A^1 3694, f. 39.

44. SHD A^1 3677, f. 140, 3 February 1769.

45. AD de la Loire-Atlantique C 392, n. 36. From 22 May 1774.

46. AD de la Loire-Atlantique C 322, n. 28, "Société patriotique et desintéressée pour l'entreprise du spectacle à Nantes" (1785), art. 10.

47. Rougemont, *La Vie théâtrale en France*, 183.

48. These numbers are based on named individuals who either alone or with others directed stages in the following cities: Lyon (1687–1789), Rouen (1763–89), Dijon (1703–89), Montpellier (1750–89), Metz (1729–89), Strasbourg (1750–89), Lille (1718–89), Lorient (1751–89), Bordeaux (1732–89), Versailles (1768–89) and Brest (1764–89). These are the cities for which such information about eighteenth-century directors is provided in the scholarship. Due to source limitations, not all directors could be identified and some years within these ranges are unaccounted for. Lefebvre, *Histoire du théâtre de Lille*, 1: 204–371, and 2: 1–59; *Trois siècles d'opéra à Lyon*, 20; Tribout de Morembert, *Le Théâtre à Metz*, 41–118; Debauve, *Théâtre et spectacles à Lorient*, 13–27, 44–69; Jourda, *Le Théâtre à Montpellier*, 20–21; Bouteiller, *Histoire . . . des théâtres de Rouen*, 1: 7–188; Lagrave, *La Vie théâtrale à Bordeaux*, 133–46; Deck, *Histoire du théâtre français à Strasbourg*, 27–30; Gouvenain, *Le Théâtre à Dijon*, 75–131; Villard, *Le Théâtre Montansier à Versailles*, 11–50; Kernéis, "Contribution à l'histoire de la ville et du port de Brest," 108–219.

49. See, for example, Lefebvre's brief biographical sketches of the directors in Lille in *Histoire du théâtre de Lille*, 1: 258–371, and those provided in Fuchs, *Lexique des troupes de comédiens*.

50. Although contemporaries often emphasize the instability of provincial stages in this era because of the turnover of directors, the length of various directors' tenure at the helm of large theater and opera companies in France in fact changed relatively little into the nineteenth and twentieth centuries. For comparison, see lists of directors in *Trois siècles d'opéra à Lyon*, 20–21; Segond and Arrouas, *L'Opéra de Marseille*, 250–51.

51. For examples of financial crises and bankruptcies facing troupes performing in Toulon, Thionville, and Strasbourg, see BMCF 2 ATO Province 1774, Lamare [to CF], 7 February 1774, and Com. div. "Rousselet," 11 December 1749; ARS Archives de la Bastille 11921 "Baugran," 106–7.

52. When directors failed to honor their commitment and the Nantes stage went unoccupied for eighteen months in the late 1750s, this was considered unusual and troubling enough for the governor to take the matter into hand. Destranges, *Le Théâtre à Nantes*, 22–23.

53. Quoted in Leroy, *Les Comédiens de province en Picardie*, 52.

54. Quoted in Lefebvre, *Histoire du théâtre de Lille*, 1: 339.

55. "Denesle" in Fuchs, *Lexique des troupes de comédiens*, 55; Gouvenain, *Le Théâtre à Dijon*, 110–32; Clothilde Tréhorel, "Le Théâtre à Dijon," in *Les Arts de la scène & la Révolution française*, ed. Philippe Bourdin and Gérard Loubinoux (Clermont-Ferrand: Presses Universitaires Blaise-Pascal, 2004), 163–79, esp. 165.

56. These women's success in such a public profession places them among the small group of particularly prominent women entrepreneurs and public figures of this era such as the fashion designer Rose Bertin and Madame du Coudray, the

royal midwife who taught throughout the provinces. See Clare Haru Crowston, "The Queen and Her 'Minister of Fashion': Gender, Credit, and Politics in Pre-Revolutionary France," *Gender and History* 14 (2002): 92–116, and Nina Rattner Gelbart, *The King's Midwife: A History and Mystery of Madame du Coudray* (Berkeley: University of California Press, 1998).

57. The directing profession has received remarkably little scholarly attention. Martine de Rougemont raises the challenges posed by lack of sources in *La Vie théâtrale en France*, 183–86, 191–92. The directors of the fairground and boulevard theaters in Paris are considered in Root-Bernstein, *Boulevard Theater and Revolution*, and Laurent Turcot, "Directeurs, comédiens et police: Relations de travail dans les spectacles populaires à Paris au XVIIIe siècle," *Histoire, économie et société* 23 (2004): 97–119. Among individual directors only Marguerite Brunet, known as Mlle Montansier or La Montansier, has been the subject of extensive biographical study. These works include Dicta Dimitriadis, *La Montansier: Biographie* (Paris: Mercure de France, 1995), and Patricia Bouchenot-Déchin, *La Montansier: De Versailles au Palais-Royal: Une femme d'affaires* (Paris: Perrin, 1993). Madame Destouches-Lobreau receives attention in Vallas, *Un Siècle de musique et de théâtre à Lyon*, esp. 285–321, 383–401.

58. Natalie Zemon Davis, *Society and Culture in Early Modern France: Eight Essays* (Stanford: Stanford University Press, 1975), 94; also idem, "Women in the Crafts in Sixteenth-Century Lyon," *Feminist Studies* 8 (1982): 46–80, 70; Olwen Hufton, "Women and the Family Economy in Eighteenth-Century France," *FHS* 9 (1975): 1–22; Merry Wiesner, *Women and Gender in Early Modern Europe* (Cambridge: Cambridge University Press, 1993), 110; Deborah Simonton, *A History of European Women's Work, 1700 to the Present* (London: Routledge, 1998), 47–69. Recent assessments of women occupying positions of authority in the workplace include Daryl Hafter, "Female Masters in the Ribbonmaking Guild of Eighteenth-Century Rouen," *FHS* 20 (1997): 1–14, and Clare Crowston, *Fabricating Women: The Seamstresses of Old Regime France, 1675–1791* (Durham: Duke University Press, 2001).

59. See note 48. Philbert is mentioned in Gorce, *L'Opéra à Paris*, 105. On other women in the profession, see additional directrices who authored letters or were mentioned in BMCF Register and 2 ATO Dossiers Province 1774–1789, and the files in Com. div.

60. This account draws on Vallas, *Un Siècle de musique et de théâtre à Lyon*, 285–99, 310–21, 383–401, and "Destouches" in Fuchs, *Lexique des troupes de comédiens*, 62–63.

61. This was for the 1776–77 season. Vallas, *Un Siècle de musique et de théâtre à Lyon*, 398–99.

62. AM Lyon 3 GG 98, n. 13, "Mémoire signifié Pour Michelle Poncet Destouches, épouse du sieur Jean Lobreau," p. 4.

63. AM Lyon 3 GG 98, n. 13, p. 28; Vallas, *Un Siècle de musique et de théâtre à Lyon*, 300.

64. AM Lyon BB 346 f. 234, 6 June 1780. On her retirement, see also f. 217 v–220 v, and Vallas, *Un Siècle de musique et de théâtre à Lyon*, 400–402. On her death, see Vingtrinier, *Le Théâtre à Lyon*, 62.

65. On La Montansier's early life, see Dimitriadis, *La Montansier*, 11–45; and Bouchenot-Déchin, *La Montansier*, 11–44.

66. On her business practices, see Bouchenot-Déchin, *La Montansier*, 53–54, 70.

67. In time, she enjoyed sole rights to entertain audiences in cities including Versailles, Nantes, Lorient, Rennes, Angers, Tours, Orléans, Saumur, Alençon, Amiens, Le Havre, Caen, Evreux, Rouen, and Le Havre. Ibid., 125–26.

68. Dimitriadis, *La Montansier*, 85–95.

69. Bouchenot-Déchin, *La Montansier*, 125–26; Dimitriadis, *La Montansier*, 79, 71; Villard, *Le Théâtre Montansier à Versailles*, 16.

70. Bouchenot-Déchin, *La Montansier*, 124–28.

71. Quoted in Dimitriadis, *La Montansier*, 218.

72. I did not find any letter from provincial actors and directors to the Comédie-Française in the BMCF register or files that directly comments on the gender of a director in a positive or negative tone.

73. Joseph-Abraham Bénard Fleury, *Mémoires de Fleury de la Comedie Française, 1757 à 1820*, ed. J.-B.-P. Lafitte (Paris: Ambroise Dupont, 1836–38), 6 vols., I: 135.

74. Ibid., I: 140.

75. Ibid., I: 194–95.

76. AM Lyon 3 GG 101, n. 130, Villeroy to Tolozan de Montfort, 22 February 1789.

77. AM Lyon 3 GG 98, n. 13, "Mémoire signifié Pour Michelle Poncet Destouches," and n. 15, "Arrèt du Conseil d'État du Roi," 1779.

78. Vallas, *Un Siècle de musique et de théâtre à Lyon*, 399.

79. BMCF Com. div. "Mlle Destouches," 24 April 1780, Destouches-Lobreau to Richelieu.

80. Ibid., Richelieu to Monsieur de la Ferté, 29 April 1780.

81. Destouches-Lobreau's nephew debuted 9 August 1780. He was accepted as a member in 1787. Georges Monval, ed., *Comédie-Française, 1658–1900: Liste alphabétique des sociétaires depuis Molière jusqu'à nos jours* (Paris: Bureaux de l'amateur d'autographes, 1900), 47.

82. ARS Archives de la Bastille 11866, "Jansolin," f. 192–208.

83. BMCF 2 ATO Province 1786, Armand de Verteuil to CF, 8 August 1786.

84. Of the analyses of provincial repertories that have been made, most have been based on fragments of repertories found in newspapers and archives and therefore they remain impressionistic. The exception is Henri Lagrave's excellent in-depth studies of the Bordeaux theater repertory, based on the Lecouvreur manuscript. Even this exceptional work, however, faces certain limitations because it is based on just one city, making it difficult to generalize from this data. Lagrave, *La Vie théâtrale à Bordeaux*, 281–308, and Henri Lagrave, "La Saison 1772–1773 au théâtre de Bordeaux: Étude du repertoire," in *La Vie théâtrale dans les provinces du Midi: Actes du IIe colloque de Grasse, 1976*, ed. Yves Giraud (Paris: Jean-Michel Place, 1980), 209–21; Leroy, *Les Comédiens de province en Picardie*, 115–61; and Fuchs, *La Vie théâtrale en province: Personnel et répertoire*, 119–48.

85. BM Bordeaux Ms 1,015 "État des pieces jouées dans la troupe de comédie établie sous les orders de Monseigneur le Maréchal duc de Richelieu . . . de 1772 à 1798" (known as the Lecouvreur manuscript); AM Toulouse GG 943, "Catalogue des comedies, tragedies, operas, drames, et autres pieces en tout genre, qui ont eté jöüeès, et des divers Ballets qui ont eté executes, sur le Théatre de la Comédie à Toulouse, En l'annèe commencée le lundy 24 avril 1786"; Lyon AM 3 GG 100,

"Spectacles de Lyon, Recette & Dépense, années 1787 à 1788, 2e année du Privilège de M. Le Conte." These three sources provide the basis for the analysis below. The repertory information for Toulouse is for the 1786–87 year, while the Lyon data is from the 1787–88 year. Additional information, including genre designations, for the titles provided in these sources was obtained using the Calendrier électronique des spectacles sous l'ancien régime et sous la révolution [CÉSAR] database, http://www.cesar.org.uk/cesar2/home.php.

86. Ibid. As theater companies intensified production, the pressure for variety resulted in larger repertories. For the 1766–67 season in Lyon, when the resident troupe performed fewer days per week, Olivier Zeller identified a smaller repertory of 172 different titles. See "Géographie sociale, loisir, et pratique culturelle: Abonnés et abonnements au théâtre de Lyon (1761–1789)," *RHMC* 44 (1997): 580–600, esp. 593.

87. A. Joannidès, *La Comédie-Française de 1680 à 1900: Dictionnaire général des pièces et des auteurs* (New York: B. Franklin, 1971), "Table chronologique des pièces, 1787" (n.p.). Joannidès presents the company's repertory based on the calendar year, rather than the theater year.

88. AM Lyon 3 GG 98, "Observations tendantes à convertir l'année de Comédie de 1786 à 1787 en un état d'année commune."

89. This is based on box office revenues from 317 performances, rounded to the nearest livre. The average income was about 624 livres. Calculated from Lyon AM 3 GG 100, "Spectacles de Lyon, Recette & Dépense, Années 1787 à 1788, 2e année du Privilège de M. Le Conte."

90. Lagrave, *La Vie théâtrale à Bordeaux*, 284.

91. Lagrave, "La Saison 1772–1773," 219.

92. On the popularity of this work, recognized as one of Grétry's masterpieces, see Philippe Vendrix, ed., *Grétry et l'Europe de l'opéra-comique* (Liège: Pierre Mardaga, 1992).

93. This analysis is based on the sources presented in note 85.

94. Jean-François Marmontel, however, was a fairly close second, with 467 performances for Molière's 491. Lagrave, *La Vie théâtrale à Bordeaux*, 281–309, esp. 285–86 and 296.

95. On Molière's rising reputation after 1760, see Mechele Leon, *Molière, the French Revolution, and the Theatrical Afterlife* (Iowa City: University of Iowa Press, 2009) 27, 100–101, 128–29.

96. Between 1750 and 1789, the Comédie-Française debuted between three and thirteen works each calendar year, out of a total performance repertory of between roughly 120 and 150 plays. Calculated from Joannidès, *La Comédie-Française*.

97. Ravel notes the number of printed plays in *Contested Parterre*, 6.

98. On these societies and the construction of a musical canon in eighteenth-century England, see William Weber, *The Rise of Musical Classics in Eighteenth-Century England: A Study in Canon, Ritual, and Ideology* (Oxford: Clarendon Press, 1992), 189–97.

99. John Lough, *Paris Theatre Audiences in the Seventeenth and Eighteenth Centuries* (London: Oxford University Press, 1957), 264–68; Lagrave, *La Vie théâtrale à Bordeaux*, 298–301.

100. In Lyon and Toulouse, for example, of the six dramatists who were most frequently performed during the season studied, five were the same: Michel-Jean Sedaine, Jean-François Marmontel, Monvel (Jacques-Marie Boutet), Molière, and Desfontaines (François-Georges Fouques Deshayes). For Toulouse in 1786–87, these were Sedaine (39 performances), Marmontel (31), Molière (26), Monvel (25), Desforges (Pierre-Jean-Baptiste Choudard), and Desfontaines (tied at 24). For Lyon in 1787–88, the most frequently performed authors were Monvel (31), Marmontel (30), Sedaine (29), Molière (29), Desfontaines and Dumaniant (Antoine-Jean Bourlin) (22 each). AM Toulouse GG 943, "Catalogue des comedies, tragedies, operas, drames, et autres pièces"; Lyon AM 3 GG 100, "Spectacles de Lyon, Recette & Dépense, Années 1787 à 1788, 2e année du Privilège de M. Le Conte."

101. Together, lyric and dance performances increased from approximately one-third of the Bordeaux repertory in the mid-1770s to one-half during the late 1780s. This is based on Lagrave's extensive repertory study in *La Vie théâtrale à Bordeaux*, 281–302.

102. Fuchs, *La Vie théâtrale en province: Personnel et répertoire*, 124.

103. On the prestige that came from writing for the Comédie-Française, as well as the complex systems of remuneration for playwrights, see Brown, *Field of Honor*, 35–120. Only during the Revolution, when they began to pay performance fees to playwrights, did provincial directors come to fully appreciate the financial advantages they enjoyed under this earlier system. See Flachat, *Pétition à l'Assemblée nationale: Presentée par les comédiens des spectacles de Lyon, Marseille, Rouen, Nantes, Brest, Toulouse, Montpellier, Strasbourg, Lille, Metz, Dunkerque, Genève, Orléans et Grenoble* (n.p., n.d).

104. The *Mercure de France*, France's most widely circulating periodical, regularly featured reviews of works performed at the Comédie-Française, the Comédie-Italienne, and the Opera.

105. Fuchs found at least thirty-six pieces that debuted in provincial cities between 1729 and 1789. See Fuchs, *La Vie théâtrale en province: Personnel et répertoire*, 123–26.

106. See the entry on *Mahomet* in the CÉSAR database; Lough, *Paris Theatre Audiences*, 266.

107. Fuchs, *La Vie théâtrale en province: Personnel et répertoire*, 125.

108. Lagrave, *La Vie théâtrale à Bordeaux*, 298; Fuchs, *La Vie théâtrale en province: Personnel et répertoire*, 125.

109. Quoted in Lough, *Paris Theatre Audiences*, 265–66.

110. All works that could be identified in the repertories in Lyon and Bordeaux had French titles or were written by French playwrights or librettists with the exception of Shakespeare's *Hamlet*, which was almost undoubtedly performed using the rather liberal verse translation by Jean-François Ducis that was in the repertory of the Comédie-Française. Among such works in Toulouse, only Carlo Goldoni's comic opera *La Buona figliola* (The Good Girl) was listed on the repertory in Italian. On the rise of the French language in France during the early modern era, see Paul Cohen, "Courtly French, Learned Latin, and Peasant Patois: The Making of a National Language in Early Modern France" (PhD diss., Princeton University, 2001).

111. This influence can be seen as all the more important given that public theaters generally preceded the founding of local newspapers. René Merle, "Fonction sociale du théâtre français et du théâtre dialectal dans le Sud-Est, de la fin de l'Ancien Régime à 1840," *Provence historique* 40 (1990): 157–72, quote from 157.

112. Ibid., esp. 163–64.

113. Quoted in *L'Art du théâtre à Valenciennes*, 44.

114. Quoted in Bouteiller, *Histoire . . . des théâtres de Rouen*, 88. For similar sentiments, see compliment reproduced in Lefebvre, *Histoire du théâtre de Lille*, 1: 362.

115. Monnet, *Supplément au Roman comique*, 73.

116. Such poor taxes were undoubtedly modeled on the *quart des pauvres* that was long assessed on productions at the Comédie-Française. After 1757, the royal theater paid sixty thousand livres to the Hôpital of Paris. Directors in Marseille paid fifteen thousand livres a year to the poor, while in Bordeaux the director paid nine thousand livres a year. Brown, *Field of Honor*, 115; AM Lyon 3 GG 99, "Questions relatives à l'entreprise des spectacles de Marseille. Réponces," November 1787; and "Questions relatives à l'entreprise des spectacles de Bordeaux," December 1787.

117. Strasbourg took on direct management of the theater from 1751 to 1755 and Metz from 1753 to 1757. In each case, the city then handed responsibility over to an independent director. Deck, *Histoire du théâtre français à Strasbourg*, 30; Tribout de Morembert, *Le Théâtre à Metz*, 71–81.

118. AM Lyon 3 GG 98, n. 19, 9 February 1730.

119. Ibid.

120. Rental income from dependencies was evaluated by the city in AM Lyon 3 GG 98, "Extrait des Registres du Conseil d'Etat 22 janvier 1777." The percentage of the operating budget is based on the 1764 operating budget of 170,000 livres. Vallas, *Un Siècle de musique et de théâtre à Lyon*, 309.

121. On theater subsidies by municipal governments in the nineteenth century, see Cohen, *Urban Government and the Rise of the French City*, 138–40.

122. AD du Rhône 1 C 202, "Spectacles de Lyon," extract from "Soumission du sieur fourdau, addressé a M. Le Contrôleur Général," 20 November 1775.

123. AM Lyon 3 GG 98 "Extrait des Régistres du Conseil d'Etat," 22 January 1777.

124. Ibid.

125. AM Lyon 3 GG 98, "À M. le duc de Villeroy, gouverneur de la ville de Lyon," from "René Le Conte, entrepreneur des spectacles de la ville de Lyon."

126. Ibid. See also AM Lyon 3 GG 98, "Lettre de Melle Destouches, directrice des spectacles de Lyon à Messieurs les abonnés."

127. AV Strasbourg AA 2161, "Monseieur le marquis de Paulny," May 1754. Subsidies are also discussed in AA 2162, "Copie de la letter écrite par Mgr. le marquis de Paulny à M. de Lucé Intendant en Alsace le 25 février, 1756," and the memoire from 1785.

128. Tribout de Morembert, *Le Théâtre à Metz*, 80 and 82. Evidence of the presence or absence of municipal financial support is difficult to locate, yet direct statements from directors or authorities that no subsidies were offered to the theater companies in Lille, Besançon, Marseille, and Bordeaux can be found in the following: AV Strasbourg AA 2162, de Paulny to de Lucé, intendant en Alsace, 25 February 1756; Lefebvre, *Histoire du théâtre de Lille*, 1: 270; AM Lyon 3 GG 99, "Questions relatives à l'entreprise des spectacles de Bordeaux. Réponces," December 1787; and "Questions relatives à l'entreprise des spectacles de Marseille. Réponces," November 1787.

129. Zeller, "Géographie sociale, loisir, et pratique culturelle," 587, 590, 596.

130. Ibid., 586.

131. Lagrave, *La Vie théâtrale à Bordeaux*, 217–19. AD de la Loire-Atlantique C 392, n. 20, "État de la troupe de Longo, année 1784 à 1785."

132. AM Lyon 3 GG 100, "Spectacles de Lyon, Recette & Dépense, années 1787 à 88, 2e année du privilège de M. Le Conte."

133. AD de la Loire-Atlantique, C 392, n. 20. This provides box office receipts from 20 April 1784 to 26 November 1784.

134. *Affiches* were a routine expense on theater budgets. See, for example, AM Lyon 3 GG 100, "Spectacles de Lyon, état de la recette et dépences de l'année 1784 à 1785." That year the theater company spent 1,348 livres on *affiches*.

135. Newspaper advertisements for theaters appeared from time to time in many local newspapers, including the *Journal de Provence*. On such advertising, see also Lagrave, *La Vie théâtrale à Bordeaux*, 253–54 and 341–51; Lefebvre, *Histoire du théâtre de Lille*, 1:322. This form of advertising was not, however, without problems. Lagrave notes that in the *Journal de Guienne* announcements concerning the theater repertory were irregular and quite frequently incorrect. The Rouen newspaper attempted to advertise theatrical performances in 1786, but stopped because the repertory was so often changed at the last minute. Bouteiller, *Histoire . . . des théâtres de Rouen*, 131. On discussions of theater in journals and newspapers, see also Ambard, *La Comédie en Provence*, 16–17; Tribout de Morembert, *Le Théâtre à Metz*, 109–17; Vallas, *Un Siècle de musique et de théâtre à Lyon*, 411–23.

136. Quéruau-Lamerie, *Notice sur le théâtre d'Angers*, 80; Lefebvre, *Histoire du théâtre de Lille*, 2:2–3. See also printed advertisements for the theater of Valenciennes from the late 1770s and early 1780s, in which two out of eighteen exemplars feature poems for the ladies, in BMCF "Programmes province," Valenciennes, 16 March 1781 and 24 July 1782.

137. M. Klairwal, *Prologue pour l'ouverture de la nouvelle salle de spectacles d'Amiens, par M. Klairwal, représenté le . . . 21 janvier 1780* (Amiens: J.-B. Caron fils, 1780), 29.

138. In Lyon, in 1761, women's yearlong subscriptions cost seventy-two livres while those for men cost 120 livres; in 1786, women's subscriptions cost ninety-six livres, while those for men cost 144 livres. In Lille, women paid twelve livres a month, while men paid eighteen livres. Women's subscriptions in Bordeaux were only twelve livres a month, as opposed to twenty-four for men. Lefebvre, *Histoire du théâtre de Lille*, 1:380; Lagrave, *La Vie théâtrale à Bordeaux*, 273; Zeller, "Géographie sociale, loisir et pratique culturelle," 586 and 591.

139. In Lyon, in 1787–88, 161 women purchased annual subscriptions as opposed to 441 men. AM Lyon 3 GG 100, "Spectacles de Lyon, Recette & Dépense, Année 1787 à 88, 2e Année du Privilège de M. Le Conte."

140. On the stigmas actors faced, see *Extrait historique pour servir à l'essai d'un plan de régie générale, pour les spectacles de province, par un comédien de province* (Geneva: n.p., 1767), 1–22.

141. On representations of actresses during the Old Regime, see Lenard Berlanstein, *Daughters of Eve: A Cultural History of French Theater Women from the Old Regime to the Fin de Siècle* (Cambridge: Harvard University Press, 2001). Monnet, for example, wrote about the "adventures" of Lyon actresses who were kept by local elites, one of whom purportedly maintained four lovers at a time, in *Supplément au roman comique*, 101–4.

142. Denis Diderot, "Entretiens sur le Fils naturel" [1757], in *Oeuvres esthétiques*, ed. Paul Vernière (Paris: Éditions Garnier Frères, 1965), 69–175; Jean Le Rond d'Alembert's "Geneva," first published in volume VII of the *Encyclopédie*, reprinted in Rousseau, *Politics and the Arts: Letter to M. d'Alembert*, 4–5.

143. Quoted in Tribout de Morembert, *Le Théâtre à Metz*, 96–97.

144. AM Toulouse GG 943, "Compliment de cloture du théâtre," 31 March 1787. Similar sentiments appeared in Fleury's compliment for the opening of that season, GG 943, 24 April 1786.

145. AM Lyon 3 GG 98, "Lettre de Mlle Destouches, Directrice des Spectacles de Lyon, à Messieurs les Abonnées."

146. Quoted in Bouteiller, *Histoire . . . des théâtres de Rouen*, 1: 118.

147. Quoted in ibid., 188.

148. AM Lyon 3 GG 98, "Lettre de Mlle Destouches."

149. See also Lefebvre, *Histoire du théâtre de Lille*, 2: 58.

150. This was common knowledge for any director. In proposing a program for the centralization and reform of French theater, the *Extrait historique pour servir à l'essai d'un plan de régie générale* proposed that traveling troupes be allocated to cities only for as long as "comedy can be played there without a loss" (22).

151. Quoted in Leroy, *Les Comédiens de province en Picardie*, 27.

152. Favart, *Mémoires et correspondance*, 2: 45, Favart to Durazzo, 28 December 1762.

153. *Extrait historique pour servir à l'essai d'un plan de régie générale*, 21.

154. Bouteiller, *Histoire . . . des théâtres de Rouen*, 8–12, 20, 177–86; Vogt, *Le Théâtre à Nancy*, 8–9.

155. In addition to Paris, metropolitan cities with resident theater companies included Lyon, Lille, Strasbourg, Bordeaux, Marseille, Nantes, Toulouse, Metz, Nancy, Versailles, Brest, Rouen, Lorient, and Montpellier. Traveling companies performed in other cities on regional circuits that included routes such as Montpellier, Nîmes, and Arles (before 1788), and Reims, Troyes, Châlons-sur-Marne, and Langres. Lagrave, *La Vie théâtrale à Bordeaux*, 265; AN H 1359; Lefebvre, *Histoire du théâtre de Lille*, I: 258, 386–88; AD de la Loire-Atlantique C 321, n. 36–37; AM Toulouse GG 943; Debauve, *Théâtre et spectacles à Lorient*, 44, 58, 70; AV Strasbourg AA 2162, "Questions de la ville de Besançon, réponses," 1782; Tribout de Morembert, *Le Théâtre à Metz*, 43, 79; P. Fromageot, *Le Théâtre de Versailles et La Montansier* (Versailles: Aubert, 1905), 29–30; Jourda, *Le Théâtre à Montpellier*, 20–21, 36; B., "Le Théatre de Reims," *Revue de Champagne et de Brie* 17 (1884): 105–9, esp. 107.

156. Borsay, *English Urban Renaissance*, 120; Rosenfeld, *Strolling Players and Drama in the Provinces*.

157. AM Lyon 3 GG 100, "Spectacle. État de la recette des spectacles de Lyon depuis le 30 mars 1761, ouverture du théâtre, jusque et compris le 26 jan.er 1762," and "Spectacles de Lyon, Recette & Dépense, Année 1787 à 88, 2e année du Privilège de M. Le Conte." On the intensification of performance in Lyon during this time, see also Olivier Zeller, "L'Intensification de la vie théâtrale à Lyon (1761–1788)," *Cahiers d'histoire* 42 (1997): 193–216.

158. Lagrave, *La Vie théâtrale à Bordeaux,* 141, 281; Ambard, *La Comédie en Provence*, 94. In Toulouse, the troupe performed 307 days during this season. AM Toulouse GG 943, "Catalogue des comedies, tragédies, operas, drames, et autres pièces," 1786. In theory, the troupe in Nantes performed daily, although it took more holidays and

breaks. In September and October of 1784, for example, they performed twenty-six times each month. AD de la Loire-Atlantique C 392, n. 20, "Etat de la troupe de Longo, Année 1784 à 1785."

159. Jourda, *Le Théâtre à Montpellier*, 36.

160. Lagrave, "La Saison 1772–1773," 212.

161. Calculated from financial information given by Lagrave, *La Vie théâtrale à Bordeaux*, 221 and 224.

162. AM Lyon 3 GG 100, receipts and expenses for 1761–62, 1784–85.

163. AM Lyon 3 GG 98, "Lettre de Mlle Destouches."

164. AM Lyon 3 GG 101, n. 144. Madame Destouches-Lobreau to M. de la Verpillière, Prévôt des marchands, 16 April 1764.

165. Ibid.

166. Ibid., n. 145, 11 May 1764 (emphasis in original).

167. Ibid., n. 147, 9 June 1764.

168. Ibid., n. 149, 1 July 1764.

169. Ibid., n. 150, 30 July 1764.

170. Ibid., n. 149, 1 July 1764.

171. Ibid., n. 151, 7 August 1764.

172. *Trois siècles d'opéra à Lyon*, 20. On the financial losses of the directors in Lyon in the 1780s, see, for example, AM Lyon 3 GG 98, "À M.gr le Duc de Villeroy," from René Le Conte.

173. AM Lyon 3 GG 101, n. 155.

174. Lagrave, *La Vie théâtrale à Bordeaux*, 222; AM de Lyon 3 GG 100, "Spectacles de Lyon année 1782 à 1783," "Tableau de la troupe du spectacle de Lyon pour l'année 1787 à 88."

175. AM Lyon 3 GG 98, Letter to the duc de Villeroy, from Le Conte.

176. On theater rentals and debt, see AM Lyon 3 GG 99, "Questions relatives à l'entreprise des spectacles de Bordeaux. Réponces," December 1787, and AM Lyon 3 GG 101, n. 220. In Marseille, as discussed in chapter 1, the joint-stock company running the theater troupe panicked when the owners of the new playhouse initially demanded 82,500 livres a year in rent with a collateral of over one million livres, an amount that was later reduced.

177. The cost of oil and candles for the new Marseille theater, for example, came to the very substantial sum of twenty thousand livres a year. AM Lyon 3 GG 99, "Questions relatives à l'entreprise des spectacles de Marseille. Réponces," November 1787. For complaints about these rising costs and their impact on the bottom line of the theater business, see AM Lyon 3 GG 98, Lettre de Mlle Destouches.

178. Directors' use of the privilege to collect the quart des spectacles is discussed in chapter 3. On adding additional boxes and raising subscription prices in the late 1780s, see AM Lyon 3 GG 101, nos. 111, 120, 121, 131.

179. Quoted in Vallas, *Un Siècle de musique et de théâtre à Lyon*, 403–4.

180. AM Lyon 3 GG 98, Letter to de Villeroy from Le Conte.

181. Jacques-Thomas Mague de Saint-Aubin, *La Réforme des théâtres, ou Vues d'un amateur sur les moyens d'avoir toujours des acteurs à talens sur les théâtres de Paris & des grandes villes du royaume, & de prévenir les abus des troupes ambulantes, sans priver les petites villes de l'agrément des spectacles* (Paris: Guillot, 1787), 40. For a brief biography, see Alphonse Leveaux, *Mague de Saint-Aubin: Notice biographique* (Compiègne: H. Lefebvre, 1876).

5. The Work of Acting

1. BMCF 2 ATO Carton 198 Théâtres de Province, XVIIIe–XIXe, Consultations des Comédiens français, Dossier Province 1774. Mme Marion [to Comédie-Française], 25 July 1774.

2. Quoted in Gustave Lhotte, *Le Théâtre à Lille avant la Révolution* (Lille: L. Danel, 1881), 53.

3. BMCF 2 ATO Province 1774. Mme Marion [to CF], 25 July 1774.

4. Ibid.

5. The BMCF contains a register of issues and conflicts brought before the royal theater—the Registre concernant les consultations de la province R 137, 1—and a set of dossiers containing letters and other materials organized by year in 2 ATO Carton 198, Théâtres de Province, XVIIIe–XIXe, Consultations des Comédiens français. The labels of these dossiers were not standardized. For these notes I refer to these sets of sources as either Registre R 137, 1 or 2 ATO Province and the year(s) in question. In addition, a separate collection of letters was filed under Comédiens divers hors Comédie-Française (Com. div.), usually under the name of the individual letter writer. On the relationship between the Comédie-Française and provincial actors and directors, see also Jules Bonnassies, *La Comédie-Française et les comédiens de province aux XVIIe et XVIIIe siècles: Contestations-débuts* (Paris: Léon Willem, 1875).

6. Unflattering contemporary accounts of professional performers range from Jean-Jacques Rousseau's *Letter to M. d'Alembert on the Theatre* to a pornographic libel of the famous Mademoiselle Clairon of the Comédie-Française. Even Diderot, a playwright and an ardent supporter of the stage, acknowledged that "an actor [who is a] gallant man, an actress [who is a] respectable woman are such rare phenomena." Pierre Alexandre Gaillard de La Bataille's *Histoire de Mademoiselle Cronel dite Fretillon, actrice de la comédie de Roüen*, 4 vols. (The Hague: Aux depens de la compagnie, 1741–43); Denis Diderot, *Paradoxe sur le comédien*, ed. Ernest Dupuy (Geneva: Slatkine Reprints, 1968), 147. Scholarship on actors and actresses has tended to reinforce the image of the actor as dissolute and undisciplined, and the actress as essentially a *femme publique*. Root-Bernstein, *Boulevard Theater and Revolution*, 141–65; Berlanstein, *Daughters of Eve*, 33–83.

7. On the excommunication of actors and their diminished civil status, see Rougemont, *La Vie théâtrale en France*, 205–6, and McManners, *Church and Society in Eighteenth-Century France*, 2: 312–42. According to contemporary legal experts such as Joseph-Nicolas Guyot, even the Comédie-Française did not receive an official legal corporate standing until the troupe's new regulations of 1757 were registered by the Parlement of Paris in 1761. This status did not extend to actors working elsewhere or to the profession as a whole. "Comédien," in Joseph-Nicolas Guyot, *Répertoire universel et raisonné de jurisprudence civile, criminelle, canonique, et bénéficiale*, 17 vols. (Paris: Visse, 1784), 4: 15; Louis Marcerou, *La Comédie française: L'Association des comédiens français (étude corporative)* (Paris: Librairie de France, 1925), 63–64. In contrast to actors, painters and sculptors in Paris enjoyed both an academy and corporate status. See Charlotte Guichard, "Arts libéraux et arts libres à Paris au XVIIIe siècle: Peintres et sculpteurs entre corporation et Académie royale," RHMC 49 (2002): 54–68.

8. Charles Collé, *Journal et mémoires de Charles Collé*, ed. Honoré Bonhomme, new ed., 3 vols. (Paris: Firmin Didot Frères, 1868), 3: 3–4.

9. This poem, which appeared in the *Affiches de Provence* on 14 November 1779, is reprinted in Ambard, *La Comédie en Provence*, 95.

10. Root-Bernstein uses these terms when describing the theater professionals of the Paris Boulevard stages in *Boulevard Theater and Revolution*, 167, 144. Laurent Turcot likewise adopts a more autocratic vision of labor relations in French theater than the one presented here in "Directeurs, comédiens et police."

11. BMCF 2 ATO Province 1774, Mme Marion [to CF], 25 July 1774.

12. Although early seventeenth-century contracts demonstrate that some actors did apprentice, this practice largely ended by the 1620s. Mongrédien, *La Vie quotidienne des comédiens*, 12.

13. For one example of such a contract, signed in September 1783 between the actor St. Vallié and Felix Gaillard, entrepreneur privilégié du Roy pour les spectacles de Bordeaux, see BMCF 2 ATO Province 1784, St. Vallié [to CF], 17 April 1784.

14. The joint-stock company managing Marseille's theater company allocated twenty-four thousand livres for this purpose beyond the other costs of directing and managing the troupe. Bordeaux's directors estimated annual recruitment costs at thirty thousand livres. AM Lyon 3 GG 99, "Questions relatives à l'entreprise des spectacles de Marseille/Réponces," November 1787, and "Questions relatives à l'entreprise des spectacles de Bordeaux," December 1787.

15. BMCF 2 ATO Province 1780–81, Clairys de Carom [to CF], 8 March 1782. See also Clairanval's discussion of forming a troupe in Angoulême, Province 1773, 5 January 1773.

16. BMCF 2 ATO Province 1784, 4 November 1784. On the common practice of signing contracts in September, see AM Bordeaux GG 1004 e, "Mémoire pour le sieur Chevalier Peicam Danseur, attaché au Spectacle de Bordeaux," 1.

17. BMCF 2 ATO Province 1784, Du Vergez [to CF], 9 January 1784.

18. The café and its colorful denizens are described in an essay entitled "Café de la rue des Boucheries," in Louis-Sébastien Mercier, *Tableau de Paris, tome 11*, new ed. (Amsterdam: n.p., 1789), 85–90; and in Louis-Marie Prudhomme, *Miroir historique, politique et critique de l'ancien et du nouveau Paris et du département de la Seine* (Paris: n.p., 1807), 3rd ed., 6 vols., 4: 73. Joseph Laglaine describes living next to the café years earlier as a young student and being unable to withstand the attraction of the stage, in a letter dated 7 October 1822, reproduced in Antoine Chelin, *Le Théâtre à l'Ile Maurice: Son origine et son développement* (Port-Louis, Ile Maurice: Mauritius Printing Company, 1954), appendix VIII, 96–97.

19. Mague de Saint-Aubin, *La Réforme des théâtres*, 4–5.

20. Ibid., 6–9, 30–31.

21. Papillon de la Ferté, *Journal*, 198.

22. Favart, *Mémoires et correspondance*, 2: 149–50; BMCF 2AG 1763, letter from Papillon de la Ferté to the duc de Duras, 27 September 1763.

23. Letter of 23 June 1772 from François Fleury to Charles Dedon, the syndic of Metz, quoted in Tribout de Morembert, *Le Théâtre à Metz*, 83.

24. These averages are compiled from salary lists in budgets for troupes performing in Brest (1768–69); Montpellier, Nîmes, and Arles (1772–73); Lyon (1772–73); Amiens, Abbeville, Douai, Cambrai, and Arras (1773–74); Pau and Bayonne (1774–75); Nantes (1784–85); Lyon (1787–88); and Rouen (1787–88). The data set represents a total of 251 yearlong engagements for actors, actresses, and singers, including 150 men and 101 women. Salaries for individuals ranged between four hundred and

eight thousand livres a year, and averaged 2,417 livres. The median salary for the 220 performers who were working on individual rather than family contracts was twenty-two hundred livres. The Brest salaries were part of a proposed budget that may not have been enacted and the salaries for Rouen include both salary and projected proceeds from benefit performances that were contractually guaranteed to various actors and actresses, estimated at four hundred livres each. I did not include orchestral musicians or dancers, who were often hired on a month-to-month basis. BNF Ms Naf 9411, f. 289; Bouteiller, *Histoire. . . des théâtres de Rouen*, 1: 177–79; Ducéré, "Le Théâtre bayonnais," 329; Ancely, *Histoire du théâtre et du spectacle à Pau*, 67–68; Lhotte, *Le Théâtre à Douai*, 81–82, 99–100; AD de la Loire-Atlantique C 392 n. 20, n. 31, "État de la troupe de Longo, année 1784 à 1785"; AM Lyon 3 GG 99, n. 1 and 3 GG 100, "Tableau de la Troupe du spectacle de Lyon pour l'année 1787 à 1788."

25. Lagrave, *La Vie théâtrale à Bordeaux*, 312–13.

26. For lower salary, see BMCF Com. div. "Alexandre," 1749. Salaries for the later era are based on the data cited in note 24 above.

27. Actors can hardly be characterized as generally poorly paid, as Rougemont asserts in *La Vie théâtrale en France*, 203. Wages in other occupations taken from Alasseur, *La Comédie-Française*, 124–28, and Michael Sonenscher, *Work and Wages: Natural Law, Politics, and the Eighteenth-Century Trades* (Cambridge: Cambridge University Press, 1989), 204–5.

28. Alasseur, *La Comédie-Française*, 149.

29. Papillon de la Ferté, *Journal*, 199–200.

30. Hafter, "Female Masters in the Ribbonmaking Guild," 2. On women's work in France, see also Daryl Hafter, *Women at Work in Preindustrial France* (University Park: Pennsylvania State University Press, 2007).

31. Of the women in this sample, 94 percent earned six hundred livres or more a year. See note 24. According to Olwen Hufton, women's earning potential in provincial cities was limited. A woman working as a servant might earn between fifty and one hundred livres a year, in addition to her room and board. Women who made stockings or lace might earn somewhere between twenty and two hundred livres a year. Hufton, "Women and the Family Economy in Eighteenth-Century France," 6, 13, 16. In Paris, seamstresses who had completed three-year apprenticeships earned annual salaries between roughly sixty and 270 livres, and in some cases may also have received food and lodging. Crowston, *Fabricating Women*, 91–94.

32. See note 24 above. Salaries for the eighty-four women whose salaries were listed independently ranged between four hundred and eight thousand livres a year, averaging 2,447 livres. Salaries for the 136 men spanned the same range, and came to an average of 2,349 livres. Actresses' median salary came to 2,300 livres, higher than the median for actors of 2,140 livres. I established a third category for those hired together as couples or in a family group, all for a single salary, which made it difficult to assign a specific salary to an individual actor or actress in the family. In fact, these families fared best of all, with thirteen husband-and-wife pairs, one mother with daughter, and one couple with child (thirty-one performers in all) hired for an average salary of 2,634 livres each. On women's earnings in other trades, see Hufton, "Women and the Family Economy," 13.

33. Contemporary British actresses, too, enjoyed remarkable earning potential and learned to leverage celebrity to their economic advantage through hard-nosed negotiations. See Felicity Nussbaum, *Rival Queens: Actresses, Performance, and the*

Eighteenth-Century British Theater (Philadelphia: University of Pennsylvania Press, 2010), esp. 31–60.

34. Favart served as a talent scout for the comte de Durazzo, who was the director for the imperial theaters in Vienna. Favart, *Mémoires et correspondance*, 1: 239, Favart to M. le C. de Durazzo, 24 January 1762.

35. Ibid., I: 259, 30 April 1762.

36. BMCF Com. div. "Mlle Destouches," "Copie d'une lettre de Mad. Montrose Dalainval," n.d.

37. Ibid., "Copie d'une letter."

38. BMCF 2 ATO Province 1785, Duverger [to CF], 13 January 1785.

39. Favart, *Mémoires et correspondance*, 2: 132–33, Favart to M. le C. de Durazzo, 29 July 1763; 2: 178, Favart to M. le C. de Durazzo, 21 December 1763; 2: 146–47, Favart to M. le C. de Durazzo, 27 September 1763.

40. BMCF Com. div. "Mlle Destouches," n.d. Montrose's contract was signed 25 August 1778 in Cadiz. Although Montrose signed the contract for the Lyon stage, illness and a deteriorating political situation made it impossible for her to make the trip to France. The director contacted the Comédie-Française about how much Montrose should pay for breach of contract.

41. See BMCF Registre R 137, 1: 23 July 1779. This was reaffirmed in 1787 and 1789.

42. BMCF 2 ATO Province 1774. Lamare [to CF], 7 February 1774.

43. Ibid.

44. BMCF Com. div. "Ganie," 6 April 1786.

45. BMCF 2 ATO Province 1786, Sr. Armand de Verteuil [to CF], 8 August 1786.

46. BMCF Com. div. "Berville," 28 June 1781.

47. Mague de Saint-Aubin, *La Réforme des théâtres*, 3.

48. Bouteiller, *Histoire. . . des théâtres de Rouen*, 1:184; Ancely, *Histoire du spectacle à Pau*, 67–68; Alasseur, *La Comédie-Française*, 149; and BMCF Com. div. "Dorny," letter of 8 February 1776.

49. BMCF Com. div. "Mlle Rinville, femme Le Roy," letter of 27 June 1774.

50. BMCF Com. div. "De Villeneuve," letter of 2 May 1780.

51. Quoted in Fuchs, *La Vie théâtrale en province: Personnel et repertoire*, 38.

52. Mlle Raucourt, quoted in ibid.

53. In one such crisis, a leading singer in the Lyon theater, "unhappy, aggrieved (*chagrinée*)" after being poorly received in a role, refused to go on the following evening in the opera that was scheduled. When her director insisted, she violently threw him out of her dressing room. AM Lyon 3 GG 101 n. 167, Collot d'Herbois to the Prévôt des marchands, 31 December 1787.

54. The BMCF 2 ATO Province 1719 contains a letter from provincial actors to the royal troupe asking for advice on a contract dispute that dates from 1719.

55. BCMF Registre R 137, 1: 2 June 1777; Bonnassies, *La Comédie-Française et les comédiens de province*, 7–10. Internal regulations established by the royal actors in 1729 note that responsibility for responding to queries from provincial actors was to be given to certain members of the troupe. In this sense, provincial arbitration became a formal obligation at this point. The 1766 clause on this subject specifies that the issues raised and the decisions of the actors were to be transcribed in a special

register to be kept in one of the armoires in their meeting room. Unfortunately, the registers of such arbitration at the BMCF begin only in 1772.

56. Marcerou, *La Comédie-Française*, 67.

57. The BMCF 2 ATO Province 1786, for example, contains responses from all three of these parties.

58. BMCF Com. div. "Dannery et al.," 5 April 1777. The Comédie-Italienne was also given a similar responsibility in their "Reglemens pour la Comédie Italienne" dating 20 June 1774, AN O^1 848, n. 11. However, this register has not been found nor has corroborating evidence suggesting that the Comédiens italiens maintained such a register. Letters to the Comédie-Française from singers and dancers, as well as those asking about role distribution in opéras-comiques, suggest that the Comédie-Française handled most, if not all, disputes.

59. BMCF 2 ATO Province 1775, Dutilleul [to CF], 15 February 1775.

60. They also responded to French-speaking companies in Warsaw, Munich, Naples, and elsewhere. Based on the cities of origin noted in the Registre R 137, 1; the dossiers from province 1772–89; and the letters in Com. div.

61. Friedland, *Political Actors*, 3, 198. On prerevolutionary attempts by actors to make a case for basic civil rights, such as giving testimony in a court of law, see BMCF *Mémoire et consultation sur l'état des comédiens, rélativement aux effets civils* (Paris: Michel Lambert, 1768).

62. Brown, *Field of Honor*, 121–208, esp. 136; Papillon de la Ferté, *Journal*, 207, 209–10, 232, 325, 329.

63. Favart, *Mémoires et correspondance*, 2: 150, Favart to M. le comte de Durazzo, 13 October 1763.

64. Bonnassies, *La Comédie-Française et les comédiens de province*, 27.

65. William Sewell introduced the idea of a "corporate idiom" in *Work and Revolution in France: The Language of Labor from the Old Regime to 1848* (Cambridge: Cambridge University Press, 1980), 16–39.

66. On oral contracts, see Amalia Kessler, *A Revolution in Commerce: The Parisian Merchant Court and the Rise of Commercial Society in Eighteenth-Century France* (New Haven: Yale University Press, 2007), 61. The contracts transcribed in correspondence that survived in the collection of the BMCF had not been notarized. Rather, they include language attesting that the contract is to have the same strength and authority as though it had passed before a notary.

67. BMCF Registre R 137, 1, 28 March 1778. On verbal contracts, see BMCF Com. div. "Rousselet," and 2 ATO Province 1783, Désicourt [to CF], 16 November 1783.

68. BMCF Registre R 137, 1, 21 June 1779.

69. BMCF 2 ATO Province 1773. Response by CF to Laon troupe, n.d.

70. BMCF 2 ATO Province 1784, St. Vallié [to CF], 17 April 1784; Province 1776, Dufresne et al. [to CF], 9 April 1776; Province 1780–81, Piri et al. [to CF], 2 April 1780; Province 1786, Sr. Armand de Verteuil [to CF], 8 August 1786.

71. See, for example, BMCF 2 ATO Province 1774, contract for Dlle Poupard, femme Martin, October 1774; Registre R 137, 1, 22 February 1779.

72. More than fifty separate inquiries and disputes about roles were addressed to the Comédie-Française. This description of hiring is based on the contracts and letters in the BMCF collection and BMCF Registre R 137, 1, response from CF of 10 June 1775.

73. BMCF Com. div. "Delaval." He wrote from Liège on 12 June 1779. In this case, the response of the royal company was not preserved, but because he was hired to perform *en chef* or in alternation, Delaval may have had a case.

74. BMCF 2 ATO Province 1784, Desroches [to CF], 22 July 1784.

75. BMCF 2 ATO Province 1785 and 1787, decisions by CF of 24 January 1785 and 23 July 1787.

76. BMCF 2 ATO Province 1774, decision by CF, 25 July 1774.

77. BMCF 2 ATO Province 1788, decision of 28 January 1788, reaffirmed on 22 June 1789.

78. BMCF Registre R 137, 1, 8 June 1776. The issue of illness would be raised again in 1784 and 1785.

79. BMCF 2 ATO Province 1772. [Director of the troupe in Lille to CF], 7 November 1772. See also Province 1773, decision of 2 August 1773.

80. BMCF Registre R 137, 1, response by CF, 15 May 1775. See also BMCF Com. div. "Montansier," 20 May 1782.

81. BMCF Registre R 137, 1, 15 May 1775.

82. BMCF 2 ATO Province 1774, Mme Marion [to CF], 25 July 1774; and Province 1775, Dutilleul [to CF], 15 February 1775; Com. div. "de Villeneuve," 2 May 1780. This was also true for the French troupes performing in cities and courts such as Geneva and Munich. Authorities in Brussels, for example, asked for decisions from the King's Players, wanting their advice concerning precedent. Province 1780–81, Piri et al. to CF, 2 and 15 April 1780.

83. Kessler, *Revolution in Commerce*, 128–35.

84. BMCF Registre R 137, 1, 11 April 1778. They repeated this assertion in 1785.

85. BMCF 2 ATO Province 1785. Response by CF, 7 February 1785. As early as 1773, an actor named Diancourt wrote that his directors claimed to have no "higher judges." BMCF 2 ATO Province 1773. See also case of Brest in Province 1788, response by CF, 16 May 1788.

86. The work experiences of actors and their relationships with the directors who employed them can be compared with those of journeymen and seamstresses with their masters and mistresses discussed in Michael Sonenscher, *Work and Wages*, and idem, "Journeymen's Migrations and Workshop Organization in Eighteenth-Century France," and Cynthia Truant, "Independent and Insolent: Journeymen and Their 'Rites' in the Old Regime Workplace," in *Work in France: Representations, Meaning, Organization, and Practice*, ed. Steven L. Kaplan and Cynthia Koepp (Ithaca: Cornell University Press, 1986), 74–96 and 131–73; Steven Kaplan, *The Bakers of Paris and the Bread Question, 1700-1775* (Durham: Duke University Press, 1996), part 2; and Crowston, *Fabricating Women*, esp. 74–112, 297–342.

87. On struggles between masters and journeymen over this issue, see Truant, "Independent and Insolent," 140. A royal order to debut at one of the king's theaters constituted for provincial actors and directors an important exception to the usual operation of the theater market. Such an order could happen at any time during the year, and it might deprive a theater company of one of its most talented performers indefinitely, at great cost. On tensions between provincial directors and the royal theaters (and especially their administrators) on this issue, see Papillon de la Ferté, *Journal*, 143–44, 181, 199, 398.

88. Unlike Truant's journeymen, for whom the well-being of the community took precedence over the aspirations and liberties of the individual, actors attempted a more difficult, and less cooperative, balancing of the two. Truant, "Independent and Insolent," 173.

89. Sewell, *Work and Revolution*, 20–21.

90. For example, of the seventy guilds in Rouen, both men and women served together as masters in only five of these. Although women did serve as officers in some of these mixed-sex guilds, others prohibited women from even attending the general assemblies of masters. In Paris, only a single guild was genuinely mixed-sex, reserving an equal number of elected leadership positions for women and men. Daryl Hafter, "Gender Formation from a Working Class Viewpoint: Guildwomen in Eighteenth-Century Rouen," *Proceedings of the Annual Meeting of the Western Society for French History* 16 (1989): 415–22, 418; Hafter, *Women at Work*, 222–27; Crowston, *Fabricating Women*, 181. Lenard Berlanstein has noted that actresses' power within the royal company was curtailed somewhat in the 1760s with the creation of a leadership committee that included seven actors and just two actresses. Lenard Berlanstein, "Women and Power in Eighteenth-Century France: Actresses at the Comédie-Française," *Feminist Studies* 20:3 (1994): 475–506, 489. Nonetheless, women were regularly given a voice in these matters. As mentioned above, the entire company, which included significant numbers of women, participated in many decisions regarding provincial matters.

91. Out of approximately 196 issues and individual files that remain in the company records, forty can be identified as having been written by women alone. Women constituted approximately three-eighths of the performers in provincial acting companies and about 10 percent of directors.

92. The question of women's contracts—and their legality and enforceability in various circumstances—was raised before the Comédie-Française. Unmarried actresses, including those who were minors, signed binding contracts in their own names. In keeping with legal tradition, married actresses required permission from their husband, at least theoretically, to execute such a contract, although such permission could be assumed if the husband did not protest. On women's legal ability to execute binding contracts in theory and practice during the Old Regime, see Kessler, *Revolution in Commerce*, 142–43.

93. BMCF 2 ATO Province 1785, response by CF, 23 May 1785.

94. Pregnancy for unmarried women was in this way treated differently than illness: sick actors were paid even when they could not perform, for the duration of the contract. BMCF 2 ATO Province 1772, response by CF, 7 November 1772.

95. Among the many works that explore the extensive influence of Rousseau on contemporary understandings of gender and of women's place in the "natural" order, see especially Joel Schwartz, *The Sexual Politics of Jean-Jacques Rousseau* (Chicago: University of Chicago Press, 1984); Joan B. Landes, *Women and the Public Sphere in the Age of the French Revolution* (Ithaca: Cornell University Press, 1988), 66–89; Dena Goodman, *The Republic of Letters: A Cultural History of the French Enlightenment* (Ithaca: Cornell University Press, 1994), 39, 53–56.

96. On the use of such tactics by the Parisian seamstresses' guild, see Clare Haru Crowston, "Engendering the Guilds: Seamstresses, Tailors, and the Clash of Corpo-

rate Identities in Old Regime France," *FHS* 23:2 (2000): 339–71, esp. 347, 366–67; and *Fabricating Women*, esp. 244–55, 412–15.

97. Chappuzeau, *Le Théâtre françois*, 97.

98. Louis Riccoboni, *De la réformation du theâtre* (Paris: n.p., 1743), esp. 41–48 and 98–116. See also Nicolas-Edme Rétif de la Bretonne, *La Mimographe, ou Idées d'une honnête-femme pour la réformation du théâtre national* (Amsterdam: Changuion, 1770); and Louis-Sébastien Mercier, *Du Théâtre, ou Nouvel essai sur l'art dramatique* (Amsterdam: E. Van Harrevelt, 1773), 359–66.

99. In addition to their official duties, many of the King's Players were involved with private theater societies in Paris, another source of personal income and competition for the royal actors' energies. Mague de Saint-Aubin estimated in 1787 that more than thirty private theater societies existed, some of which sought to bring in royal performers for guest appearances. *La Réforme des théâtres*, 62.

100. For a well-documented biography of Lekain (also known as Le Kain), see Jean Jacques Olivier, *Henri-Louis Le Kain de la Comédie-Française, Illustré de soixante-six gravures d'après les documents de l'époque* (Paris: Société française d'imprimerie et de librairie, 1907).

101. Based on BNF Fonds français Ms 12532, Lekain, "Journal de la Comédie tenu pour mon seul usage depuis le 27 décembre 1747 jusqu'au 23 mars 1765," and BNF Fonds français Ms 12533, Lekain, "Journal de tous les rôles que j'ai joués depuis le mois d'avril 1765 jusqu'à la fin de mars 1777."

102. These expenses included buying one's share in the troupe at a cost of nearly nine thousand livres. BMCF Dossier Lekain and Olivier, *Henri-Louis Le Kain*, 46–47; Marcerou, *La Comédie française*, 62. The amount of company profits that were paid out per share to vested members can be found in Alasseur, *La Comédie-Française*, 125–26.

103. Several years after Lekain was accepted into the royal company, when Voltaire denounced the system that prevented such a talented actor from receiving the compensation that he deserved, he observed, "You would earn more in *province* than in Paris: it is an insufferable shame." Letter from Voltaire to Lekain, 5 January [1757], in Henri-Louis Lekain, *Mémoires de Lekain, précédés de réflexions sur cet acteur, et sur l'art théatral, par F. Talma* (Paris: Ponthieu, 1825), 250.

104. Olivier, *Henri-Louis Le Kain*, 67.

105. From the *Mercure dijonnais* for the month of April 1753, quoted in Gouvenain, *Le Théâtre à Dijon*, 93–94, and Olivier, *Henri-Louis Le Kain*, 67–68.

106. Ibid.

107. BNF Fonds français Ms 12532–33. During the first fifteen years of his membership in the royal troupe, the percentage of Lekain's Paris and court performances out of his overall yearly performances remained, for the most part, at or above 90 percent. During the final decade of his career, the actor's health declined and he gave far fewer performances even as his celebrity grew. During this time, provincial performances and those abroad comprised as much as a quarter to a third of his total stage appearances in a given year.

108. [François Antoine] de Chevrier, *Almanach des gens d'esprit par un homme qui n'est pas sot, Calendrier pour l'année 1762 et le reste de la vie* (London: Jean Nourse, 1762), 25.

109. Lekain also performed in nine locales outside of France. BNF Fonds français Ms 12532 and 12533.

110. AM Lyon 3 GG 98, Letter from Mlle Destouches, Directrice des spectacles de Lyon, to Messieurs les Abonnés, n.d. Over the course of the 1780s, Lyon directors paid out roughly ten to twenty thousand livres annually as "honoraria to visiting talents." AM Lyon 3 GG 100, budgets for 1782 through 1788. A letter from 1783 suggests that although the top ranks of performers were receiving five to six hundred livres per performance, for a longer term engagement involving both Marseille and Aix Madame Saint-Huberty might have been willing to accept four hundred livres a day, together with round-trip travel expenses from Paris. Sainval aînée, who usually received six hundred to seven hundred livres per evening, may have earned as much as eighteen hundred livres in a single day in Brest. Edmond de Goncourt, *Madame Saint-Huberty d'après sa correspondance et ses papiers de famille* (Paris: Bibliothèque Charpentier, 1900), 115; Kernéis, "Contribution à l'histoire de la ville et du port de Brest," 214.

111. Paul Courteault, "Mademoiselle Clairon et Le Kain à Bordeaux," *Actes de l'Académie nationale des sciences, belles-lettres et arts de Bordeaux* 4:2 (1914–15): 237–56, esp. 249.

112. Between the 1750s and the 1780s, members of the royal company received shares that ranged between four thousand livres and twenty-six thousand livres a year. Even during the 1780s, when annual profit shares regularly topped twenty thousand livres, the actors earned only about two thousand livres in a month. Alasseur, *La Comédie-Française*, 197–99.

113. City ordinances often regulated the amount prices could be raised, usually by a third or more during such extraordinary performances. Lefebvre, *Histoire du théâtre de Lille*, 1: 379. For Madame Dugazon's performance in Toulouse in 1785 prices were doubled, yet the theater was completely full. Cradock, *La Vie française à la veille de la Révolution*, 186.

114. See, for example, BMCF Dossier Lekain, "Placard Annonçant la venue de Le Kain à Lille."

115. Jourda, *Le Théâtre à Montpellier*, 33, 36.

116. Lekain performed a similar repertory of leading roles in playhouses throughout France. Based on BNF Fonds français Ms 12532 and Ms 12533. See also the repertory performed by Madame Dugazon in Amiens in 1788: Leroy, *Les Comédiens de province en Picardie*, 160.

117. BMCF Dossier Lekain, "Placard Annonçant la venue de Le Kain à Lille."

118. "Lettre écrite de Rouen, à M. Delagarde, Auteur du Mercure pour l'article des spectacles," *Mercure de France*, June 1763, p. 198.

119. Ibid.

120. "Lettre à M. De La Garde, Pensionnaire adjoint au privilège du Mercure pour la partie des spectacles," *Mercure de France*, June 1765, pp. 181–84.

121. BM Bordeaux Ms 1,015, "État des pieces jouées," 1786–87 season; AM Toulouse GG 943 "Catalogue des comedies, tragedies, operas, drames, et autres pieces."

122. Kernéis, "Contribution à l'histoire de la ville et du port de Brest," 209.

123. Saint-Huberty also performed in Strasbourg and Toulon. On the tours of Saint-Huberty and Sainval aînée, see *Trois siècles d'opéra à Lyon*, 56–61; BM Bordeaux Ms 1,015, "État des pieces jouées," 1786–87 season; AM Toulouse GG 943, "Catalogue." On Saint-Huberty's relatively modest salary at the Paris Opera, which was raised in the 1780s from fifty-five hundred to eight thousand livres a year, see

Hugh Williams, *Later Queens of the French Stage* (London: Harper & Brothers, 1906), 290–94, 306–8, 311.

124. AM Lyon GG 101 n. 229, De La Luze to Tolozan, prévôt des marchands, 10 January 1789.

125. Ibid.

126. AM Lyon GG 101 n. 232, De La Luze to Tolozan, prévôt des marchands, 23 February 1789.

127. Letter from l'abbe Duverney to Lekain, 26 June 1772, in *Mémoires de Lekain*, 334.

128. Quoted in Vallas, *Un Siècle de musique et de théâtre à Lyon*, 411.

129. Quoted in Grimm et al., *Correspondance littéraire*, 14: 207.

130. Goncourt, *Madame Saint-Huberty*, 146–48.

131. Quotes are from Grimm et al., *Correspondance littéraire*, 14: 208; and Karamzine, *Lettres d'un voyageur russe*, 100–102. The latter describes the rapture and transports of Lyon crowds during performances by the Parisian ballet dancer Vestris in the spring of 1790.

132. Quoted in Papillon de la Ferté, *Journal*, 207 (19 October 1767).

133. Letter from Voltaire to Lekain, 14 April 1755, in *Mémoires de Lekain*, 248, and Olivier, *Henri-Louis Le Kain*, 122–23.

134. Papillon de la Ferté, *Journal*, 328 (1 July 1772).

135. Jean-Baptiste Firmin, *Parallèle entre Talma et Le Kain: Esquisse: Suivi de quelques réflexions sur l'art dramatique* (Paris: Haut-Coeur, 1826), 15.

136. Collé, *Journal et mémoires*, 3: 348.

137. One critic complained that "they were paying [Lekain] in Paris, while he declaimed in Brussels." Firmin, *Parallèle entre Talma et Le Kain*, 16.

138. Rousseau, *Politics and the Arts: Letter to M. d'Alembert*, 26, 100.

139. Berlanstein, *Daughters of Eve*, 33–58.

140. Jennifer J. Popiel, *Rousseau's Daughters: Domesticity, Education, and Autonomy in Modern France* (Durham: University of New Hampshire Press, 2008), 1–3, quote from 7; Rousseau, *Politics and the Arts: Letter to M. d'Alembert on the Theatre*, 80–85, 90–92.

141. Rousseau, *Politics and the Arts: Letter to M. d'Alembert on the Theatre*, 81.

142. Kaplan, *Bakers of Paris*; Sarah Maza, *Servants and Masters in Eighteenth-Century France: The Uses of Loyalty* (Princeton: Princeton University Press, 1983). Cissie Fairchilds, in contrast, argues that relations between masters and servants during the later eighteenth century became more contractual, defined by a "language of a market economy" that suggested the equality of employer and employee. *Domestic Enemies: Servants and Their Masters in Old Regime France* (Baltimore: Johns Hopkins University Press, 1984), 151–52.

143. Mague de Saint-Aubin, *La Réforme des théâtres*, 40.

144. BMCF 2 ATO Province 1774, Lamare [to CF], 7 February 1774.

145. In the letters and petitions in the BMCF dossier 2 ATO Province for 1774 alone, the term "right" or "rights" is used at least twenty-five times by actors, directors, and the King's Players. *Pace* Laurent Turcot, who emphasizes the "total power" of the director, "Directeurs, comédiens et police," 115.

146. BMCF 2 ATO Province 1774, Duclos [to CF], 12 April 1774, and Province 1789, Mademoiselle Lachataigneraye [to CF], 25 May 1789.

147. Lynn Hunt, *Inventing Human Rights: A History* (New York: W. W. Norton, 2007), 22–26.

148. Kessler, *Revolution in Commerce*, 8 (quote) and 287–89.

149. T. C. W. Blanning, *The Culture of Power and the Power of Culture: Old Regime Europe, 1660-1789* (Oxford: Oxford University Press, 2002), 135.

150. BMCF 2ATO Province 1774, response by CF of 8 August 1774.

6. Consumers of Culture

1. Johann Georg Fisch, *Briefe über die südlichen Provinzen von Frankreich* (Zurich: n.p., 1790), 85–86, 459–60, 538–39, quote 538. My thanks to Beatrix Brockman for her assistance with this translation. On theater in Toulon during this era, see also A.-Jacques Parès, *Aperçu sur les spectacles de Toulon avant la Révolution* (Toulon: Société nouvelle des imprimeries toulonnaises, 1936), 18–22.

2. Fisch, *Briefe*, 538–39.

3. Ibid.

4. References to elites from these backgrounds attending performances in various provincial cities can be found in AM Lyon 3 GG 99, lists indicating individuals who should receive free entry to performances, 1780–85; Zeller, "Géographie sociale, loisir, et pratique culturelle," 581, 594–600; Lagrave, *La Vie théâtrale à Bordeaux*, 268–76; Albert Depréaux, "Une Querelle à la comédie d'Orléans en 1783," *Bulletin de la Société archéologique et historique de l'Orléanais* 19 (1920): 75–88, esp. 78–83; Rittaud-Hutinet, *Vision d'un future*, 134–37; AN H 1359 n. 112.

5. Specific mention of individuals from these backgrounds present in parterre audiences appears in police reports and other contemporary sources noted in Édouard-Hippolyte Gosselin, *Recherches sur les anciens théâtres du Havre et d'Yvetot* (Rouen: Ch.-F. Lapierre, 1875), 8–9; Ravel, *Contested Parterre*, 174; Charvet, *Recherches sur les anciens théâtres de Beauvais*, 49–50; Debauve, *Théâtre et spectacles à Lorient*, 35–38; François Métra et al., *Correspondance secrète, politique et litéraire, ou memoires pour servir à l'histoire des cours, des sociétés, et de la littérature en France, depuis la mort de Louis XV*, 18 vols. (London: John Adamson, 1787–90), 14: 363–64; Decombe, *Le Théâtre à Rennes*, 33–42.

6. Rittaud-Hutinet, *Vision d'un future*, 134–37; Depréaux, "Une Querelle," 78–83; Cradock, *La Vie française*, 125, 159, 205; Ducéré, "Le Théâtre bayonnais," 189–90.

7. On military personnel and sailors in provincial playhouses, see Fuchs, *La Vie théâtrale en province au XVIIIe siècle*, 204–10; Bossuat, "Le Théâtre à Clermont-Ferrand," 140–46; Lefebvre, *Histoire du théâtre de Lille*, 2: 34–37. In Nantes, captains of commercial vessels went to the theater. AM Nantes FF 283, n. 7, 13 March 1775, and n. 26, 12 September 1786. In Marseille, mention is made of common sailors and workers in the theater balcony, Rittaud-Hutinet, *Vision d'un futur*, 145.

8. J.-P. Bardet makes this statement specifically about Rouen in *Rouen aux XVIIe et XVIIIe siècles*, 252. This sentiment is echoed, however, by other scholars including Maillard, "Le Théâtre à Angers," 118. Assertions by contemporaries that playhouses fostered social unity can be found in AD de la Haute-Garonne 1 C 311, n. 1 (1765); and *Délibération du conseil de ville tenu pour la construction de la salle de spectacle* (1759), quoted in Bossuat, "Le Théâtre à Clermont-Ferrand," 146.

9. Observation from 1788 quoted in Vallas, *Un Siècle de musique et de théâtre à Lyon*, 446.

10. Ravel presents a detailed study of Parisian parterre audiences and their behaviors in *Contested Parterre*, esp. 13–66.

11. Roche, *A History of Everyday Things* and *Culture of Clothing*; Jones, "Great Chain of Buying."

12. AM Bordeaux Bib F 4/28, *Épître à M. de C . . . sur l'inauguration de la nouvelle salle des spectacles de Bordeaux, et le prologue intitulé Le jugement d'Apollon* [par Marandon].

13. On the challenges of studying eighteenth-century audiences, see Ravel, *Contested Parterre*, 6–8. The scarcity of sources for provincial audiences is also noted in *L'Art du théâtre à Valenciennes*, 47, and Lagrave, *La Vie théâtrale à Bordeaux*, 268.

14. This list of annual and monthly subscribers is included in AM Lyon 3 GG 100, "Spectacles de Lyon: Recette et Dépense, Année 1787 à 1788."

15. AM Lyon 3 GG 99, "Observations pour M. le lieutenant général sur l'entrée au spectacle."

16. On the "multitude of abuses" related to free entries to the theater, see correspondence from the duc de Villeroy, as well as free entry lists, in AM Lyon 3 GG 99.

17. By the 1780s, the right to issue free entries had often passed from the city officers into the hands of the royal governor. For examples of these lists, see AM Lyon 3 GG 99, "État des entrées au spectacle de Lyon," 1785; AM Bordeaux, BB 140, f. 76–80, "Spectacle: Entrées gratuites," 14 September 1784.

18. Quoted from "Un Projet d'ordre à établir et de réforme à faire" (1788), reproduced in Bouteiller, *Histoire . . . des théatres de Rouen*, 1: 176.

19. For example, the theater in Lille in 1787 had six categories ranging from fifteen sous to four livres. Lefebvre, *Histoire du théâtre de Lille*, 2: 23–27.

20. Corbun exaggerated only slightly when he complained that only in Lyon and Bordeaux were tickets as expensive as in Paris, in *Le Voeu de l'humanité*, 56. Ticket prices for twenty-six eighteenth-century French playhouses are provided in Clay, "Theater and the Commercialization of Culture," 336–38. Tickets for the Paris boulevard theaters during this era cost between six and twenty-four sous. Isherwood, *Farce and Fantasy*, 167, 181.

21. In Bordeaux's new Grand Théâtre of 1780, for example, the theater could hold about nine hundred spectators in the parterre and paradis together, and eight hundred in all other seats. AM Bordeaux GG 1004 a, Letter from shareholders to Richelieu, 8 April 1780.

22. This price for Lyon's most expensive boxes dates from 1739; during the 1780s the first boxes, parquet, and amphitheater cost three livres. Vallas, *Un Siècle de musique et de théâtre à Lyon*, 224, 444; Lagrave, *La Vie théâtrale à Bordeaux*, 216.

23. There were twelve price categories for the Paris Opera, starting at three livres. Johnson, *Backstage at the Revolution*, 41.

24. Cities in which ticket prices dropped following the inauguration of a new, larger playhouse include Lorient and Nantes, where prices were lowered from twenty to twelve sous (for soldiers in the paradis in Lorient to just six sous), and Lyon, where ticket prices dropped from twenty-four to twenty sous. Debauve, *Théâtre et spectacles à Lorient*, 36–37; Destranges, *Le Théâtre à Nantes*, 18, 37; Vallas, *Un Siècle de musique et de théâtre à Lyon*, 224, 444.

25. On the prices of food at Parisian establishments, see Rebecca Spang, *The Invention of the Restaurant: Paris and Modern Gastronomic Culture* (Cambridge: Harvard University Press, 2000), 66 and 267 n. 76; on the price of black market books, see Darnton, *Forbidden Best-Sellers*, 34; on clothing prices, see Roche, *Culture of Clothing*, 357–58.

26. On provincial wages in the late eighteenth century, see Roche, *History of Everyday Things*, 63–72.

27. On manufacturing workers in the parterre, see Ernest Charvet, *Recherches sur les anciens théâtres de Beauvais. Note additionnelle* (Beauvais: D. Pere, 1882), 21. On artisans, clerks, and assistants, see Bossuat, "Le Théâtre à Clermont-Ferrand," 141–43; on a clerk, a spectator *sans état*, and another who had been out of work for three months, see AM Nantes FF 283 n. 6, 26 February 1773; n. 20, 26 October 1783; n. 21, 27 October 1783.

28. Fairchilds, "Production and Marketing of Populuxe Goods," 228–48.

29. Spang, *Invention of the Restaurant*, 272 n. 65, and 22.

30. Censer, *French Press,* 189–91; Jones, "Great Chain of Buying," 17.

31. Roche, *Culture of Clothing*, 357–59.

32. In Zeller's analysis of this list, he was able to identify 204 out of a total of 441 male subscribers. "Géographie sociale, loisir, et pratique culturelle," 594–95.

33. Ibid.

34. The actor Choudart-Desforges quoted in Lagrave, *La Vie théâtrale à Bordeaux*, 269.

35. Roche, *Le Siècle des lumières en province*, I: 99–105, 193, 197. Maillard, for example, contrasts the very limited participation in the Académie d'Angers with the broad theatergoing public, in "Le Théâtre à Angers," 118. Contrast with Caradonna, *Enlightenment in Practice*.

36. As reported by Siméon-Prosper Hardy, the lawyer Blondel made this claim before the Parlement of Paris. Quoted in Bailey Stone, "Robe against Sword: The Parlement of Paris and the French Aristocracy, 1774–1789," *FHS* 9 (1975): 278–303, esp. 282–84. John Shovlin kindly brought this reference to my attention.

37. Ibid. Pernot Duplessis filed this suit against the comte de Moreton-Chabrillant, charging that he had been publicly insulted, forcibly detained, and denied his seat in the theater on the evening of 9 April 1782. The trial apparently drew a large and diverse crowd. The court ruled in favor of Duplessis, and Moreton-Chabrillant was required to acknowledge that he had wrongfully insulted a man of honor and to pay a fine of six thousand livres.

38. John Shovlin, "The Cultural Politics of Luxury in Eighteenth-Century France," *FHS* 23:4 (2000): 577–606, quote from 583.

39. On the procession and its decline in eighteenth-century urban life, see Robert Schneider, *The Ceremonial City: Toulouse Observed, 1738–1780* (Princeton: Princeton University Press, 1995), 111–93.

40. Corbun, *Le Voeu de l'humanité*, 72.

41. Alexandre-Balthasar-Laurent Grimod de La Reynière, *Tableau de Lyon en 1786, par Grimod de La Reynière, Addressé sous forme de lettre à Mercier, Auteur du Tableau de Paris* (Lyon: Imp. de la Boitel, 1843), 12.

42. Quoted in Fray-Fournier, *Le Théâtre à Limoges*, 23. This sentiment was echoed in Rouen. Bouteiller, *Histoire . . . des théâtres de Rouen*, 176.

43. AN H 1359 n. 112, Mémoire, 1785.

44. Cradock, *La Vie française*, 190.

45. Servants wearing livery were actually banned from entering some provincial playhouses, even when paying. In a few cases, theater regulations banned servants entirely, although this provision must have been difficult to enforce. In Nantes, where this had been the case, the regulations were changed in 1788 so that prohibitions no longer applied to occupations or categories of people: henceforth, only servants *wearing* livery and wigmaker-barbers *wearing* their powdery clothes were denied entry. Contrast AM Nantes FF 115 n. 8, Arrest de la Cour, 3 February 1779, p. 4; and n. 12, "Arrest de réglement, Pour la police extérieure et intérieure du théâtre de la Ville de Nantes," 15 March 1788.

46. AN H 1359, p. 112, Mémoire.

47. AM Bordeaux FF 70, Letter from Richelieu, 8 January 1771; Parès, *Aperçu sur les spectacles de Toulon*, 19.

48. Cradock, *La Vie française*.

49. Zeller, "Géographie sociale, loisir et pratique culturelle," 586.

50. AM Lyon 3 GG 99, "Liste des personnes." Although only a few women on this list are titled marquise or countess, a majority of these women's names bear the "de" that suggested nobility.

51. Quoted in Vallas, *Un Siècle de musique et de théâtre à Lyon*, 446.

52. Piozzi and Johnson, *French Journals of Mrs. Thrale*, 78.

53. Ibid.

54. Letter from Jeanne-Marguerite Caron (known as Tonton) to her sister Julie, written in the mid-1750s, quoted in Louis de Loménie, *Beaumarchais et son temps: Études sur la société en France au XVIIIe siècle*, 2 vols. (Paris: Michel Lévy Frères, 1856), 1: 54.

55. This contemporary requested better lighting in the house so as to better see the women present. Quoted in Bouteiller, *Histoire . . . des théâtres de Rouen*, 1: 176–77.

56. On women's special role in polite society, and the "restraining force" they presented, see Goodman, *Republic of Letters*, 90–135.

57. Ibid., 101 and (quote) 130.

58. The *Mercure dijonnais* quoted in Gouvenain, *Le Théâtre à Dijon*, 94. For similar observations in Montpellier, see also Jourda, *Le Théâtre à Montpellier*, 33.

59. Quoted in Vallas, *Un Siècle de musique et de théâtre à Lyon*, 446.

60. Lagrave, *La Vie théâtrale à Bordeaux*, 273–74. In Valenciennes, Beauvais, and elsewhere, we find middling women going to the theater with their husbands. *L'Art du théâtre à Valenciennes*, 50; Charvet, *Recherches sur les anciens théâtres de Beauvais*, 130–31.

61. Depréaux, "Querelle à la comédie d'Orléans," 78, 81.

62. Cradock, *La Vie française*, 159.

63. Quoted in B., "Le Théatre de Reims," *Revue de Champagne et de Brie* 17 (1884): 105–9, 106.

64. Quoted in Augustin Fabre, *Les Rues de Marseille*, 5 vols. (Marseille: E. Camoin, 1868), III: 385.

65. Corbun, *Voeu de l'humanité*, 44.

66. Lagrave, *La Vie théâtrale à Bordeaux*, 274.

67. Cradock, *La Vie française*, 186.

68. Rousseau, *Politics and the Arts: Letter to M. d'Alembert*, esp. 57–65, 75–92, 109–13.

69. Louis-François-Marie Bellin de La Liborlière, *Vieux souvenirs du Poitiers d'avant 1789* (Poitiers: chez tous les libraires, 1846), 155.

70. For scholarship on Masonic lodges and provincial academies in Old Regime France, see chapter 1, note 76.

71. For example, women subscribers to the Lyon theater more than doubled between the late 1760s and the late 1780s. Zeller, "Géographie sociale, loisir, et pratique culturelle," 586.

72. Ibid.

73. On the gendering of practices of consumption in the realm of fashion during this era, see Jones, *Sexing La Mode*, esp. part II.

74. Maillard, "Le Théâtre à Angers," 111.

75. During the 1770s and 1780s, police regulations typically specified the hour the performance would begin, usually at 5:30 p.m. The police did investigate delays, as seen in AM Nantes FF 283 n. 17, procès-verbal of sieur Desmarais.

76. This lighting was not always considered sufficient for the purposes of watching stage or spectators. Bouteiller, *Histoire . . . des théâtres de Rouen*, 1: 176–77. Mrs. Cradock complained that French playhouses were generally quite dark, in *La Vie française*, 99, 117. On the importance of seeing and being seen at the theater, see AN H 1359, n. 112, Mémoire.

77. In Bordeaux, actors and actresses of the troupe complained of "the excessive cold and the perpetual wind" in the new playhouse, which ruined their voices and threatened their health. AM Bordeaux GG 1004 e, letter to "Messieurs les Actionnaires des Spectacles de Bordeaux."

78. Cradock, *La Vie française*, 117.

79. Quoted in Jourda, *Le Théâtre à Montpellier*, 33.

80. Cradock, *La Vie française*, 143, 153.

81. Ibid., 280.

82. Young, *Travels in France*, 125.

83. Ibid., 190.

84. Lough, *Paris Theatre Audiences*, 228–29; AM Nantes FF 283 n. 16, 20 Dec. 1779.

85. AM Nantes FF 283 n. 26, 12 September 1786.

86. F.-B. Hoffman quoted in Fabre, *Les Rues de Marseille*, 379–80.

87. For such behaviors, see the procès-verbaux in AM Nantes FF 283 nos. 6–32; Lagrave, *La Vie théâtrale à Bordeaux*, 255–59; Depréaux, "Une Querelle à la comédie d'Orléans," 76–77; Vallas, *Un Siècle de musique et de théâtre à Lyon*, 431–32; *L'Art du théâtre à Valenciennes*, 47–50.

88. AM Nantes FF 283, n. 6, 26 February 1773, and n. 29, 26 May 1787.

89. Nantes FF 283, nos. 8, 13, 27.

90. Piozzi and Johnson, *French Journals of Mrs. Thrale,* 79.

91. See, for example, Vallas, *Un Siècle de musique et de théâtre à Lyon*, 429; AM Nantes FF 283 n. 19, 15 January 1781; Lhotte, *Le Théâtre à Lille*, 53.

92. AM Nantes FF 283, n. 20, 27 October 1783.

93. Quoted in Lagrave, *La Vie théâtrale à Bordeaux*, 259.

94. This 1776 regulation on the policing of the theater is reproduced in Armand Bénet, "Le Théâtre à Rouen à la fin de l'ancien régime, d'après les archives des d'Harcourt," *RSBAD* 23 (1899): 791–814, quote from 810.

95. AM Nantes FF 283 n. 24, procès-verbal of Dlle Guerin, 6 August 1785; Lefebvre, *Histoire du théâtre de Lille*, 2: 56–57.

96. Lagrave, *La Vie théâtrale à Bordeaux*, 259.

97. Internal troupe regulations intended to ensure that actors, singers, and dancers were on time and ready to perform the work that had been advertised became increasingly common. Those who were late or unprepared faced steep fines. See AM Bordeaux GG 1004 b, "Status et reglemens nouveaux, Portant sur les acteurs, actrices, & tous autres sujets . . . 1782." On the pressure felt by directors whose actors were ill, overworked, or simply uncooperative, see AM Lyon 3 GG 101 n. 167, Collot d'Herbois to the Prévôt des marchands, 31 December 1787.

98. AM Nantes FF 115 n. 12, Arrest de réglement, 1788; Fabre, *Les Rues de Marseille*, 380.

99. See, for example, AM Nantes FF 283, n. 7, 13 March 1775; Charvet, *Recherches sur les anciens théâtres de Beauvais*, 50, 129; Ducéré, "Le Théâtre bayonnais," 189–90.

100. AM Nantes FF 283 n. 27, 8 October 1786; Fabre, *Les Rues de Marseille*, 368–69.

101. Lagrave, *La Vie théâtrale à Bordeaux*, 255; Karamzine, *Lettres d'un voyageur russe*, 100–101.

102. This event took place in 1780. Quoted in Bossuat, "Le Théâtre à Clermont-Ferrand," 143.

103. On this and other clashes between officers and civilian spectators in Marseille, see Fabre, *Les Rues de Marseille*, 367–79.

104. Friedland, *Political Actors*, 25–28. On the silencing of audiences in the late eighteenth and early nineteenth century, see also James Johnson, *Listening in Paris*, and Marc Baer, *Theatre and Disorder in Late Georgian London* (Clarendon Press, 1992), 166–88.

105. Friedland, *Political Actors*, 28.

106. Provincial audiences shared this belief with their counterparts in Paris and London. Ravel, *Contested Parterre*; Baer, *Theatre and Disorder*, 166–88.

107. "Consultation" by lawyers Barlet and Roman-Tributiis (1774), quoted in Fabre, *Les Rues de Marseille*, 379.

108. E. P. Thompson, "The Moral Economy of the English Crowd in the Eighteenth Century," *Past and Present* 50 (1971): 76–136.

109. As one governor explained, both tradition and decency dictated that at the theater "people invested with authority always have the most prominent seats." AD de la Loire-Atlantique C 392 Police des Spectacles, n. 37, 17 March 1772.

110. Maza, *Private Lives and Public Affairs*, 314. Other scholars who, drawing on Habermas, use this metaphor include Landes, *Women and the Public Sphere*, 18–19, and Roger Chartier, *Cultural Origins*, 33.

111. Beam, *Laughing Matters*, 77–141.

112. AM Bordeaux FF 70, letter from the duc de Richelieu, to the mayor and city officers of Bordeaux, 24 October 1769.

113. AM Nantes FF 115 n. 8, Arrest de la Cour, 3 February 1779, p. 7.

114. *Ordonnance du roi pour régler le service dans les places et dans les quartiers. Du 1er mars 1768*, 178.

115. On this conflict between municipal and military authorities, see Fuchs, *La Vie théâtrale en province au XVIIIe siècle*, 167–82.

116. Ravel, *Contested Parterre*, 133–60; Fabre, *Les Rues de Marseille*, 368; Lagrave, *La Vie théâtrale à Bordeaux*, 200.

117. Even a city as large as Lille had no specific regulations for policing the theater before 1767. Lefebvre, *Histoire du théâtre de Lille*, I: 259 and II: 23; AM Nantes FF 115, n. 2, "Ordonnance de Police, concernant le spectacle," 18 April 1771; "Consignes de la Place de Cambrai (14 March 1783)," in Fuchs, *La Vie théâtrale en province au XVIIIe siècle*, 208–10; *L'Art du théâtre à Valenciennes*, 49, 85.

118. AM Bordeaux FF 70, police regulation of 14 July 1745.

119. Ordonnance de police, 14 February 1759, reprinted in Lagrave, *La Vie théâtrale à Bordeaux*, 203.

120. See, for example, AM Nantes FF 115 n. 12, Arrest de réglement, 1788. This increased from just thirteen less than a decade earlier.

121. Ravel, *Contested Parterre*, 172.

122. On policing as principally a concern of the state, see Fuchs, *La Vie théâtrale en province au XVIIIe siècle*, 167–82; Ravel, *Contested Parterre*, 9.

123. AM Nantes FF 115, n. 4, Letter to Messieurs tenant le Bureau de Police from the *commissaires* of the enterprise of the theater, 4 April 1771; n. 5, "Projet de réglemens pour la police intérieure et extérieure du spectacle"; and n. 2, "Ordonnance de police, concernant le spectacle," 18 April 1771. A second reason for directors to ask for heightened regulation was to impose order and discipline on their actors, as in Marseille. E. Isnard, "Notes sur la vie théâtrale à Marseille au XVIIIe siècle," *Bulletin de la Société de l'Histoire du Théâtre* (1935): 5–13 and 37–49, esp. 48–49.

124. *L'Art du théâtre à Valenciennes*, 49, 85.

125. Fuchs, *La Vie théâtrale en province au XVIIIe siècle*, 175.

126. See, for example, the "Ordonnance pour les Spectacles du 4 avril 1787" from Lille, which highlights these contractual issues. Lefebvre, *Histoire du théâtre de Lille*, II: 23–29, quote from 27, and AM Nantes 115 n. 12, Arrest de réglement, 1788.

127. AM Bordeaux FF 70, "Ordonnance de MM. les Maire, Lieutenant-de-Maire et jurats, gouverneurs de Bordeaux, juges criminels et de police, concernant la police des spectacles," 31 March 1780. In context, these provisions seem to refer to men's dress. Is it important to note, however, that at this time women wore dresses known as the *redingote* and the *manteau*. These new feminine styles also would have been considered to be inappropriately informal for the theater. On clothing styles during the Old Regime, see Roche, *Culture of Clothing*, especially 134–48, and Crowston, *Fabricating Women*, 36–41. My thanks to Clare Crowston for clarifying this point.

128. AM Bordeaux FF 70, "Ordonnance," 1780.

129. AM Bordeaux GG 1004 b, "Consigne qu'observera au spectacle de la ville de Bordeaux, le Suisse nommé Bersier," 1783.

130. Quoted in Depréaux, "Une Querelle à la comédie d'Orléans en 1783," 76–77.

131. "Consignes de la Place de Cambrai, 1783," reprinted in the appendix to Fuchs, *La Vie théâtrale en province au XVIIIe siècle*, 208. An emphasis on decency also

appears in AM Nantes FF 115, "Extraits des Registres de Parlement," 14 November 1778.

132. AM Bordeaux FF 70, 14 July 1745.

133. AM Nantes FF 115, n. 2 "Ordonnance de Police, Concernant le Spectacle," 18 April 1771. This language is echoed later in the decade in n. 8, "Arrest de la Cour," 1779.

134. Lagrave, *La Vie théâtrale à Bordeaux*, 200.

135. Compare ibid., 201, and Ravel, *Contested Parterre*, 162–64.

136. AM Nantes FF 283, nos. 6, 10, 11, 14, 15, 20, 23, 27.

137. Ibid. One individual who was arrested in Nantes complained of the injustice of pinning the blame on him when he was simply imitating the actions of all those around him. N. 21, procès-verbal of René O'Sullivan, 27 October 1783.

138. These findings, based on AM Nantes FF 283, are consonant with Laurent Turcot, "De la definition du lieu théâtrale populaire: Police et spectateurs du boulevard à Paris au XVIIIe siècle," *RHT* 231 (2006): 261–86, esp. 274. In Paris, he finds, more than half of those arrested for disrupting performances in Parisian boulevard theaters between 1774 and 1789 were released and only around one-third imprisoned.

139. On such methods, see procès-verbaux in AM Nantes FF 283. See also the discussion of policing the theater in Bayonne in Ducéré, "Le Théâtre bayonnais," 187–91.

140. For examples of municipal authorities pushing directors to meet demands by audiences as, in their words, "the only way to quell the disorder and calm our citizens," see Lagrave, *La Vie théâtrale à Bordeaux*, 260 (quote); Lefebvre, *Histoire du théâtre de Lille*, 2: 19–20.

141. Lefebvre, *Histoire du théâtre de Lille*, 1: 302; Kernéis, "Contribution à l'histoire de la ville et du port de Brest," 214–15.

142. Ordinance from 1785 published in the *Journal de Lyon*, in Vingtrinier, *Le Théâtre à Lyon*, 70–71.

143. Tribout de Morembert, *Le Théâtre à Metz*, 117.

144. Ibid.; Vingtrinier, *Le Théâtre à Lyon*, 70–71; Lefebvre, *Histoire du théâtre de Lille*, 2: 21–22; Kernéis, "Contribution à l'histoire de la ville et du port de Brest," 214–15.

145. AM Bordeaux, FF 70, Richelieu to the mayor and *jurats* (aldermen) of Bordeaux, 18 February 1771 and 26 February 1773.

146. Ibid., 26 February 1773.

147. Fuchs, *La Vie théâtrale en province au XVIIIe siècle*, 174.

148. Thompson, "Moral Economy of the English Crowd," 78; and Colin Lucas, "The Crowd and Politics between 'Ancien Regime' and Revolution in France," *JMH* 60 (1988): 421–57.

149. These incidents are discussed in Ravel, *Contested Parterre*, 170–84; Fuchs, *La Vie théâtrale en province au XVIIIe siècle*, 177–78; Max Fuchs, "Deux incidents au Théâtre de Marseille (1772–1778)," *Extrait des Mémoires de l'Institut Historique de Provence* (Marseille: Institut Historique de Provence, 1932), 3–36; Charvet, *Recherches sur les anciens théâtres de Beauvais*, 48–51, 128–35.

150. This claim is more plausible for the case of Marseille, where it seems likely that a soldier's weapon discharged accidentally, leading the other soldiers to believe they were under attack and to begin firing. In Angers, the officers in charge publicly threatened spectators before the show began. Ravel, *Contested Parterre*, 175; AN Mar B³ 602, n. 253, 30 November 1772.

151. Ravel, *Contested Parterre*, 184.

152. Maillard, "Le Théâtre à Angers," 117; Charvet, *Recherches sur les anciens théâtres de Beauvais*, 50–52, 134–35.

153. Following the incident in Beauvais, the duc de Gesvres assured the municipal officers that he would place the "just reclamations of the citizens" before the eyes of the king so that restitution could be made for this offense. In Marseille and Angers, following these episodes of conflict and violence, the public theaters emerged once again as disorderly, contested spaces. Charvet, *Recherches sur les anciens théâtres de Beauvais*, 135 (quote); Maillard, "Le Théâtre à Angers," 117; Fabre, *Les Rues de Marseille*, 3: 378–79.

154. *Pace* Ravel, who suggests that both local and royal authorities typically deployed violent force to control theater audiences. *Contested Parterre*, 161–62.

155. Métra et al., *Correspondance secrète*, 14: 363–64.

156. AM Nantes, FF 283, n. 29, 27 May 1787.

157. Two complementary accounts of this event, relying on different sets of sources, are given by Armand Bénet, "Le Théâtre à Rouen," 799–806, and Bouteiller, *Histoire . . . des théâtres de Rouen*, 1: 136–60, quote from 136.

158. This letter is quoted in Bouteiller, *Histoire . . . des théâtres de Rouen*, 1: 136–39, quotes from 137–38.

159. Ibid.

160. Bénet, "Le Théâtre à Rouen," 801.

161. Quoted in ibid.

162. Bénet, "Le Théâtre à Rouen," 802.

163. Ibid.

164. Bénet, "Le Théâtre à Rouen," 801–2. Excerpts from two such songs, sung to the tunes of popular vaudeville and theater songs, are included in Bouteiller, *Histoire . . . des théâtres de Rouen*, 1: 154–55. On the subversive uses of song during the Old Regime, see Robert Darnton, *Poetry and the Police: Communication Networks in Eighteenth-Century Paris* (Cambridge: Harvard University Press, 2010).

165. Bénet, "Le Théâtre à Rouen," 803.

166. *Journal de Normandie*, 5 May 1787.

167. Quoted in Bénet, "Le Théâtre à Rouen," 803.

168. Ibid., 804–5.

169. Ibid., 802–5.

170. Quoted in ibid., 803–4.

171. "Lettre de la dame Montansier au Rédacteur," *Journal de Normandie*, 25 April 1787.

172. Ibid.

173. Ibid.

174. *Journal de Normandie,* 28 April 1787.

175. Ibid.

176. AD de la Seine-Maritime 1B 5533, letter (undated) from Dlle. Montansier to the Procureur général du Parlement de Normandie.

177. Bouteiller, *Histoire . . . des théâtres de Rouen*, 1: 195–96.

178. Ravel, *Contested Parterre*, 98.

179. In 1783, when angry spectators in Bordeaux proposed a three-month strike against the theater over the director's refusal to hire a popular opera singer, this "seditious" assembly explained this action as "a punishment against the Sieur Gaillard, one of the directors of the theater, for not having appeared on the stage when the parterre asked him to last Monday." Protests convulsed the city for several days and royal troops were brought to the city limits, but the strike and demonstrations petered out. AM Bordeaux FF 70, "Declaration faite aux Maire et jurats, par Sr. Etienne Alliez," 28 May 1783; Lagrave, *La Vie théâtrale à Bordeaux*, 258–60.

180. Quoted in Kernéis, "Contribution à l'histoire de la ville et du port de Brest," 224.

181. On this incident, see ibid., 214–28.

182. Ibid., 215.

183. Quoted from ibid., 220. See also Fuchs, *La Vie théâtrale en province au XVIIIe siècle*, 179–82.

184. Kernéis, "Contribution à l'histoire de la ville et du port de Brest," 222.

185. The honorific boxes were not included in this demand. Ibid., 225-26.

186. Ibid., 226-227. Controversy over policing of the Théâtre de la Marine continued into the Revolution. See Fuchs, *La Vie théâtrale en province au XVIIIe siècle*, 181–82.

187. Pierre Bernadau, *Les Débuts de la Révolution à Bordeaux d'après les tablettes manuscrites de Pierre Bernadau*, ed. Michel Lhéritier (Paris: Société de l'histoire de la Révolution française, 1919), 29. Members of the audience in Bordeaux made escalating demands on the directors, even threatening commercial protest if such demands were not met. Lagrave, *La Vie théâtrale à Bordeaux*, 258–62. On the dangers of allowing an overzealous public to dictate the terms of cultural production, see AM Bordeaux GG 1004 e, Letter from de Beaunoir to the mayor and *jurats*, 7 March 1789.

188. AN H 1359, n. 185, letter of 29 April 1789. These audience demands took on greater political significance given that during the late 1760s and early 1770s, the municipal authorities had repeatedly sought to display a similar tapestry in front of their *loge* when they were at the theater, yet Versailles repeatedly forbade them to do so. Fuchs, *La Vie théâtrale en province au XVIIIe siècle*, 191.

189. Jones, *Great Nation*, 405.

190. AN H 1359, n. 185.

191. AN H 1359, n. 184, Jacques Necker to the mayor and *échevins* (municipal councilors) of Marseille, May 1789. See also the case of Brest, where Secretary of State for the Navy La Luzerne applauded the peaceful resolution of the theater strike during the spring of 1789. La Luzerne further instructed the commander, the comte d'Hector, to cultivate goodwill with the public: "So that no more discussion is raised on this matter and so that the theater is continually supported by the city residents, it is essential that you take in hand that all conform exactly to the dispositions prescribed by the regulation." Quoted in Kernéis, "Contribution à l'histoire de la ville et du port de Brest," 227.

7. The Production of Theater in the Colonies

1. *Affiches Américaines* [*AA*], 23 April 1766, p. 145.

2. Ibid. On the history of theater in the city prior to the inauguration of the theater, see Moreau de Saint-Méry, *Description*, I: 344, 356.

3. On the place of the gens de couleur or free people of color in the playhouses of Saint-Domingue, see Moreau de Saint-Méry, *Description*, I: 358, 361–65; II: 880–82, 987, 1100; AN Col. F³ 274, fols. 883–88, "Projet d'établissement d'un spectacle à Saint-Marc."

4. On musicians, including free people of color and slaves, who performed at colonial theaters, see Bernard Camier, "Musique coloniale et société à Saint-Domingue dans la seconde moitié du XVIIIème siècle" (PhD diss., Université des Antilles-Guyane, 2004), 82–154, 253–80, 304; Jean Fouchard, *Le Théâtre à Saint-Domingue* (Port-au-Prince: Imprimerie de l'État, 1955), 345–46.

5. Moreau de Saint-Méry, *Description*, II: 984–85, 1308, 1099, 879.

6. Colonial cities that enjoyed public playhouses during the late Old Regime included Le Cap, Port-au-Prince, Les Cayes, Saint Marc, Léogane, and Jacmel in Saint-Domingue; Saint-Pierre and Fort-Royal in Martinique; Basse-Terre and Pointe-à-Pitre in Guadeloupe; and Port-Louis in the Indian Ocean colony of Île de France. In addition to these cities, newspapers also note professional troupes performing at least briefly in Petit-Goâve, in Saint-Domingue. There were no professional public theaters in Québec City or in Montréal until the nineteenth century. For the theaters of Saint-Domingue, see below. For those elsewhere in the French colonies, see Bernard Camier, "Les spectacles musicaux en Martinique, en Guadeloupe et en Dominique dans la seconde moitié du XVIIIème," *Bulletin de la Société d'histoire de la Guadeloupe* 130 (2001): 3–25; Chelin, *Le Théâtre à l'Ile Maurice*, 2; Lewis Waldo, *The French Drama in America in the Eighteenth Century and Its Influence on the American Drama of that Period, 1701–1800* (Baltimore: Johns Hopkins University Press, 1942), 19–47.

7. Estimation based on Fouchard, *Artistes et repertoire*, 93–269.

8. In the United States public theaters were closed in 1774 during the prelude to the War of Independence, and only reopened after the conflict. They began to feature resident companies during the mid-1790s. The Coliseum in Mexico City performed six nights a week during the 1780s as opposed to the three or more nights a week in Le Cap. That playhouse, however, held only eight hundred spectators, just over half of the capacity of the public playhouse in Le Cap. Moreover, outside of Mexico City regular public theaters operated only in a handful of the largest cities such as Veracruz and Puebla. Juan Pedro Viqueira Albán, *Propriety and Permissiveness in Bourbon Mexico*, trans. Sonya Lipsett-Rivera and Sergio Rivera Ayala (Lanham, Md.: SR Books, 2004), 31–32, 42, 44, 58; Hildburg Schilling, *Teatro profano en la Nueva España: Fines del siglo XVI a mediados del XVIII* (Mexico: Imprenta Universitaria, 1958), 11–45; Felicia Hardison Londré and Daniel J. Watermeier, *The History of North American Theater: The United States, Canada, and Mexico: From Pre-Columbian Times to the Present* (New York: Continuum, 1998), 39–89.

9. Jean Fouchard produced the groundbreaking scholarship on theatrical life in the colony in *Le Théâtre à Saint-Domingue* and *Artistes et repertoire des scènes de*

Saint-Domingue (Port-au-Prince: Imprimerie de l'État, 1955). Although Fouchard's work has informed scholarship on cultural life in Saint-Domingue for the past half century, his important contributions have been largely ignored by scholars of French theater. Colonial theaters have recently attracted renewed attention in works such as Bernard Camier and Laurent Dubois, "Voltaire et Zaïre, ou le théâtre des Lumières," and in Camier's deeply researched doctoral thesis, "Musique coloniale et société à Saint-Domingue."

10. When analyzing the relationship between the French state and its provincial subjects, scholars of French cultural life have effectively used colonialism as a comparative framework. See Weber, *Peasants into Frenchmen*, 485–93, and Gerson, *Pride of Place*, 146–48, 266–67.

11. Catherine Hall, "Introduction: Thinking the Postcolonial, Thinking the Empire," in *Cultures of Empire: Colonizers in Britain and the Empire in the Nineteenth and Twentieth Centuries*, ed. Catherine Hall (New York: Routledge, 2000), 1–33, esp. 23.

12. On concerns about the "Frenchness" of the colony and its inhabitants, see John Garrigus, "Redrawing the Color Line: Gender and the Social Construction of Race in Pre-Revolutionary Haiti," *Journal of Caribbean History* 30 (1996): 28–50.

13. Frederick Cooper and Ann Laura Stoler, "Between Metropole and Colony: Rethinking a Research Agenda," in *Tensions of Empire: Colonial Cultures in a Bourgeois World*, ed. Frederick Cooper and Ann Stoler (Berkeley: University of California Press, 1997), 1–56, quotes from 16.

14. For a brief biography of Moreau de Saint-Méry and a discussion of this and other writings by him, see the editors' introduction to his *Description*, i–xlvii. Moreau de Saint-Méry explicitly argues that free men and women of mixed heritage were first admitted to the public theater in Le Cap in 1766 in *Description*, I: 362. Because racial categories were more fluid earlier in the century, it is possible that the amateur theater in Le Cap may have allowed individuals of color to participate prior to the 1760s without labeling them as such. I thank Sue Peabody for clarification of this point. On the hardening of attitudes of racial difference around midcentury, see Garrigus, "Redrawing the Color Line," 28–30, and John Garrigus, *Before Haiti: Race and Citizenship in Saint-Domingue* (New York: Palgrave Macmillan, 2006), 141–70.

15. Stewart King, *Blue Coat or Powdered Wig: Free People of Color in Pre-Revolutionary Saint Domingue* (Athens: University of Georgia Press, 2001), xvii.

16. In addition to the institutions mentioned here, free people of color were also excluded from various professions such as medicine and from holding public office. After 1765, they were no longer commissioned as officers in the colonial militias, although they did maintain leadership roles as noncommissioned officers. James E. McClellan III, *Colonialism and Science: Saint Domingue in the Old Regime* (Baltimore: Johns Hopkins University Press, 1992), 259–72, esp. 262; King, *Blue Coat*, 62; Garrigus, *Before Haiti*, 291. On new restrictions on free blacks and mulattoes in France, see Sue Peabody, *"There Are No Slaves in France": The Political Culture of Race and Slavery in the Ancien Régime* (New York: Oxford University Press, 1996).

17. Paul Ulric Du Buisson, *Nouvelles considérations sur Saint-Domingue, en réponse à celles de M. H. D. Par M. D. B.* (Paris: Cellot & Jombert, 1780), 80. The expense of bringing actors and actresses from Europe was also noted in AN Col. C^{8B} 15, fol. 43 bis-52, Fouché de Clairval, "Mémoire concernant l'établissement d'un spectacle à Saint-Pierre de la Martinique, 1780."

18. A colonial livre was worth two-thirds as much as a *livre tournois*, the currency commonly used in France.

19. Moreau de Saint-Méry recorded that the expenses for the Le Cap theater society between 1771 and 1783 totaled 2,829,025 livres, or an average of 235,752 livres a year, although he later wrote that the expenses were at least 280,000 livres a year. *Description*, I: 357, 366; II: 998. These expenses can be compared with the annual budgets of provincial theater companies discussed in chapter 4.

20. In 1770, a strong earthquake abruptly ended a performance in Saint Marc. In Port-au-Prince, the house where plays were performed was destroyed by an earthquake at some point between 1767 and 1771. Ibid., II: 881, 985.

21. The populations of these cities are given in McClellan, *Colonialism and Science*, 3, 49, 75–76, 82.

22. Moreau de Saint-Méry, *Description*, I: 344.

23. Ibid., I: 356.

24. Initially, performances in Le Cap took place twice a week, on Sundays and Thursdays, while occasional benefit performances on behalf of an actor or musician took place on an alternate evening. In 1775, the shareholders decided to add a third weekly performance on Tuesdays. The theater was also the site of dances and balls. Moreau de Saint-Méry, *Description*, I: 359.

25. CAOM Collection Moreau de Saint-Méry [Coll. MSM] F³ 184, "Traité & Accords Entre les actionnaires du Spectacle du Cap, Arrets & autres pieces relatives à cet Etablissement, 1771." My sincere thanks to Bernard Camier for generously sharing with me a copy of this document and several others from the CAOM referenced below.

26. Ibid.; Moreau de Saint-Méry, *Description*, I: 357.

27. CAOM Coll. MSM F³ 184, "Traité & Accords"; Du Buisson, *Nouvelles considérations*, 82.

28. CAOM Coll. MSM F³ 184, "Traité & Accords." Meetings were advertised in newspaper notices inviting the shareholders to gather at a specific day and time "to deliberate on the affairs concerning the society." See, for example, notices in the *Supplément aux Affiches Américaines [SAA]*, 1 April 1775; and in the *AA*, 27 February 1781 and 27 March 1781.

29. Moreau de Saint-Méry, *Description*, I: 357 and note.

30. AN T 210, 3, Papiers la Ferronnays. The petition, dated 28 June 1774, is signed by Daniel Dutrejet, Lavanis, and Drieux.

31. CAOM Coll. MSM F³ 184, "Traité & Accords."

32. Michel-Réné Hilliard d'Auberteuil, *Considérations sur l'état présent de la colonie française de Saint-Domingue. Ouvrage politique et législatif; Présenté au Ministre de la Marine*, 2 vols. (Paris: Grangé, 1776–77), II: 110 and note.

33. Moreau de Saint-Méry, *Description*, I: 357 in note.

34. Joint-stock theater companies came forward in Saint Marc and Les Cayes to support local theatrical life. In Martinique, the first theater was established in the early 1770s by "a company of négociants," which paid to construct the playhouse and financed the company. Du Buisson, *Nouvelles considérations*, 82. Moreau de Saint-Méry, *Description*, II: 881–83, 1308–09; AN Col. C⁸ᴮ 15, Fouché de Clairval, "Mémoire," Saint-Pierre, Martinique, 1780.

35. Camier, "Musique coloniale et société à Saint-Domingue," 16.

36. Moreau de Saint-Méry, *Description*, II: 984–89.

37. Ibid., III: 1308–09.

38. Ibid., II: 879–80.

39. Ibid., II: 880–83.

40. A public theater had opened in Léogane in the 1760s, but it closed within eighteen months. Theater was revived there briefly in 1771–72, before being reintroduced in 1786. Ibid., II: 1099–1101.

41. In addition to these professional theaters, a *comédie bourgeoise* or amateur theater society was established in the city of Jérémie in 1787. Fouchard, *Le Théâtre à Saint-Domingue*, 113–15; Moreau de Saint-Méry, *Description*, III: 1385.

42. Du Buisson, *Nouvelles considérations*, 83. Moreau de Saint-Méry includes a brief description of actors' contract and salary information for Le Cap in *Description*, I: 360. When currency differences are accounted for, these actors' salaries compared favorably to those in most midsized provincial cities discussed in chapter 5, where average salaries during this era came to about twenty-four hundred livres.

43. AN Col. C^{8B} 15, Fouché de Clairval, "Mémoire."

44. Moreau de Saint-Méry, *Description*, I: 360. For two particularly popular actors, Du Buisson claimed, the proceeds from their benefit performances ran as high as eighteen thousand colonial livres. *Nouvelles considérations*, 81.

45. Based on the brief biographies of approximately three hundred colonial actors and actresses compiled by Fouchard, it is evident that many performers worked in more than one colonial city during their career; *Artistes et repertoire*, 1–87.

46. AN Col. Coll. MSM F^3 278, f. 109–10.

47. BMCF 2 ATO Province 1774, Letter from Deval to CF, 15 April 1774.

48. Although his wife subsequently disappears from the historical record, Joseph Deval later returned to France where he managed a traveling troupe for the prominent provincial director Gallier de Saint-Gérand during the early 1780s. BMCF 2 ATO Province 1774, and "Saint-Gérand" in Comédiens divers, hors Comédie-Française. The Devals' contract is included with their letter, dated 15 April 1774. In these documents, the husband is referred to variously as Deval, Duval, and Duvalt.

49. Camier, "Musique coloniale et société à Saint-Domingue," 299. Camier, too, observes that theater in Saint-Domingue was founded on private enterprise and was only loosely supervised by the state.

50. Ibid., 243.

51. Female directors led theater troupes in Saint Marc and Les Cayes, as well as in Guadeloupe. See Moreau de Saint-Méry, *Description*, II: 881; III: 1308; AN Col. F^3 232, fols. 553–54.

52. Moreau de Saint-Méry, *Description*, I: 356–57.

53. Du Buisson, *Nouvelles considérations*, 80. On theater repertory in Saint-Domingue, see Fouchard, *Artistes et repertoire*, 91–259, and *Le Théâtre à Saint-Domingue*, 219–32. On finances, see AN T 210, 3, Papiers la Ferronnays, 28 June 1774, and CAOM F^3 184, "Traité & Accords."

54. Moreau de Saint-Méry refers to "gifts" by the made by the government in *Description*, I: 357; Fouchard, *Le Théâtre à Saint-Domingue*, 15–20.

55. CAOM Coll. MSM, F^3 187, fols. 66 bis-84, "Dossier Mesplès."

56. AN Coll. MSM F³ 187 fols. 1578–80, "Ordonnance pour l'établissement d'un spectacle dans la ville du Port-au-Prince, du 28 juin 1777."

57. The royal government paid fifty thousand colonial livres to the former owners. The repairs made to the "theater belonging to the King" cost eighteen thousand colonial livres. AN Col. F³ 278, fols. 431–35. See also F³ 279, fol. 475–81, "Ordonnance de MM. les Administrateurs"; and Moreau de Saint-Méry, *Description*, II: 986.

58. Gabriel Debien, *Esprit colon et esprit d'autonomie à Saint-Domingue au XVIIIe siècle* (Paris: Larose, 1954); Charles Frostin, *Les Révoltes blanches à Saint-Domingue aux XVII et XVIII siècles (Haïti avant 1789)* (Paris: L'École, 1975).

59. *Almanach général de tous les spectacles de Paris et des provinces pour l'année 1791* (Paris: Froullé, 1791), 293.

60. These behaviors are recorded and described in AN Col. Coll. MSM F³ 273 f. 315, "Ordonnance du Juge du Police 31 mars 1769, St. Marc"; Moreau de Saint-Méry, *Description*, 1: 364–65; and Fouchard, *Le Théâtre à Saint-Domingue*, 194–95, 261–62. They can be compared with the audience practices described and discussed in chapter 6.

61. On this incident, the boycott it sparked, and the complex political fallout, see Moreau de Saint-Méry, *Description*, 1: 364–66, and *Loix et constitutions des colonies françoises de l'Amérique sous le vent*, 6 vols. (Paris: chez l'auteur, 1784–90), VI: 734–35, 778.

62. I borrow this frame of comparing theatergoing in Saint-Domingue and France from Camier and Dubois, yet extend it to provincial cities in addition to Paris. I include here only the five public playhouses that were most regularly active, excluding the city of Jacmel, about which little is known. My numbers therefore differ slightly from theirs. "Voltaire et Zaïre," 44.

63. The Bordeaux theater held a maximum of 1,726 spectators for a population of eighty-three thousand, while the Le Mans theater, smaller than anticipated, held about six hundred spectators for a population of 13,800. Rougemont, *La Vie théâtrale en France*, 223; Lepetit, *The Preindustrial Urban System*, appendix B; Lagrave, *La Vie théâtrale à Bordeaux*, 233; Deschamps La Rivière, *Le Théâtre au Mans*, 33.

64. In the colony, the cheapest daily tickets for whites typically cost one gourde, while tickets for the gens de couleur usually cost half a gourde. One gourde equaled eight livres five sous in colonial currency, or roughly five and a half *livres tournois*. Fouchard, *Le Théâtre à Saint-Domingue*, 172–73; Moreau de Saint-Méry, *Description*, I: 356.

65. For example, see McClellan, *Colonialism and Science*, 3–5, 75–107. On the city's status as "one of the most important [cultural centers] in the eighteenth-century Americas," see also Laurent Dubois, *Avengers of the New World: The Story of the Haitian Revolution* (Cambridge: Belknap Press of Harvard University Press, 2004), 24.

66. Moreau de Saint-Méry invokes the great distances that separated France from the colonies in *Loix et constitutions*, I: vii.

67. Justin Girod-Chantrans, *Voyage d'un Suisse dans différentes colonies d'Amérique pendant la dernière guerre, avec une table d'observations météorologiques faites à Saint-Domingue* (Neuchatel: Imprimerie de la Société Typographique, 1785), 324, 323.

68. With this influx of immigrants, by the late eighteenth century more than 75 percent of the whites living in the colony had been born in France. McClellan, *Colonialism and Science*, 49.

69. Hilliard d'Auberteuil, *Considérations sur l'état présent de la colonie*, II: 33. On the nature of these expatriates, see also Pierre Victor Malouet, baron de, *Collection de mémoires et correspondances officielles sur l'administration des colonies, et notamment sur la Guiane française et hollandaise*, 6 vols. (Paris: Baudouin, 1801), IV: 128–29.

70. My interpretation of urban life and of colonial society has been shaped by C. L. R. James, *The Black Jacobins: Toussaint L'Ouverture and the San Domingo Revolution*, 2nd ed. (New York: Vintage Books, 1989), 28–44.

71. Alexandre-Stanislas Wimpffen, baron de, *Saint-Domingue à la veille de la Révolution*, ed. Albert Savine (Paris: La Michaud, 1911), 174, 67.

72. Ignacio Gala, *Memorias de la colonia francesa de Santo Domingo, con algunas reflexiones relativas a la isla de Cuba* (Madrid: Hilario Santos Alonso, 1787), 80–81. Wimpffen made similar observations in *Saint-Domingue à la veille de la Révolution*, 80.

73. Michel Hector and Claude Moïse, *Colonisation et esclavage en Haïti: Le régime colonial français à Saint-Domingue (1625-1789)* (Port-au-Prince: Henri Deschamps, 1990), 156.

74. Quoted in Pierre de Vaissière, *Saint-Domingue: La société et la vie créoles sous l'ancien régime (1629–1789)* (Paris: Perrin et Cie., 1909), 298. Wimpffen seconds this in *Saint-Domingue à la veille de la Révolution*, 80.

75. Quoted in Fouchard, *Le Théâtre à Saint-Domingue*, 234.

76. Hilliard d'Auberteuil, *Considérations sur l'état présent de la colonie*, II: 35–36.

77. *Les Veuves créoles* (Amsterdam: Merlin, 1768). A performance of this play in Saint-Domingue was advertised in the *Supplément de l'Avis du Cap*, 1 May 1769. Fouchard, *Artistes et répertoire*, 119. On this play and its context, see Jérôme Brillaud, "*Les Veuves créoles* et le théâtre à la Martinique au XVIIIe siècle," *Travaux de Litérature: Les Amériques des écrivains français* 24 (2011): 143–52.

78. *Les Veuves créoles*, 25–26.

79. Ibid., 14.

80. Ibid., 22.

81. Moreau de Saint-Méry, *Description*, I: 367.

82. Fouchard, *Le Théâtre à Saint-Domingue*, 297–99.

83. Camier, "Musique coloniale et société à Saint-Domingue," 16.

84. Fouchard, *Le Théâtre à Saint-Domingue*, 219–30, and *Artistes et répertoire*, 93–253.

85. Moreau de Saint-Méry *Description*, I: 356.

86. Quoted in Fouchard, *Le Théâtre à Saint-Domingue*, 9.

87. Quoted in *AA*, 11 September 1781. For examples of announcements advertising Parisian performances of a play or opera as well as provincial successes and court performances, see *AA,* 12 February 1766; 4 June 1766; 2 October 1781; 30 October 1781; 13 November 1781; *SAA*, 5 January 1785.

88. *Avis du Cap*, 5 December 1768.

89. *SAA (PAP)*, 31 July 1781. These examples, written more than a decade apart, indicate that performances in both Le Cap and Port-au-Prince were characterized as re-creating metropolitan theater. For additional examples, see also *SAA*, 5 January 1785, and, implicitly, *AA*, 26 February 1785.

90. *AA*, 6 November 1781.

91. *Avis du Cap*, 4 April 1768. See also the advertisement for Sieur and Dame Berthier, "Actors awaited from France," who had recently arrived on a three-year contract, in *AA*, 18 June 1785.

92. See, for example, *AA*, 18 June 1766, and *SAA (PAP)*, 12 February 1785.

93. A[lexandre] P. M. de Laujon, *Souvenirs de trente années de voyages à Saint-Domingue, dans plusieurs colonies étrangères, et au continent d'Amérique*, 2 vols. (Paris: Schwartz et Gagnot, 1835), I: 164.

94. In addition to Ribier, Moreau de Saint-Méry mentions Volange, a notable performer of the Variétés Amusantes, a theater on the Paris Boulevard, as well as two actors who had performed with the Comédie-Italienne. Volange also toured in metropolitan France, performing in Metz, for example, in 1788. *Description*, I: 366; Tribout de Morembert, *Le Théâtre à Metz*, 117. Ribié's contract for his 1791 tour is in the AN Minutier central ET XXII 62 Notaire BERTELS. On the actor and his return in 1791, see also Fouchard, *Le Théâtre à Saint-Domingue*, 247–57.

95. *Almanach général de tous les spectacles*, 293.

96. AN T 210, 3, Papiers la Ferronnays, 28 June 1774. Hilliard d'Auberteuil argued, in contrast, that these social tensions contributed to the financial difficulties of several stages in *Considérations sur l'état présent de la colonie*, II: 109.

97. On these competing populations and the conflicts among them, see McClellan's discussion of Saint-Domingue society in *Colonialism and Science*, esp. 47–51; Dubois, *Avengers*, 18–35; and Colin Dayan, *Haiti, History, and the Gods* (Berkeley: University of California Press, 1995), 144–47.

98. AN T 210, 3, Papiers la Ferronnays, Dutrejet et al., 28 June 1774.

99. Ibid.

100. See article addressing the question: "Is a theater necessary in the large cities of the French colonies, and in particular in Port-au-Prince?" *AA (PAP)*, 29 April 1786.

101. Colonist Brueys d'Aigalliers quoted in Fouchard, *Le Théâtre à Saint-Domingue*, 8.

102. CAOM Collection Moreau de Saint-Méry F³ 184, "Traité & Accords."

103. AN T 210, 3, Papiers la Ferronnays, 28 June 1774.

104. Moreau de Saint-Méry, *Description*, I: 360, 361, 362, 367 (quote from 367). Du Buisson witnessed 268 women at the theater in Le Cap. *Nouvelles considérations*, 82.

105. On eighteenth-century theories of race, including discussions of degeneration, see William B. Cohen, *The French Encounter with Africans: White Response to Blacks, 1530–1880* (Bloomington: Indiana University Press, 1980), 60–99; Michèle Duchet, *Anthropologie et histoire au siècle des Lumières* (Paris: Albin Michel, 1995), 214–57; Cornelius de Pauw, *Recherches philosophiques sur les américains*, 2 vols., ed. Michèle Duchet (Paris: Jean Michel Place, 1990), I: 181.

106. Dayan, *Haiti, History, and the Gods*, 25.

107. AN Col. C⁸ᴮ 15, Fouché de Clairval, Saint-Pierre, Martinique, 1780. For a contrasting view critical of the effects of theater in Saint-Pierre, and in particular on the gens de couleur, see AN Col. C⁸ᴬ 79: 180–81, "Extrait des Registres de la Chambre d'Agriculture en l'Isle Martinique du 23 juillet 1787."

108. Ibid. Although their specific plan was not adopted, the racial concerns raised by this group may well have resonated with colonial officials. Just seven years later a new theater was constructed in Saint-Pierre, financed in part with support from the colonial administration. AN Col. C⁸ᴮ 15: 53.

109. Cooper and Stoler, "Between Colony and Metropole," 7.

110. On Moreau de Saint-Méry's obsessive interest in racial intermixing, see especially Doris Garraway, "Race, Reproduction and Family Romance in Moreau de

Saint-Méry's *Description. . . de la partie française de l'isle Saint-Domingue,*" *Eighteenth-Century Studies* 32 (2005): 227–46.

111. Garrigus, "Redrawing the Color Line," 29.

112. Dayan, *Haiti, History, and the Gods*, 143.

113. On the restrictions that gens de couleur confronted, see John Garrigus, "Colour, Class, and Identity on the Eve of the Haitian Revolution: Saint-Domingue's Free Coloured Elite as *Colons américains*," *Slavery and Abolition* 17:1 (1996): 20–43, esp. 26; King, *Blue Coat*, 158–79; Auguste Lebeau, *De la condition des gens de couleur libres sous l'ancien régime* (Poitiers: A. Masson, 1903); Hector and Moïse, *Colonisation et esclavage en Haïti*, 159–60.

114. On this shift in policy toward gens de couleur, see Garrigus, "Redrawing the Color Line," 29–30, and Lebeau, *De la condition des gens de couleur libres*. Some scholars suggest that gens de couleur often disregarded sumptuary regulations that forbade them from adopting "the dress, hairstyles, style, or bearing of whites" as well as other restrictive legislation. See King, *Blue Coat*, 168–69 (quote); and Dominique Rogers, "On the Road to Citizenship: The Complex Route to Integration of the Free People of Color in the Two Capitals of Saint-Domingue," in *The World of the Haitian Revolution*, ed. David Patrick Geggus and Norman Fiering (Bloomington: Indiana University Press, 2009): 65–78.

115. Moreau de Saint-Méry, *Description*, II: 987, 1100, 880, 882; I: 362.

116. Ibid., I: 362.

117. Ibid., I: 367; AN Col. F³ 274, f. 883–88, "Projet d'établissement."

118. CAOM Coll. MSM F³ 184, "Traité & Accords."

119. This was the case in Port-au-Prince, Les Cayes, and Saint Marc. Moreau de Saint-Méry, *Description*, I: 359; II: 987, 1309; AN Col. F³ 274, f. 883–88, "Projet d'établissement."

120. Moreau de Saint-Méry specifies that ten boxes were reserved for free blacks and people of color, and that although each box could comfortably accommodate six, they often held eight. *Description*, I: 358. Scholars such as Dominique Rogers have emphasized the growing economic prominence of free people of color at this time. "On the Road to Citizenship," 66–67, 75–76.

121. Moreau de Saint-Méry, *Description*, I: 361–62. On the financial benefits of inviting mulatto women to the theater, see also Fouchard, *Le Théâtre à Saint-Domingue*, 183, n. 1. Despite seating restrictions, colonial playhouses, their cafés, and the environs served as prime spaces for mixed-race sociability. Camier and Dubois, "Voltaire et Zaïre," 47.

122. Moreau de Saint-Méry, *Description*, I: 358–59.

123. Hilliard d'Auberteuil, *Considérations sur l'état présent de la colonie*, II: 110n; Moreau de Saint-Méry, *Description*, I: 357; Fouchard, *Le Théâtre à Saint-Domingue*, 15–20.

124. Both changes were enacted during the summer of 1775. Ibid., I: 359, 362.

125. Hilliard d'Auberteuil, *Considérations sur l'état présent de la colonie*, II: 110. On Hilliard d'Auberteuil's controversial writings, see Gene E. Ogle, "'The Eternal Power of Reason' and 'the Superiority of Whites': Hilliard d'Auberteuil's Colonial Enlightenment," *French Colonial History* 3 (2003): 35–50.

126. Hilliard d'Auberteuil, *Considérations sur l'état présent de la colonie*, II: 110. This account was published in 1776, very shortly after the admission of free blacks.

127. Ibid., and Du Buisson, *Nouvelles considérations*, 85.

128. Hilliard d'Auberteuil, *Considérations sur l'état présent de la colonie*, II: 111, note.

129. AN Col. C⁸ᴬ 79, fols. 177–87, "Extrait des Registres de la Chambre d'Agriculture en l'Isle Martinique du 23 Juillet 1787."

130. On displays of wealth by gens de couleur in colonial society, see King, *Blue Coat*, 168–72.

131. Moreau de Saint-Méry, *Description*, I: 362 (emphasis in original).

132. Ibid., I: 362.

133. Du Buisson, too, recognized the agency of the free people of color in policing racial boundaries. Slaves did not attend the theater anywhere in Saint-Domingue, he argued, because the gens de couleur would never have permitted them to do so. *Nouvelles considérations*, 85.

134. Hilliard d'Auberteuil argued that gens de couleur attended "at the invitation of MM. the Shareholders." *Considérations sur l'état présent de la colonie*, II: 111.

135. Camier and Dubois, "Voltaire et Zaïre," 46.

136. Fouchard, *Le Théâtre à Saint-Domingue*, 181.

137. Camier, "Musique coloniale et société à Saint-Domingue," 114, 259–61, 267–68, 277, 279–80.

138. Moreau de Saint-Méry, *Description*, II: 1100–1101 (quote 1101).

139. Quoted in Camier and Dubois, "Voltaire et Zaïre," 46.

140. On the campaign by free coloreds to assert their virtue and reform colonial racism during the late 1780s, see Garrigus, *Before Haiti*, 218–25. On the heightened economic status and wealth of the *libres de couleur* during the 1780s, see Rogers, "On the Road to Citizenship."

141. Moreau de Saint-Méry is explicit that this singer's debut was a novelty for colonial society in *Description*, II: 989.

142. *SAA*, 4 May 1785.

143. On the career of Minette, who was baptized Elisabeth Alexandrine Louise, see Moreau de Saint-Méry, *Description*, II: 989; and Fouchard, *Le Théâtre à Saint-Domingue*, 303–44. Bernard Camier examines her parentage and social background in "Minette: Situation sociale d'une artiste de couleur à Saint-Domingue," *Généalogie et histoire de la Caraïbe* 185 (2005): 4638–40.

144. Du Buisson, *Nouvelles considérations*, 80–81. King describes this as an era of economic downturn for the colony in *Blue Coat*, xvii.

145. Du Buisson puts the number of soldiers stationed in Saint-Domingue around 1780 at eight thousand. *Nouvelles considérations*, 109.

146. Quoted in Fouchard, *Le Théâtre à Saint-Domingue*, 318. See also Bernard Camier, "Minette (1767–1807): Artiste de couleur à Saint-Domingue," *Revue de la Société haïtienne d'histoire et de géographie* 205 (2000): 1–11.

147. Camier, "Minette: Situation sociale," 4640.

148. *AA (PAP)*, 18 October 1783; Camier and Dubois, "Voltaire et Zaïre," 54–55.

149. Moreau de Saint-Méry, *Description*, II: 1101; Fouchard, *Le Théâtre à Saint-Domingue*, 340–43.

150. Fouchard, *Le Théâtre à Saint-Domingue*, 347; Laujon, *Souvenirs*, I: 166–67.

151. Scholars have disputed the meaning of her career. Whereas Fouchard has presented Minette's success as a sign of the "slow and sure ascension" of the gens de couleur, Camier and Dubois, in contrast, have drawn attention to the controversy sparked by the professional theatrical debut of a young woman who was light skinned, socially prominent, and from a prosperous family, as evidence of the humiliating barriers that constrained the social advancement of people of color in Saint-Domingue prior to the Revolution. Fouchard, *Le Théâtre à Saint-Domingue*, 302, see also 303–4, 344–47; Camier and Dubois, "Voltaire et Zaïre," 54–56, 68.

152. Moreau de Saint-Méry, *Description*, II: 989.

153. Fouchard, *Le Théâtre à Saint-Domingue*, 312–40; and *SAA*, 5 June 1781, 31 July 1781, and 25 September 1781. In these early notices, Minette is often referred to as "the young debutant," rather than by name.

154. Jean-Paul Martini, *L'Amoureux de quinze ans, ou la Double fête*, libretto by Pierre Laujon (Paris: Veuve Duchesne, 1771); André Grétry, *Zémire et Azor, Comédie-ballet en vers et en quatre actes*, libretto by Jean-François Marmontel (Paris: Vente, 1772); François-Joseph Gossec, *Toinon et Toinette*, libretto by Jean-Augustin Julien Desboulmiers (Avignon: Louis Chambeau, 1767); M. Blaise, *Isabelle et Gertrude, ou les Sylphs supposés*, libretto by Charles-Simon Favart (Avignon: Louis Chambeau, 1772); Giovanni Paisiello, *L'Infante de Zamora, comédie en quatre actes*, libretto by Nicolas-Étienne Framery (Paris: Durand, 1781); Nicolas Dalayrac, *Nina, ou la Folle par l'amour*, libretto by Benoît-Joseph Marsollier des Vivetières (Paris: Peytieux, 1789).

155. Laujon, *Souvenirs*, I: 166–67.

156. On the integration and assimilation of free people of color during the late Old Regime, see Rogers, "On the Road to Citizenship," esp. 75–76.

Epilogue

1. "Budget 2008 du ministère de la Culture et de la Communication, 26 septembre 2007," http://www.culture.gouv.fr/culture/actualites/index-budget08.html.

2. "Budget 2012 du ministère de la Culture et de la Communication, mercredi 28 septembre 2011," http://www.culturecommunication.gouv.fr/Espace-Presse/Dossiers-de-presse/Budget-2012-du-ministere-de-la-Culture-et-de-la-Communication/%28language%29/fre-FR.

3. Fumaroli argues that theater lay at the origins of the ministry in the 1950s. *L'État culturel*, 147.

4. "Budget 2008."

5. http://www.comedie-francaise.fr/la-comedie-francaise-aujourdhui.php?lang=en&id=493. The Arts Council England (ACE), which provides government subsidies to arts groups, disburses some 370 million pounds annually to English theater organizations. In 2010–11 these ACE funds constituted on average approximately 30 percent of funded theaters' operating budgets: "Regularly Funded Organizations: Key Data from the 2010/11 Annual Submission," p. 34, available at http://www.artscouncil.org.uk/artforms/theatre/. Earned income remained

the largest source of income (53–54%) for these companies. The Lincoln Center for the Performing Arts in New York receives less than 5 percent of its operating funds from the federal government: http://www.lincolncenter.org/load_screen. asp?screen=support. It is, of course, important to note that American arts groups are aided indirectly by the federal policy of providing substantial tax exemptions to private donors to arts institutions.

6. Jacques Rigaud, *L'Exception Culturelle: Culture et pouvoirs sous la Ve République* (Paris: B. Grasset, 1995); Poirrier, *L'État et la culture*, 9. Germany, also recognized for its strong public support for music, opera, and the performing arts, has adopted a more decentralized system in which individual states, or *Länder*, and municipal governments play a much greater role (and the federal government a less prominent role) than in France. See Peter Ullrich and Wolfgang Wöhlert, "Germany," in *The World Encyclopedia of Contemporary Theatre*, ed. Don Rubin, Peter Nagy, and Philippe Rouyer (London: Routledge, 2000), esp. 351–55; Katrin Sieg, "German Theatre and Globalization," in *Theatre in the Berlin Republic: German Drama since Reunification*, ed. Denise Varney (Oxford: Peter Lang, 2008), 307–24, 314–15.

7. John Rockwell, "French Culture under Socialism: Egotism or a Sense of History? (Cultural Desk)," *New York Times*, 24 March 1993.

8. Among the many works concerning France's cultural policies during the twentieth century and the controversies surrounding them, see especially Fumaroli, *L'État culturel*; Poirrier, *L'État et la culture*; Pierre-Michel Menger, "L'Hégémonie parisienne: Économie et politique de la gravitation artistique," *AESC* (1993): 1565–1600, esp. 1586–98; David Loosely, *The Politics of Fun: Cultural Policy and Debate in Contemporary France* (Oxford: Berg Publishers, 1995), 157–245.

9. François-Joseph Grille, *Les Théâtres: Lois, règlemens, instructions, salles de spectacle, droits d'auteur, correspondans, congés, débuts, acteurs de Paris et des départemens* (Paris: A. Eymery, 1817), 216–25.

10. During the first two years of the Revolution in Saint-Domingue, the principal stages remained open. During the fall of 1791, in the midst of the massive slave uprising, the theater in Port-au-Prince burned down and the Le Cap stage was closed, only to be lost in the fires that ravaged that city two years later. When the Le Cap theater was rebuilt under the authority of Toussaint Louverture in 1797, a troupe featuring predominantly black actors performed for an audience that included former slaves who had become revolutionary citizens. Fouchard, *Le Théâtre à Saint-Domingue*, 28–35, 74, 348–49.

11. Hemmings, *Theatre and State*, 160–75, quote from 162. Theatrical production and practices outside of Paris during the Revolutionary and Napoleonic eras have been largely neglected. Cyril Triolaire lays important groundwork in his deeply researched *Le Théâtrale en province pendant le Consulat et l'Empire* (Clermont-Ferrand: Presses Universitaires Blaise Pascal, 2012).

12. "Instruction sur les théâtres" of May 1815, originally promulgated on 30 August 1814, in Grille, *Les Théâtres*, 261–65.

13. Ibid., 53. On the continuity in theater policies between Napoleon and Louis XVIII and later French regimes, see also Hemmings, *Theatre and State*, 3–4.

14. Marc Précicaud, *Le Théâtre lyrique à Limoges, 1800–1914: Recueil de texts, d'archives et de journaux locaux* (Limoges: Presses universitaires de Limoges, 2001), 19.

15. On the establishment of subsidies for municipal theater troupes, which rose steeply over the course of the nineteenth century, see Hemmings, Theatre and State, 144–52; Cohen, *Urban Government and the Rise of the French City*, 138–40. Limoges illustrates this trend. When the municipal council was asked by the resident theater company for a subsidy in 1818, it refused. Subventions, introduced under pressure from the minister of the interior, rose from just six hundred francs in 1820 to as much as forty-three thousand francs in 1897. Précicaud, *Le Théâtre lyrique à Limoges*, 166–72.

16. Hemmings, *Theatre and State*, 110–12, 162–63; F. W. J. Hemmings, *The Theatre Industry in Nineteenth-Century France*, (Cambridge: Cambridge University Press, 1993), 195–98; Précicaud, *Le Théâtre lyrique à Limoges*, 97–105.

17. Denise Z. Davidson, *France after Revolution: Urban Life, Gender, and the New Social Order* (Cambridge: Harvard University Press, 2007), 75–130; Sheryl Kroen, *Politics and Theater: The Crisis of Legitimacy in Restoration France, 1815–1830* (Berkeley: University of California Press, 2000); Cohen, *Urban Government and the Rise of the French City*, 127–46.

18. *Extrait historique pour servir à l'essai d'un plan de régie generale pour les spectacles de province*, esp. 22–26; Mague de Saint-Aubin, *La Réforme des théâtres*. See also the prospectus for an official correspondence and placement bureau, authorized by the crown, that would have required directors and actors to participate in a national employment registry: *Établissement seul autorisé par le Gouvernement, d'un Bureau d'adresse et d'indication pour les directeurs de spectacles et acteurs de province* (Paris: Ballard et fils, 1788), reprinted in Ducéré, "Le Théâtre bayonnais sous l'ancien régime," 415–18. This project was initiated by two entrepreneurs who likely modeled it on the corporate employment offices discussed in Sonenscher, *Work and Wages*, 284–86. This bureau was apparently interrupted by the Revolution, for after 1788 I have found no further evidence of its existence.

19. The work was performed in Lyon on 5 July 1785; in Lille on 10 July 1785; in Rouen on 20 August 1785; and in Nantes on 24 August 1785. Colonial audiences, who were kept abreast of the play's popularity in newspaper articles, could attend performances in Le Cap on 11 June 1785 and in Port-au-Prince just one month later. Pierre Augustin Caron de Beaumarchais, *La Folle journée, ou le Mariage de Figaro, comédie en cinq actes et en prose* (Paris: Ruault, 1785); Pierre Grosclaude, *La Vie intellectuelle à Lyon dans la deuxième moitié du XVIIIe siècle: Contribution de l'histoire littéraire de la province* (Paris: A. Picard, 1933), 249; Cradock, *La Vie française à la veille de la Révolution*, 247; Bouteiller, *Histoire complète et méthodique des théâtres de Rouen*, 99; Vogt, *Le Théâtre à Nancy*, 11; Lefebvre, *Histoire du théâtre de Lille*, I: 355; *SAA*, 12 February 1785, 1 June 1785; *AA*, 18 June 1785; Lagrave, *La Vie théâtrale à Bordeaux*, 209, 262; *L'Art du théâtre à Valenciennes*, 46.

20. William H. McNeill, *Keeping Together in Time: Dance and Drill in Human History* (Cambridge: Harvard University Press, 1995).

21. My thinking about public opinion has been influenced by Darnton, *Poetry and the Police*, esp. 129–39.

22. Jones, "Great Chain of Buying," 26, 39.

23. Quoted in Stone, "Robe against Sword," 284.

24. Joan Landes argues that the Habermasian public sphere was "essentially, and not just contingently, masculinist" in *Women and the Public Sphere*, 1–13 and 39–65,

quote from 7. On women's exclusion from the literary public sphere, see also Goodman, *Republic of Letters*, 233–80. Carla Hesse, in contrast, sees a commercializing cultural sector as generating new opportunities for women, although she locates this development in the publishing industry after 1789. *The Other Enlightenment: How French Women Became Modern* (Princeton: Princeton University Press, 2003), 31–55. Dominique Rogers points to the extensive economic opportunities enjoyed by the free people of color in prerevolutionary Saint-Domingue as an indicator of their integration into society in "On the Road to Citizenship."

25. Michael B. Miller, *The Bon Marché: Bourgeois Culture and the Department Store, 1869–1920* (Princeton: Princeton University Press, 1981), esp. 165–89.

26. Mague de Saint-Aubin, *La Réforme des théâtres*, 55 (emphasis in original). This author opposed, on commercial terms, such audience disruption of theatrical performances, arguing that he, too, had paid and deserved the right to enjoy a performance in peace and to come to his own assessment of its quality.

27. Mercier, *Du Théâtre*, 3–4.

28. Marie-Joseph Chénier, *De la liberté du theater en France* (n.p.: 1789), 5.

29. D'Alembert quoted in Chartier, *Cultural Origins*, 27; Mona Ozouf, "L'Opinion publique," in *The French Revolution and the Creation of Modern Political Culture*, ed. Keith Michael Baker, vol. 1, *The Political Culture of the Old Regime* (Oxford: Pergamon Press, 1987), 419–34.

30. On the role of authors in the making of a literary public, see Chartier, *Cultural Origins*, 157–62, quote from 159.

31. Baker, *Inventing the French Revolution*, 198–99.

32. I borrow this term from William Doyle, *Old Regime France, 1648–1778* (Oxford University Press, 2001), 251.

33. On the end of royal oversight and patronage for the royal stages of Paris, see Brown, *Field of Honor*, 349, and Johnson, *Backstage at the Revolution*, 37–82. Root-Bernstein notes that during the Revolution a number of the more prestigious Parisian theater companies sought and eventually received subsidies from the state, in *Boulevard Theater and Revolution*, 201–7. As its status and authority declined, the Comédie-Française stopped arbitrating labor disputes. Letters to the troupe declined precipitously after 1789. When the theater established new internal regulations in 1791, the actors dropped any reference to responsibility for their provincial colleagues. Bonnassies, *La Comédie-Française et les comédiens de province*, 16.

34. Quote from Carlson, *Theatre of the French Revolution*, v. See also Root-Bernstein, *Boulevard Theater and Revolution*, 197–233. Maslan notes that over one thousand new plays were written during the Revolution, in *Revolutionary Acts*, 15.

35. On actors' rights, see Friedland, *Political Actors*, 211–27, 258–69. On politics and audience activism, see also Jones, *Backstage at the Revolution*, 37–60; Maslan, *Revolutionary Acts*; and Pierre Bernadau in Lhéritier, ed., *Les Débuts de la Révolution à Bordeaux*, 74. The essays in *Les Arts de la scène et la Révolution française*, ed. Philippe Bourdin and Gérard Loubinoux (Clermont-Ferrand: Presses Universitaires Blaise Pascal, 2004) explore the complex relationship between the Revolution and theater from numerous angles.

36. Frantz and Sajous d'Oria list twenty-six new playhouses inaugurated in France between 1790 and 1799, eleven of which were located in Paris, in *Le Siècle*

des théâtres, 194–95. On the continuing popularity of Old Regime playwrights, plays, and operas during the Revolution, see Emmet Kennedy, Marie-Laurence Netter, James P. McGregor, and Mark V. Olsen, *Theatre, Opera, and Audiences in Revolutionary Paris: Analysis and Repertory* (Westport, Conn.: Greenwood Press, 1996), esp. 90; and Deck, *Histoire du théâtre français à Strasbourg*, 73–75.

37. Traditionally, scholars of French theater have viewed the Revolution as a moment of rupture in the practices of the French theater industry. In doing so, most give particular weight to the destruction of the royal theaters' privileges in 1791 and to the politicization of the stage, most notably during the Terror. Although I do not wish to deny that the Revolution had important implications for the French stage, most spectacularly in Paris, I propose that when France as a whole is taken into account the structures of theatrical production remained quite similar even as economic and political circumstances changed so dramatically. Perhaps the greatest innovation of the revolutionary state was its explicit use of theater as a tool of nationalism, enlisting theater companies directly to educate citizens in the values of the Republic. Yet even as the Commission of Public Instruction, established under the authority of the Committee of Public Safety, urged in 1794 that theatrical performances "speak the language of Liberty" and "make the laws and the *patrie* loved," it also advised that the material organization of France's theaters—administrative and financial matters—remain in the hands of theater professionals. BNF Bibliothèque-Musée de l'Opéra, *Commission d'Instruction Publique. Spectacles. Extrait des registres des arrêtés du comité de Salut Public de la Convention nationale,* 18 Prairial, 5 Messidor, An II (N.p.: n. pub., n.d.).

38. Maslan, *Revolutionary Acts*, vii and 2.

39. Here, I invoke the concept of culture as a "tool kit," a "repertory of competencies" that is essentially performative in nature, discussed in the introduction to Gabrielle Spiegel, ed., *Practicing History: New Directions in Historical Writing after the Linguistic Turn* (New York: Routledge, 2005), 1–31, 20.

Appendix

1. Although theater troupes did perform in Orléans during the eighteenth century, they seem to have done so in a converted playhouse about which I have been unable to locate information. For this reason, Orléans does not appear on the timeline. The data provided here is more extensive than that found in Fuchs, Frantz and Sajous d'Oria, or Rabreau (*Apollon dans la ville*, 210), while also correcting several errors. It is compiled from Ancely, *Histoire du théâtre et du spectacle à Pau*, 26–28; AN Col. C[8] A 87, fol. 9; Pierre Barrière, *La Vie intellectuelle en Périgord, 1550–1880* (Bordeaux: Éditions Delmas, 1936), 487; Émile Biais, "Le Théâtre à Angoulême (quinzième siècle-1904)," *RSBAD* 28 (1904): 279–333, data on 290; BMCF Com. div., "Saint-Pierri," 1774; Caillet and Duplan, *Spectacles à Carpentras*, 35–37; Camier, "Les Spectacles musicaux en Martinique"; Cardevacque, *Le Théâtre à Arras*, 40–46, 96–99, 113; Charvet, *Recherches sur le anciens théâtres de Beauvais*, 45; Clerambault, "Le Théâtre à Tours," 81–91, 83; Chelin, *Le Théâtre à l'Ile Maurice*, 2; Desprez de Boissy, *Lettres sur les spectacles*, I: 601; Ducéré, "Le Théâtre bayonnais," 229–30; Gosselin, *Recherches sur les anciens théâtres du Havre*, 16; Fouchard, *Le Théâtre à Saint-Domingue,*

113–14; Fromageot, *Le Théâtre de Versailles*, 8, 30; Frantz and Sajous d'Oria, *Le Siècle des théâtres*, 47–193; Fuchs, *La Vie théâtrale en province*, 20–27, 39, 105–7; Jourda, *Le Théâtre à Montpellier*, 12; Gosselin, *Recherches sur les anciens théâtres du Havre*, 16–33; Gouvenain, *Le Théâtre à Dijon*, 79–80; Lagrave, *La Vie théâtrale à Bordeaux*, 170–75; Lecocq, *Histoire du théâtre de St.-Quentin*, 37; Lhotte, *Le Théâtre à Lille*, 33; Mesuret, *Le Théâtre à Toulouse*, 10–17; Mongrédien and Robert, *Les Comédiens français du XVIIe siècle*, 309–26; Moreau de Saint-Méry, *Description*, I: 356–59 and II: 879, 984–85, 1099, 1100–1101, 1308, 1385; Moulin, *L'Architecture civile*, 73; Jean Nattiez, "Les salles et le matériel dans les théâtres de Picardie (1780–1860)," *RHT* 13 (1961): 246–49; Jean Quéniart, *Culture et société urbaines dans la France de l'Ouest au XVIIIe siècle* (Paris: Klincksieck, 1978), 489; E. Quéruau-Lamerie, "Notes sur le théâtre à Laval au XVIIIe siècle," *Bulletin de la Commission historique et archéologique de la Mayenne* 39 (1923): 66–79, 89–108, data on 78; Teil and Heyraud, *Saint-Étienne et le théâtre*, 10–12; *Trois siècles d'opéra à Lyon*, 31–32; Tribout de Morembert, *Le Théâtre à Metz*, 34–35, 42; Vogt, *Le Théâtre à Nancy*, 5–6.

BIBLIOGRAPHY OF PRIMARY SOURCES

Archival Sources

Archives de la Ville et Communauté urbaine de Strasbourg. Series AA 2161, 2162. Ms 6 R 26.

Archives départementales de la Haute-Garonne. 1 C 311.

Archives départementales de la Loire-Atlantique. C 321–323, 392.

Archives départementales de la Sarthe. 111 AC 611.

Archives départementales de la Seine-Maritime. 1B 5533.

Archives départementales du Rhône. 1 C 202.

Archives municipales de Bordeaux. Bib F 4/28. BB 140. DD 37. FF 70. GG 1004 a, b, e. R 12.

Archives municipales de Lyon. BB 321, 336, 346. GG 98–101.

Archives municipales de Nantes. BB 105. CC 218. FF 115, 283. GG 289, 676, 678.

Archives municipales de Saumur. 4M92, 4M93.

Archives municipales de Toulouse. GG 943.

Archives nationales. Series AJ^{13} 2, 13, 18. Series H 39, 1359. Series O^1 848. Series Marine B^2 367, 381; B^3 338, 483, 540, 577, 592, 598, 599, 602. Series Colonies C^{8A} 79, 87; C^{8B} 15. Collection Moreau de Saint-Méry Series F^3 273, 274, 278, 279. Series T 210, 3, Papiers la Ferronnays. Minutier central ET XXII 62 Notaire BERTELS.

Bibliothèque de l'Arsenal. Paris. Ms 6394. Archives de la Bastille. Ms 11866, 11921. Fonds Rondel.

Bibliothèque municipale de Bordeaux. Ms 1015.

Bibliothèque municipale de Lyon. Fonds Coste 50 (1462).

Bibliothèque municipale de Nantes. Fonds Ancien. 50103, 50106.

Bibliothèque-Musée de la Comédie-Française. Paris. 2 ATO Carton 198 Théâtres de Province, XVIIIe–XIXe, Consultations des Comédiens français. Registre concernant les consultations de la province R 137, 1. Comédiens divers hors Comédie-Française. Dossier "Lekain." Programmes province.

Bibliothèque nationale de France. Paris. Salle des manuscrits. Nouvelles acquisitions françaises Ms 9411; Fonds français Ms 12532, 12533.

Centre des Archives d'Outre-Mer. Aix-en-Provence. Collection Moreau de Saint-Méry. F^3 184, 187.

Newberry Library. Chicago. Case folio FRC 9730.

Service historique de la Défense. Chateau de Vincennes. Series A^1 1391, 1395, 3147, 3396, 3677, 3697, 3694, 3699. A^2 20. Y^a 255.

Print Sources

Affiches Américaines (variants include *Avis du Cap, Supplément aux Affiches Américaines*), 1766–89.

Affiches du Mans, 1774–89.

Almanach général de tous les spectacles de Paris et des provinces pour l'année 1791. Paris: Froullé, 1791.

Aubignac, François Hédelin, abbé d'. *La Pratique du théâtre par l'abbé d'Aubignac.* Amsterdam: Jean Frederic Bernard, 1715 [1657].

Bachaumont, Louis Petit de, et al. *Mémoires secrets pour servir à l'histoire de la république des lettres en France.* 36 vols. London: John Adamson, 1780–89.

Beaumarchais, Pierre Augustin Caron de. *La Folle journée, ou le Mariage de Figaro, comédie en cinq actes et en prose.* Paris: Ruault, 1785.

Bernadau, Pierre. *Les Débuts de la Révolution à Bordeaux d'après les tablettes manuscrites de Pierre Bernadau.* Edited by Michel Lhéritier. Paris: Société de l'histoire de la Révolution française, 1919.

Blaise, M. *Isabelle et Gertrude, ou les Sylphs supposés.* Libretto by Charles-Simon Favart. Avignon: Louis Chambeau, 1772.

Blondel, Jacques-François. *Architecture françoise.* 4 vols. Paris: Charles-Antoine Jombert, 1752.

——. *Cours d'architecture, ou Traité de la décoration, distribution & construction des bâtiments; Contenant les leçons données en 1750, & les années suivantes.* 6 vols. Paris: Desaint, 1771–77.

Bricaire de la Dixmerie, Nicolas. *Lettres sur l'état présent de nos spectacles, Avec des vues nouvelles sur chacun d'eux, particulièrement sur la Comédie Françoise & l'Opéra.* Amsterdam: Duchesne, 1765.

Chappuzeau, Samuel. *Le Théâtre françois, Accompagné d'une préface et de notes par Georges Monval.* Paris: J. Bonnassies, 1876 [1674].

Chaumont, Chevalier de. *Exposition des principes qu'on doit suivre dans l'ordonnance des théâtres modernes.* Paris: Jombert, 1769.

Chénier, Marie-Joseph. *De la liberté du théâtre en France.* N.p., 1789.

Chevrier, [François Antoine] de. *Almanach des gens d'esprit, par un homme qui n'est pas sot, Calendrier pour l'année 1762 et le reste de la vie.* London: Jean Nourse, 1762.

Cochin, Ch. N. *Projet d'une salle de spectacle pour un théâtre de comédie.* Paris: Jombert, 1765.

Collé, Charles. *Journal et mémoires de Charles Collé.* Edited by Honoré Bonhomme. New ed. 3 vols. Paris: Firmin Didot Frères, 1868.

Commission d'Instruction Publique. Spectacles. Extrait des registres des arrêts du Comité de salut public de la Convention nationale, 18 Prairial, 5 Messidor, An II. N.p., n.d..

[Corbun, M.] *Le Voeu de l'humanité, ou Lettres sur le spectacle de Bordeaux.* Bordeaux: Pallandre aîné, 1778.

Cradock, Anna Francesca. *La Vie française à la veille de la Révolution (1783–1786). Journal inédit de Madame Cradock.* Translated from the English by O. Delphin Balleyguier. Paris: Perrin, 1911.

Dalayrac, Nicolas. *Nina, ou la Folle par l'amour.* Libretto by Benoît-Joseph Marsollier des Vivetières. Paris: Peytieux, 1789.

Desprez de Boissy, Charles. *Lettres sur les spectacles: Avec une histoire des ouvrages pour & contre les théâtres.* 6th ed. 2 vols. Paris: Boudet, 1777.

Diderot, Denis. *Oeuvres esthétiques.* Edited by Paul Vernière. Paris: Éditions Garnier Frères, 1965.

——. *Paradoxe sur le comédien.* Edited by Ernest Dupuy. Geneva: Slatkine Reprints, 1968 [published posthumously in 1830].

Du Buisson, Paul Ulric. *Nouvelles considérations sur Saint-Domingue, en réponse à celles de M. H. D. Par M. D. B.* Paris: Cellot & Jombert, 1780.

Dumont, Gabriel Pierre Martin. *Parallèle de plans des plus belles salles de spectacles d'Italie et de France, avec des détails de machines théâtrales.* New York: B. Blom, 1968 [1773].

Duthoy, J.-J. "A Lille, à la fin du XVIIIe siècle. Documents inédits concernant Michel Lequeux, les artisans-sculpteurs lillois, le plan d'urbanisme de l'Intendant Calonne." *Revue du Nord* 65 (1983): 507–14.

Encyclopédie, ou Dictionnaire raisonné des sciences, des arts et des métiers. Edited by Denis Diderot and Jean Le Rond d'Alembert. 17 vols. Paris: Briasson, 1751–65.

Extrait historique pour servir à l'essai d'un plan de régie générale, pour les spectacles de province, par un comédien de province. Geneva, 1767.

Favart, Charles-Simon. *Mémoires et correspondance littéraires, dramatiques et anecdotiques, de C.S. Favart.* 3 vols. Geneva: Slatkine Reprints, 1970 [1808].

Firmin, Jean-Baptiste. *Parallèle entre Talma et Le Kain: Esquisse: Suivi de quelques réflexions sur l'art dramatique.* Paris: Haut-Coeur, 1826.

Fisch, Johann Georg. *Briefe über die südlichen Provinzen von Frankreich.* Zurich, 1790.

Flachat. *Pétition à l'Assemblée nationale; Presentée par les comédiens des spectacles de Lyon, Marseille, Rouen, Nantes, Brest, Toulouse, Montpellier, Strasbourg, Lille, Metz, Dunkerque, Genève, Orléans et Grenoble.* N.p., n.d.

Fleury, Joseph-Abraham Bénard. *Mémoires de Fleury de la Comedie Française, 1757 à 1820.* Edited by J.-B.-P. Lafitte. 6 vols. Paris: Ambroise Dupont, 1836–38.

Gaillard de La Bataille, Pierre-Alexandre. *Histoire de Mademoiselle Cronel dite Fretillon, actrice de la comédie de Roüen.* 4 vols. The Hague: "Aux depens de la compagnie," 1741–43.

Gala, Ignacio. *Memorias de la colonia francesa de Santo Domingo, con algunas reflexiones relativas a la isla de Cuba.* Madrid: Hilario Santos Alonso, 1787.

Garrick, David. *The Diary of David Garrick, Being a Record of His Memorable Trip to Paris in 1751.* Edited by Ryllis Clair Alexander. New York: Benjamin Blom, 1971.

——. *The Journal of David Garrick Describing His Visit to France and Italy in 1763.* Edited by George Winchester Stone Jr. New York: Modern Language Association of America, 1939.

Girod-Chantrans, Justin. *Voyage d'un Suisse dans différentes colonies d'Amérique pendant la dernière guerre, avec une table d'observations météorologiques faites à Saint-Domingue.* Neuchâtel: Imprimerie de la Société Typographique, 1785.

Gossec, François-Joseph. *Toinon et Toinette.* Libretto by Jean-Augustin Julien Desboulmiers. Avignon: Louis Chambeau, 1767.

Grétry, André. *Zémire et Azor, Comédie-ballet en vers et en quatre actes.* Libretto by Jean-François Marmontel. Paris: Vente, 1772.

Grille, François Joseph. *Les Théâtres: Lois, règlemens, instructions, salles de spectacle, droits d'auteur, correspondans, congés, débuts, acteurs de Paris et des départemens.* Paris: A. Eymery, 1817.

Grimm, Friedrich Melchior et al. *Correspondance littéraire, philosophique, et critique.* 16 vols. Paris: Garnier frères, 1877–82.

Grimod de La Reynière, Alexandre-Balthasar-Laurent. *Tableau de Lyon en 1786, par Grimod de La Reynière, Adressé sous forme de lettre à Mercier, Auteur du Tableau de Paris.* Lyon: Impr. de la Boitel, 1843.

Guyot, Joseph-Nicolas. *Répertoire universel et raisonné de jurisprudence civile, criminelle, canonique, et bénéficiale.* New ed. 17 vols. Paris: Visse, 1784–85.

Habasque, Francisque. *Documents sur le théâtre à Agen, 1585–1788.* Agen: Imprimerie Veuve Lamy, 1893.

Hilliard d'Auberteuil, Michel-Réné. *Considérations sur l'état présent de la colonie française de Saint-Domingue. Ouvrage politique et législatif; Présenté au Ministre de la Marine.* 2 vols. Paris: Grangé, 1776–77.

"Histoire des salles: Documents inédits, XVIIIe siècle. Jeux de Paume, Marchés d'aménagement en théâtres." *RHT* 4 (1948–49): 271–72.

Journal de Normandie, 1787.

Journal de Paris, 1783.

Karamzine, Nicolaï. *Lettres d'un voyageur russe.* Translated from the Russian by Vladimir Berelowitch. Paris: Quai Voltaire, 1991 [1792].

Klairwal, M. *Prologue pour l'ouverture de la nouvelle salle de spectacles d'Amiens, par M. Klairwal, représenté le . . . 21 janvier 1780.* Amiens: J.-B. Caron fils, 1780.

La Rochefoucauld, François de. *Voyages en France de François de la Rochefoucauld (1781–1783).* Edited by Jean Marchand. 2 vols. Paris: Champion, 1938.

La Tour, Bertrand de. *Réflexions morales, politiques, historiques, et littéraires, sur le théâtre.* 10 vols. Avignon: Marc Chave, 1763–66.

Laujon, A[lexandre] P. M. de. *Souvenirs de trente années de voyages à Saint-Domingue, dans plusieurs colonies étrangères, et au continent d'Amérique.* 2 vols. Paris: Schwartz et Gagnot, 1835.

Ledoux, Claude-Nicolas. *L'Architecture considérée sous le rapport de l'art, des moeurs et de la législation.* 2 vols. Paris: F. de Nobele, 1961 [1804].

Lekain, Henri-Louis. *Mémoires de Lekain, précédés de réflexions sur cet acteur, et sur l'art théatral, par F. Talma.* Paris: Ponthieu, 1825.

"Lettre de M. le marquis de Monteynard à tous les commandants des provinces frontières du 13 janvier 1772." *RHT* 13 (1961): 48.

*Lettre d'un citoyen de la ville de Saint-Quentin, à M**, Sur l'établissement d'une salle de spectacles dans la même ville.* Saint-Quentin, 1774.

Louis, Victor. *Salle de spectacle de Bordeaux.* Paris: Esprit, Libraire, 1782.

Mague de Saint-Aubin, Jacques-Thomas. *La Réforme des théâtres, ou Vues d'un amateur sur les moyens d'avoir toujours des acteurs à talens sur les théâtres de Paris & des grandes villes du royaume, & de prévenir les abus des troupes ambulantes, sans priver les petites villes de l'agrément des spectacles.* Paris: Guillot, 1787.

Malouet, Pierre Victor, baron de. *Collection de mémoires et correspondances officielles sur l'administration des colonies, et notamment sur la Guiane française et hollandaise.* 6 vols. Paris: Baudouin, 1801.

Martini, Jean-Paul. *L'Amoureux de quinze ans, ou la Double fête.* Libretto by Pierre Laujon. Paris: Veuve Duchesne, 1771.

Mémoire et consultation sur l'état des comédiens, rélativement aux effets civils. Paris: Michel Lambert, 1768.

Mercier, Louis-Sébastien. *Du Théâtre, ou Nouvel essai sur l'art dramatique.* Amsterdam: E. Van Harrevelt, 1773.

——. *Panorama of Paris: Selections from "Le Tableau de Paris," by Louis-Sébastien Mercier.* Edited by Jeremy D. Popkin. Translated by Helen Simpson and Jeremy D. Popkin. University Park: Penn State University Press, 1999.

——. *Tableau de Paris. Tome 11.* New ed. Amsterdam, 1789.

Mercure de France, 1763–80.

Métra, François, et al. *Correspondance secrète, politique et litéraire, ou Memoires pour servir à l'histoire des cours, des sociétés, et de la littérature en France, depuis la mort de Louis XV.* 18 vols. London: John Adamson, 1787–90.

Monnet, Jean. *Supplément au Roman comique.* 2 vols. London: 1772.

Moreau de Saint-Méry, M. L. E. *Description topographique, physique, civile, politique et historique de la partie française de l'isle Saint-Domingue.* Edited by Blanche Maurel and Etienne Taillemite. 3 vols. Paris: Société française d'histoire d'outre-mer, 1984 [1797–98].

——. *Loix et constitutions des colonies françoises de l'Amérique sous le vent.* 6 vols. Paris: chez l'auteur, 1784–90.

Oberkirch, Henriette Louise von Waldner. *Mémoires de la baronne d'Oberkirch sur la cour de Louis XVI et la société française avant 1789.* Edited by Suzanne Burkard. Paris: Mercure de France, 1989.

Ordonnance du roi pour régler le service dans les places et dans les quartiers. Du 1er mars 1768; Suivi du décret impérial du 24 décembre 1811, relatif à l'organisation et au service des états-majors des places, et annotée des lois, décrets, ordonnances, arrêtés, règlements et autres dispositions qui ont modifié la matière jusqu'à ce jour. Paris: Librarie militaire J. Dumaine, 1855.

Paisiello, Giovanni. *L'Infante de Zamora, comédie en quatre actes.* Libretto by Nicolas-Étienne Framery. Paris: Durand, 1781.

Papillon de la Ferté, Denis Pierre Jean. *Journal de Papillon de la Ferté, intendant et contrôleur de l'argenterie, menus-plaisirs, et affaires de la chambre du roi (1756–1780).* Edited by Ernest Boysse. Paris: Paul Ollendorff, 1887.

Patte, Pierre. *Essai sur l'architecture théâtrale: ou, De l'ordonnance la plus avantageuse à une salle de spectacles, relativement aux principes de l'optique & de l'acoustique.* Paris: Moutard, 1782.

Pauw, Cornelius de. *Recherches philosophiques sur les américains.* 2 vols. Edited by Michèle Duchet. Paris: Jean Michel Place, 1990 [1770].

Piozzi, Hester Lynch (Thrale), and Samuel Johnson. *The French Journals of Mrs. Thrale and Doctor Johnson.* Edited by Moses Tyson and Henry Guppy. Manchester: Manchester University Press, 1932.

Prudhomme, Louis-Marie. *Miroir historique, politique et critique de l'ancien et du nouveau Paris et du département de la Seine.* 3rd ed. 6 vols. Paris, 1807.

Recueil des édits, arrêts, lettres-patentes, déclarations, règlemens et ordonnances, Imprimés & mis à exécution par ordre de M. l'intendant ou par les différens tribunaux de la ville de Lille. Lille: N.-J.-B. Peterinck-Cramé, Imprimeur ordinaire du Roi, 1785.

Recueil de planches, sur les sciences, les arts libéraux, et les arts méchaniques, avec leur explication. 11 vols. Paris: Briasson, 1762–72.

Rétif de la Bretonne, Nicolas-Edme. *La Mimographe, ou Idées d'une honnête-femme pour la réformation du théâtre national.* Amsterdam: Changuion, 1770.

Le Réveil d'Apollon, Prologue en vers libres, Représenté à l'ouverture de la nouvelle salle de spectacle de Lyon. N.p., 1756.

Riccoboni, Louis. *De la réformation du théâtre.* Paris, 1743.

Rondel, Auguste. *Quelques renseignements sur la construction de l'Opéra de Marseille et sur son inauguration, le 31 octobre 1787. Suivis de* L'Union du commerce et des arts, *Prologue composé pour l'ouverture du nouveau théâtre de Marseille et représenté pour la première fois le 31 octobre 1787 par M. Ponteuil, Comédien du Roi.* Marseille: Imprimerie provençale Guiraud, 1924.

Roubaud, Claudine. *L'Opéra de Marseille: Recueil de documents d'archives.* Marseille: Service éducatif des archives municipales, 1987.

Roubo, André-Jacob. *Traité de la construction des théâtres et des machines théâtrales.* Paris: Cellot & Jombert, 1777.

Rousseau, Jean-Jacques. *Politics and the Arts: Letter to M. d'Alembert on the Theatre.* Translated from the French by Allan Bloom. Ithaca: Cornell University Press, 1960.

Savary des Bruslons, Jacques. *Dictionnaire universel de commerce, d'histoire naturelle, et des arts et métiers.* 4 vols. Paris: Veuve Estienne, 1750.

Scarron, Paul. *Le Roman comique, par M. Scarron.* New ed. 4 vols. London, 1781.

Soufflot, J. G. *L'Oeuvre de Soufflot à Lyon: Études et documents.* Lyon: Presses universitaires de Lyon, 1982.

Les Spectacles de Paris, ou Calendrier historique & chronologique des théâtres; pour l'année 1766. Paris: Veuve Duchesne, 1766.

Les Veuves creoles. Amsterdam: Merlin, 1768.

Voltaire (François-Marie Arouet). *Oeuvres complètes de Voltaire.* 70 vols. Paris: Imprimerie de la Société littéraire-typographique, 1785–89.

Wimpffen, Alexandre-Stanislas, baron de. *Saint-Domingue à la veille de la Révolution.* Edited by Albert Savine. Paris: La Michaud, 1911 [1797].

Young, Arthur. *Travels in France During the Years 1787, 1788 & 1789.* Edited by Constantia Maxwell. Cambridge: Cambridge University Press, 1950.

Index

Note: Page numbers in *italics* indicate illustrations.

Abbeville theater, *16,* 25–26, 118
absolutism, 3–4, 6, 166, 266n27; theater
　culture and, 38, 70–73, 166, 182, 193,
　226–27
Académie Royale de Marine, 78
academies, provincial, 2, 8, 32–33, 57, 175,
　199, 245n33, 253n76
Acquaire, Madame (singer), 221
Acquaire, Monsieur (director), 202
actors/actresses: audience cabals against, 80,
　132, 134, 179, 183, 186, 207, 233; careers
　of, 134–37, 141–43; contracts of, 99,
　102, 113, 129, 135–41; excommunication
　of, 134, 285n7; labor arbitration for, 10,
　132–35, 143–49, 160–62, 205;
　pregnancy benefits for, 151, 291n94;
　professionalization of, 149–52; salaries
　of, 102, 129–30, 133, 137–39, 155–56,
　162, 199, 204, 286n24; sick benefits for,
　147–48; prejudices against, 124–25, 134,
　159–60, 282n141; star system of, 4–5,
　152–59; troupe management by, 99–100.
　See also audiences; directors
advertisements, 123–24, *124,* 282nn134–35
Agen, *16,* 21, 91
Aix-en-Provence, *16,* 55, 64, 101, 259n36
Albanel, Christine, 225
Alençon, *16,* 25
Amiens, *16,* 108, 126
Anderson, Benedict, 7, 245n29
Angers theater, *16,* 88–89, 186–87,
　303n150
antitheatricality, 12, 62–63, 134, 219.
　See also actors; excommunication, of
　actors; religious concerns about theater
army, 69–70, 73–82, 92–94, 165, 187;
　garrisons, 4, 17–19, 21, 69–70, 73, 182;
　officers' seating, 85–87; subscriptions by,
　69–81
Arras theater, *16,* 86–87, 242n8

Arthaud, Monsieur (theater owner), 195,
　205
audiences, 122–26, 163–67, 176–81;
　advertising for, 123–24, *124,*
　282nn134–35; boycotts by, 166, 187–94,
　208, 233, 304n179; civility of, 77, 173,
　184; dress codes for, 184, 298n45,
　301n127, 312n114; in French colonies,
　195–99, 207–15, 305n6; heckling by, 3,
　132, 134, 143, 165–66, 178–86, 207–8,
　233. *See also* actors; subscriptions
Austrian Succession, War of, 74–75
Auxerre theater, 24
Avignon theater, *16,* 242n8, 274n14

Baker, Keith Michael, 245n24
ballet, 25, 90, 96; at Bordeaux, 50, 62, 67,
　116, 117; at Lyon, 117; at Montpellier,
　177; at Nantes, 107; at Rouen, 189, 191;
　at Toulouse, 106, 117
Bardet, Jean-Pierre, 261n62, 295n8
Bayonne, *16,* 19, 34, 102, 267n54
Beam, Sara, 242n5
Beaumarchais, Pierre-Augustin Caron de,
　173; *Le Barbier de Séville,* 61; *The Marriage
　of Figaro,* 229
Beaupré, Mademoiselle (actress), 140
Beik, William, 73
Belle-Isle, maréchal de, 19, 83
Benabou, Erica-Marie, 267n52
Bénard, Abraham-Joseph "Fleury" (actor),
　111
Bénard, Charles Joachim (architect), 35
Berlanstein, Lenard, 159, 291n90
Bertin, Rose, 276n56
Berville, Monsieur (actor), 142
Besançon, *16,* 18, 21, 122; theater of,
　61–62, 178, 261n73
Blondel, Jacques-François, 42, 45, 64
Bordeaux, *16,* 117; population of, 54, 55

Bordeaux theater, 19–21, 27, *50,* 50–52,
179–80; ballet at, 50, 62, 67, 116, 117;
boutique rentals at, *59,* 60, 63; boycott
of, 304n179; building of, 43, 51–52,
104–5; design of, 46, 50, 58–60, *59*;
financing of, 200; inauguration of,
50–51, 57; interior of, 56–57, *170,*
261n68; labor disputes at, 149; La Rochefoucauld on, 66; operating budget for,
104, 123, 127, 186n14; ordinances of,
182, 184–86, 184, 301n127; Parisian
artists at, 156–57; performance schedules
for, 127; profitability of, 106; prostitutes
at, 174; rents from, 63, 262n83; repertory
of, 114–17, 278n84; salaries at, 137–39;
seating arrangements at, 208, 242n8,
296n21, 309n63; success of, 177; ticket
prices at, 168
Bourdon, Honoré "Neuville," 111, 188–91
boutique rentals, *59,* 60, 63
boycotts, by theatergoers, 166, 187–94, 208,
233, 304n179
Brest, *16,* 19, 73
Brest theater, 18, 68–71, 77–82, 228;
bankruptcy of, 71, 95–96; boycott of,
192–93; precursor of, 68, 264n1, 265n13;
proposal for, 68–69, 78; salaries at, 138;
seating arrangements at, 82; ticket prices
at, 79
Breteuil, baron de, 84
Brewer, John, 243n9, 244n19
British theaters, 42, 45, 178; modern
subsidies for, 225, 314n5; state patronage
of, 19; seating arrangements in, 172;
traveling troupes and, 2, 127
Brunet, Marguerite "La Montansier,"
25–27, 108–13, 126, 141; biographies
on, 277n57; Rouen theater boycotts and,
188–91
Buirette de Belloy, Pierre-Laurent, 266n41

Cailhava, Jean-François, 144
Cain, Henri Louis. *See* Lekain, Henri
Calais theater, 80, 86, 266n41
Calendrier électronique des spectacles sous
l'ancien régime et sous la révolution
(CÉSAR) database, 279n85
Cambrai, *16,* 242n8
Camier, Bernard, 196, 211, 220
carabiniers (cavalry officers), 31, 74
Carnival season, 25–26
Casanova, Giovanni Giacomo, 174–75

Caumartin, Antoine-Louis-François
Lefebvre de, 83
censorship, 118, 227, 229
Chabrillan, comte de, 37
Châlons-sur-Marne theater, *16, 53,*
259n36
Chappuzeau, Samuel, 100
Chartier, Roger, 13
chefs de troupe, 73, 99–102, 274n17
Chénier, Marie-Joseph, 232
Chesneau-Desportes, Mathieu, 14, 34–35
Chinon, Monsieur (director), 200–201
Choiseul, duc de, 76–78
Chomel, Monsieur (lawyer), 26
Clairon, Mademoiselle (actress), 142–43,
285n6
Claris de Florian, Jean-Pierre, 115
Clavel, Anne-Antoinette-Cécile "Madame
Saint-Huberty," 156–59
Clément, Claude, 202
Clermont-Ferrand, *16,* 19, 49, 180
Cochin, Charles-Nicolas, 49
Coigny, maréchal de, 93
Colbert, Jean-Baptiste, 3, 71, 78
Collé, Charles, 118, 134, 159, 193–94
Collot d'Herbois, Jean-Marie, 211
Comédie-Française, 4, 72, 91, 150, 225;
archives of, 9; founding of, 2, 116; labor
arbitration by, 133–35, 143–52, 160–62,
205; monopoly on debuts of, 117–18;
provincial recruits for, 109, 112–13,
125–26; repertory of, 114, 116; during
Revolution, 233–34; salaries at, 138–39;
seating arrangements at, 178; theater
buildings of, 38, 45, 65–66, 258n27;
ticket prices at, 168
Comédie-Italienne, 4, 44–45, 72, 151;
opéra-comique and, 103–4; repertory of,
115, 118
consumerism, 3–6, 54–57, 232, 243n9;
theater boutiques and, 60, 63; theater
boycotts and, 187–94, 208, 233, 304n179;
theater seats and, 57–58, 82–87, 165–75
contracts, acting, 99, 102, 113, 129, 135–41.
See also rental contracts
Cooper, Frederick, 198, 215
Corbun, M., 296n20
Corneille, Pierre, 4, 125, 132
Corsica, *16,* 248n10
Coulom, Jean-Baptiste, 24
Coyer, abbé, 65
Cradock, Anna Francesca, 172, 174, 175, 177